SITUATING SOCIAL THEORY

Second edition

SITUATING SOCIAL THEORY

Second edition

Tim May and Jason L. Powell

 Open University Press

Open University Press
McGraw-Hill Education
McGraw-Hill House
Shoppenhangers Road
Maidenhead
Berkshire
England
SL6 2QL

email: enquiries@openup.co.uk
world wide web: www.openup.co.uk

and Two Penn Plaza, New York, NY 10121—2289, USA

First published 1996

A catalogue record of this book is available from the British Library

ISBN-13: 978-0-33-5210770 (pb)
ISBN-10: 0-33-521077-5 (pb)

Typeset by Kerrypress, Luton, Bedfordshire
Printed and bound in the UK by Bell and Bain Ltd, Glasgow

The *McGraw·Hill* Companies

Contents

Acknowledgements   vii
Introduction   1

PART I SITUATING SOCIAL THEORY

1   The Enlightenment and the development of social theory   7
2   Seven traditions of renewal, modification and critique   36

PART II CONTEMPORARY THEORIES ON SOCIETY AND SOCIAL LIFE

3   Symbolism and performance in everyday life   71
4   Social life as accomplishment   88
5   Reproducing society in social relations   105
6   Habitus, capital and field: society in social relations   122
7   Action, networks and intermediaries   139
8   The linguistic turn in critical theory   154
9   Where did all the women go?   175
10   The making of the modern subject   197
11   Beyond modernity?   216

PART III THEORIES IN ACTION

12   Emotion in social relations   243
13   Globalization   257

Conclusion: Looking back and looking forward   271

Bibliography   285

Index   XX

Acknowledgements

Jason would like to thank his friends and his family for their unstinting support in giving him the ideas and space to contribute to this second edition. Thanks to my Mum, Grandad, Stella and Rob for their continuing support. Finally, I would also like to thank Tim for his staunch support and friendship.

Tim would like to express his thanks to Jason for working with him in producing this second edition. I have enjoyed the discussions that have resulted and it is good to make theory work for you and not just do work for theory. I would also like to record my thanks to my friends at SURF (Centre for Sustainable Urban and Regional Futures) – Beth, Simon, Mike and Vicky – for their support and for allowing me some space in a very busy environment to complete the book. Finally, my thanks to Vicky for discussions on ideas of the self and to Dee, Calum and Cian. Calum and Cian ensure that any celebrations that may result from writing a book are kept in check. When I have asked them if they would like to know about it's content their responses have been unprintable!

Introduction

This book contextualizes and engages with what we understand by social theory in its rich and diverse perspectives. An informed use of social theory is to examine taken-for-granted assumptions, explore the basis and content of interpretations of the social world, its structural dynamics and the place of human agency within it. Social theory is core to establishing frameworks for understanding in social science, interpreting human action and how social processes are contested and negotiated, as well as the interplay between various levels at which social relations take place from the micro to macro and individual to societal.

In approaching the writing of this book, there are two key questions that need to be considered. First, how does one make sense of the complicated nature of social theory? If we use a metaphor, a 'life-jacket' is needed which enables a committed reader to 'swim' through a conceptual pool, or swamp, depending upon their perspective! The life-jacket should provide buoyancy and provide its wearer with the confidence to continue on their journey. One of the aims of the book is to provide such a life-jacket through being equipped with the conceptual tools to analyse the social world. It also aims to convey the importance and significance of social theory for the disciplined study of society and social relations.

The social analyst who is armed with 'thinking tools' seeks to understand the relationship between personal troubles, public issues and how biography and history intersect (Bauman and May 2001; Mills 1970). The role of the social analysts is to reveal the connections between what is going on in the world and what may be happening within ourselves; in other words, 'to grasp history and biography and the relations between the two within society' (Mills 1970: 33). The ability to analyse experiences or issues from different levels of analysis and to see the intersection of these levels and their mutual influences, lies at the very heart of socio-theoretical endeavours.

At the same time, there are features of social theory which render its study difficult. First, all theories are not simply neutral mediums for interpretation. They contain a 'persuasive' power which seeks to render their accounts either superior over, or different from, those of others. Second, as will become apparent, social theory not only seeks to account for the dynamics of society, but also reflects upon how knowledge about the social world is possible, as well as the nature of 'social reality' (questions of epistemology and ontology, respectively). Third, social theories vary according to the cultural and intellectual traditions under which they are conceived and from which they draw their inspiration.

As a result of these characteristics, its study can appear to be inward-looking, frustrating, narrow, inapplicable and its ideas incommensurable and unduly 'philosophical'. Yet to theorize is a practice which either reflects upon, or assumes, the nature of knowledge and ideas of human action and consciousness. This means that there is a fine line between philosophy and social theory; which, it should be added, is a characteristic of sciences in general (Williams and May 1996). Therefore, in order to situate social theory, an understanding of the history and relationship between philosophy and social theory, as well as its cultural antecedents, is required. The other important point to note is that theories often mirror the norms and values of their creators and their social times, reflecting culturally dominant views of what should be the appropriate way to analyse social phenomena (Ritzer 2004).

Mapping the terrain

The book itself is divided into three parts. The first part has two chapters, the second has ten chapters and the third, two chapters and a conclusion. Part I is called 'Situating social theory'. This is designed as a springboard into the second part because it is necessary to know the history and issues within social theory before examining various schools of thought which currently exist on its terrain. Therefore, it differs from conventional accounts because it is explicitly designed to provide the historical antecedents of ideas in Part II. We also seek to engage in reflection by situating emotion and globalization in social theory. By illuminating these two central elements in social life we provide a platform for highlighting how social theories can be deployed to enhance our understanding of the contemporary world.

Chapter 1 is a historical tour of the development of social theory from the Enlightenment to the turn of the twentieth century. Chapter 2 then focuses upon the issues which have been raised during the twentieth century by examining eight traditions within social and philosophical thought, all of which have a bearing on the form and content of contemporary social theory. There is no simple line which can be drawn between these two chapters, but they raise issues which the theories and theorists in Part II have sought to tackle in a novel and detailed fashion.

The purpose of Part II is to provide an exposition of a number of contemporary ideas. Each chapter is divided into the following sections. First, the development of the respective theories are examined by situating them within the discussions contained in Part I of the book. Second, there is an examination of some of the issues which their ideas raise in order that a greater insight into their strengths and weaknesses may be achieved.

Chapters 3 and 4 focus upon 'micro' theories due to their concern with the creation of the social world by individuals interacting with each other in everyday life. In this section, we have chosen to concentrate on two schools of thought: ethnomethodology and symbolic interactionism. We shall examine the underlying assumptions of these theories, as well as the criticisms which have emanated from other schools of thought and social thinkers: in particular, the works of Erving Goffman.

Chapters 5 and 6 examine the ideas of two social theorists who have sought to tackle the dualism between action and structure. They consider the main theoretical assumptions of Giddens and Bourdieu. Here we find not only an adherence to the creative capacities of people, but also a notion of social structure in terms of its ability to both enable and constrain their actions.

We might also add that it is not just about human behaviour and actor network theory looks at post-humanist issues within social action. Chapter 7 thus explores the rise and consolidation of actor network theory (ANT) and its positionality of actors as both human and non-human entities.

Chapter 8 moves on to examine the work of Jürgen Habermas, who sits within the tradition of critical theory. As will become apparent, he has modified this tradition in significant respects. Nevertheless, as with social theory in general, it is said to lack an adequate consideration of the role of women in society. It is for this reason that Chapter 9 is devoted to an understanding of feminist theories which, as will be noted throughout the book, challenge much of the taken-for-granted notions upon which ideas and practices routinely draw.

Chapters 10 and 11 seek to encapsulate those schools of thought which have challenged the assumptions of modernity and the Enlightenment project. For this reason, there is an examination of the works of Michel Foucault in Chapter 10, while Chapter 11 considers the broad school of thought known as postmodernism.

In Part III, we reflect upon the journey we have undertaken and consider the implications of current changes in social relations for the future direction of social theory. To undertake this, we examine 'emotion' and 'globalization'. One represents what is taken to be a personal issue, whilst the other is assumed to be significant in terms of its impact upon our lives. In Chapter 12, therefore, we reflect on how situating social theory within the traditions and contemporary ideas identified throughout the book provides an important frame of reference for highlighting the ways in which emotion is constructed and experienced. Chapter 13 focuses on theorizing 'globalisation'. Theorizing globalization provides an essential context of how we understand and interpret the future implications for how global changes impact on how we experience the modern world.

Finally, we conclude with a critical review of the theories identified within the book and point to a reflexive social theory that must embrace how diverse human experiences are continually reframed by our relationship with ourselves, each other and the changing contours of the social and natural world.

Social theory is a rich, diverse and complicated subject which attracts as much, if not more, misunderstanding, as it does controversy. It is envisaged that this book will contribute, in some way, to moving beyond this to show social theory for what it is: an important means of enhancing our understanding of social relations and explanations of society which should be both challenging and challenged.

PART I

Situating social theory

1 The Enlightenment and the development of social theory

This chapter and Chapter 2 offer historical overviews of the themes that have emerged in the development of social theory in order to situate current ideas in terms of their past influences. At the same time it is noted that an injustice will be committed if the reader simply concludes that the writings of 'past' social theorists are not still of importance in understanding contemporary times.

It follows that in situating social theory according to the context of its production, theorists are not viewed as disembodied from their theories, but implicated in their production through addressing the problematics of their own historical times (Harrington 2005). Second, the works of these thinkers have not only acted as catalysts for current thought, but also structured its agenda. Their works enable theoretical discourse by operating to 'fix' prior debates which then facilitate theoretical discussion without recourse to continual elaboration, one such example being works on capitalism. These will either explicitly refer to, or be compared with, Karl Marx's (1818–83) original analysis which represents the most systematic critical account of the genesis and consequences of this form of organizing social relations.

The Enlightenment may be characterized as a catalyst for the development of particular styles of social thought. It does not represent a set of ideas which can be clearly demarcated, extracted and presented as a list of essential definitions, but represents a general shift in thought:

> In its simplest sense the Enlightenment was the creation of a new framework of ideas about man, society and nature, which challenged existing conceptions rooted in a traditional world-view, dominated by Christianity.
>
> (Hamilton 1992: 23)

These ideas, when fused with governmental practice, produced some core themes. First, a concept of freedom based upon an autonomous human subject who is capable of acting in a conscious manner. Second, the pursuit of a universal and foundational 'truth' gained through a correspondence of ideas with social and physical reality. Third, a belief in the natural sciences as the correct model for thinking about the social and natural world over, for example, theology and metaphysics. Fourth, the accumulation of systematic knowledge within the progressive unfolding of history. Collectively, these changes acted as catalysts and/or informed the scientific study of human societies. Therefore, it follows that they need to be considered in more detail before moving on to examine the development of social theory in differing contexts. For this purpose, there follows a brief examination of these cultural transformations and philosophical ideas.

The power and relevance of these cultural shifts cannot be underestimated in their effects upon modern times:

> I believe that we are all to a greater or lesser extent children of the Enlightenment, and that it is from this standpoint that civilized members of Western society – the heirs to a humane tradition more than two centuries old – almost necessarily judge the political and social movements of their own time.
>
> (S. H. Hughes 1979: 27)

Even postmodernists, who challenge the dominance and assumptions of modernism, are forced to engage with it for it permeates our contemporary ideas and practices. To paraphrase Marshall Berman (1993), we cannot ignore or turn away from it, for it is the only world that we have. This is the world which became an object of inquiry for the social sciences. Emerging modes of political practice, however, contained within them both positive and negative elements.

In negative terms, the Western Intellectual Tradition (Bronowski and Mazlish 1970) may be characterized as one which invokes assumptions which are assumed to be applicable to all societies, or through which 'other' people may be evaluated according to its dominant intellectual, political, social and economic standards. Coupled with this, the idea of modernity evokes the development of capitalism and industrialization, as well as the establishment of nation states and the growth of regional disparities in the world system (B. S. Turner 2006). The period has witnessed a host of social and cultural transformations. Indeed, William Du Bois, an American social theorist, recognized this double–edge to its force and for this reason worked towards a multicultural social theory which would not exclude whole groups of people via its unexamined assumptions (Du Bois 1989).

In general terms, battle lines have now been drawn between the defenders of the project of modernity or enlightenment (Habermas 1992a), its detractors (Baudrillard 2005; Lemert 2006; Lyotard 1984; Seidman 2001) and those thinkers who, through their historical and philosophical excavations, have questioned the comfortable certitudes upon which modern practices and ideas have based themselves (Derrida 1978; Foucault 1992). In the following history of social theory, we will also find those thinkers who regarded modernity as an opportunity (Comte, Marx and Durkheim) and those who were more ambivalent in their evaluations (Montesquieu, Weber and Simmel).

When did these changes start? We cannot state a time at which the Enlightenment and what has been called 'the modern age' or 'modernity' began:

> How old is modernity? is a contentious question. There is no agreement on dating. There is no consensus on what is to be dated. And once the effort of dating starts in earnest, the object itself begins to disappear.
>
> (Bauman 1991: 3).

We still need some idea of its genesis. These broad changes have been examined in two ways. First, through the history of ideas, and second, through examining transformations in social practices. In terms of the former, Kroker and Cook (1988) have travelled back to the work of the theologian Augustine, who they describe as 'the Columbus of modern experience' (1988: 37). They argue that modernity is characterized as the search for a theory of representation whereby it becomes possible to explain a variety of human experiences in different contexts. Augustine placed this in question:

> To suggest a historical thesis, it is our position that Augustine was the first postmodern thinker. ... Refusing the alternatives of rationalism and materialism, or tragic idealism and dogmatic skepticism, Augustine demonstrated the fatal flaw in enlightenment modernism: its absence of a directly experienced creative principle which could serve to unify the warring tendencies in Western experience. ... When enlightenment returns in the seventeenth century, it reawakens the fatal flaw in Western metaphysics, and thus experience, which Augustine had laid to rest for a period of eleven centuries.
>
> (Kroker and Cook 1988: 28)

In terms of social practices Toynbee (1954) saw the emergence of a modern age in the ways of life of European people on the Atlantic coast in the fifteenth century, while Stephen Toulmin (1990, 2003) regards it as a shift from an understanding of 'argumentation' in Renaissance humanism, towards a concern with 'proofs' and universal logic. Marshall (1994) argues that there are three historical periods to modernity, the first being from the sixteenth to eighteenth centuries, the second being with the French Revolution and the accompanying rapid changes in social and political life and the third giving rise to a 'world culture of modernism' with its growing turmoil and uncertainty.

Shifting this emphasis towards the experiential aspects of modernity has witnessed one nineteenth-century writer describing it as 'ephemeral, fugitive, contingent' (Baudelaire quoted in D. Sayer 1991: 9). This continues into the twentieth century with Michel Foucault (1926–84) describing it as more of an 'attitude' which informs practices, rather than any actual period of history:

> And by 'attitude', I mean a mode of relating to contemporary reality; a voluntary choice made by certain people; in the end, a way of thinking and feeling; a way, too, of acting and behaving that at one and the same time marks a relation of belonging and presents itself as a task.
>
> (Foucault 1984: 39)

This experiential focus also permits a comparison between 'discontinuities' in contemporary social institutions and their effects on daily lives, with traditional social orders which are seen to have represented both stability and continuity (Giddens 1990; Stones 2005).

In these attempts to pinpoint a meaning for and genesis of modernity, one of the central characteristics of the debate appears to be 'the extent to which key terms have evaded clarification' (Smart 1990: 16). Nevertheless, there remains a relationship between emerging ideas in this period and the development of social thought.

Catalysts to the Enlightenment project

The journey begins with Immanuel Kant (1724–1804). Kant added power to the search for a universal truth through his inheritance of two philosophical traditions: rationalism and empiricism. Rationalism was represented by the work of René Descartes (1596–1650).

Using a method of doubt, Descartes asked how it is that people 'know' that the knowledge they possess is true? After all, people disagree over experiencing the same thing: to one person a plate may be hot, to another only warm. Further, it is often difficult to tell the difference between dreams and reality – a recurring dream can eventually come to seem like reality itself. As such, the senses distort reality. Therefore, how can social or physical reality be known with any degree of certainty? The basis for knowledge is reason. As experiences play tricks on the mind, they cannot be considered a satisfactory foundation for knowledge.

Kant was also influenced by the idea that knowledge of the social and physical worlds is gained through experience. One of the most famous thinkers in this school of thought (known as empiricism) was the Scottish philosopher David Hume (1711–76). Hume drew a distinction between 'impressions' and 'ideas'. The former, he argued, have more influence upon understanding. While complex ideas do not necessarily resemble impressions – a mermaid may be imagined without necessarily having seen one – the parts that make up complex ideas are themselves derived from impressions and impressions, in their turn, from experience. It is from a multitude of experiences in social life that ideas are then derived (see Chappell 1968).

Kant's resultant fusion of reason and empiricism is complex. For the purposes of this journey, what is of importance is that his work contains a *focus imaginarius* as a 'built in feature of the human mind'. This is concerned with 'absolute truth, pure art and humanity as such' (Rorty 1989: 195–196). Freedom is derived from an individualism which regards human subjects as autonomous and transcendental through the exercise of reason. In this way, a link is established between scientific knowledge and moral rules (each governed by 'laws'):

> Everything in nature works according to laws. Only a rational being has the capacity of acting according to the conception of laws; i.e, according to principles. This capacity is will. Since reason is required for the derivations of actions from laws, will is nothing else than practical reason.
>
> (Kant quoted in Albrow 1987: 167–168)

Kant concluded that the material world causes sensations, but mental apparatuses order these and provide the concepts through which people understand their experiences in the 'phenomenal' world (the 'noumenal' world being beyond experience). Out of this fusion of ideas comes an ability to reflect upon nature and society in a rational manner:

> Rational mastery of nature and society presupposed knowledge of the truth, and the truth was a universal, as contrasted to the multi-fold appearance of things or to their immediate form in the perception of individuals. This principle was already alive in the earliest attempts of Greek epistemology: the truth is universal and necessary and thus contradicts the ordinary experiences of change and accident.
>
> (Marcuse 1969: 17)

Reason is the guarantor of universal knowledge. Add to this the Cartesian claim of a universal standard against which truth could be objectively measured, independent of the objects of scientific inquiry, then the Enlightenment comes to represent an ascending history of the scientific colonization over 'valid' knowledge. This requires that 'other' forms of knowledge are supplanted in the quest for objectivity, defined as 'the basic conviction that there is or must be some permanent, ahistorical matrix or framework to which we can ultimately appeal in determining the nature of rationality, knowledge, truth, reality, goodness, or rightness' (Bernstein 1983: 8).

Equipped with reason, scientists could emerge as the legislators, not simply the interpreters of knowledge concerning the social and physical worlds (Bauman 1987). Science could establish the difference between 'truth' and 'falsity'. Via Kant's a priori categories of thought, the individual could make sense of their empirical world and the worlds of culture and nature become distinguishable:

> As a result, the individual (not only the Cartesian mind) emerged as the subject, as subject of the world. Experiencing the world, the individual could claim to have a transcendental source of certainty within himself. He could set out to realize himself by realizing the world within himself.
>
> (Luhmann 1986: 317)

The development of reason can also be related to how human subjectivity was structured under the consolidation of the rise of occidental modernity, where, beginning in the seventeenth and eighteenth centuries, the social sciences, industrial capitalism and bureaucratic politics synchronized novel ways of objectifying 'individuals' and 'populations' in western societies (Dumas and Turner 2006). The emergence of western rationality was accompanied by a growth of scientific traditions such as positivism, each intellectualizing the nature and extent of individuality. Empirical observation, reason and science are major themes of the Enlightenment project. It was the Age of Reason in the second half of the eighteenth century with the idea of progress elaborated by Kant, Turgot, Condorcet and others that gave rise to modernity. The French Revolution in 1789 gave momentum to a new consciousness and the Industrial Revolution provided its material substance (Munck 2002).

This modern world, this new social order, was characterized by a new dynamism, a rejection of earlier traditions, a belief in progress and the potential of human reason to promote freedom. Increasing rationality would enhance social understanding, order and control, justice, moral progress and human happiness (Layder 2006). Coupled with this was Descartes's metaphysical axiom *'Cogito, ergo sum'* (I think, therefore I am), which extolled the capacity of individual reason as the foundation of awareness and the locus of knowledge. As a rationalist philosopher and mathematician, Descartes forcefully separated between 'mind' and 'body' and thereby articulated a Cartesian dualism that has provided a pivotal feature of western society.

Central to this Cartesian epistemology is a systematic belief in the supremacy of logical reason over illogical nature; Enlightenment philosophy assumes that the rational self has an 'inner' relationship with the mind and an 'outer' relationship with the body. Therefore the individual is conceived not as part of 'who we are' but part of nature, hence an object to be controlled. With the Kantian philosophy of ethics, reason is identified with morality for it provides the principles for knowledge, certainty and universal law, whereas the body is identified with feelings and emotions that are, according to Kant, external forms of determination; a lack of freedom that takes individuals away from the path of pure reason (Dumas and Turner 2006).

The notion of transcendence went on to act as a basis for objective and universal knowledge, reinforcing the Cartesian method in which experience is deemed to be 'real' only if deeply entrenched within consciousness and entirely detached from the corporeal (Seidman 2001). Reason and rationality now became regarded as the source of a taken–for–granted superiority:

> Mental life comprised for Descartes, above all, rational calculation, intuitive ideas, intellectual deliberations, and sensory inputs: we can accept responsibility for the validity of our calculations, but not the emotions that disturb or confuse our inferences
>
> (Toulmin 1990: 40)

The causes and consequences of modernity are not only cultural and social, but also economic. As Munck (2002) points out, another driving force was capitalism with its constant quest for new raw materials, new sources of labour power, new technologies and new applications that might attract new consumers. From the outset modernity promised to change the world and each innovation spawned another. However, alongside this, differentials, in terms of who may have access to and be able to deploy 'reason', served as a sophisticated legitimization function between 'scientific experts' and 'subjects' of knowledge given the dichotomous relationship between individuals will tend to define themselves via their position or identity.

We now have a combination of influences with which to contextualize social theory. However, these were interpreted according to different political and intellectual cultures. These diluted, modified and challenged these insights. It is to an understanding of this process to which we now turn.

Society: the object of study

In Italy there was a social theorist who was already anticipating three trends that were to emerge in the nineteenth century. First, an interest in the nature of social development and social origins. Second, the merging of history and philosophy into a 'science of society'. Third, the attempt to discover rational-empirical causes for social phenomena in place of metaphysical or theological ones (Bottomore and Nisbet 1979: 563).

Giambattista Vico (1668–1744) was no ally of the dominant ideas of his era, particularly Cartesianism. Perhaps for this reason he was little understood or read in his own time. Nevertheless, Vico had an influence on later thinkers such as Auguste Comte (1798–1857), Robert Michels (1876–1936) and Georges Sorrel (1847–1922). His argument was that social theory should be centred around a human subject whose actions could be understood only in relation to the whole of society. In other words, the individual could not be abstracted from their social context. People were social creatures whose feelings came from their socio–cultural environment. These feelings were 'sensory topics' which

> provide the 'roots' of a 'civil society'; they constitute the shared sense which arises among a social group who already share a set of circumstances – and it is against the background of such feelings as these that any conceptualization of what we take our human nature to be can be judged for its adequacy.
>
> (Shotter 1993: xiii–xiv)

In England at this time, an inspiration for feminist ideas was apparent in the writings of Mary Astell (1668–1731) and, later, Mary Wollstonecraft (1759–97). In 1694 Astell wrote 'A Serious Proposal to the Ladies' (K. M. Rogers 1979). Differences between the sexes were not attributed to some examined idea of 'nature' or 'reason', upon which so many thinkers had drawn from the Greeks onwards (Griffiths and Whitford 1988; P. Johnson 1993; Okin 1980) but to the power that men held over women in society. If Descartes has proclaimed reason in all, then it must also be available to women:

> It was this notion that the feminists seized upon so avidly. Mary boldly proclaimed the radical thesis that God had given all mankind the same intellectual potential – whether ancient or modern, rich or poor, male or female. Circumstances determine the extent to which men and women may exercise their rational faculties, but the faculties are present in all.
>
> (Kinnaird 1983: 34)

Nearly one hundred years later, in 1792, Wollstonecraft (1989) called for women to enjoy the changes occurring within society. In the spirit of modernity she argued that women should aspire to the realm of reason over that of pleasing men's desires, a relationship which serves to reinforce their subordination. These tensions between reason and emotion form, as we shall see in Chapter 2, a central part of the feminist critique of social theory.

In Scotland the so-called 'Scottish School' of Adam Ferguson (1723–1816), John Millar (1735–1801), David Hume and Adam Smith (1723–90), centred around Edinburgh, contributed to the Scottish Enlightenment. This group added to the idea that society was an object of study, with its own underlying properties, which should be examined through observation. They saw a link between social context and human actions. Hume characterized society in terms of customs and between social customs and ideas a link may be discovered. Overall, Hume's work may be seen in terms of the dissection of human nature in order that he might advance the understanding of history: 'In this sense, Hume's thinking was totally secular and empirical' (Heilbron 1995: 102).

In the case of Ferguson, it was the study of groups which formed the basis of his ideas. Indeed, he regarded conflict as a characteristic of society long before later 'conflict' theorists such as Max Weber (1864–1920) and Georg Simmel (1858–1918). Further, his ideas on the division of labour predated those of Marx and Emile Durkheim (1858–1917). In Ferguson's view, the increased division of labour which came with modernity possessed the potential for progress, as well as a threat to social stability.

Although more rationalist in orientation than England or Scotland, French social theorists incorporated the challenge to rationalist epistemology from empiricism. The individualism of Descartes and Kant, when fused with the experiences of the French Revolution, were not a sufficient basis for a cohesive social order. Diverse as the ideas of French scholars became, these influences led to the emergence of some core themes:

> Instead of a God-ordained society they spoke of reason; instead of regarding sin as inherent in man, they pinned their faith to human perfectibility and believed that education could the human personality; instead of the privileges of the different orders, they insisted upon egalitarianism.
>
> (Beloff 1954: 176)

One of the main representatives of this tradition was Charles Montesquieu (1689–1755). His main concern was with human freedom and how government could be most efficiently organized to secure it. He was also interested in the connections between people's opinions and the nature and structure of society. In the process, people were viewed

> not as a multitude of individuals under one government, but as a community distinguishable from others by their manners and institutions. All institutions, political, religious, domestic, economic, and artistic, are, in his eyes, intricately related to one another, so that any considerable change in one is bound to affect the others.
>
> (Plamenatz 1963: 256)

Through systematic study, Montesquieu wished to see how, in ways previously unsuspected, society forms people as 'social creatures'. At the same time, he did not view society in terms of progressive development. This distinguishes his thought from the Enlightenment idea of progress found in the work of Comte. Where Comte emphasized unity, Montesquieu remained aware of diversity.

In Comte's time the climate of opinion was more favourable to new ideas than it was for Montesquieu (Bierstedt 1979). Indeed, Comte is a central figure in the intellectual lineage of structuralism. This may be characterized in terms of 'the relation is more important than the parts' (Bottomore and Nisbet 1979: 558). This places structuralism at odds with the individualistic emphasis of other socio–theoretical traditions, in particular, those in nineteenth-century England.

Comte was to embrace the positive-rationalist idea of social progress, together with a belief in the scientific method for the purposes of studying and reconstructing the social, political and economic spheres of human life. Such was his faith in Positive Philosophy, which he learnt through his work with Saint-Simon, that he refused to read newspapers or books which had a bearing on his work; all part of his system of 'cerebral hygiene' (Bosanquet 1967). He was a pioneer of positivism which

> in its classical nineteenth-century form is an empiricist interpretation and systematization of the sciences combined with a general theory of history and society which can be understood as theoretical articulation of a definite set of political problems.
>
> (Benton 1977: 28)

In this way Comte added power to one of the central pillars of the Enlightenment: that is, the superseding of metaphysical and theological thought by science. This rejection of speculative thought placed sociology, as the highest science, firmly within the natural scientific paradigm. His view of 'social physics', with its theme of social statics (the science of order) and social dynamics (the science of progress), rejected the idea that social elements existed in separation from one another. As such, the individual subject could not exist separately from the society of which they were a part:

> there must always be a spontaneous harmony between the whole and the parts of the social system, the elements of which must inevitably be, sooner or later, combined in a mode entirely comfortable to their nature.
>
> (Comte in Parsons et al. 1965: 126–127)

This torch of positivism was taken up and held in different ways in the works of the English utilitarian philosopher John Stuart Mill (1807–73) and the social theorist Herbert Spencer (1820–1903), both of whom were influenced by the political culture of English individualism. Mill developed his positivism based on the idea that although society was constantly changing, human nature was itself fixed. The task of social science became to explain observations and construct social laws as deduced from a constant human nature. In the case of Spencer, he held an evolutionary view of society through combining a radical individualism with a collectivist organicism – as derived from biology – of society's social structures and institutions. Contrast the following with the quote from Comte above:

> Society is made up of individuals; all that is done in society is done by the combined actions of individuals; and therefore, in individual actions only can be found solutions of social phenomena.
>
> (Spencer 1969: 49)

Spencer was widely read in Victorian England, probably due to the support his ideas gave to the indivdualism of laissez-faire capitalism. The system of economic exchange was then provided with an intellectual legitimacy for its functioning, promises and effects. The same could hardly be said of a contemporary of Spencer's: Karl Marx.

From consciousness to capitalism

In Comte's positivism and structuralism there is a 'philosophy of history' (P. Burke 1980). Each of the aspects in his work – the unfolding of history, the condemnation of individualism, a belief in science and progress towards more enlightened times – are also characteristics of Marx. Here, however, the parallels end. His ideas were formed not only through the influences of Saint-Simon, but also in his encounters with the German idealist philosopher Georg Hegel (1770–1831) and with what are known as the 'English political economists' (see Barber 1981):

> His belief in history ... more than anything else, distinguishes him from his predecessors and above all from Kant. ... Reality is to be understood in becoming and therefore in history. For the dialectical process, in which truth came from the coming together of opposing views, was only the mirror of a dialectical process in reality.
>
> (Lindsay 1967: 58)

People become viewed as historical beings, not philosophical abstractions. Nevertheless, where Hegel was to emphasize consciousness, Marx was to emphasize actual human existence in given social situations. For Marx it was not ideas which formed society but, on the contrary, the actual material conditions under which people lived. Marx came to consider the 'dialectic of history' in opposing terms to Hegel. To understand this, it is first necessary to consider Hegel's work in some more depth.

For Hegel reason could become manifest in history. History unfolds in dialectic from thesis and antithesis to a synthesis. Two Enlightenment ideals are worth noting here: progress and freedom from an external world. Human 'being' must be defined, not in terms of something external to people, but in ways which depend upon an internal relation within and between each other. This is where his concept of 'mind' and its historical unfolding towards self-consciousness enters.

The Phenomenology of Mind (Hegel 1967a) is a study of how minds appear to themselves (phenomenology being the study of how things appear to people). Kant had argued that reality could never be known as it was, but comprehended only through the a priori categories of thought (space, time and causation). These are not part of reality, but the means through which it is grasped. Kant thus started with the idea of a 'reality' and 'that knowledge is some kind of instrument or medium by which we grasp reality' (Singer 1983: 50). This presupposes a difference between human beings and the reality they inhabit. Despite this, knowledge is still regarded as being part of reality. The question remains, however, as to how reality can be known by people, given their separation from it?

The Kantian answer to this question is that the instruments through which people seek to gain knowledge of reality must be known. It is this which forms the basis of Hegel's critique of Kant's epistemology:

> We ought, says Kant, to become acquainted with the instrument, before we undertake the work for which it is to be employed; for if the instrument be insufficient, all our trouble will be spent in vain. ... But the examination of knowledge can only be carried out by an act of knowledge. To examine this so-called instrument is the same thing as to know it. But to seek to know before we know is as absurd as the wise resolution of Scholasticus, not to venture into the water until he had learned to swim.
>
> (Hegel quoted in Singer 1983: 51)

The starting–point for knowing reality is now consciousness of that reality. Upon examination, the limitations of consciousness may be discovered. This will enable the development of a more sophisticated form of consciousness and so on, until 'absolute knowledge' is reached. Therefore, it is not necessary to be content with a Kantian 'appearance of reality'. Instead, knowledge can be gained of reality itself, for Hegel regards knowledge as historically constituted. 'Being' is linked with history and the 'Real' is the 'Rational': 'History is the substance of society, since the substance of society is nothing more than continuity. Humanity's being therefore lies in its historicity' (Heller 1984: 28).

Hegel then links this with politics (Hegel 1967b). For clarity of exposition, we can say that the 'idea' or 'ideal' is to realize our potential in reality. This is freedom from a bond with nature through the development of self-consciousness. However, as people are socially constituted (the development of our personalities is a societal, not individual matter for Hegel) there must be a relation between our internal consciousness and the external sphere of the society which we inhabit. In other words, there must be a social means through which we are recognized as 'free agents'. The means is 'possession' and its social manifestation is 'property' (see Ryan 1986). Yet there must be some regulatory relation between the seeking of individual ends and the wider society in order that it is maintained and reasonably stable. Aside from property, an answer to how this relationship is achieved is found in writings on the state.

The state is seen as a fusion between self-consciousness and the manner in which it is objectively manifested in social, political and economic relations. The rights of the individual and universal reason can thereby be united and the social problems created by a competitive society tempered. What Hegel termed 'civil society' can be moderated by this higher unity. Its absence would exacerbate a tendency towards what he called an 'alienation of the spirit': that is, the duality within people to regard their freedom as freedom from the constraints of the material world and to strive to be purely spiritual while, at the same time, recognizing that they are part of that world and thus cannot escape from it, nor transcend it.

To finally link Hegel to Marx we must do so via the work of Ludwig Feuerbach (1804–72). Feuerbach was a 'Young Hegelian' who examined 'religion' and 'God', but in so doing adopted a position opposed to it. Broadly speaking, he argued that God was a creation of human beings and not the other way round. Marx also reversed Hegel's idealism, but as applied to the state. As people had created God, so they had created the state. Hegel argued that social relations were dependent upon the 'idea of the state' manifested in reason. Marx, on the other hand, argued that consciousness did not create institutions, but the material conditions under which people actually lived: 'With me ... the ideal is nothing else than the material world reflected by the human mind, and translated into forms of thought' (Marx 1983: 29):

Marx reached the conclusion that it was not spiritual attitudes, but external conditions, the wealth men enjoyed or lacked, the ways they had to labour, which shaped society. Epochs were controlled not by conceptions of man but by material ends and means. The ruling interests and difficulty of men was relating to the *world*, not to the *self*.

(G. A. Cohen 1984: 22, original italics)

The explanation for civil society is now found in the material conditions of social life. History was not the unfolding of a 'dialectic of spirit', but a dialectic resulting from changes in the means of production. This is the guiding thread of Marx's social theory:

> In the social production of their life, men enter into definite relations that are indispensable and independent of their will, relations of production which correspond to a definite stage of development of their material productive forces. The sum total of these relations of production constitutes the economic structure of society, the real foundation, on which rises a legal and political superstructure and to which correspond definite forms of social consciousness.
>
> (Marx 1980: 181)

Given this, Marx was critical of philosophy in terms of both Hegel's idealism and Feuerbach's materialism (Marx 1961, 1964). Social theory now needs to explain the context of people's actions so that thought and practice can fuse in what he termed 'praxis'. The scientific validity of this theory rests upon its capacity not only to explain social life, but also to change it.

To achieve these aims Marx had to embark upon an empirical examination of capitalism, as well as a critique of the economic theory which provided for its legitimacy. Political economy, which assumed the existence of private property, did so without explaining the cause of the division between labour and capital in the first instance. Economic exchange is not some 'accidental fact': 'The only wheels which political economy sets in motion are *greed* and the *war amongst the greedy* – competition' (Marx 1981: 62, original italics). In a similar way, society, the state and social relations are not manifestations of some 'spirit', but of the ways in which people organize their societies on the basis of the means of production (the 'base'). This, in turn, structures all other relations within society (the superstructure). Labour and the need to sell labour to capital, for the extraction of surplus value, in order to survive, oils the capitalist machine to the benefit of the few, not the many. Although Hegel was correct to connect 'being' to social relations and to restore history and meaning to the human realm, he was wrong to view this in terms of something called 'will'. For Marx, the implications of this position were clear:

> What is society, whatever its form may be? The product of men's reciprocal action. Are men free to choose this or that form of society? By no means. Assume a particular state of development in the production faculties of man and you will get a particular form of commerce and consumption. Assume particular stages of development in production, commerce and consumption and you will have a corresponding social constitution.

(Marx to Annenkov, 28 December 1846, in Marx and Engels 1953: 40)

Alienation also has a different origin. Hegel's outstanding achievement was to see the connection between self and social environment, but he was wrong to see labour only in terms of 'mental' labour. People are distinguished from all other living things through their ability to produce, but in a manner which takes account of their needs. They create through their labour, but capitalism, as a system of production, is dehumanizing. People become alienated from each other and the world in which they live through the use of their labour by a system which expropriates and abstracts it from their daily lives. Nor is private property the affirmation of self-development, but its very denial. The link between 'being in society' and the system under which people live is now established in a material, not idealist sense:

> What Marx saw as capitalism's most basic contradiction, between its increasingly social productive forces and its enduringly privatized mode of appropriation, reaches deep: into our selves. Modernity constitutes individuals as subjects not through but in opposition to the real sociality which concretely defines and differentiates them.
>
> (D. Sayer 1991: 72)

Capitalism now defines the character of modernity and capital becomes: 'the demiurge of the modern world' (D. Sayer 1991: 12). Marx noted how the division of labour 'seizes upon, not only the economic, but every other sphere of society'. It provides, at the expense of everything else, an 'all engrossing system of specializing and sorting men' (Marx 1983: 334). In this analysis, there was the potential for change. The end point of history is not self-consciousness, but communism. Here, co-operation and freedom from alienation would exist.

Despite the power of argument two questions, in particular, remain. First, how is capitalist society to be condemned, if it also contains within it the seeds for a better future? As Alisdair MacIntyre puts it: 'if the moral impoverishment of advanced capitalism is what so many Marxists agree that it is, whence are these resources for the future to be derived' (1985: 262)? This has led to a number of debates over the relationship between Marxism and morality (see Lukes 1985; McLellan and Sayers 1990). Second, does Marx's work inevitably imply the need for revolution, or could a better society be obtained through revisionism?

Attempts to answer these questions have moved through a myriad of ideas, which include the work of critical analysis to help the demise of capitalism on its way (Lukács 1971). In the case of the 'revisionist-controversy', this was sparked by the writings of Bernstein, leading to a debate involving key Marxist figures at the turn of the twentieth century: for example, Kautsky, Luxemburg and Hilferding (see Laclau and Mouffe 2001).

Four schools of thought then emerged within Marxist thought: the orthodox school; the revisionist school; the Austro-Marxists and Lenin and the Bolsheviks (Bottomore 1979). All of which leads to a rich history of Marxist thought (see Kolakowski 1978a, 1978b).

The use of work to come to terms with the nature of modernity and its propensity for change is a continual feature of social and political thought. In terms of our immediate journey, when it comes to an absence of a consideration of the ethical realm in social life, over the predominance of the economic realm, we find one social theorist who, like many European social thinkers at the turn of the twentieth century, was looking for new sources of inspiration. As S. H. Hughes puts it regarding this phenomenon:

> in asking themselves whether Marxism could properly be considered a science, they were inevitably led to pose the further question of what one meant by a science of society and the extent to which such a body of scientific knowledge was attainable at all.
>
> (S. H. Hughes 1979: 73–74)

Ethics and social integration

As we have seen, for Comte, societal development was governed by social laws. With Hegel, history was conceived of in terms of the progress of the mind, with an ultimate dialectical progression towards self-consciousness. For Marx, history was seen in terms of progress but, in an inversion of idealism, then theorized in terms of the actions of people in concrete social situations. When it comes to the work of Emile Durkheim, however, he was to emphasize the ethical aspects of social life. In Durkheim's hands, morality was to become a defining characteristic of modern society that expresses its collectively held needs. Durkheim attempted early in his career to establish an academic niche for his embryonic social science that would be distinct from its roots in moral philosophy and separate from its related and already established discipline, psychology. 'Almost single-handed [Durkheim] forced the academic community to accept sociology as a rigorous and scientific discipline' (Swingewood 1991: 97). By defining his own work in scope and method, he created the 'boundaries' of a social theory that were distinct from those of other emerging social sciences such as economics, political science, and anthropology. The 'revolutionary character' of Marx was one of the main reasons that Durkheim dismissed Marxism as a viable means for improving the moral or social condition in modern society. He felt that deep social change is always the result of long-term social evolution, not a sudden revolution from the working class.

Durkheim differed with Marx not only in how social improvements should be made, but also in terms of the theoretical, methodological, and substantive approaches that sociology should take in its empirical observation of the social world. Just as the natural sciences look for physical forces that influence the world we perceive with our senses, social sciences look at social facts as external forces which exerted moral constraint on individuals. In this manner, Durkheim established the context of sociology as the study of 'moral phenomena', such as anomie, collective conscience and social currents and looked for structural manifestations (social facts) that influence and, more importantly, constrain individuals (Ritzer 2000: 187).

Durkheim employed his science of moral phenomena with the prospect of reintroducing and upholding a moral order within modern society. Durkheim's opinion was that 'the characteristic problem facing the modern age is to reconcile the individual freedoms which have sprung from the dissolution of traditional society with the maintenance of the moral control upon which the very existence of society depends' (Giddens 1972b: 99). For this reason, his theories centred on the ideas of social cohesion (solidarity), moral order (law, anomie, collective conscience), and the role of ideas (religion) and most importantly their influence on the social life of individuals.

Durkheim's own intellectual legacy was Montesquieu, Comte and Spencer, not Hegel and English political economy. There is also the political context in which he lived. As with Comte before him, this was a time of considerable change in France. Whereas for Comte it was the legacy of the French Revolution, for Durkheim it was events such as the Dreyfus Affair, defeat in the Franco-Prussian War (1870–71) and the German annexation of Alsace–Lorraine. Here is a writer who has been characterized as an idealist, a materialist, a social realist and a neo-Kantian (Lukes 1981). His social theory has been seen as a link between French conservatism and systematic sociology (Nisbet 1970: 13) as well as there now being critical and radical interpretations of his work (M. Gane 1992; Pearce 1989). Despite these contradictory interpretations, there is one thing that can be said about Durkheim's work with certainty: in his hands, social theory and, in particular, sociology were to receive major boosts.

Durkheim's work was organized around three goals. First, the establishment of sociology as a scientific discipline. Second, the foundation of a basis for the unity and unification of the social sciences. Third, the provision of an empirical, rational and systematic basis for modern society's civil religion (Tiryakian 1979). Together with French intellectual figures such as Le Play, Proudhon and Comte, Durkheim contributed to the development of a normative social theory which sought to integrate morality and economic life for the purpose of social stability. This was a key feature of the liberal left in French social thought, translating into the political question as to how the traditional structures of society were to be incorporated and adapted to fit emergent forms? In terms of his third goal, his work may thus be characterized as contributing to the moral integration of the Third Republic. Aside from those already mentioned, what were the influences on his work towards this end?

First, there were the rigorous historical methods of Gabriel Monod and Fustel de Coulanges (Lukes 1981: 58–65). To this can be added the influence of the German social thinker Albert Schaffle and his idea of society as an 'organism'. However, while defending Schaffle's socialism against the charge that it was collectivist and authoritarian, the idea of an organism was a metaphorical, not literal device. On this Durkheim was clear. Society is not a set of material relations in the sense in which an organism is governed 'mechanically', but it is a set of relationships of ideas which neither are reducible to the persons who make up that society, nor can be separated from them. If moral order was to be regained following the transition from a traditional community (mechanical) to the interdependent modern society (organic), a temporary period in his opinion due entirely to a lack of moral cohesion brought upon by the cult of individuality and the specialization of labour, it would do so more easily if it were guided by a morally conscious democratic state advised and counselled by an empirically based moral science (Ritzer 2000).

In his encounters with socialism, Durkheim was always to emphasize morality over economics. This stemmed from the need to find 'a substitute for traditional Christian teachings, so as to legitimate itself and win the broader support of new generations of schoolchildren, wrestling them away from the moral authority of the Catholic Church' (Tiryakian 1979: 195). Without a moral basis for society, France would represent, as it had in the First and Second Republics, the exercise of power in the hands of one person, with the alternative being anarchy as manifested in a proletarian uprising. The solution to this problem lay in a rational and systematic inquiry into the causes, consequences and conditions for social order.

In this quest Kant was to be an important inspiration, but this was Kant mediated not through the works of Hegel, but through the writings of Charles Renouvier (1815–1903). Renouvier was a thinker from whose philosophy, it has been claimed, no less than the political culture of the Third Republic was derived (Lukes 1981: 55). His concerns were then reflected in Durkheim's writings:

> his uncompromising rationalism; his central concern with morality and his determination to study it 'scientifically'; his neo-Kantianism emphasizing the compatibility of the determinism of nature with the freedom presupposed by morality; his Kantian concern with the dignity and autonomy of the individual together with his theory of social cohesion based on the individual's sense of unity with and dependence on others; his preference for justice over utility and denial that the first can be derived from the second; his notion of

existing society being in a state of war and his view of the State's role being to establish 'social justice' in the economic sphere.

(Lukes 1981: 55)

Renouvier was critical of Kant's idea that experience was given via the a priori categories of thought. Instead, as in the works of Vico, Montesquieu and Marx, what if reason and categories of thought are not given a priori, but produced socially? From a structuralist vantage point, a change in the structures of society would then mean an alteration in experiences. This emphasis was to form a central pillar of Durkheim's social theory whereby the philosophical, sociological and political fuse.

Durkheim's 'sociological epistemology' would allow him to derive a new approach to ethics that would be capable of providing a basis for stability in times of change. Accepting that people are rational and 'free', rationality would be exercised through the construction of laws applicable to all. Society would then be the transcendental source and not universal reason as such. Society would possess an authority not only because it transcended each individual, but also because it was also contained within them. It possessed a twofold source of morality: 'It was a set of facts-in-the-world from which correct moral inferences could be made and it was the authority for moral judgements' (Hawthorn 1976: 121).

Together with his nephew Marcel Mauss (1872–1950) Durkheim saw sociology as the correct means for deriving moral forms within society. From a political point of view he argued for a harmony between the individual and the state and against the utilitarian individualism of Spencer and others. For Durkheim, this would result in what the philosopher Thomas Hobbes (1588–1679) referred to as the 'war of all against all'. At the same time, Durkheim defended the individual against large impersonal institutions. For instance, in a review of Merlino's *Formes et essences du socialisme* (1898), he argued that the state, if it is to remain 'normal', should be moderated by autonomous, restricted groups: for example, professional associations. He takes up Merlino's assertion that the individual and the state are necessarily antagonistic to each other:

> Nothing could be more contrived than this so-called antagonism, the idea of which Merlino is quite wrong to borrow from orthodox economics. The truth is that the State has been quite the opposite – the liberator of the individual. It is the State which, as it grew stronger, freed the individual from private and local groups which tended to absorb him: the family, the city, the corporation, etc.
>
> (Durkheim 1992: 57)

In the scientific pursuit of establishing a causal relationship between the moral reality of 'modern' turn-of-the-century France and the social forces that created that order (or disorder), Durkheim employed comparative method (for example, comparing totemism to modern monotheistic religions) and the construction of dichotomies (such as normal versus pathological) to investigate the social world. As Seidman (2001) points out, the comparative method, properly understood, is the very framework of the science of society and is inseparable from a scientific sociology. As a result Durkheim established the methods it would employ in the observation of social facts and to establish causality in the pursuit of questions on the relationship between the individual and society. In the Preface to the first edition of *The Division of Labour in Society* he writes:

> This work has its origins in the question of the relation of the individual to social solidarity. Why does the individual, while becoming more autonomous, depend more upon society? How can he be at once more individual and more solidarity?
>
> (Durkheim 1964: 37)

The moral dimension to social life continually returns in his work. For instance, in the increasing division of labour, as represented in the transition from mechanical to organic solidarity, we find that the emergence of modernity leads to a greater recognition of a need for each other. This 'togetherness' 'was the coming thing, rather than something which we were losing' (Gellner 1988: 30). The laissez–faire ideal would not bring peace to people and Durkheim viewed Marx as sharing this economistic approach to social life which ignored the moral dimension and the 'fact' that the division of labour not only limits people's activity, but also increases it (Durkheim 1964: 305). Indeed, in comparing their writings on anomie and alienation we can say that: 'Social constraint is for Marx a denial and for Durkheim a condition of human freedom and self–realization' (Lukes 1967: 142). Through employing Charles Darwin's (1809–82) ideas, he reconciles a greater population density without an exacerbation of social conflict. An increased specialization of labour is argued to counteract the tendency towards conflict, as it enables coexistence in the performance of different services, yet in parallel to each other (Durkheim 1964: 266–267).

The balance between autonomy and togetherness is actuated through 'moral individualism'. The source of this is Christianity, or Protestantism to be more exact:

> Since for the Christian, virtue and piety do not consist in material procedures, but interior states of the soul, he is compelled to exercise a perpetual watch over himself. ... Thus of the two possible poles of thought, nature on the one hand, and man on the other, it is necessarily around the second that the thought of Christian societies has come to gravitate.
>
> (Durkheim quoted in Giddens 1971: 115–116)

Comte was thus criticized for calling for a return to traditional times. The march of individualism could not be stopped and a new bridging system was required between the individual and society. Durkheim was clearly aware of the tensions which existed between pre-modern and modern forms of society. His belief in the potential harmonic position between the individual and society has frequently been stressed over the tensions he saw within society: for example, he has been characterized as a consensus theorist, in contrast to the conflict ideas of Marx, Weber and Simmel. Yet a motor of societal progress is expressed in terms of anomie, while he notes the role of desire and feeling in human relations, in contrast to the usual neo-Kantian readings of his work.

This emphasis on desire and feeling leads into the writings of the German philosopher Arthur Schopenhauer (1788–1860), who wrote on the 'will' and 'irrationalism' in social thought. Progress is seen in his work not as the triumph of reason, but as the furtherance of the power of the 'will'. After all, myths, habits and rituals should not, as both Thorstein Veblen (1857–1929) and Sigmund Freud (1856–1939) recognized, be simply dismissed as irrelevant or uninteresting in the study of social life. If this reading of Durkheim is accepted, he recognized the tensions in modernity between will and reason. Is it this which gave rise to his desire to find a new basis for social solidarity in the France of his day, without recourse to the egoistic tendencies in modern western societies.

At this point we can make a link here from Durkheim to another leading social theorist: Max Weber. Schopenhauer influenced Friedrich Nietzsche (1844–1900), who refused the Hegelian revision of a philosophy of history. In so doing: 'He renounces a renewed revision of the concept of reason and *bids farewell* to the dialectic of enlightenment' (Habermas 1992a: 86, original italics). The influence of Marx and Nietzsche is to be found in the writings of Max Weber.

The forward march of rationalization

Like Durkheim, Weber did not believe in a class revolution. Despite being contemporaries, however, they had little influence upon each other and were influenced by separate disciplines: Durkheim from French post-Enlightenment philosophy and Weber from the German historical school (Callinicos 2000). For Weber there are no historical laws, or any resolution of history through revolution. This has given rise to wide-ranging debates over his ideas, their meaning and applicability to contemporary times (Lash and Whimster 1987; Ray and Reed 1994). At the same time, he became an inspiration for a number of scholars (Dahrendorf 1959; Goldthorpe and

Marshall 1992; Rex 1961; Ritzer 2000). We may distinguish Weber, in part, from either Marx or Durkheim because of his unwillingness to see science as a means for prescribing ends:

> Science today is a 'vocation' organized in special disciplines in the service of self-clarification and knowledge of interrelated facts. It is not the gift of grace of seers and prophets dispensing sacred values and revelations, nor does it partake of the contemplation of sages and philosophers about the meaning of the universe. This, to be sure, is the inescapable condition of our historical situation. We cannot evade it as long as we remain true to ourselves.
>
> (Weber in Gerth and Mills 1970: 152)

We are led away from history as resolved by the 'mind' (Hegel), or the actions of people with common interests (Marx), or by the laws of historical evolution (Saint-Simon, Comte and Durkheim). Instead, history is resolved by 'will' (Hawthorn 1976). The link between modernity, rationality and progress is now cast into the realm of uncertainty. Weber becomes a theorist of 'fate' (B. S. Turner 1981) for whom modernity came to represent the forward march of rationalization. This can stifle the individual, but is a condition from which they cannot escape:

> Weber saw historical change as the unintended effect of endless social processes and contingent circumstances ... this world-view is a social liberalism which asks us, given the complexity and uncertainty of knowledge, to behave responsibly – that is, as agents with 'personality' who are forced to make choices in conditions of unreliable knowledge.
>
> (Holton and Turner 1989: 9)

These tensions are also apparent in the writings of two of Weber's contemporaries: Georg Simmel and Ferdinand Tönnies (1855–1936). The nature of Simmel's work has made for a myriad of interpretations. It has been characterized as 'fragmentary' and 'unsystematic' (Frisby 1992a, 1992b), while he is said to be the first sociologist of modernity (Frisby 1991) as well as the first sociologist of postmodernity (Weinstein and Weinstein 1991). As for Tönnies, he employed the ideas of 'community' (*Gemeinschaft*) and 'society' (*Gesellschaft*) to consider the changes from a rural to an industrial Germany in the forward march of modernity. The former is characterized by a 'natural will' of habit and instinct, wwhile the latter is characterized by a 'rational will' which is instrumental in terms of its selection of means for ends. For Tönnies, there were ramifications for the ways in which individuals then related to one another. Parallels become evident in both of their works with Weber in terms of a concern for the fate of the individual in modern society.

It is the sheer range of intellectual influences which informed German social theory at this time which leads to this range of interpretations. When it comes to Weber, to the neo-Kantians and Nietzsche, we may add Marx, or more accurately those Marxists who were busy interpreting his work. In addition, Freund (1979) notes two other influences. The first of these derives from the distinction which is made between the state and civil society (which Marx had criticized). This is basic to an understanding of German intellectual culture at this time. Broadly speaking, the institution of the state is seen as 'the source of all liberty, while society is the field of economic activity, which is the source of dependence and servitude' (Freund 1979: 151).

The second influence was that of psychologism and historicism. According to the former, society could be studied in terms of a collective psychology. The focus here is upon, for example, languages, myths, habits, customs and so on, which permits one to speak of a 'spirit' in Hegelian terms. Wilhelm Dilthey (1833–1911), for instance, sought to discover an epistemological basis for the human sciences through their being rooted in 'inner' experience, rather than a natural-scientific 'outer' experience. This focus on understanding social life and the meanings for the individuals who comprise it, led him to develop a 'descriptive psychology'. Historicism is then of importance due to a focus on the 'lived experience' of people. As such, history could not be ignored in the process of social inquiry.

It was in economics that an influential historical school emerged and from this discipline Weber had emerged (at one time he referred to himself as a 'social economist': Holton and Turner 1989). Together with the work of Windelband and Rickert on the role and meaning of history in knowledge, this fusion of intellectual cultures – psychologism, historicism, neo-Kantianism, Nietzsche and Marx – led him to reject all attempts at finding an 'inner meaning' or objective social laws in history. His methodological writings exhibit a combination of Dilthey's idea of the meaningful 'inner' experiences of people (understanding), together with an analysis of the observed regularities of human behaviour in terms of the natural scientific idea of cause and effect (Weber 1949).

To the above we must add the changing political and economic culture of Germany in order to fully situate Weber's work. As with Durkheim, Weber's writings took place against the background of political problems. In particular, Weber was concerned to analyse the conditions of industrial expansion in Germany in the post-Bismarckian era. This led to an emphasis in his political sociology on two aspects: first, the furtherance of the German nation state, and second, that all politics is, in the last analysis, a struggle for power (*Macht*):

> As a witness of Bismarck's unification of Germany and the virtual elimination of the liberal, middle-class movements from positions of

> political influence, Weber became convinced that great goals could be achieved only by power politics. For the rest of his life he set a premium upon examining political life without illusions, looking at it as a struggle between individuals and groups with conflicting beliefs and interests, always decided in the end by the reservoir of power available to the winning side and by its greater ability to use that power effectively.
>
> (Bendix 1977: 7)

In charting these reactions to modernity, clear differences emerge between Weber and the other thinkers considered so far. His emphasis on the never ending nature of power struggles and his unwillingness to reduce the political sphere to the economic separate him from both Durkheim and Marx. In addition, although a defender of the objectivity of social science, he acknowledged the 'extra-scientific' dimension to its practice: for example, the cultural values which exist within particular societies and the ways in which they affect the reception of particular ideas.

The above noted, we also find a common reaction in the work of Weber and Durkheim. For both 'have their origin in an attempt to defend – or rather re-interpret – the claims of political liberalism within the twin pressures of Romantic hypernationalistic conservatism on the one side, and revolutionary socialism on the other' (Giddens 1971: 244). This shared quest was one of generating a liberal political consciousness in the face of the forward march of modernity. Here, we also find similarities with Marx who, after all, took aim at Romantic conservatism and utilitarian ideas. This emphasis not only allows for a modification of Marx and Durkheim's insights, but also provides for a re-examination of the relationship between Marx and Weber (Lowith 1993; D. Sayer 1991).

Although differences do exist between Marx and Weber, Weber told one of his students in the later years of his life:

> One can measure the integrity of a modern scholar, and especially of a modern philosopher, by how he sees his own relationship to Nietzsche and Marx. Whoever does not admit that he could not accomplish very important aspects of his work without the work that these two have performed deceives both himself and others. The world in which we ourselves exist intellectually is largely a world stamped by Marx and Nietzsche.
>
> (Weber quoted in Mommsen 1992: 54)

This fusion proved to be a 'massive, but brittle, intellectual synthesis' (Giddens 1972a: 58). Yet it is a dynamic which permits two outcomes. First, it renders Weber's work of contemporary importance to understanding social life. Second, it allows a questioning of the simple distinction which can be made between Marx and Weber on the grounds that the former was a materialist and the latter an idealist critic of Marx. Weber, for example, refers not just to the importance of ideas in examining social relations, but also of material interests – as is manifest in his observations on the Russian Revolution (Beetham 1974).

This situation is compounded through a failure to locate their works in terms of the social content in which they wrote. Weber read of Marx through the lenses of Friedrich Engels (1820–95) and Karl Kautsky (1854–1938), both of whom tended to perpetuate a view of Marx as somewhat mechanistic in his conceptions of society and social relations. What was lost in this interpretation was the element of praxis. After all, Marx provided 'a theory for practical orientation, requiring human action to become reality' (Mommsen 1992: 56). On this basis, Weber and Marx share an anthropological concern with the whole question of the relationship between the individual, modernity and social reality. For one, this reality was characterized as self-alienation, for the other, by a process of rationalization in which the individual found themselves increasingly trampled by vast impersonal forces.

As capitalism was the main characteristic of modernity for Marx, so rationalization was for Weber. In particular, what he referred to as formal rationality: that is, the application of rational calculable principles to everyday action. In contrast to the usual preoccupations of the Marx versus Weber debate: 'a more appropriate approach to Weber's sociology may be located in the problems of modernization and modernity, and that we should regard rationalization as the process which produced modernism' (B. Turner in Holton and Turner 1989: 69). This theme was given special emphasis in Weber's writings on religion and the emergence of capitalism (Weber 1985). In the 'last analysis', it was rationalization which gave rise to capitalism and under which all else is subsumed, including those elements prioritized by Marx:

> Weber did not regard capitalism as a power made up of 'relations' of the forces and means of production which had become autonomous, so that everything else could be understood therefrom in terms of ideology. According to Weber, capitalism could only become the 'most fateful' power in human life because it had itself already developed within the framework of a 'rational way of life'.
>
> (Lowith 1993: 63)

Here are echoes of Kant and Hegel fused with a Nietzschean fatalism. Human meaning and values were declining in the modern world. This was a situation which might be rectified by powerful leadership. To recap, it was Hegel who historicized Kant, leaving his abstract considerations on transcendental reason to became rooted in the unfolding of human history. Brunkhorst (1992) argues that in Weber's social history of religion we find a Hegelian objective 'spirit' (in this case, of capitalism) as a correlate of Kant's abstract concept of a 'categorical imperative' (simply put, the duty to act according to a universal moral law regardless of the consequences of one's actions). However, we should note that Weber would not guarantee an outcome for this process through his refusal to employ Enlightenment principles without qualification:

> 'Scientific' pleading is meaningless in principle because the various value spheres of the world stand in irreconcilable conflict with each other. ... I do not know how one might wish to decide 'scientifically' the value of French and German culture; for here, too, different gods struggle with one another, now *and for all times to come*.
>
> (Weber in Gerth and Mills 1970: 147–148, emphasis added)

Modernity now appears tinged with disenchantment, not absolute progress. Formal rationality increasingly undermines substantive rationality, which involves 'a conscious belief in the absolute value of some ethical, aesthetic, religious, or other form of behaviour, entirely for its own sake and independently of any prospects of external success' (Weber in Parsons et al. 1965: 1063).

The Protestant ethic is the key element in the rise of capitalism for Weber. This leads to the unintended consequence of an increased rationalization of social life. Weber's social theory can thus be read as preoccupied with the everyday world of human culture (Smart 2007). History moves from the personal to the impersonal, leaving human meanings and values in its wake. Ironically, what starts as an irrational quest for salvation, ends up as the 'iron cage of rationality': 'The premiums were placed on 'proving' oneself before God ... and 'proving' oneself before men in the sense of socially holding one's own within the Puritan sects' (Weber in Gerth and Mills 1970: 321). This drive towards self–perfection has a high cost:

> No one knows who will live in this cage in the future, or whether at the end of this tremendous development entirely new prophets will arise, or there will be a great rebirth of old ideas and ideals, or, if neither, mechanized petrification, embellished with a sort of convulsive self–importance. For of the last stage of this cultural development, it might well be truly said: specialists without spirit, sensualists without heart; this nullity imagines that it has attained a level of civilization never before achieved.
>
> (Weber 1985: 182)

Summary: the legacy for social theory

The Enlightenment formed a backdrop against which the development of social theory could be evaluated. It would be incorrect, however, to characterize this as a determining relationship. This was a relationship which was modified according to the cultural and political circumstances and intellectual traditions in which social theorists worked. It is these very aspects of social theory which provide it with the power of insight, relevance and critique.

Writers such as Montesquieu, Hume, Smith and Ferguson, in their different ways, viewed people as 'social creatures', not metaphysical entities capable of floating freely over their social universes. This affected the nature of the relationship between the individual and society which witnessed a journey from Montesquieu, through Comte's structuralism, to Spencer's methodological individualism. In the process, ideas on how history unfolded, what the future might be, how it might best be secured, what constituted valid knowledge and what it was to be human, were illuminated.

Marx considered the relationship between the individual and society in dialectical terms. For this purpose, he drew upon the work of Hegel, whose achievement was:

> to link a philosophical idea of rationality, couched in the broadest possible terms to comprehend mind, consciousness, the following of rules, the essence of what it was to be human, with everyday understanding of people about their practical business of learning skills, trading goods, getting married or engaging in state activities.
> (Albrow 1990: 112)

Hegel challenged the idea of absolute truth and error characteristic of 'the traditional, foundational picture of knowledge' (Sayers 1989: 34). Marx took this on board, but applied a more materialist than idealist reading, ultimately viewing capitalism as the defining characteristic of modernity. For Marx, walking in the shadows of the Enlightenment, history would still unfold, but towards communism, not the idealist concept of self-consciousness. Yet if we jettison the tendential determinism associated with his ideas of history, it is perhaps not surprising that one recent biography notes that a special issue of the New Yorker in 1997 hailed Marx as the person who has taught us most about the dynamics of capitalism and as long as it persists, his work will be relevant (Wheen 1999).

Durkheim, like Marx, was concerned with the fate of the individual in modern life. However, he was also concerned with the future of social solidarity in the France of his time. Changes in society required new modes of social integration which would respect individual autonomy, but without recourse to egoism. This moved him away from an economic, to an ethical focus in human affairs. Indeed, Durkheim's greatest influence on the development of social science was probably the idea of society as an 'actively moralizing force' (Bauman 1989: 172).

In Weber's work neo-Kantianism became fused with Nietzsche. Although committed to the idea that social science should start with the subjective meanings that people attach to their social lives, Weber was concerned with the fate of individuals in the forward march of modernity. Therefore, can this journey be characterized as one which travelled from the optimism of the early Enlightenment to one of pessimism? Put in these terms, this might not be unreasonable. However, if Weber appeared as a pessimist, he was not a full-blown fatalist. He drew the boundaries of science far tighter than had many of his predecessors. Science could not enter into the realm of value judgements. At best, it might help to decide upon the best means for the achievement of pre-selected ends.

We might now observe that at the end of this journey there appears a common thread among thinkers at the end of the nineteenth century. This *fin de siècle* spirit parallels that of recent times: 'a deliberate breaking away from the seriousness of tradition ... and a seemingly liberal concern with what might still be termed socialist, democratic, humanistic ideals of justice and equality' (Meštrović 1992: ix). This characterization is not without its problems. Indeed, we would probably not want to live in the pre-Enlightenment world, given the choice. Yet there are reasons for having reservations about the legacy the Enlightenment has left us. For example, a culture in which we are always looking for the most effective or efficient means for our ends often forgets to give adequate thought to those ends themselves. Cost–benefit analysis applied to environmental issues is often a case in point; the dispelling of 'myth' has led to a certain 'disenchantment', a loss of the sense of magic; the search for universal political and moral principles can now appear suspect (Powell 2005). 'Whose justice? Which rationality?' (MacIntyre 1988).

As we shall see later on, but highly pertinent to evaluating the Enlightenment characterization as progress, Theodor Adorno and Max Horkheimer wrote:

> In the most general sense of progressive thought, the Enlightenment has always aimed at liberating men from fear and establishing their sovereignty. Yet the fully enlightened earth radiates disaster triumphant. The program of the Enlightenment was the disenchantment of the world; the dissolution of myths and the substitution of knowledge for fancy ... What men want to learn from nature is how to use it in order wholly to dominate it and other men. That is the only aim. Ruthlessly, in despite of itself, the Enlightenment has extinguished any trace of its own self-consciousness. The only kind of thinking that is sufficiently hard to shatter myths is ultimately self–destructive. Power and knowledge are synonymous.
>
> (Adorno and Horkheimer 1979: 55)

Yet the Enlightenment does serve to question the idea that past social theorists simply built their ideas upon the comfortable certitudes of something called the 'Enlightenment' and that their ideas therefore no longer speak to contemporary concerns. Those who have proclaimed the 'end of history', now find themselves turning to thinkers such as Weber and Durkheim to explore the culture basis to economic development (Fukuyama 1995). In continuing this history of social theory, we will find that revisions and critiques are plentiful. In the process, ideas regarding the promise of modernity and the relationship between the individual and society were to be viewed in new and illuminating ways.

2 Seven traditions of renewal, modification and critique

Together with the intellectual legacies considered so far, the traditions of thought examined in this chapter had profound implications for the future direction of social theory. This is not an easy history to document and for this reason the chapter is divided into two main sections.

In the first section of the chapter we shall examine three traditions of thought: hermeneutics, phenomenology and pragmatism. For ease of understanding the first two are examined in one section. Although there are clear differences between and within these three traditions, they all contributed to a shift in theoretical focus towards understanding the role of history, human action, meaning and language in everyday life. In the second section, four traditions of social thought are considered: critical, structuralist, systems and feminist theories. Each of these have also added to and informed the direction of modern social theory. In order to specify how these traditions are connected to ideas in Part II of the book, each section will conclude with a summary discussion.

Modification and critique in three traditions

Hermeneutics and phenomenology: history, consciousness and being

Although there were differences among the neo-Kantians, they did share a scepticism regarding the possibility of utilizing a model of the natural sciences for the development of a 'science of society'. In so doing, they placed Enlightenment 'scientism' in question: ' "Scientism" means science's belief in itself: that is, the conviction that we can no longer understand science as one form of possible knowledge, but rather must identify knowledge with science' (Habermas 1989a: 4). The challenge to scientism, in terms of a separation between the realm of nature and human activity, informed the writings of Dilthey. This, however, leaves two questions. First, if the social sciences could no longer march in the shadow of the natural sciences, what was the alternative? Second, what implications does this have for the direction of social theory?

Dilthey's answer to the first question was to turn to an assessment of the scientific validity of historical writings. In the process, he sought nothing less than to provide new epistemological foundations for the human sciences. In this attempt, the influences so characteristic of German thought at this time emerged in his ideas: 'Kantian memories, strict historical training, a nostalgia for the spiritual world of the Enlightenment, a respect for the aims of positivist investigation, and, still hovering in the background, the misty pan-theism of Romantic theology' (S. H. Hughes 1979: 193).

This latter influence came from Friedrich Schleiermacher (1768–1834) in whose writings the seeds of hermeneutics, defined as the theory and practice of interpretation, were laid. The question was how to produce a scientifically based hermeneutics? For this purpose texts had to be situated and interpreted in the social context in which they were produced. It would then be possible to replicate a central characteristic of science: to move beyond 'particularity' to the 'general'. To achieve that:

> it is necessary to rise above, not only the particularity of texts, but also the particularity of the rules and recipes into which the art of understanding is dispersed. Hermeneutics was born with the attempt to raise exegesis and philology to the level of a *Kunstlehre*, that is, a 'technology' which is not restricted to a mere collection of unconnected operations.
>
> (Ricoeur 1982: 45, original italics)

From a hermeneutic point of view, the social analyst must then start with a text and seek to understand it through an act of interpretation which connects them with the author and what was known by them when they constructed the text. What is often referred to as the circle involves a relationship between the part and the whole or, to put it another way: 'the relation between an isolated expression or work and the pre-given totality of language or literature' (J. B. Thompson 1981: 37).

This move also paved the way for a general inquiry into the nature of human understanding. Therefore, in seeking to fulfil his aims, Dilthey moved from the perspective of individualistic psychology, to an historicist view based on Hegel's objective 'mind' or 'spirit' as indicative of a given age: 'Every single human expression represents something which is common to many and therefore part of the realm of objective mind … the individual always experiences, thinks, acts, and also understands, in this common sphere' (Dilthey quoted in Outhwaite 1975: 26–27).

Dilthey could now argue that the human sciences could respect both individuality and universality through their ability to locate the 'inner' experiences of people in terms of their history. This contrasts with positivism, whose scientific aim is to explain the 'outer' observable patterns of human behaviour in terms of the relations of cause and effect. Nevertheless, how are these 'understandings' to be validated?

A solution to this problem was the adoption of *verstehen* (interpretative understanding). This allows the social sciences to possess something in addition to the physical sciences through their ability to understand the meaning of an event for social actors. After all, the natural sciences explain an event by considering it as *'the effect of a cause'* (Strasser 1985: 2, original italics). To study human relations, on the other hand, must involve 'understanding what makes someone tick' or how they 'feel or act as a human being' (Taylor 1981: 30). A precondition of theoretical development then becomes an understanding of the consciousness which informs human actions.

Adding a voice to this breakdown of the unity of the human and natural sciences was the philosopher Edmund Husserl (1859–1938), whose concerns were, once again, defence of the 'legitimacy and dignity of the human sciences' (Nuyen 1990). Husserl's route was to seek to establish 'truth' in the realm of human consciousness. This led him to a concern with perception in the attempt to grasp something called 'true understanding'. The method he advocated for this purpose was to question, or suspend, any presuppositions regarding society by adopting the strategy of 'bracketing'. People would then be freed from their historical context and enabled to uncover a 'true under-standing' which is pre-theoretical and free from prejudice. Given this:

> Phenomenology asks us *not* to take received notions for granted. It asks us to *question* them – to question nothing less than our culture, that is, our way of looking at and being in the world in which we have been brought up.
>
> (Wolff 1979: 500, original italics)

Without bracketing experiences in this way the result would be, in what Husserl called the 'natural attitude' of everyday life, people simply taking-for-granted the world around them.

Husserl's teacher, Franz Brentano (1838–1916) stressed the idea of 'intentionality' in human psychology whereby consciousness is always directed towards 'something'. Husserl then took Descartes' act of perception and added an important dimension: the 'thing' which is perceived. As such, objects of thought, including society and social relations, are viewed as being constituted in and through consciousness. In contrast to positivism, there is no separation of the social world from the act of perception, for it is an object of 'consciousness'. Husserl thereby transforms Descartes' famous statement into *ego cogito cogitata*, translated as 'I think, and what I am thinking are the objects of my thoughts' (Strasser 1985: 124).

'Knowing' is now reduced to a perceiving subject. For this reason, a phenomenologically informed social theory is required to focus upon a description and understanding of subjective perceptions, not an explanation of objective conditions. Questions such as 'What is social reality?' are then replaced by two different questions. First, 'How does reality come to be constituted by mental operations as a known object?' Second, 'How do we go about constructing our ideas of what reality is?' (T. Johnson et al. 1984: 78).

Although discussions of phenomenology are found under the broad heading of 'interpretivist social theory', there are important variations in its unfolding history. After all, in their different ways, Husserl and Dilthey were still pursuing an Enlightenment ideal: that is, the search for 'true' knowledge. Their approach was to be challenged and modified in the writings of Martin Heidegger (1889–1976), who moved the focus of phenomenology from epistemology to ontology. In the process he was critical of Kant. He argued that we are not only observers of an external world mediated through our consciousness (Husserl), but also members of a world who exist as 'beings-in-time'. This moves away from Dilthey's neo-Kantian preoccupations with method, to the study of what Heidegger called *Dasein* (Williams and May 1996). This is best described as 'pre-understanding': 'the *place* where the question of being arises, the place of manifestation; the centrality of *Dasein* is simply that of a being which understands being' (Ricoeur 1982: 54, original italics).

This is not an easy notion to grasp. For our purposes, however, what Heidegger is criticizing is the concept of a 'transcendental ego'. He does not attempt to 'solve' the subject–object dichotomy by prioritizing human consciousness, as had Husserl and Dilthey, because understanding is seen as part of a 'mode of being'. It emerges, for example, from the gap which exists between where people are located in time and the possibilities which are available to them for the future. These possibilities are then 're-projected' into the present which can become 'an object of potential questioning, challenge, and change' (Bauman 1978: 166). The implication being that social theory should cast its gaze upon historically given subjects who exist in a 'lifeworld' in which a series of possibilities for social action are then contained. The practices within the lifeworld contain interpretations of, as well as methods of coping with, social relations. Hermeneutics is now the act of interpreting people's everyday interpretations.

Making connections with Part II

Hans-Georg Gadamer (1900–2002) is largely responsible for the contemporary interest in hermeneutics. Following Heidegger, Gadamer (1975) does not see hermeneutics as a method for study, but part of the condition of human existence. These arguments have had an effect on the development of the social sciences. For instance, Jürgen Habermas (born 1929) seeks to develop a 'depth hermeneutics' which draws upon but is also critical of Gadamer. Heidegger's ideas appear in the work of Jacques Derrida (1930–2004), Michel Foucault and Norbert Elias (1897–1990), whose 'process' theory represents a critique of the subject–object dualism in social thought (see Elias 1991; Mennell 1992). Additionally, structuration theory will be shown to be ontologically based in terms of an emphasis upon human 'being' and 'doing', while Pierre Bourdieu (1930–2002) considered the implications of Heidegger's philosophy for generating a theory of human practice.

A more general phenomenological input into social theory is apparent in the work of Alfred Schutz (1899–1959). Schutz was a central figure in the development of phenomenological social theory. Schutz rejected positivism as a model for the human sciences and was critical of the concept of *verstehen*. He did not view this as a method for 'doing' social science, but social science should study how people interpret the social world. In other words, how it is that people produce social life in a meaningful way. As Berger and Luckmann put it:

> Commonsense contains innumerable pre-and quasi-scientific inter-pretations about everyday reality, which it takes for granted. If we are to describe the reality of commonsense we must refer to those interpretations, just as we must take account of its taken-for-granted character – but we do so within phenomenological brackets.
>
> (Berger and Luckmann 1967: 20)

Together with Peter Winch (1926–97), who imported the insights of the philosopher Ludwig Wittgenstein (1889–1951) into social science, Schutz added to the focus of social theory on the rule-following and meaningful nature of human actions in everyday life.

Pragmatism: action, consciousness and the self

Little in the way of American social thought was noted in Chapter 1; aside, that is, from a reference to Veblen. North America was left to be 'imported' into European social theory via Alexis de Tocqueville's (1805–59) interests in democracy. All of this was to change in the nineteenth century with the work of those such as William Sumner (1840–1910) and Edward Ross (1866–1951). Nevertheless, this did not involve travelling down a Hegelian-historicist road; one reason being that they regarded their own revolution, in contrast to that of the French, as a success (Ross 1991). This was to change with events such as the American Civil War and the process of industrialization.

Towards the end of his life Durkheim devoted a set of lectures to pragmatism for two main reasons. First, he saw in pragmatism an attack on rationalism which had informed so much of French intellectual life and was thus a threat to French culture in general (Joas 1993). Second, he viewed pragmatism as undermining the idea that 'true' knowledge was possible (Durkheim 1983: 1). Contained with these lectures was a veiled attack on his contemporary Georges Sorel (1847–1922), who distrusted intellectualist formulations and insisted 'on the origin in *practical action* of all valid social theory' (S. H. Hughes 1979: 176, original italics). Given this we must ask what are the main elements of pragmatism which provoked such reactions? One approach to this question allows us to compare pragmatism with German-idealist attempts to ground epistemology in human consciousness:

> the basic idea of pragmatism, namely that it is actions rather than consciousness which are the foundations of thought, was developed in the 1870s by a group of young thinkers in Cambridge, Massachusetts, and was first publicly voiced by Charles Peirce in 1878.
>
> (Joas 1993: 95)

Charles Peirce (1839–1914) began his studies with the prejudices that people actually possess in everyday life, not with Descartes' abstract method of 'doubting'. The Cartesian solitary ego then became replaced by a 'cooperative search for truth for the purpose of coping with real problems encountered in the course of action' (Joas 1993: 19). A similar argument also evolved in the work of John Dewey (1859–1952). For Dewey, ideas and actions should be judged according to the social situations which give rise to them. In contrast to the top-down approach of metaphysical speculation, the social sciences should now concern themselves with the concrete social conditions under which actions take place. To add to this, William James (1842–1910) sought to critique the idea of consciousness as a resolution to the object dilemma:

> Consciousness, he says, 'is the name of a nonentity, and has no right to a place among first principles' ... he is not denying that our thoughts perform a function which is that of knowing. ... What he is denying might be put crudely as the view that consciousness is a 'thing'.
>
> (Russell 1955: 840)

The consequences of these positions are far-reaching. Pragmatism displaces the relationship between thought and reality in terms of how truthfully one may be represented by the other. Thinking is now seen as a social, not solitary act, which takes place within a 'community of others'. Over time, however, this insight became distorted such that knowledge was to be judged in terms of its 'use-value', leading to 'two pragmatisms' (Mounce 1997).

At this point we may detect a link between pragmatism and Marx's concept of praxis. That said, Marx would not have accepted the 'instrumentalism' of this position such that: 'knowledge should be judged as more or less "useful" rather than as true or false' (A. Sayer 1992: 70). The parallels with Heidegger's reflections, on the other hand, are more readily apparent:

> At the center of the first section of *Being and Time* stands the analysis of the concept of world. From the perspective of manipulation, and in general of non-objectifying, practical dealings with physical components of the lifeworld, Heidegger explicates a concept of world as a network of involvements reminiscent of Pragmatism.
>
> (Habermas 1992a: 148, original italics)

Heidegger and the pragmatists may be seen to be calling upon social theory to shift its attention away from consciousness towards people's adaptions and methods of coping with the world in their everyday lives.

Making connections with Part II

The clearest way in which the influence of pragmatism may be traced in social theory is via the work of George Herbert Mead (1863–1931), the Chicago School and the symbolic interactionists. These are the subjects of Chapter 3. Mead's work, in particular, represents the desire to overcome the subject–object dualism in social thought. To recall the discussion so far. Following Kant, the individual had been considered as both 'a *world-generating* and *autonomously acting subject*' (Habermas 1992b: 158, original italics). As Mead goes on to suggest, the conceptualization of the subject then 'fell between the cracks' of a transcendental ego, apparently capable of surveying the world around it through the exercise of reason and an empirical ego, who simply exists as one among many in the social world.

In Mead's work we will find neither an interest in utility-oriented action (towards a desired end) nor a Kantian style moral-individual action (transcendental ego), but an examination of the relationship between consciousness and action. Social action is not conceptualized in terms of an orientation to a predetermined end, for the very consciousness which formulates an individual's ends cannot take place outside of the context of the action itself:

> Rather, the setting of an end can only be a result of reflection on resistances encountered by the variously orientated behaviour of a life form whose world is always already schematized in a practical manner prior to all reflection.
>
> (Joas 1993: 248)

Social 'selves' are viewed as being formed through a process of confronting the world of which the individual is a part in dialectic relation between subject and object. Only by encountering objective conditions are people able to gain a sense of 'who' they are.

There are a further six ways in which connections between pragmatism and modern social theory can be drawn. First, in Peirce's work on semiology (the study of signs and their systems) the idea of 'indexicality' appeared. This suggests that we may understand an utterance only in the context in which it is made. As we shall see, this is part of the theoretical armoury of ethnomethodology. Second, there is Habermas's theory of communicative action. While his critical theory has foundationalist aspirations, the linguistic aspects of his work contain a pragmatist theory of meaning which revolves around the assertion 'that to understand an utterance is to understand the claim it raises' (Cooke 1994: 95). Third, pragmatism forms an essential part of the ideas of the contemporary 'anti-foundationalist' American philosopher Richard Rorty (1982). Despite his own reservations on this trend in social thought (Rorty 1993) his works have added to the 'postmodern turn' in social theory. Fourth, Alfred Schutz used James' ideas in order to develop his phenomenological social theory. Fifth, pragmatism existed in the critical thought of Charles Wright Mills (1916–62) who called for a fusion of the practical and intellectual within social science (Mills 1970). Finally, alongside the ideas of Durkheim, phenomenology, linguistics and ethology, we shall uncover its influence in the works of Erving Goffman (1922–82).

Having examined these philosophical schools in terms of their implications for the development of social theory, attention is now turned to four traditions of social thought which represent the journey of renewal, modification and critique in the Enlightenment project.

Four traditions in social thought

Critical theory: for (and against) modernity

The term critical theory has been used in a plethora of contexts with different meanings but always probes beneath the everyday surface of social reality to find what might be hidden there. It has been used to denote a mode of enquiry into culture and history in order to access deeper levels of meaning and understanding. Within the context of social theory, it has been used to describe an 'attempt to grapple seriously with the historical embeddedness of all theory, where a full understanding demands an appreciation of the historical and cultural conditions ... on which the theorist's own intellectual activity depends' (Calhoun 2000: 537). In a specific sense, it has been used to describe the work of the Frankfurt school of social theorists who were to attempt to fuse Marx and the work of Freud (Layder 2006). Critical theory aims to bring to consciousness an awareness of capitalist exploitation, bureaucratic domination and to create a popular demand for liberation. It also aims to bring to our consciousness oppression of which we may or may not have been aware, and it calls for 'criticism of life' to resist and transform the existing systems of domination and exploitation (Powell and Moody 2003: 11).

The fundamental aim of critical theory is the dismantling of existing forms of oppression (Habermas 1992b). Quite simply, racism, genocide, increasing environmental pollution and possible nuclear holocaust cannot be the truth of human existence. Searching for truth means going beyond this apparent reality. Thus, truth lies in attempts to change the world via a critique of established reality. A critical theoretical analysis is true in so far as it helps change the world and make it a more human place in which to live. So while reality may lie quite beyond human comprehension and can never be reduced to words, truth is the living of each moment of human life to its maximum potential, the unfolding of reality from its potential to a lived practice or actuality of human existence. In contrast to critical theory, much of sociology remains at the level of the 'facticity of the given' (Marcuse 1964: 170). Such analysis has the effect of justifying the status quo whether it intends to do so or not.

Coupled with this is the notion that the truth of a theory is the degree to which it is responsive to human values (Habermas 1992a). Praxis is the key concept that differentiates critical social theory from the ahistorical gathering of so-called 'facts' whose activities characterize positivism and empiricism. Praxis refers to the ideal of conscious practical action: that is, making the critique of alienation speak for popular needs and leading to concrete actions to transform social relations. Ultimately, knowledge cannot be divorced from social reality and values.

Under the auspices of its second director, Max Horkheimer (1895–1973), the Institute for Social Research at Frankfurt came to centre its interests on six broad areas. First, the seeking of explanations for the absence of a unified working-class movement in Europe. Second, an examination of the nature and consequences of capitalist crises. Third, a consideration of the relationship which existed between the political and the economic spheres in modern societies. Fourth, to provide an account for the rise of Fascism and Nazism as political movements. Fifth, to study socialization in families in terms of ego development. Finally, to undertake a sustained critique of the link between positivism and science (adapted from Held 1990: 35).

In order to adequately examine these questions a new theoretical approach was required which involved a 'refusal to champion vulgar idealism as an antidote to vulgar materialism' (Jay 1973: 294). This involved a return to the Hegelian strand in Marxism in order that the concept of human praxis might be recovered from overly materialist readings of Marx. Yet between Hegel and the Frankfurt School stood such figures as Schopenhauer and Nietzsche, both of whom had questioned the Enlightenment project. Therefore, it was necessary to engage with these ideas in order to recover the promise of Marxism.

To these intellectual antecedents and aims we must add the political context in which these scholars wrote in order to fully situate their work. In Nazi Germany, the Institute found itself under threat with the result that its leading members, including Theodor Adorno (1903–69), Max Horkheimer and Herbert Marcuse (1898–1979) emigrated to the United States (Adorno and Horkheimer returned after the Second World War). Here they found the self-confidence of bourgeois liberal-capitalism with its apparent ability to absorb and neutralize proletarian consciousness. To analyse how this occurred necessitated a consideration of culture which, up to this point in time, had been largely devalued in Marxist circles (see Raymond Williams 1961).

The work of these scholars was interdisciplinary, accompanied, as noted, by a rejection of 'scientific Marxism', together with critiques of positivism and interpretivism. As Horkheimer said of the relationship between social philosophy and positivism:

> Contemporary social philosophy, as we have seen, is in the main polemically disposed toward positivism. If the latter sees only the particular, in the realm of society it sees only the individual and the relations between individuals; for positivism, everything is exhausted in mere facts. These facts, demonstrable with the means of analytic science, are not questioned by philosophy.
>
> (Horkheimer 1993: 7)

Positivism turns human relationships into nothing more than abstract categories through a failure to examine the conditions under which they develop and are sustained. In this sense it represents part of the increasing desire to control the social and natural worlds in the name of profit (Adorno et al. 1976). What makes critical theory 'critical' is precisely this recognition of the connection which exists between knowledge and human interests.

Interpretivist social theories were inadequate due to an exclusive concentration upon the process of self-understanding and self-consciousness, the result being that they exhibit an uncritical acceptance of dominant forms of consciousness within given societies and fail to consider the structural determinants of human actions, as well as the role of the unconscious and power and control in human relations. Indeed, in another direction, critiques of this type led to attempts to fuse phenomenology and Marxism (Paci 1972) and an emphasis upon ideological mechanisms of control as apparent in the works of Georg Lukács (1885–1971) and Antonio Gramsci (1891–1937). It was Gramsci who employed the concept of hegemony whereby it is held that the bourgeoisie exercises its social control through both coercion and consensus within institutions. What presents itself as common sense is actually symptomatic of ideological distortion (Gramsci 1971). This notion still inspires cultural studies (Nelson and Grossberg 1988) as well as leading to a framework for 'post-Marxist' politics (Laclau and Mouffe 2001).

In focusing upon ideological incorporation, Herbert Marcuse (1968a) spoke of the 'technical-administrative control' of society and took aim at a growing corpus of social theory which claimed to have witnessed a vindication of capitalism through what was known as the 'end of ideology' thesis (Bell 1960):

> The capabilities (intellectual and material) of contemporary society are immeasurably greater than ever before – which means that the scope of society's domination over the individual is immeasurably greater than ever before. Our society distinguishes itself by conquering the centrifugal social forces with Technology rather than Terror, on the dual basis of an overwhelming efficiency and an increasing standard of living.
>
> (Marcuse 1968a: 9)

It follows that the rationality of 'the system' itself had to be subjected to critique. One way in which this took place was through an investigation into the Enlightenment project. Here we find history interpreted as a journey towards a 'new kind of barbarism' whereby

> The individual is wholly devalued in relation to the economic powers, which at the same time press the control of society over nature to hitherto unsuspected heights. ... The flood of detailed information and candy-floss entertainment simultaneously instructs and stultifies mankind.
>
> (Adorno and Horkheimer 1979: xiv–xv)

On this basis Weber was criticized for confusing capitalism as a process of rationalization with reason itself (Marcuse 1968b). Instead of liberating the subject, the Enlightenment had witnessed a growing disjuncture between reason and rationality: 'The unleashed market economy was both the actual form of reason and the power which destroyed reason' (Adorno and Horkheimer 1979: 90). The result was a 'fractured' subject through self-alienation perpetuated by positivism with its fetish for collecting social facts. Modernity now represents a loss of meaning:

> For the Enlightenment, whatever does not conform to the rule of computation and utility is suspect. So long as it can develop undisturbed by any outward repression, there is no holding it. ...

> Every spiritual resistance it encounters serves merely to increase its
> strength. ... Enlightenment is totalitarian.
>
> (Adorno and Horkheimer 1979: 6)

This meta-critique noted, the question remains that having rejected interpretivist social theory how can the important analysis of mental states be
achieved? This is where Sigmund Freud enters as part of the whole history of
the relationship between psychoanalysis and social theory (see Elliott 1992).

Freud sought to supplant the idea of the conscious process of human
thought with a theory of the unconscious. While he acknowledged that an
unconscious process could be inferred only from observing patients, he
believed it to play a dominant role in the determination of behaviour. He
thus placed the idea of the 'conscious subject' into question, but for different
reasons than any we have noted so far:

> According to Freud ... we are not who or what we think we are: we
> do not know our own centers; in fact, we probably do not have a
> center at all. Psychoanalysis undermines notions about autonomy,
> individual choice, will, responsibility, and rationality, showing that
> we do not control our own lives in the most fundamental sense.
>
> (Chodorow 1986: 88)

This focus moves away from an understanding of the solitary ego in the
social world, to the self-misunderstanding person who fails to see the causes
of their own symptoms. Indeed, Freud's whole metapsychological project can
be read as one which sought to show 'who we are', while psychoanalysis is a
practice for the development of autonomy and control in the 'self' (Chodorow 1986).

More specifically, Freud viewed all behaviour as being motivated or
caused whether it be 'neurotic' or 'normal'. This could be attributed to earlier
determinants which appeared as symptoms whose purpose was to avoid
painful memories. In the self there exists a continuous struggle between
'internality' and 'externality' or, to express it another way, between mental
structures (id, ego and superego) and life-experiences. This, however, does
not simply take place 'within' the individual, but is a response to their
physical and social environments. These may be manifest in a whole series of
'slips' (Freud 1938) and the idea of civilization itself (Freud 1969).

A Freudian approach to the unconscious and self-misunderstanding
permitted the Frankfurt theorists to concentrate on the process of ideological
distortion under capitalism, without resorting to some notion of consciousness as an explanatory framework: 'it is only through the process of
interpretation that subjects can come to know the conditions and complexi-
ties of their own existence' (J. B. Thompson 1981: 212). Despite this
utilization of Freud, we are still left with problems. Up to the time of the
Frankfurt theorists Marxists had dismissed psychoanalysis as unworthy of

attention (see Osborn 1937). After all, the problematic fusion of Marx and Freud is apparent at different levels: 'On the practical level, psychoanalysis is carried on by rich doctors on richer patients. Conceptually, it starts from the individual's problems and tends to play down social conditions and constraints' (Ollman 1979: 177).

If Freud's work was to serve the needs of critical theory, it has required modification. At this point, Leo Lowenthal and Eric Fromm enter the scene as central to this process. Fromm, for example, examined the relationship between the individual and totalitarianism (Fromm 1969). He also held throughout his life that our capacity for love and freedom: 'depends almost entirely on the given socio-economic conditions' (quoted in Jay 1973: 100). The interest in Freud was also apparent in socio-psychological studies on the structure of modern personality types (Adorno et al. 1950) as well as in the writings of Wilhelm Reich on the relationship between sexuality and capitalism (see Ollman 1979). Fromm also examined politics from a psychoanalytic point of view:

> It has been shown that this irrational acting and feeling are the result of certain instinctual impulses, of which the actor is often unconscious, but which compulsively condition him or her. It therefore seems to follow that psychoanalysis could also provide the key to an understanding of similarly conditioned social action, of similarly irrational *political* events.
>
> (Fromm in Bronner and Kellner 1989: 213, original italics)

Making connections with Part II

The critical theorists left a legacy which has been the subject of interpretations and understandings (Bronner 1994; Hoy and McCarthy 1994; Wiggershaus 1995). Of all contemporary scholars, it is Jürgen Habermas who sits most firmly within this tradition but who, as we shall see, has submitted it to extensive modification. However, if we broaden our horizons to trace a critical 'intent' in the development of social theory, the picture becomes less restrictive. For instance, Pierre Bourdieu sits within a tradition which runs from Marx to the Frankfurt School (Calhoun 1995) and critique of what appears to be self-evident remains apparent in his later works (Bourdieu 2000, 2005); Nancy Fraser and Axel Honneth have clear critical intentions in their work on recognition and redistribution (Fraser and Honneth 2003), as does the critical realism of Roy Bhaskar (1993) and Margaret Archer (1995, 2003). There are also the ideas of Michel Foucault, whose own words suffice here:

> As far as I'm concerned, I think that the Frankfurt School set problems that are still being worked on. Among others, the effects of

power that are connected to a rationality that has been historically and geographically defined in the West, starting from the sixteenth century on. The West could never have attained the economic and cultural effects that are unique to it without the exercise of that specific form of rationality.

(Foucault 1991a: 117)

While the Frankfurt scholars were writing, another tradition was active in French intellectual life. Starting with an examination of language and working through to anthropology, it culminated in the works of a Marxist thinker who, unlike the above, sought to expunge any Hegelian trace in Marxism to provide it with a 'scientific' status.

Structuralism: farewell to the subject?

The French intellectual climate was undergoing rapid change in the post-Second World War period. Existentialism and phenomenology were vying for intellectual ascendancy with mixtures of Marxism, the psychoanalysis of Freud and Jacques Lacan (1901–83) and interpretations of the structuralist writer Ferdinand de Saussure (1857–1913).

Structuralism may be distinguished from other traditions by noting its contention that knowledge cannot be grounded in individuals or their historically given situations. Conceptually, structuralism asserts that the structure of discourse itself produces 'reality' – that we can think only through language, and therefore our perceptions of reality are all framed by and determined by the structure of language. Structuralism also rejects empiricism for its failure to distinguish between the appearance of a phenomenon and its underlying 'reality'. It is a 'science of relationships' with the emphasis of holistic structuralism being upon the interconnections or interdependencies between different social relations within society (Runciman 1973). This position holds that we cannot understand the dynamics of a society by studying each of its parts in isolation. Instead, we can explain its parts only through their relationship with other constituent elements in a given system. To give an everyday example: we stop at a set of traffic lights because we contrast the signs with each other. Red signifies that we should 'stop' because it is contrasted with green which means 'go': 'When we see red we see red-and-not-green' (Keat and Urry 1975 :124).

Saussure, the founder of modern structural linguistics, separated the regularities or codes of language (*la langue*) from its usage by an individual who externalizes the underlying system (*la parole*). Saussure argued that there is no consciousness before language. He considered the relationship between thought and language via a comparison with a sheet of paper: 'thought is the front and the sound the back; one cannot cut the front without cutting the back at the same time; likewise in language, one can neither divide sound from thought nor thought from sound' (Saussure in Easthope and McGowan 1992: 7).

Language itself is grasped through an ability to assimilate and order a system of signs which are its basic units. Signs are divided into two parts: the signifier (the sound) and the signified (the idea or concept to which the sound refers). The latter does not refer to an actual object in the material world, but the way in which the system of language, through its signs, organizes the world, with signs becoming defined by their differences within the language system itself. In this way, the conscious individual is supplanted by a system of language which is prioritized over its manifest utterances in individual speech-acts. Given that the relationship of signs depends upon a network internal to the language system itself, they are seen to possess value before signification. Thus, within language, there are no absolutes, only relations of mutual dependence (as with our traffic light example):

> The idea or phonic substance that a sign contains is of less importance than the other signs that surround it. Proof of this is that the value of a term may be modified without either its meaning or its sound being affected, solely because a neighboring term has been modified.
>
> (Saussure in Easthope and McGowan 1992: 13)

As language is self-referential, it can be studied as an internal system through which both subjectivity and the social world are produced. Saussure envisaged that this may be applied to the non-linguistic realm as part of the science of semiology. It is the development of this insight that explains much of the history of twentieth-century structuralist thought. Consider, for example, observing a game of chess. It may be concluded that people adhere to common rules. An analysis of those rules would then indicate the strategies of the players, with a direct involvement in the game not being necessary for explanatory purposes. The same can be said of an analysis of food:

> The menu, for instance, illustrates very well this relationship between language and speech: any menu is concocted with reference to a structure (which is both national – or regional – and social); but this structure is filled differently according to the days and the users, just as a linguistic 'form' is filled by free variation and combinations which a speaker needs for a particular message.
>
> (Barthes in Lemert 1993: 343)

This focus upon language without reference to a speaking subject uncovers an affinity with Freudian psychoanalysis. Whereas Freud prioritized the unconscious processes of human behaviour over consciousness, Saussure prioritized the system of language over the intentions and meanings for an individual speaker. Paul Ricoeur (1913–2005) refers to this joint combination of attacks on the theory of the subject as the 'semiological challenge' (Ricoeur 1982: 35).

Lévi-Strauss (1963) starts his study of 'myths' with a dilemma: that is, their content is contingent but why, given this, are they so similar throughout the world? This is explained through the prioritization of form over content. In using the methods of Freud, he seeks to account for diverse social phenomena in the logic of the human mind itself. He argues that myths are not reducible to individual consciousness, but are themselves a product of a 'collective unconsciousness' (the influence of Durkheim being mediated here via Mauss). This exists prior to individuals and is constraining upon their actions and thoughts. Myths then work to organize social relations and they have a cognitive function (Stehr 2005).

In the study of myths Lévi-Strauss argues that he has uncovered the universal structures of the human mind. These structures are derived from binary oppositions. The very ability of people to think is governed by dualisms: for example, between raw and cooked; us and them; ideal and material, etc. While there may be cultural variations in the content of these oppositions, their underlying form is universal. Here we can detect a neo-Kantianism. Although not rooted in consciousness, verbal categories are considered as the mechanisms which link the universal structures of the human mind to the universal structures of culture. However, in this process the subject is displaced by structures beyond their conscious apprehension. This position is also found in the work of Louis Althusser (1918–90).

In contrast to Jean-Paul Sartre's (1905–80) existential interpretation (Sartre 1960) the structuralist reading of Marx enjoyed an enormous resurgence in Althusser's (1969) arguments. His aim was to recover the scientific element of Marxism from the tradition of existentialism, without succumbing to the problems of a materialist philosophy of history. To achieve this he employed a 'symptomatic reading' of Marx (a term borrowed from Freud). Broadly speaking, he argued that there was an 'epistemological break' in writings – between the early (pre-1845) and 'mature' Marx. The latter provided the scientific basis for an explanation of history thereby constituting a dismissal of the Hegelian legacy.

While Engels had added to the one-sided materialist interpretations of Marx, he also wrote:

> According to the materialist conception of history, the *ultimately* determining element in history is the production and reproduction of real life. More than this neither Marx nor I have ever asserted. Hence if someone twists this into saying that the economic element is the *only* determining one, he transforms this proposition into a meaningless, abstract, senseless phrase.

> (Engels to Block, in Marx and Engels 1953: 498, original italics)

Althusser took this qualification as indicative of the 'relative autonomy' of the ideological and political spheres from that of the economic. How does this translate into structuralist language?

The answer to this question may be seen in the relationship between the system (society) and its constituent parts (people). Society pre-exists the individual and ideological practices provide the means through which people relate to the world around them. What Althusser calls 'Ideological State Apparatuses' consist of the family, media, educational and religious institutions, which in turn constitute who we are, how we think of ourselves and may even be the origin of our individual traits. In other words, they both work through us and yet enable us to recognize ourselves. We even learn the idea of the autonomous bourgeois subject from families and therapists. Speaking of which, Althusser used concepts from the writings of the psychoanalyst Jacques Lacan. Where Althusser sought to conceive of Marxism without Hegel's absolute subject, so thought of psychoanalysis without Freud's ego (Sarup 1993). Now, in the works of Althusser and his contemporary Nicos Poulantzas (1936–79), who sought to employ Althusserian concepts (Poulantzas 1978), structures do not come from the universal categories of the human mind (Lévi-Strauss) or from language (Saussure), but from the history of class societies.

Making connections with Part II

Whether through critique, revision or contrast, structuralism has generated extensive interest. In terms of contrasts, we can compare it with the utilitarian-based exchange theories of those such as Homans (1961) and the 'rational-choice' model of human behaviour which has enjoyed a well-argued defence in the work of James Coleman (1990). Revisions include the neo-structuralist Mary Douglas (1970, 1978) but her intellectual debt is more to Durkheim given an emphasis on ritual and symbol in social life.

By the mid 1970s Althusser's legacy had withered and the critiques were numerous. These included the French Marxist Henri Lefebvre (1901–91) and English historian E. P. Thompson (1924–93). Yet it can be argued that his legacy is apparent in the most productive area of contemporary Marxism: the analytic Marxism of Cohen, Elster and Erik Olin Wright, among others (see Mayer 1994). It is argued that the questions they pursue are only possible when Hegelianism is abandoned. In this sense, this school could be termed 'post-Althusserian Marxism' (Callinicos 2000).

As for critical contrast, the structuralist 'dissolving' of the subject has informed ideas on the social 'self' and the agency–structure debate. Anthony Giddens, for example, accepts the problems of prioritizing a 'philosophy of consciousness' in social theory, but does not accept the idea of a 'subject-less history'. As a thinker steeped in the traditions of French social thought, Pierre Bourdieu was clearly influenced by structuralism. Nevertheless, he aims to return agents, rather than subjects, back into the terrain of social theory. Structuralist connotations will also be found in Habermas's idea via his use of the work of the structural psychologist Jean Piaget (1896–1980) and is apparent in critical realism (Archer 1998). Critical realism suggests that individuals cannot manage without a concept of truth. There is a pre-existing external reality about which it is the role of science to tell us. True, we must be cautious about claims to objective reality, alert to ideological distortions, and aware that the world is a messier, more complicated place than the accounts of physicists would suggest (Layder 2006). At same time, Michel Foucault is often interpreted as working within the 'structuralist' tradition.

Structuralism also appeals in the realms of literary criticism, cultural studies and history, the latter being exemplified in the work of the Annales historians (see Clark 1991) who have influenced the world-systems analysis of Immanuel Wallerstein (1990). In terms of literary criticism, Jacques Derrida's (1930–2004) engagement with and critique of structuralism in terms of the arbitrary character of signs has provided the catalyst for an enormous growth of interest in textual analysis (Kamuf 1991; Norris 1987). For one writer, Derrida has been responsible for starting an 'anti-humanism in the humanities' of almost epidemic proportions (Schwartz 1990). Finally, Jean Baudrillard (1929–2007) treated commodities as systems of signs which have a reference only to each other. Hence, as will be noted in Chapter 10, he criticized Marxism for concentrating on production and exchange, rather than consumption and style in contemporary mass society.

Lévi-Strauss developed his methods against the idea that society was essentially stable. He also prioritized structure over function. Yet the inspiration for normative functionalism, which we shall consider in examining the work of Talcott Parsons (1902–79), also stemmed from the structuralist writings of Comte and Durkheim. This found its twentieth-century expression in the work of the social anthropologists Bronislaw Malinowski (1884–1942) and A. R. Radcliffe-Brown (1881–1955).

Systems theory

The emphasis of functionalism, as with structuralism, tends towards the synchronic and holistic. On the other hand, normative functionalist explanations downplay the search for origins or causes of social phenomena in favour of seeing cultures as total systems of functionally interrelated parts. Teleological explanation is then employed whereby the statement: 'the function of X is to maintain Y, implies that X has some kind of causal influence on Y' (Dore 1973: 66). This may be illustrated through the Durkheimian argument that religion exists to provide the moral foundations of society. In order to see how this develops in one particular direction, attention will be focused on the writings of Talcott Parsons.

Parsons perceived a convergence in social and economic theory around the turn of the twentieth century. This centred upon a concern with the subjective experiences and actions of individuals combined with the Hobbesian problem of social order expressed in terms of the question: how are diverse interests in a society possible? Parsons then embarked upon the building of bridges between dualisms in social thought; in particular, between positivism, which ultimately regards human action as a passive adaption to the social world and utilitarianism, where only an actor's orientation to an end is required to understand their actions. According to this idea, social order results from the egoistic pursuit of ends from which is supposed to emerge the 'public good'. Parsons, as Durkheim before him, found this theory to be fundamentally flawed. After all, the pursuit of private ends would be best achieved by 'force and fraud' from which social chaos, not order, would emerge. He thus sought an explanation which moved away from the simplistic notion that action was motivated by self-interest. What form did this take?

Parsons' (1937) theory of action contained four parts. First, the actor. Second, the desired state of affairs towards which their action is oriented (this is the teleological aspect of the act). Third, the social situation in which the action takes place. Here, those social situations over which they have control are called 'means', while those over which they have no control, he calls 'conditions', including not only the physical environment, but also biological potential and limitations. Fourth, a 'normative orientation'. This normative orientation he regards as the 'motor' of social action (Parsons in Hamilton 1985: 73–78). Social action is thus conceptualized in terms of the use of means to reach desired ends in a process infused with societal norms. The Hobbesian problem is then resolved via a process in which the actor is seen to possess a sensitivity to the meanings in their environment which they then take account of their action:

> These normative rules both define what immediate ends should and should not be sought, and limit the choice of means to them in terms other than those of efficiency. Finally, they also define standards of socially acceptable effort. This system of rules, fundamental to any society ... is what I call institutions. They are *moral* norms, not norms of efficiency.
>
> (Parsons in Hamilton 1985: 62, original italics)

In Parsons' 'second phase' (Hamilton 1983) in which he published *The Social System* (Parsons 1951) the emphasis of his thought then shifted towards 'social structure', defined as:

> a system of patterned expectations of the behavior of individuals who occupy particular statuses in the social system. ... Such a system of patterned legitimate expectations is called by sociologists a system of roles. In so far as a cluster of such roles is of strategic significance to the social system, the complex of patterns which define expected behaviour in them may be referred to as an institution.
>
> (Parsons in Hamilton 1985: 126–127)

Analytic focus is now less upon the actor's rationality and more a specification of what is meant by 'normative orientation' in the choice of actions. Parsons is now more concerned with the means through which social organization may be explained in functionalist terms. Social stability is conceptualized in terms of social institutions which provide 'behavioural forces' which act as linking mechanisms between actions and systems. These institutions ensure 'that action can be sufficiently regularized so as to be compatible with the functional requirements of a society' (Parsons in Hamilton 1985: 127).

In these terms cultural patterns provide the framework for choices between courses of action. These options were reduced by Parsons to four dilemmas, each containing two responses with a definite meaning for the actor concerned. They are: affectivity versus affective neutrality; universalism versus particularism; achievement versus ascription and specificity versus diffuseness (a fifth, self-orientation versus collectivity-orientation, was later dropped). These may be manifest in the following way: the choice to set aside feelings or become more involved in a relationship; to judge an object according to general or specific criteria; to judge an object either in terms of its use, or in terms of a quality independent of its benefit and finally, to come into contact with others only in specific contexts or in many contexts, in which case relationships are more diffuse.

For Parsons the above could be used to categorize modes of action at increasing levels of abstraction: from the personality system, to the normative requirements of the social system and the value-patterns of the cultural system.

Within his overall convergence thesis, Parsons viewed Freud and Durkheim as working on the same problem. What was needed was a fusion of the internalization–externalization process which linked the needs-dispositions of personality with those of the social system. However, this did not mean that there exists a simple correspondence between the structure of personalities and social institutions because: 'persons occupying the same well-defined status in the social system will be found to cover a wide range of personality types' (Parsons in Hamilton 1985: 127). The need exists, therefore, for 'motivating mechanisms' which take account of such diversity.

Although his preoccupation with social integration is still apparent, following the influence of the physiologist Lawrence Henderson (1878–1942), he now begins to see societies more as organisms. For Parsons all theories involved two elements: the static and the dynamic. The static aspect is, as with structuralism, the structure of the social system. Its dynamic elements are the means through which the static categories are linked; this is the concept of function. The relationship between subsystems of action and the social system as a whole is now of interest where functions provide the links between the dynamic and structural aspects of a social system. An emphasis upon cybernetics, defined as the study of communication between different elements in a social system, now becomes evident in his work.

Drawing on the work of Robert Bales and together with Edward Shils, Parsons then argued that each system, from the unit-act to the social system as a whole, had four functional problems. These were listed in order of significance as: pattern maintenance; goal attainment; adaption and integration (AGIL). Pattern-maintenance is concerned with socialization and its focus is upon the structural category of social values. Stability is the key here, involving 'tension-management' due to the potential of 'strain' between personality and the needs of the social system. Goal-attainment is accomplished by the state and polity for the purposes of establishing goals and the motivating elements in the system towards their achievement. Meeting the needs of the system in terms of the acquisition and distribution of resources is required to ensure equilibrium. In a situation of a plurality of goals, however, the question of their 'cost' relative to others will arise. Therefore, a need exists for the economic system to maximize 'generalized disposability in the process of allocation between alternative uses' (Parsons 1965: 40). Lastly, as systems are differentiated and segmented into more or less independent units, there is the question of their adjustment and contribution to the effective functioning of the social system as a whole. Norms are then required to establish coherence and control between subsystems. As Parsons notes: 'In a highly differentiated society, the primary focus of the integrative function is found in its system of legal norms and the agencies associated with its management, notably the courts and the legal profession' (Parsons 1965: 40).

In sum, the functional maintenance of the social system is achieved through four functional prerequisites. For the purpose of social stability, values then link the need-dispositions of personality with that of the social system which, in turn, is linked via role-expectations to cultural consensus. Husserl's 'transcendental subject' is now replaced by a 'transcendental actor' given that Parsons sees society and culture as the transcendental conditions for human action (Bauman 1978). By starting with meaningful action and then moving on to consider the cultural and social systems as co-ordinating mechanisms for that action, neither the individual nor society are prioritized. Therefore, contrary to popular interpretations, he does not simply abandon the individual for the social system over the course of his work. It is more productive for the development of understanding social relations, to see his work as moving from an analysis of action to social interaction within social systems as a whole.

Making connections with Part II

Perhaps the first point to note in reflecting upon Parsons' work was his optimism: 'industrial society is the end of a long road, the culmination of a slow process of maturation. It is the most finished form of society because social organization and human rationality find their finest expression within it' (Rocher 1974: 158).

We do not discover a longing for a bygone age of community in the face of the forward march of industrialism. On the contrary, the focus on values in modern society was undertaken without a nostalgia for the pre-modern. Yet Parsons was also aware of the major shifts within modern societies towards the expressive and symbolic. In that sense he anticipated some of the modern versus postmodern debates in contemporary social theory (B. S. Turner and Robertson 1991).

In terms of his more direct influences, Habermas, while subjecting his work to extensive critique, also utilizes the AGIL schema and systems' ideas (Habermas 1975). He writes: 'no theory of society can be taken seriously today if it does not at least situate itself with respect to Parsons' (Habermas 1987: 199). Part of this is explained by Parsons' conceptual bridge building between continental and Anglo-American social theory (Sciulli 1985) and we find the systems theorist Niklas Luhmann (1927–98) interpreting Parsons in a way which owes more to Heidegger than Husserl. The social system is then seen to require increased mechanisms of control as society becomes more complex and existential anxiety is exacerbated. Systems are then differentiated from each other with communication, which is not reducible to individuals, being paramount (Luhmann 1993). For the neo-functionalist Jeffrey Alexander, however, the system is then over-determined for, in Luhmann's conservative emphasis, no conflict is considered outside of the demands of the system (Alexander et al. 2004). Therefore, we should note that for the more liberal-minded Parsons, 'culture is always a system analytically separated from society' (Alexander 1984: 402).

In the United States Robert Merton (1910–2003) was to modify the functionalist tradition (Merton 1968). In particular, his preference for a 'middle-range theory', more amenable to empirical testing, was in tune with American intellectual culture (Bershady 1991). Further, one of Parsons' graduate students, Harold Garfinkel (born 1917), went on to consider the gaps in his action theory and became the founder of ethnomethodology. Whether in terms of continental or Anglo-American social theory, or as a theorist against which to sharpen theoretical axes, his legacy cannot be ignored.

Embodied in Homans' (1973) article, 'Bringing Men Back In', is the criticism that Parsons gives us an over-determined view of social relations which was to lead some to a rejection of social structural analysis in favour of action, rather than a more productive examination of the relations that exist between them (López and Scott 2000). While a more productive reading has been suggested, its acknowledgement permits me to employ some licence for the purpose of continuity in this unfolding history. Homans may or may not be correct, but what of 'bringing back in' the other half of the population: women?

Feminisms: social theory and social practice in question

The potential for Enlightenment thought to marginalize whole groups of people was noted at the beginning of Chapter 1. Indeed, within feminist thought there exists a consensus that the intellectual and political cultures which have evolved over time have been invented by and for men. For some, the entire social universe of women's lives, including language and meanings, are viewed as saturated with male power (Marshall and Witz 2004).

There are two important issues to consider here. First, how power imbalances shape theoretical construction in terms of being reflective of more generally inequalities within society. Second and relatedly, how a group's place within the social structure influences the theoretical attention they afford particularly phenomena. For example, men in general remain the principle holders of economic and political power and this is replicated across history and the present. Men make up a large majority of corporate executives, top professionals and holders of political power. Globally, men held 93 per cent of cabinet-level posts in 1996 and most top positions in international agencies (Longino and Powell 2004). In western culture men continue to control technologies such as the Internet (consider the major corporate 'owners' of Microsoft and Netscape – the two owners are men with a combined personal wealth of £97 billion – an amount which outstrips the combined GNP of most non-western nation states) and weaponry (Smart 2007). With only limited exceptions it is men who have historically staffed and controlled the agencies of military force and judicial systems such as armies, intelligence agencies, police, prison and court systems (Connell 2000).

This section aims to bring attention to the ways in which theorists, in general, draw upon their 'background assumptions' (Gouldner 1971) to reproduce dominant ideas of men and women and from there, particular images of social relations. Biography and autobiography become important topics for this focus. For instance, in her study of housework, Ann Oakley takes Marx to task for the contradictions between the way in which he lived his life and the generation of his theoretical and political ideas (Oakley 1974), while Pam Odih (2007) discusses the limitations of labour process theory for understanding the relations between gender and capitalism. By not reflecting in this manner, social theorists and scientists in general are found to produce partial accounts and explanations which then masquerade as generalizations (Haraway 1991; Harding 2006). In the social sciences this has resulted in a lack of consideration of a whole range of core social activities fundamental to an understanding of social relations: 'areas like domestic work, or reproduction, or intimate relationships' (Oakley in Mullan 1987: 194).

Given the above, one aim of feminist theory is to focus upon an explanation for the exclusion of women from the considerations of social theory and social life in general. In the twentieth century this scholarship was inspired by those such as Virginia Woolf (1882–1941) and Simone de Beauvoir (1908–86) and then in what is known as second-wave feminism. Writers within this genre include Eva Figes (1978), Shulamith Firestone (1988), Betty Frieden (1965), Germaine Greer (1970), Kate Millett (1969) and Juliet Mitchell (1966).

From an historical viewpoint, feminist ideas were born out of the daily struggles of women in their everyday lives. These are then mobilized for the purpose of critically investigating the prevailing social order. Take, for example, the history of North American feminism. In the nineteenth century the women's movement aligned itself with the slavery abolition movement (Hole and Lévine 1979). Sojourner Truth, once a slave herself, then illustrated the 'double jeopardy' that Black women faced when she spoke at a Women's Rights Convention in 1851:

> I think that between the Negroes of the South and the women of the North all talking about rights, the white men will be in a fix pretty soon ... That man over there says that women need to be helped into carriages and lifted over ditches, and to have the best place every-where. Nobody ever helped me into carriages, or over mud puddles, or gives me any best place ... and ain't I a woman? ... I have borne thirteen children and seen most all sold off into slavery, and when I cried out with my mother's grief, none but Jesus heard – and ain't I a woman?
>
> (quoted in Almquist 1979: 433)

Feminism takes particular aim at the alleged separation of theoretical justifications and social practices for the purpose of contributing to political change. This separation is often maintained for the purpose of enabling a 'distance' to be achieved in the analysis of society and social relations. From this arises notions of objectivity. Yet upon examination, the basis of this strategy is seen to rest upon unexamined assumptions concerning differences between the sexes. For instance, consider the culture–nature divide. In terms of the Enlightenment quest to differentiate ourselves from nature, women have been reflected in social and political thought via the view that culture is symptomatic of the 'rational man' and nature is closer to the 'emotional woman' (Marshall and Witz 2004).

Distinctions of this type are a topic for feminist theory. It is not suggested that biological differences do not exist between the sexes, but that these gain significance: 'within the framework of culturally defined value systems' (Ortner 1982: 489). Fused with their institutional reproduction within society, these ideas produce both social situations and images of women's place within society:

> the organisation of work, the division of labour, the ways in which political and social stability were envisaged, and the respective roles of husband and wife in childrearing. … The divisions between male and female, science and nature, did not remain at the level of theorising but set the terms for a whole range of concrete struggles which are still being enacted today in the Western World.
> (Brown and Jordanova 1981: 239)

In these terms, the masculine becomes the sign of reason and is contrasted with the feminine as the sign of emotion. One is then a standard against which the 'other' is measured. As Lois McNay argues: 'A masculinist cultural hegemony is maintained through a process which involves the constantly practised differentiation of itself from what it believes it is not – the feminine' (McNay 1994: 37).

After all, we have found that a central way in which humanity has been considered is through the ability to exercise reason. In subtle ways, however, the 'knowers' of the Cartesian subject have been assumed to be men:

> Thus it would seem, if this assumption were right, that being emotional, or close to one's body and feelings, would mean being less rational, and therefore less free, and therefore less able to fully participate in all aspects of human life as a mature adult – less than fully human.
> (Griffiths 1988: 132)

In subjecting such ideas and practices to critical scrutiny, feminists seek to show that the ideas of 'men' and 'women' are social, political and historical constructs and not based upon so-called 'natural' differences.

For Dorothy Smith (1988, 1999) the cultural language and analysis of classical sociologists is that of men, male activities and experiences. For feminists, a major problem is that the classical 'scientific' definitions of the social world exclude large parts of human action and interaction (Marshall and Witz 2004). It presupposes a belief in individual difference and personal agency. It builds upon the concept of individuality developed in early-modern Europe with colonialism and capitalism (Gilroy 2001). This idea that men and women are qualitatively different did not exist until the eighteenth century and bourgeois ideology of separate spheres. With the rise of 'Enlightenment', we witnessed images of 'white masculinity'. It was at this point that notions of reason, science, progress, and masculinity were merged into a unified concept of 'manhood'. Reason and objectivity also provided the moral legitimacy for the rise of capitalism and the modern organization of society. For philosophers such as Kant, reason tempered by science could overcome feelings and intuition. At the time of Enlightenment, utilitarian doctrines were gaining momentum enshrined by 'success is happiness'. As industrial capitalism and the world of machines grew and flourished, this rationality included competition, planning, and goal attainment for men (Marshall and Witz 2004).

One aspect of the long history of modernity was the development of a separation between the public and private spheres. These had not always been separated in traditional societies, although there was usually a sex-based division of labour, often associated with a patriarchal system of male dominance. With the development of capitalism, cities and industry, a public sphere dominated by men and male activities developed and expanded. Women generally became restricted to the private sphere of household and family, and had limited involvement in political, economic, or even public social life. While some women were involved in more public activities, in the nineteenth century there were movements to restrict the participation of women in public life – for example, factory legislation and the family wage.

The notion of 'family' exists in two interrelated forms: first, 'familialism' – a widespread ideology of gender roles which run along lines of ideas of 'domesticity' and 'breadwinning'; second, as economic groups, the 'family' organizes domestic and personal life providing functions that underpin capitalism: for example, by providing child care, family care and domestic labour. The state has and still draws on not only capitalism to help it in its answers for production, but also ideologies deriving from science in order to legitimize male and female roles and responsibilities to preserve the existing social and moral order.

Women in the eighteenth and nineteenth centuries in England and North America were not recognized as individuals in legal structures or social theories (D. E. Smith 1988). Historically, Mary Wollstonecraft has been called the 'first feminist' or 'mother of feminism'. In her 1792 *Vindication of the Rights of Women*, now considered a classic of feminist history, Wollstonecraft accepts the definition of her time that women's sphere is the home, but she does not isolate the home from public life. For Wollstonecraft, the public life and domestic life are not separate, but connected. The home is important to Wollstonecraft because it forms a foundation for social life and public life. For her, the state and public life enhances and serves both individuals and the family; men have duties in the family and women have duties to the state.

This also required an overhaul of concept of reason as a male dominated activity. In doing so, Wollstonecraft was also providing a critique of Enlightenment philosophers such as Kant who did not believe that such individual liberty was for women. Woman, for Kant, was incapable of reason, and only man could be trusted to exercise thought and reason. Thus, women could not be citizens. Yet Wollstonecraft makes her position clear: only when women and men are equally free and equally dutiful in an exercise of their responsibilities to family and state, can there be true freedom.

Coupled with this, in the nineteenth century, Mill and Taylor, along with some early US feminists such as Elizabeth Cady Stanton and Susan Anthony, argued that the equality of women required full citizenship for women. This included giving women enfranchisement in 'democratic process'. After 1865, when Mill was in the English Parliament, he fought for women's suffrage. He also fought 'to amend the laws that gave husbands control over their wives' money and property'. He supported the campaign for birth control information to be available and was active in other campaigns that were aimed at assisting women and children (D. E. Smith 1988). Famously, the suffragette movement in the early twentieth century also added a key voice in pointing to the activities of women and striving for political action that represented women in society as a whole.

The operation of patriarchy, defined broadly as the exercise of male power which serves to oppress women, has been reduced to the dynamics of capitalist relations. Yet feminist scholarship has shown that capitalism has particular effects not only upon women as a whole, but upon working-class women in particular (Rowbotham 1973). This stands in contrast to the idea that the working-class forms a homogeneous group in relation to the means of production. From a historical viewpoint, it has been argued that the sexual division of labour actually predates capitalism (Barrett 1988). Findings of this type thus throw doubt upon the ability of Marxism to explain the roles and positions of women in society.

Those feminists who seek to use Marxism for the purpose of such explanation have reacted to this state of affairs in differing ways. Some, while finding analytic mileage in writings, find it difficult to stick to the letter of his works because the oppression of women, as a distinct class, did not concern him (Delphy and Leonard 1992; Gibson-Graham 1996). Overall, the necessity of modification renders the marriage between Marxism and feminism somewhat 'unhappy' (Weinbaum 1978). Either it should become 'healthier' or it will result in 'divorce':

> The struggle against capital and patriarchy cannot be successful if the study and practice of the issues of feminism is abandoned. A struggle aimed only at capitalist relations of oppression will fail, since their underlying supports in patriarchal relations of oppression will be overlooked.
>
> (Hartmann in Humm 1992: 109)

Whatever the ways in which feminist theories manifest themselves, it is clear that in meeting mainstream theory there is general agreement over the necessity for critique, modification or abandonment, depending upon the perspective from which the relationship is viewed. Therefore, in the encounter between Marxism and feminism new ideas have emerged. Take, for example, socialist feminisms which comprise

> a set of interventions by feminists into socialist and especially Marxist theory, which aims to analyse and end the oppression of women in capitalist society. As such Socialist Feminism is built upon key texts, writers, political events, and organizations which comprise the Marxist tradition. It is these which have helped shape the agenda for Socialist Feminist debates and reformulations of Marxism.
>
> (L. C. Johnson 1990: 304)

Similarly, out of a confrontation with Freud's work, psychoanalytic feminisms have developed while within the writings of radical feminists two themes, in particular, become apparent. First, women as a distinct social group are oppressed by men, where patriarchy is taken to be the structure of oppression. Second, given the problems of incorporating male theories for the purposes of developing feminist ideas, radical feminism is seen to be created by women for the purposes of their liberation: 'So reproduction, marriage, compulsory heterosexuality, and motherhood are primary sites of attack and envisaged positive change' (Rowland and Klein 1990: 273). Given this, differences between Marxist, Socialist, radical and psychoanalytic theories frequently centre upon whether ideas generated by men can be used to explain the position of women in society. This, in turn, clearly relates to the political question of what is required in order to achieve women's equality. The theoretical and political are thereby fused.

Making connections with Part II

The development of feminisms has necessitated a recovery of women's ideas from their historical marginality (Spender 1983). Further, there exists a continual need to maintain a link between theory and practice for the purposes of social, political and economic change. In its historical unfolding over several hundred years, feminist ideas have worked towards this end in a variety of ways.

In the first instance, there was the call for an incorporation of women into the changes taking place with the rise of modernity. In the works of both Wollstonecraft and de Beauvoir, for example, reason and liberalism combined in order that women may gain equality with men. However, on whose terms? If this is to utilize existing legislation, then are laws to be seen as neutral instruments? This is a highly problematic assumption given the nature of patriarchal relations. Here we witness another direction being formulated within the broad feminist agenda. A stress upon a more gendered view of social relations also appears, which

> glorified differences between men and women. ... Emphasis was placed on what is essential to women; by seeing the world through a woman's eyes, by allowing for a women's standpoint, we see not only a new perspective but one that is significantly better, more inclusive, and more life affirming. The celebration of women's traits, when linked to the idea that the marginalized and oppressed have an interpretive edge, gives women an epistemological or epistemic privilege.
>
> (Farganis 1994: 23)

The aim of this new generation of ideas was to erode 'the old distinctions between men and women' (Mitchell 1986: 45). This, as discussed, took place via a critique of the very grounds upon which dominant modes of thought and practice had based themselves. For some, this necessitated concentrating on patriarchy as the oppressive mechanism to the exclusion, for example, of the economic sphere. For others, as will become apparent in Chapter 9, this emphasis was too one-dimensional.

What we now find is a terrain of feminist social theory which has been influenced by a rich history of ideas. In some cases, paralleling a current trend in social theory, the recognition of differences and diversities between women has led to the abandonment of any explanatory metanarratives which seek to account for the experiences of all women. The essential category 'women' as a social class and their relationship with men then gives way to an examination of the differences between women. Once the coherence of women's identities are questioned in this way, it has ramifications for any political movement which assumes a degree of homogenous characteristics among a group which may act as a unifying catalyst for change. Many of the contributors to one feminist reader thus question the use of Enlightenment rationality for the development of feminist theories in general (Marshall and Witz 2004).

To the contemporary theoretical landscape of socialist, radical, Marxist, liberal and psychoanalytic feminisms, we must now add both postmodern and poststructuralist feminisms. Given this, it is accurate to talk of 'isms', not feminism (Humm 1992). Therefore, in Chapter 9 we shall outline the development and modification of feminist ideas since the mid to late 1960s. This history will then be continued in Chapters 10 and 11 where the issues raised by poststructuralist and postmodernist social theories are examined.

Summary: the legacy for contemporary social theory

In the beginning of this journey we found Dilthey's hermeneutics as a neo-Kantian defence of the dignity of the human sciences. Dilthey, combined with Hegel, placed history firmly within the realm of social-theoretical development. This was a 'turn' in the Enlightenment project because it focused social theory on human understanding and away from a more positivist orientation on the externally observed regularities of human behaviour.

Phenomenology then entered our intellectual terrain and found us travelling from Husserl's transcendentalism to Heidegger's existentialism. Husserl, along with Dilthey, worked on an Enlightenment-based epistemological problematic. The result was that he prioritized 'consciousness' and added to the more subjectivist and action-oriented approach to social theory. This views society as 'the creation of its members; the product of their construction of meaning, and of the action and relationships through which they attempt to impose that meaning on their historical situations' (Dawe 1970: 214).

Heidegger then subjected the divorce of knowledge (epistemology) from 'being' (ontology) to critique. In following the implications of this position social theory could no longer assume a unitary 'subject' who stands at the centre of the social universe. This is manifested in social theory in a number of ways. The combination of Heidegger and Nietzsche can be argued to have provided for the postmodern turn in social theory (Habermas 1992a) while Heidegger provides for a more ontologically focused social theory. This also affects how the 'subject' is conceptualized which, up to this point in time, had largely been assumed as something 'fixed':

> From Descartes's cogito, to Kant's and Husserl's transcendental ego, to the Enlightenment concept of reason, identity is conceived as something essential, substantial, unitary, fixed, and fundamentally unchanging. Yet other modern theorists of identity postulate a non substantiality of the self (Hume), or conceive of the self and identity as an existential project, as the creation of the authentic individual (Nietzsche, Heidegger, Sartre).
>
> (Kellner 1993: 142)

This challenge to the subject, combined with cultural and economic changes and critiques from other traditions of thought, has led social 'identity' to become a core topic in modern social theory (Calhoun 2000). Heidegger's critique of subject-centred consciousness also questions the mind–body duality which, since Descartes's time, had often been taken for granted. Together with the insights of feminist theory on the divide, this has added to an interest in the 'body' within social theory (Powell and Wahidin 2006). Nevertheless, this does not imply the acceptance of biological reductionism as a focal point for its development.

Moving away from the German-idealism that informed Husserl and Dewey's writings, the pragmatists tackled the subject–object dualism through concentrating on the inextricable link between consciousness and action in everyday life. Therefore, although developed in the United States, the potential existed for an alliance with both Nietzsche and Heidegger in a critique of the Enlightenment. This inspiration, from variants of pragmatism in our age of uncertainty, have moved the focus away from a search for foundations for social theory and ideas of 'absolute truth', to the notion that truth is dependent on what is 'useful' for action.

In another direction, phenomenology was found to stress a humanism through viewing the human subject as the source of knowledge (humanism also denotes secular atheism: see Blackman 1967, 1968). In Chapter 1 we found Marx stressing a dialectic between human agency and material circumstances. At one level this gave rise to a humanist-Marxism, while the issue of structural or system determination versus a more action-oriented social theory, informed the work of the critical theorists who sought to recover the Hegelian and emancipatory aspects of his work. In so doing, they had to encounter thinkers who had challenged Enlightenment thought. In seeking to illuminate a number of central problematics, they needed to overcome the materialist-idealist dichotomy in social thought and take account of both objective and subjective factors in social life. This was achieved without a resort to consciousness by utilizing Freud's work. This also represented a critique of Cartesianism. In the resulting synthesis of ideas, an increased scepticism over the potential for emancipation within the Enlightenment project became evident via the argument that reason and rationalization were at increasing odds with each other.

Marx has also been read as a structuralist. As a general tradition of thought, this travelled in two directions. First, there were the works of Saussure and Lévi-Strauss, both of whom worked outside of the Marxist tradition. Their ideas had implications for the study of social life through, in particular, a dissolving of the 'subject'. At the same time a neo-Kantian theme could be traced in the ideas of Lévi-Strauss. Second, there was Althusser who, in returning to work, argued that there was an 'epistemological break' in his writings which provided for a 'scientific' Marxism.

A neo-Kantianism was also found in the work of Parsons. He perceived a convergence in social thought at the turn of the century and sought to overcome a dichotomy between positivism and utilitarianism in order to develop an action-oriented social theory. While the subject of sustained criticism, Parsons brought the Anglo-American and continental traditions of social thought together. His ideas were then traced in the work of Luhmann, Habermas, Merton and Alexander. More generally, they have acted as an intellectual grinding wheel against which other social theories have sharpened their insights.

Feminism then entered this journey of ideas. Here was a body of thought whose beginnings reach far back into history. Yet these are the very voices that have been eclipsed through a series of unexamined presuppositions, replicated in everyday discourse, which are assumed to exist between the sexes. The implications of feminist critiques are wide-ranging. In particular, scientific thought and practice both reflect and justify a view of society which often excludes from consideration half of the population. This also opens up questions concerning the whole relationship between social theory and masculinity (Connell 2000) as well as the ways in which women and non-white peoples are excluded from dominant modes of thought and practice.

Collectively, these are a heady brew of ideas with which to travel into the terrain of contemporary social thought. Nevertheless, some clear themes have emerged. There is the question of the focus of social theory. Should it explain society without recourse to understanding the subjective interpretations of individuals, or should it seek to understand these everyday meanings, or can it achieve both?

With this general theme in mind, our aim is now to examine the terrain of contemporary social thought. Each chapter will start by tracing the antecedents of the theories covered, with a view to the above discussions, while considering how they have developed in distinct and illuminating ways. We shall then consider some critiques and modifications to the ideas examined in order that a greater overall understanding is achieved in relation to both their strengths and weaknesses.

PART II

Contemporary theories on society and social life

3 Symbolism and performance in everyday life

Social theory tends to do one of two things with 'motive' in terms of explaining social action. First, it is ignored on the grounds that it is a matter for psychology (anti-reductionist). Second, it incorporates it on the grounds that any genuine explanation must include the individual. This all relates to the role of social structure. An apparent gap between the individual and social structure is a central dilemma in social life. In social theory it is usually referred to as the structure–agency debate whereby human action determines social structure or the other way round.

One place to start in terms of the analysis of relations is 'interaction'. Chapters 3 and 4 consider the intellectual histories of what can only be called two action-oriented social theories. This chapter will consider symbolic interactionism and the next, ethnomethodology. As with all the chapters, this exposition is not intended, nor can it be, exhaustive. Our purpose is to examine the development of their ideas on social relations by situating them within the discussions contained in Part I.

In Chapter 2 it was suggested that there were a number of different ways in which the influence of pragmatism may be found in modern social theory. Most of that section was devoted to a discussion of the work of Mead. This was a deliberate strategy. Mead's work represents a bridge between pragmatism as a philosophy and its translation into a social psychology which may be found in the symbolic interactionism of Herbert Blumer (1900–86). It is to the intellectual antecedents and subsequent development of this school of thought to which attention is now turned.

The intellectual development of symbolic interactionism

There are a number of influences on the development of symbolic interactionism. Norman Denzin (1992) dates its beginnings in four publications:

Cooley (1902), Dewey (1896), James (1890) and Mead (1910). John Petras (1968) adds to these the psychology of Baldwin, while John Lincourt and Peter Hare (1973) talk of the neglected theory of meaning in the work of one of Mead's teachers, Josiah Royce.

Paul Rock suggests that interactionism may be viewed as 'an amalgam of Simmel's formal sociology and a pragmatist epistemology' (Rock 1979: 28). Here we find the influence of Simmel being mediated through the works of Robert Park (1864–1944) and William Thomas (1863–1947), Sheldon Stryker (1980) adds to this list Weber, anthropology and the Scottish School of Hume, Smith and Ferguson, who emphasized

> the relevance of the natural (including the social) world for the emergence of the individual, the organized and internally dynamic character of the human mind, the susceptibility of the human psyche to study within the framework of science ... and the mind as an instrument for adaption or adjustment.
>
> (Stryker 1980: 20–21)

In terms of enabling some coherence to this intellectual lineage, the works of Mead, Park and Thomas form the basis of a history which develops in different directions. A second generation of interactionists then emerged, most notable Herbert Blumer and Everett Hughes. Differences in theoretical interpretation and empirical direction then arose between Blumer's Chicago School and the so-called Iowa School of interactionism, as represented by Morris Kuhn (Meltzer and Petras 1973). Third generation interactionists then arose who took their work in varying directions, thus modifying the tradition. These scholars include Erving Goffman, Howard Becker, Anselm Strauss and Barney Glaser. The modification also continues in the writings, for example, of Denzin (2007), Lofland (1976), Lyman (1991), Shott (1987) and Stryker (1980).

Given these divergences, the elements of pragmatism will be emphasized in this unfolding history. It begins by considering how Mead provided the basis for symbolic interactionist theory. To complete this intellectual lineage, however, also requires an examination of the work of Thomas and Park. Collectively, their works were to be utilized by Herbert Blumer, whose ideas on social life are examined below. In the second section of the chapter, attention will then be devoted to the modification of interactionist ideas with reference to the studies of Erving Goffman.

Mead: the dialectical formation of self in society

Under the influences of James and Cooley, Mead incorporated the subjective states of individuals into the ongoing flow of social action. This resultant link between consciousness and action then became evident in his ideas on the social self, an elaboration of which will assist in understanding the relationship between the individual and society in his work.

For Mead, the social self was divided between an 'I' and a 'me'. What Mead calls the 'I' is the 'conversational character of inner experience' and is not assumed to be 'an object in consciousness'. As he goes on to suggest, the 'I' is Kant's transcendental self or 'the soul that James conceived behind the scene' (Mead in Reck 1964: 141). The 'me', on the other hand, becomes the reply to an individual's own talk and represents

> an importation from the field of social objects into an amorphous, unorganized field of what we call inner experience. Through the organization of this object, the self, this material is itself organized and brought under the control of the individual.
>
> (Mead in Reck 1964: 140)

The result is that the 'self' is no longer considered a Cartesian subject rooted in consciousness (Mead 1930). While Mead conceptualized the mind as a tool which seeks an 'adjustive relationship' (Meltzer et al. 1975: 30) between the individual and their social environment, there is potential for misunderstanding here. Mead does not conceive of the mind in a crude behaviourist fashion such that it becomes a simple mirror of the social environment. For this purpose, he had to reject not only the mentalism of Cooley, encapsulated in the notion of the 'looking-glass self', but also the individualism apparent in the work of James (Faberman 1985). How did Mead achieve this?

To overcome both these objectivist and subjectivist tendencies, Mead argued that 'subjects' become 'objects' to themselves via symbolic communication. More specifically, language becomes seen as the medium through which people speak, hear themselves speak and thus evaluate their utterances according to the responses of others. The 'I' becomes a 'conversation' within the person and language the medium of reflexivity. This process permits a person to think of themselves as a 'whole'. The 'me', on the other hand, 'is the organized set of others' attitudes which the person assumes through communicative interchange' (Coser 1979: 310). Individuals are therefore engaged in a constant process of monitoring their actions and social selves. This produces a 'self-consciousness' in the individual, thereby overcoming any objectivist tendencies in Mead's thought:

> The self acts with reference to others and is immediately conscious of the objects about it. In memory it also reintegrates the self acting as well as the others acted upon. But besides these contents, their action with reference to the others calls out responses in the individual himself – there is then another 'me' criticizing, approving, and suggesting, and consciously planning, the reflective self.
>
> (Mead in Reck 1964: 145)

Individuals gain the ability to shape who they are by 'taking the role of others'. They conceive of themselves through the responses, attitudes and expectations of both 'significant' and 'generalized others' via symbolic communication. In the normal course of events, social interaction occurs through the ability to attribute appropriate meanings to words, gestures and actions. Young children, as the self develops, relate to a range of significant others: for example, parents and sisters and brothers. Here we see an emphasis (shared with Dewey) on the creativity of the individual through 'the conscious 'playing through' in imagination of alternative performances of action' (Joas 1993: 249).

From this 'play' stage, the child develops through to the 'game' stage which involves regulated procedures and rules. This enables the process of formation to gain stability within differing social contexts. A notion of the 'generalized other' develops which controls conduct via an expectation of the reaction of others which occurs within the self. This becomes the means through which the individual and society are inextricably interwoven. Even 'thought' itself becomes 'the conversation of this generalized other with the self' (Mead in Reck 1964: 246). However, as with Weber, Marx and Durkheim, a concern is apparent in Mead's work for the fate of the individual in the face of increasing impersonal forces. On this occasion, it is manifest in what Mead calls 'unaesthetic toil':

> The isolated man is the one who belongs to a whole that he yet fails to realize. We have become bound up in a vast society, all of which is essential to the existence of each one, but we are without the shared experience which this should entail.
>
> (Mead in Reck 1964: 301)

Thomas and the self, society and social change

In order to complete an understanding of the intellectual antecedents of symbolic interactionism, it is necessary to consider the ideas of Thomas and Park who came to their work via the humanities and periods of study in Germany. We find in Thomas's work the first important link between pragmatism and social research. Park's main legacy, on the other hand, was the provision of a macro-sociological frame of reference for future empirical studies of everyday life in American cities (Joas 1993). As a result his insights remain of significance to the study of cities in general (Vasishth and Sloane 2002).

As with Mead, Thomas and Park displayed an interest in the creative individual. For Park, such individuals were leaders who could: 'grasp basic human nature and human processes in order to know the potential and limits of change' (Fisher and Strauss 1979: 462). Although sharing these similarities, in part derived from intellectual roots in nineteenth-century European evolutionary theory, there were differences between them when it came to the conceptualization of social progress:

> For Thomas, progress was the history of social groups mounting a ladder which had problematic rungs, at different rates, and with different degrees of opposition or help from other groups. For Park, progress itself was problematic. One could be sure only of ceaseless change – the clash and accommodation of groups – but it was always possible that groups would become more democratic in spirit, more rational in direction, and more functional in organization.
>
> (Fisher and Strauss 1978: 75)

Chicago, with its changing population, was to be a rich ground upon which to explore the dynamics of social change. The result was an enormous range of empirical studies (Bulmer 1984; Kurtz 1984). Here, we shall concentrate upon the relationship between the individual and society and the nature of social change in their work. In the case of Thomas, this is enabled via a consideration of the relationship between consciousness, action, culture and social change. In Park's work, this is manifest in the relationship between social change, communication and awareness, which themselves give rise to the potential for consensus and understanding.

In Thomas's pioneering work with Znaniecki on Polish peasants in Europe and North America (Thomas and Znaniecki 1918–19), the key themes of his work emerged. In the evolution of history, from the traditional to modern periods, the relationship between the individual and society, or what Thomas calls 'life organization' and 'social organization', becomes of central importance. Under normal circumstances, people act under habit and continue in this way on a day-to-day basis; until, that is, they are confronted by 'crisis'. At this point in time there is need for a 'conscious operation' (Joas 1993: 30) on the part of the individual where new habits of behaviour are formed. However, as the individual is bound up with the collectivity, a resulting cultural ambivalence arises within them which leads to a pragmatic need to refashion the self. More generally, this necessitates that groups redefine their social situations and in so doing regain control over them – hence Thomas's idea of progress as a 'ladder with problematic rungs'.

The actual resources which are mobilized for reasserting control over social situations are derived from the society of which an individual is a part. At the same time, the social self is bounded by both space and time. The relation between subject and object is then manifest in terms of the values of a society to which an individual belongs (objective conditions) and the attitudes which an individual then adopts in response to them (subjective 'definitions of the situation'). Therefore, while social 'facts' are given and transmitted from the past, they must be understood in terms of how they are interpreted by people in given social situations. From this is derived Thomas's famous methodological maxim: 'If men define situations as real, they are real in their consequences' (Thomas and Thomas 1928: 572). It follows that if social theory is to further its understanding of social life, it must study both the objective and subjective features of social life via the relationship between social conditions and group development.

As the earlier quote indicated, progress is conceptualized in Robert Park's work as the 'clash and accommodation of groups'. At an empirical level, this is manifest as a struggle for space in urban settings: that is a pragmatic emphasis on changing and 'never self-consistent' (Park 1972: 29). In parallel to Thomas, therefore, the basis-unit of society cannot be the isolated individual, but is 'understood to be the volitional attitudes of individuals interacting in a group situation. These attitudes can either be expressed as feelings (wishes and beliefs) or as conscious ideas' (Park 1972: 31).

In this way society becomes a source not only of obligation, but also of inspiration. For Park, even an individual's ability to think is regarded as an expansion of the ideas of those who have gone before them (Park 1972: 125).

Park takes Dewey's idea of communication as the basis for maintaining a social group's unity and integrity during times of social change. As he says: 'Culture includes all that is communicable ... the essence of culture is understanding' (Park 1972: 102). What he calls 'collective representations', via communication, form the basis of collective actions out of which arise social forms which underlie symbols and social processes (the influence of Simmel is apparent here). This concern with communication and change took him in particular directions. On the one hand, he recognized that only a Durkheimian-style 'moral order' was regulated by the meanings and values extant within a social grouping. However, another form existed which was controlled by competition, or what Darwin called the 'struggle for existence' (quoted in Park 1972: 118). This form is not 'social', as defined in Deweyian terms (as exhibiting meaningful communication), but is maintained by a symbiosis which comes from the division of labour among competing groups. This is what Park termed the 'ecological order' (Park 1936).

Having identified these two forms of social order, a central question then preoccupied Park: that is, how do people overcome barriers to communication, which is the precondition of democratic communities, given the competition that existed between groups? The preoccupations of his continental predecessors are apparent at this stage for the question is framed in terms of individual creativity versus the pressure to conform in an increasingly impersonal society. In seeking a solution to this tendency, he merges knowledge and feelings within his ideas (Schopenhauer does appear in his work). Modernity is then seen to require a combination of the knowledge of other group's customs and histories, together with the exercise of compassion which comes from such understanding. This fusion, Park believed, might then permit social change by building bridges between conflict and communities (Fisher and Strauss 1979).

We now have a very rich mixture of social thought upon which to draw that still yields valuable insights on contemporary social, political and economic conditions. Having considered the main themes in the works of these three authors, attention is now turned to the development of symbolic interactionism in the work of Herbert Blumer.

The social theory of Herbert Blumer: society as symbolic interaction

In terms of this unfolding history, it is Mead's work on 'role performance' that is of interest (Mead also used this concept to derive a general theory of the social constitution of intelligence, as well as ethical development: see Joas 1985). While emphasizing the creative aspects of individual perform-ance, the concept of the 'generalized other' permits an individual to anticipate the conduct of person's occupying particular roles. However, this forms a dualism in Mead's thought. On the one hand, creativity is empha-sized and on the other, the existence of social roles is posited which create expectations upon their incumbents as to their context and form of appro-priate behaviour. This dualism permitted Talcott Parsons to draw upon Mead's ideas in linking norms and values to system needs in his action, rather than interaction, theory (J. H. Turner 1974). As will be evident, this is a very different emphasis from that found in Herbert Blumer's work.

Blumer was to emphasize creativity in role performance, the result being that he was open to the charge of selectively interpreting Mead (McPhail and Rexroat 1979). Blumer coined the term 'symbolic interaction-ism' in order to contrast it with stimulus–response models of human behaviour which were so popular at the time (Blumer 1937). He argued that the responses of human beings to their environments are mediated by meaningful interpretations. Mead's intellectual legacy thus becomes appar-ent through its ability to conceptualize what such acts of interpretation mean for a general understanding of human being, human action and human association (Blumer 1972).

The following quote encapsulates not only Blumer's interpretation of Mead, but also how he distinguishes it from either a structuralist or systems approach to social life. For Blumer, Mead's whole approach

> sees human society not as an established structure but as people meeting their conditions of life; it sees social action not as an emanation of societal structure but as a formation made by human

> actors ... it sees group life not as a release or expression of estab-
> lished structure but as a process of building up joint actions ... it sees
> the so-called interaction between parts of a society not as a direct
> exercising influence by one part on another but as mediated
> throughout by interpretations made by people; accordingly, it sees
> society not as a system ... but as a vast number of occurring joint
> actions ... all being pursued to serve the purpose of the participants
> and not the requirements of a system.
>
> (Blumer 1969: 74–75)

It is not suggested that social structures do not exist: 'Such a position would
be ridiculous' (Blumer 1969: 75). However, they become admissible only in
so far as they enter the interpretations and definitions of social actors who
pursue 'purposes'.

Given the above, we can detect three distinctive features to Blumer's
interactionist social theory. First, symbolic interactionism may be contrasted
with psychological and sociological concepts – from personalities and attitudes to social roles and structural constraints – because the interpretations
of ongoing actions involve a constant process of reorganization or adjustment in intentions and attitudes, as well as judgements as to the suitability
of norms and values to given social situations. Both pre-existing psychological and social factors are then of interest 'only in terms of how they are
handled in the interpretative process' (Blumer 1969: 66).

Second, while social life is both fluid and dynamic, forms of conduct
must be 'fitted together' to enable both the establishment and transformation of patterns of group life. Here we can see the influence of Park on
Blumer's work:

> Established patterns of group life exist and persist only through the
> continued use of the same schemes of interpretation; and such
> schemes of interpretation are maintained only through their contin-
> ued confirmation by the defining acts of others. It is highly impor-
> tant to recognize that the established patterns of group life just do
> not carry on by themselves but are dependent for their continuity
> on recurrent affirmative definition.
>
> (Blumer 1969: 67)

As such, the very ability to interpret the acts of others requires
communication and the social fixing of definitions in order that interpretations can take place in the first instance. Only then is it possible to engage in
the redefinition of acts in the continual flux of social life. This, in turn,
enables the formative aspects of human interaction which gives rise to new
relations, behaviours, conceptions, etc. Additionally, this process allows
groups to deal with the problems that they encounter in social life (Blumer
1969: 67).

Third, given the focus upon interpretation and definition in human interaction, Blumer argues that symbolic interactionism 'is able to cover the full range of the generic forms of human association' (Blumer 1969: 67). The examples of this include domination, exploitation, consensus, conflict and co-operation. This is contrasted with Parsonian systems theory with its assumption of the 'complementarity of expectations' (Blumer 1969: 68). As a result, the question of the relationship between the individual and society is not given through the inculcation of values and norms, or any structural forms which pre-exist or underlie individual actions and utterances. Instead, Blumer offers a pragmatist conception of negotiation, communication, interpretation and definition. For this reason, Lewis and Smith (1980) argue that Blumer took a 'nominalist' reading of Mead (this states that there is no independent social reality which exists separately from the 'mind'), whereas Mead can be interpreted as a 'realist' (reality exists, to some degree, independently of the mind).

In replying to this contention, Blumer (1983) seeks to further clarify the relationship between what he calls 'social' or 'joint acts' and 'individual acts'. In these terms, society is viewed as 'the fitting together of acts to form joint action' (Blumer 1969: 76). To return to an earlier point, the individual motivations which give rise to these alignments take a myriad of forms and are therefore viewed as 'the formation of workable relations' (Blumer 1969: 76). Joint actions, which range from collaborative acts between two individuals, to the acts of large corporations, fit together through the acts of interpretation and definition in pragmatic mode. By identifying the social acts which they are about to join, individuals are then able to orientate themselves. These acts of interpretation thereby guide actions, as well as serving as orientating mechanisms towards the actions of others.

The relationship between individual and joint acts involves the continual process of interpretation and definition, built up over time. This introduction of history, or what Blumer (1969) calls a 'career', is ordered through the employment of common definitions. However, lest this be seen as habitual, as with the earlier pragmatist emphasis, Blumer always sees uncertainty constantly looming in the background – no emphasis on modernity as continuity here. These uncertainties can be manifested in a number of ways. For instance, joint acts may not be initiated; they may be abandoned or transformed; the participants to such acts may not create a common definition and hence they rest on unstable premises or, even if they possess common definitions, wide discrepancies are exhibited in the course of joint actions and new situations may then arise which call for exploratory work in order that acts can, once again, be 'fitted together'. Blumer also notes that individuals who are party to joint actions may come to rely on 'other considerations' for the purposes of interpretation and definition, aside from those commonly defined by the participants.

This latter point is somewhat ambiguous. Do these 'other considerations' include the resources that people bring to interactions? If so, do these
then enable them to determine the definitions which are employed in their
social encounters? Once again, the question of the dualism in Mead's
thought, with which this section began, arises; albeit in a different form.
Quite simply, if there are 'other considerations', how does this leave the
relationship between the individual and society in terms of the notions of
creativity and constraint? This is where Erving Goffman enters our theoretical stage.

Modification and critique: exploring the interaction order

Erving Goffman was influenced by the work not only of Blumer, but also of
Everett Hughes (1971). However, to these we must add no less than the ideas
of Durkheim, Simmel, James, Schutz, Kenneth Burke (1969), social anthropologists, linguistic philosophers and ethologists! They are all mobilized to
illuminate a key feature to his work: 'the explanation for action in its
meaning for others rather than in its causal origins' (Burns 1992: 3). This is
organized around three themes: social order, social interaction and the self.
With these in mind, the purpose in this section is to examine the connections between everyday interactions (micro) and society (macro) in Goffman's work. In so doing, it will become clear that he cannot be situated
within the symbolic interactionist tradition as presented thus far.

In *The Presentation of Self in Everyday Life* Goffman (1984) quotes from a
book by William Sansom. It is an account of the ways in which Preedy, an
Englishman on holiday, projects certain impressions of himself when making
his appearance on a Spanish beach for the first time. In discussing this,
Goffman argues that such impressions are symptomatic of an act of calculation by an individual which is oriented towards significant others. These acts
of calculation are both intentional and conscious. In addition, as Blumer
noted, while significant others may be impressed, they may also 'misunder-
stand the situation', thereby reaching conclusions which bear no relation to
the person's original intent in their performance (Goffman 1984: 18). At the
same time, the traditions of a group will require particular expressions of an
individual in a given role (Goffman 1984: 18). Therefore, although impressions are 'well-designed', the individual who enacts them may do so either
consciously or unconsciously. Yet, despite this latter possibility, Goffman
argues:

> in so far as the others act as if the individual had conveyed a
> particular impression, we may take a functional or pragmatic view

and say that the individual has 'effectively' projected a given definition of the situation and 'effectively' fostered the understanding that a given state of affairs obtains.

(Goffman 1984: 18)

Although Goffman admits of the potential for actions to be unconsciously motivated or historically informed, his focus is directed upon the meanings of individual actions for significant others. In *The Presentation of Self* this even extends to the abilities of individuals to check upon the validity of a person's utterances by, for example, observing their non-verbal behaviour and interactions with others. Hidden motivations can lurk behind every appearance. Even an attention to the detail of one's dress, in order to project a particular impression of oneself to others, may have to be disguised as it is not assumed to be material to conversations in general. The intent, in other words, which underlies impression management, must remain 'hidden' (Goffman 1971: 23). Hence, Goffman prioritizes 'intentionality' in everyday conduct, over other forms of explanation, in the social arena he calls the 'interaction order': 'Social interaction can be identified narrowly as that which uniquely transpires in social situations, that is, environments in which two or more individuals are physically in one another's presence' (Goffman 1983: 4).

This is the micro-analytic arena in which Goffman's observations are so acute. It is a 'space' which comprises not 'personal' space but, more generally, the regions or social situations in which the interaction takes place. Therefore, these arenas are also defined as physical areas 'within which two or more persons find themselves in visual and aural range of one another' (Goffman 1981: 84). Meanings are then attributed to both verbal and non-verbal behaviour. The body, for example, may be mobilized to create an impression to significant others, while also enabling a space, or what Goffman (1971) calls an 'egocentric territoriality', to be produced by an individual who draws upon the cultural resources at their disposal.

Intriguing as this is, the question still arises as to whether Goffman's emphasis on intentionality still provides us with a subjectivist social theory? Linked to Robert Park acutely observed that the disposition of individuals to play out roles is an enduring and universal feature of society and that people realize their self (or selves) through the execution of such roles in society that is defined as a 'drama':

It is probably no mere historical accident that the word person, in its first meaning, is a mask. It is rather recognition of the fact that everyone is always and everywhere, more or less consciously, playing a role. ... It is in these roles that we know each other, it is in these roles that we know ourselves.

(Park in Goffman 1971: 30)

In illuminating the nature of relationship of self to society via roles, Goffman takes a very different line from Blumer. His earlier work on social interaction can actually be characterized as one which examines how the gap between the macro and micro social worlds can be closed (Burns 1992). In the interaction order, the conduct of individuals is viewed as being part of society and social order. Yet, is this not a structuralist answer in terms of the subject simply becoming a conduit through which pre-existing societal forms flow?

Goffman is neither structuralist, nor individualist. The former would assume that the interaction order is determined from 'above', while the latter would assume that it is determined from 'below' via, for example, the calculative procedures of individual actors. Both of these approaches would neglect the fact 'that we not only take other people into consideration when we act, but that we also give consideration to others' (Robin Williams 1988: 67). What Goffman does is to conceptualize this in terms of 'ritual', which he uses in two senses. First, in terms of the moral character of interaction and second, in terms of its 'standardized' or 'ritualized' character (Robin Williams 1988). Habit is apparent in the second sense with a pragmatist focus upon creativity being evident within the first. A working relationship is then established within interactions which themselves vary from setting to setting. Thus, within the interaction order there evolves a 'definition of the situation which involves not so much a real agreement as to what exists but rather a real agreement as to whose claims concerning what issues will be temporarily honoured' (Goffman 1984: 21).

In this way Goffman admits of the general properties which people possess in order to creatively contribute to the interaction order in the first place. He notes that a psychology is involved, but it is 'one stripped and cramped to suit the sociological study of conversations, track meets, banquets, jury trials, and street loitering' (1972: 3). The result is a circumscribed interaction order: 'Not, then, men and their moments. Rather moments and their men' (Goffman 1972: 3). As such, the social order provides the interaction order with the resources which it needs to sustain and reproduce itself. Ritual is the bridge between the macro and the micro or, more particularly, the Blumerian concepts of role creativity and history as manifest in the notion of 'career' (Manning 1992).

Exactly how the idea of role provides a macro–micro bridge is illuminated in Goffman's essay on 'role distance'. To paraphrase him, a 'role' is defined as those activities a person would engage in if they acted in accordance with the normative demands made upon someone in that position (Goffman 1961: 75). On the other hand, 'role performance' is the actual conduct of the person in that role. However, the issue still revolves around the notion of role as obligation and expectation. In being obliged and expected to act in certain ways, creativity, in terms of role performance, is clearly circumscribed. To emphasize the normative constraints on a particular role would clearly tend towards a Parsonian interpretation which omits the details of action in favour of theorizing it in terms of functionally related system needs.

In considering this tension, Goffman suggests that it is necessary to focus upon both role systems and the manner in which individuals manage their roles. Roles then become defined as 'the *typical* response of individuals in a particular position' (Goffman 1961: 82, original italics). What sits between the typical and actual response of an individual in a given role depends upon perceptions and definitions of the situation (Goffman 1961: 82). The researcher may then proceed to create an analytical category which allows them to 'bracket off' people whose 'common life situation' is of interest. The normative aspects of a role are then the means through which the individual is enabled to perform their role in accordance with, for example, their life chances and biography. It follows from this that the precise relationship between a person and their role in a given social situation is deliberately held open to empirical investigation: 'Individuals are almost always free to modulate what they are required to do' (Goffman 1961: 133). At the same time, the role, the place and others present will affect that performance, while 'other affiliations' will be given credit in that performance.

Two points, in particular, follow from the above. First, in terms of social identity there is no Cartesian ego. Instead, there is a focus upon the social construction and management of the self. Second, Durkheim's worlds of the sacred and profane, or Park's world of the moral and ecological, are not distinct. One is seen as a resource for the other. This is enacted by the individual through 'role distance', where the role may be prescribed, but the manner of its performance is variable. It is then open to the analyst to study the flux of everyday life: 'One can never expect complete freedom between individual and role and never complete constraint' (Goffman 1974: 269). Thus, while the desire to perform the role of mother, for example, may come from a number of sources, these could include the 'political doctrine of destiny' which serves 'to keep women in their subordinate place' (Goffman 1974: 270). On the other hand, what Goffman (1961: 85) calls 'situated roles' do enable agents to produce an impression before others, while also taking account of their activities and actions. In that sense, the very presentation of the self in everyday life becomes a constraint upon actions (Rawls 1987).

This approach to the study of roles is a clear modification to the Blumerian tradition of symbolic interactionism. Methodologically, we find a different emphasis as employed in his studies of 'total institutions' (Goffman 1968) and the analysis of everyday talk (Goffman 1981). In his most theoretical work on 'frames', Goffman (1974) argues that the reason for their use rests upon the fact that there is no 'single reality' or 'definition of the situation' which is constructed out of the interaction order. This also places him at odds, as will be noted in Chapter 4, with ethnomethodology. Instead, the analyst examines 'frames' in order to understand the 'general properties' that people draw upon in their daily interactions:

> I assume that definitions of a situation are built up in accordance with principles of organization which govern events – at least social ones – and our subjective involvement in them; frame is the word I use to refer to such of these basic elements as I am able to identify. That is my definition of frame. My phrase 'frame analysis' is a slogan to refer to the examination in these terms of the organization of experience.
>
> (Goffman 1974: 10–11)

To return to the discussions in Part I, this move allows Goffman to sidestep the epistemological problematic upon which so much social theory comes unstuck: that is, the prioritization of subject over object and vice versa. Following James, Goffman does not ask: 'What is reality'? Instead, he asks: *'Under what circumstances do we think things are real?'* (Goffman 1974, original italics). In this way, he can then move on to examine 'under what conditions such a feeling is generated, and this question speaks to a small manageable problem having to do with the camera and not what it is the camera takes pictures of' (Goffman 1974: 2).

Essentially, in suggesting that the social analyst bracket types of role, or view frames as the means through which people organize their meanings and involvements in everyday life, Goffman sits within the neo-Kantian tradition (Robin Williams 1980, 1988).

We can now say that in terms of the mobilization of particular resources that parties bring to their interactions, their representations of reality can affect reality itself. Thus, when it came to representations of gender in advertising, for example, the male norm of dominance and the female norm of submission were apparent in his analysis (Goffman 1979). At another level, non-verbal gestures, through bodily posture, can also be implicated in meaning production and power relations which then act as tactics of control and exclusion (Bourdieu 1992a, 2000).

Having briefly considered the potential for power to govern the interaction order, we just wish to finish this section by noting what will not be found in Goffman's work: that is, an explicit analysis of social structure as manifest, for example, in race and class relations. As he puts it in *Frame Analysis*:

> I am not addressing the structure of social life but the structure of experience individuals have at any moment of their social lives. *I personally hold society to be first in every way and any individual's current involvement to be second.*
>
> (Goffman 1974: 13, emphasis added)

To some commentators, this means that Goffman trivializes social life and ends up producing a somewhat conservative view of social relations (Gouldner 1971) On this aspect of his writings, it is best left to Goffman to say how his legacy should be interpreted. When it comes to the sleep of false consciousness in everyday life and to what is often called the awakening of people to their 'true' interests, his overall intention was not to 'provide a lullaby but merely to sneak in and watch the way people snore' (Goffman 1974: 14).

Summary

In terms of Mead's work, we now have new interpretations which are producing rich insights into social life. As Blumer wrote of Mead, his thought will continue to attract interest 'because of the distinctive way in which it ties together individual action and group life' (Blumer 1983: 143). This is the continuing essence to Mead's legacy for contemporary social theory and one which, as we shall see, has been utilized by Jürgen Habermas among others.

As for Blumer, his translation of the Meadian legacy was manifest in his call to situate people within the context of their actions in order that the production of meanings and definitions of the social world could be understood in their 'natural settings'. For this reason, he advocated the use of naturalistic research which was taken up and modified in various ways. However, it has been suggested that Blumer selectively interpreted Mead which led to the production of a subjectivist version of the dynamics of social life.

Whereas Mead rooted 'perception and meaning in a common praxis of subjects', Blumer focused upon 'verbal communications about definitions which is unrelated to praxis' (Joas 1985: 166). Therefore, it became a point of contention in the development of symbolic interactionism that in this interpretation and his subsequent methodological maxims, Blumer reintroduced the dichotomy between subject and object by prioritizing the former over the latter. While admitting of the existence of structures, they were thus relegated to the status of being admissible only in so far as they were apparent in consciousness (Stryker 1980). In so doing, he returned to the very dichotomy in social thought which Mead had sought to overcome. This is where Goffman stepped in.

When it came to Goffman's work, a line of continuity may be traced with Mead in terms of the development of the self in opposition to Cartesianism. The self is found in a relationship between subject and object which emerges in a community of others in which individuals are shaped and which they reshape, through their actions. In the steps of Hegel and the German idealists since Kant, it was then possible for the Meadian self to become an object of knowledge, experience and development (Joas 1985). This implies that subjects are objects to themselves. With Mead, this was apparent in relationship between the 'me' and the 'I'. For Goffman, it was more sociological in form in terms of his analyses of roles.

Although Goffman's methods were undoubtedly unorthodox, in reading his work one cannot help but gain a great deal of insight into the workings of everyday life in terms of meaning production. Goffman was to see rules of interaction not simply as produced from within social encounters, but also as producing them. He admitted of the presence of structures within social life through the manner in which encounters are 'framed' in order to interact in the first place. However, it was social interaction, not social structure, which absorbed his interests. Nevertheless, he did not presuppose symmetry of power between co-participants in the interaction order. People possessed differential access to knowledge and information which, in the 'information society', can act as a resource in interaction (Lyon 2006). Further, formal and informal rules exist which can prevent 'outsiders' joining anything from golf clubs and occupational groups to street gangs. Similarly, people are invested with skills and characteristics which they can drawn upon in influencing the actions and definitions of others. This is a legacy that has much to offer the study of social life and there is clear potential in his work for the production of a more general social theory (Layder 2006). Goffman's work is thus been deployed in a number of fields of investigation (G. W. Smith 2006).

For reasons of exposition, space and general influence on the development of social theory, we chose to emphasize Goffman in this particular journey. Yet within the development of interactionism, the same points on the relationship between social structure and social interaction could have been made in, for example, a consideration of the bounded nature of negotiations in organizations (P. M. Hall 1987; Strauss 1978, 1982). Similarly, there is the work of Howard Becker (1963) on the relationship between societal forces of social exclusion, which result from the power of a social group to define certain behaviour as antisocial, and its effects on the actions and self-definitions of those so labelled. In addition, as noted at the beginning of the chapter, those from within this tradition are now considering its merits and weaknesses through an encounter with postmodernism and poststructuralism (Lemert 2006).

There existed another route for social theory to pursue in order to devote itself to a study of the interaction order. This was to share Blumer's critique of the idea that people are often viewed as cultural dopes who are simply manipulated by structures and systems beyond their comprehension. Our focus now shifts towards an even more detailed analysis of the everyday methods that people employ in interpreting their social universes. This is a route that Schutz's phenomenology was to start, but certainly not finish.

4 Social life as accomplishment

If the actor's point of view is a prime focus for an action-oriented social theory, then language and cognition are of central importance in its development. Language, after all, is the means through which people construct their worlds, share their experiences of it, communicate with each other and reflect upon their experiences. As Alfred Schutz argued, people experience their social worlds as intersubjective ones which are then accessible to all through the mediums of intercommunication and language.

When it comes to a study of language and social life, the work of Wittgenstein cannot be ignored. Wittgenstein began his writings under the influence of Bertrand Russell, which included a brief association with what was known as the Vienna Circle of logical positivism. In his earlier work, the correspondence theory of truth was exemplified through the argument that the purpose of language was to state facts by 'picturing' them. In his later philosophy, however, he became critical of this insight (Monk 1990). The consequence of this move was that meaning was divorced from its usual basis in signification and different uses of language were collected under the generic term 'language games'. The search for hidden meanings and depth explanations became replaced by the study of the use of concepts in everyday language:

> consequent upon the abandonment of the picture theory, the distinction between sense and non-sense is made entirely internal to language. It no longer depends on any correspondence to external reality but has to do with the failure of users of the language to accord with its patterns of use.
>
> (Anderson et al. 1986: 1)

Wittgenstein's intellectual legacy has paved the way for inquiries into knowledge production and use (Bloor 1983); the use of rules in social life (Holtzman and Leich 1981) as well as developments in the methodology of the social sciences (Clammer 1976). In relation to methodology, the work of

Peter Winch (1990) came to represent yet another assault, along with those of hermeneutics and phenomenology, on the applicability of cause and effect to the study of social life (as interpreted through the idea of being determined, rather than expressing tendencies, in social relations). To this was added the 'Ordinary Language Philosophy' of Gilbert Ryle (1900–76) and John Austin (1911–60), both of whom devoted their energies to the study of language.

A combination of phenomenology and ordinary language philosophy informs the development of ethnomethodology. Therefore, the first section of this chapter contains a more in-depth examination of these influences. Following this, there is a consideration of the diversities which exist within this broad tradition of thought. This will not only enable an evaluation of its insights, but also provide a basis upon which to continue the journey through the terrain of contemporary social theory.

The making of ethnomethodology

The term 'ethnomethodology' originated from studies undertaken by Harold Garfinkel during his time at the Chicago law school in the mid 1940s. A researcher had bugged a jury room in order to listen to their deliberations. Garfinkel, in analysing the tapes, focused upon the question of 'how the jurors knew what they were doing in doing the work of jurors' (Garfinkel 1974: 15). A study of these conversations then allowed him to consider what made people jurors.

From his analysis of the jurors' deliberations, Garfinkel found that they exhibited a methodical basis exemplified by their allusions to the adequacy of the evidence as presented in the court-room. Consequently, he characterized the jurors' activities as the doing of 'methodology'. Some years later, in examining some cross-cultural area files, he found a set of words prefixed by 'ethno' (ethnobotany, ethnology, etc.). Garfinkel took this to mean, in more general terms, 'the availability to a member of common-sense knowledge of his society as common-sense knowledge of the 'whatever' (Garfinkel 1974: 16). So evolved the term 'ethnomethodology'. As a body of thought it represents 'an organizational study of members' knowledge of his ordinary affairs, of his own organized enterprises, where that knowledge is treated by us as part of the same setting that also makes it orderable'. (Garfinkel 1974: 18).

A new action theory: beyond Parsons and Schutz

As noted, influences for the development of ethnomethodology can be seen in phenomenology and linguistic philosophy. However, the original impetus came from Garfinkel's time as a graduate student with Parsons, whose neo-Kantian emphasis constructed an analytic agenda which was concerned to identify the 'real' workings of society. The questions asked of social relations were of the order of 'what' and 'why'? The former being what is said or done, which then receives an answer expressed in causal terms. However, what of the 'how'? The issue here is one of a disjuncture between the 'concreteness' of people's activities in everyday life and their analytic representation in Parsonian action theory, this result being that 'real society' becomes only 'specifiable as the achieved results of administering the policies and methods of formal, constructive analysis' (Garfinkel 1991: 13). Given this, Parsons' action theory does not render justice to the very phenomena which it sought to understand because it seeks to impose a rationality on human conduct that is separated from the practical concerns of situated everyday life.

In contrast to this sacrifice of 'concreteness' to 'generality', ethnomethodology seeks to describe an order in everyday life that does not resort to an a priori analytic framework. This approach is apparent in Garfinkel's analysis of three problems in Parsonian theory of action. First, what is the status of the actor's accounts of their own actions? Particularly when these conflict with the analytic, causal accounts offered by social scientists. Second, people share their knowledge. What is the status of this insight in a theory of action concerned to generalize beyond the particularity of a social setting? Third, people are not 'cultural dopes' manipulated as puppets on a string of normative consensus, for they make strategic choices which involve alteration in their environments. These three gaps in Parsonian theory are referred to as the problems of 'rationality', 'subjectivity' and 'reflexivity' (Heritage 1984: 23). To each of these ethnomethodology offers a unique solution.

Given these analytic failings, Garfinkel had to take a very different theoretical direction from that of Parsons. This quote, taken from Garfinkel's dissertation, indicates the nature of this route:

> At least two important theoretical developments stem from the researches of Max Weber. One development, already well worked, seeks to arrive at a generalized social system by uniting a theory that treats the structuring of experience with another theory designed to answer the question, 'What is man?' Speaking loosely, a synthesis is attempted between the facts of social structure and the facts of personality. The other development, not yet adequately exploited, seeks a generalized social system built solely from the analysis of experience structures.
>
> (Garfinkel quoted in Heritage 1984: 9)

To aim to describe these 'experience structures' has two important consequences for social theory. First, given this direction, the termination point for ethnomethodological interests actually becomes the starting point for most other social scientific practices, including theorizing about social life. Second, social action is analysed in terms of sense, with a focus on common sense, without any particular recourse for this purpose to ideas of intentionality or motive. Bearing these points in mind, we now turn to the intellectual resources that are mobilized to produce these outcomes.

Schutz argued that the object of social scientific study should be the 'natural attitude' in everyday life. *Verstehen* was not a resource for doing social science, but was the very topic which social science should devote its energies to studying. In Schutz's phenomenology, this was the common stock of knowledge that people draw upon in interpreting and ordering their social worlds. In contrast to this route, social science practitioners, such as Parsons and Weber, had projected their theories into the very phenomena which they should, in fact, be faithfully describing: for example, meaningful acts, everyday experiences and mutual understandings (Schutz 1972). It follows from the above that social phenomena are viewed as constituted as meaningful before an analyst appears on the social scene. However, while the social world is intelligible, the 'lifeworld', which people draw upon for this purpose, is taken for granted by them. These basic 'meaning structures' are then analytically rearranged by social science with the consequence that they are not accurately represented, For this reason, Schutz (1979) argued that social scientific constructs must satisfy the 'postulate of subjective interpretation'. In this way, they would then faithfully reflect these everyday meanings. In contrast to this, one strategy for the generation of interpretative social theories was to construct 'ideal types' of action which serve as bridging mechanisms between subjective meanings and relations of cause and effect.

According to Schutz, these solutions failed to address the nature of the relationship between social scientific analytic categories ('second order' constructs) and the lifeworld ('first order' constructs). A central question thus remains unanswered: that is, a determination of 'the precise nature of the *phenomenon of meaning*' through an analysis of how it constitutes social life (Schutz 1972: 13, original italics). To focus upon how meaning constitutes social life would enable social scientists 'to analyse step by step the meaning-structure of the social world' (Schutz 1972: 13). A 'phenomenological reduction' is then required which permits the researcher to see how objects are constituted out of their appearances as encountered in 'streams of consciousness'. As such, the proper subject matter of the social sciences is not only the stock of knowledge which people draw in their daily lives, but also the 'typifications' which permit them to order their experiences in the first place. Through these interpretative procedures, experiences are ordered into particular groups with certain features, so that they might be intersubjectively recognizable.

From the above we can characterize Schutz's work as inheriting Husserl's philosophical problematic and then translating it into a phenomenology of the lifeworld. At one level, this provided inspiration for the development of phenomenological social theories (Berger and Luckmann 1967; M. F. Rogers 1983). For Garfinkel, however, Schutz was to provide a basis for a descriptive, not analytic, sociology of everyday life which was to find any reference to the 'transcendental conditions' of action to be an undermining of its aims. To complete this move required that ethnomethodology draw upon linguistic philosophy.

Linguistic philosophy and ethnomethodology

It has been suggested that Parsons examined the external moderation of moral rules, without recourse to a description of everyday knowledge. Schutz, on the other hand, was concerned to examine this knowledge, but without reference to the moral dimensions of social life. In essence, Garfinkel's journey involved the abandonment of epistemology in favour of methodology. Quite simply, people get on with their daily lives by drawing upon a stock of background knowledge which makes sense of their social worlds. To 'know' what people are doing does not require any recourse to hidden motives or models of rationality, but the accurate description of everyday phenomena:

> 'know' consists really in a structure of activity. This is what the 'know' consists of. It is not that the member has it somewhere in the nervous traces or that he has it according to a theory of personal action, and that this will not permit someone to elicit what he has available to tell you. ... The 'know' resides in the ability to generate ... recognizable sentences.
> (Garfinkel in Hill and Stones Crittenden 1968: 47)

This idea of 'knowing' as available in the situated utterances of actors is found in the work of Wittgenstein, whose later studies can be read as the examination of philosopher's talk as indexical (Garfinkel and Sacks 1986). Wittgenstein suggested that philosophers cease asking questions which they cannot answer and turn instead to a study of meaning in terms of use *in situ*. In ethnomethodological parlance, this becomes translated as the abandonment of a need to use intentionality or motive to explain an action or utterance. The whole concept of an 'I', from Descartes and Kant, through to Freud, Mead and Husserl, becomes but a 'phenomenological residua' in social thought (Coulter 1979). It is a history based upon an ontological assumption which is then, illegitimately, used to explain human actions.

In contrast ethnomethodology seeks meanings in situated and practical usages in everyday life without reference to an ego. As a result, it represents a critique of aspects of the Enlightenment project. The correspondence theory of truth, according to which there is a difference between the perceiving of an object and what it 'really is', seeks to explain reality separate from the act of perception. According to the congruence theory of reality, on the other hand, there is no difference between these two parts. They are 'synonymous and interchangeable' (J. M. Atkinson 1978: 176).

The intellectual armoury for this move is found in Wittgenstein's later work. He argues that there is no private or 'inner' or transcendental referent to which the analyst might allude in determining the meaning of an expression or action. 'Nothing', Wittgenstein asserts, 'is more wrong-headed than calling meaning a mental activity' (quoted in J. B. Thompson 1981: 29). Meaning is therefore to be determined via a study of use in context where there exist 'publicly available' linguistic forms. It is these 'forms of life' which serve as backgrounds to social activity (there are parallels here between Heidegger and Wittgenstein). In this way, ethnomethodology could develop without reference to an 'I' which, if it were only public, could explain us all' (Coulter 1979: 124). Ontological, as well as epistemological assumptions, are believed to be abandoned in the process.

We may translate this as the argument that words do not stand for ideas or objects as such, but are the tools acquired within a form of life which people then draw upon as the basis for achieving intersubjective understanding. Language and social relations, in other words, become inextricably linked: 'To give an account of the meaning of a word is to describe how it is used; and to describe how it is used is to describe the social intercourse into which it enters'. (Winch 1990: 123).

As noted, this is accomplished without recourse to explanation in terms of the motive of individual egos or external relations of cause and effect. With this comes an alteration in the criteria through which social phenomena are understood:

> if the sociological investigator wants to regard them *as* social events ... he has to take seriously the criteria which are applied for distinguishing between 'different' kinds of actions and identifying the 'same' kinds of actions within the way of life he is studying. It is not open to him arbitrarily to impose his own standards from without. In so far as he does so, the events he is studying lose altogether their character as *social* events.
>
> (Winch 1990: 108, original italics)

We can now return to the theme of rationality which Garfinkel exposed in Parsons' work. If it is to be understood, then it must be situated within a form of life. The task is then to describe its form from within, not to impose an explanation from without.

Winch argues that forms of life must be rule-governed and rule-following in order that intersubjective agreement can exist in the first instance. Rules thus occupy a central place in this analysis: 'all behaviour which is meaningful (therefore all specifically human behaviour) is *ipso facto* rule-governed' (Winch 1990: 52, original italics). Following Wittgenstein, rules are viewed as publicly available and intelligible within their social context. This does not necessarily mean that agents will know the rules upon which their actions are based, nor that they will always follow particular rules, merely that all social behaviour involves the acceptance or rejection of rules.

Important possibilities in ethnomethodological analysis are now opened up through such arguments: in particular, the study of naturally occurring conversations in everyday life. Conversation analysis (or 'CA') has grown considerably since the 1960s. Under the pioneering work of Harvey Sacks (1963, 1972) this has led to a growing body of work (J. M. Atkinson and Heritage 1984; Boden and Zimmerman 1993; Lerner, 2004). The themes of the correspondence and congruence theories of reality become apparent in these studies, for the ethnomethodologist can

Armed with these intellectual antecedents, ethnomethodology focuses upon a central problematic: 'how do social actors come to know, and know in common, what they are doing and the circumstances in which they are doing it' (Heritage 1984: 76). In order to see how these dimensions work, Garfinkel exposed the interpretative procedures of interaction which people routinely draw upon by devising a series of 'breaching' experiments. In one case, students returned to their homes, for fifteen minutes to one hour, and observed the scene as if they were lodgers:

> Many students became uncomfortably aware of how habitual movements were being made; of how one was handling the silverware, or how one opened a door or greeted another member. ... Many accounts reported a variation on the theme: 'I was glad when the hour was up and I could return home to the real me'.
>
> (Garfinkel 1967: 46)

For ethnomethodology social order does not reside in the dictates of external rules as applied to situated activities. Instead it emerges from within the practical circumstances of social life. To return to one of the problems in the theory of action – the actor's rationality – the illumination of social life through models of formal rationality in social science may be required for scientific theorizing, but it is not required, as Schutz had argued: 'in theorizing activities employed in coming to terms with the affairs of everyday life' (Garfinkel 1967: 280). Everyday rationalities are data to ethnomethodologists, not impediments to their inquiries:

the activities whereby members produce and manage settings of everyday life are identical with members' procedures for making those settings 'account-able'. ... When I speak of accountable ... I mean observable-and-reportable, available to members as situated activities of looking and telling. I mean, too, that such practices consist of an endless, ongoing, contingent, accomplishment; that they are carried on under the auspices of, and are made to happen as events in, the same ordinary affairs that in organizing they describe.

(Garfinkel 1967: 1)

In this sense Weber's distinction between formal and substantive rationality is seen as a neglected one in social science (Garfinkel 1967: 281 fn). The former is employed as a model against which to judge the adequacy of routine actions. When translated, for example, into the study of formal organizations, rules are then seen as either placing limits upon actions, or something against which those actions may be judged, as opposed to being resources upon which actors routinely draw in the situated nature of their activities (Bittner 1974; Wieder 1974).

Summary

To remain faithful to the aim of understanding, ethnomethodological writings refer to indexicality, reflexivity, indifference and the documentary method of interpretation. Indexicality allows the theory of action to be tackled in a very different fashion to any we have come across before: for example, the link between particularity and generality in terms of objective mind (Dilthey). Normally indexical expressions are regarded as impediments to constructive analysis because they are seen as in need of 'remedy' in order that they make sense. However, ordinary language will make sense only by examining use in context.

As Garfinkel's experiments demonstrated, each person will assume that the other will know a setting if their situated practices 'are to serve as measures to bring particular, located features of these settings to recognizable account' (Garfinkel 1967: 8). Thus, reflexivity is a routine feature of interactions that 'Members know, require, count on, and make use of ... to produce, accomplish, recognize, or demonstrate rational-adequacy-for-all-practical purposes of their procedures and findings'. (Garfinkel 1967: 8).

Actions are not simply habitual, but subjected to 'routines' that are fragile. Because of this the actor has to be reflexive in order to continually monitor their own and others' actions and utterances to make sense of social action(s).

To study social phenomena in the above manner requires that the researcher exercises 'indifference'. The aim here is to faithfully describe the organized and routine features of natural language, whose indexical expressions are ordered and whose ordering is the direct result of the ongoing practical accomplishment of agents:

> Ethnomethodological studies of formal structures are directed to the study of such phenomena, seeking to describe members' accounts of formal structures wherever and by whomever they are done, while abstaining from all judgements of their adequacy, value, importance, necessity, practicality, success, or consequentiality. We refer to this procedural policy as 'ethnomethodological indifference'.
>
> (Garfinkel and Sacks 1986: 166)

Finally, the documentary method of interpretation, which Garfinkel gleaned from Mannheim (1952) refers to a form of reasoning, rather than a particular method of social inquiry. This allows a focus upon the way in which lay and professional accounts of social reality rest upon procedures of interpretation. Take, for example, the structuralist contention that a surface appearance stands for, and is indicative of, a deeper underlying pattern that is determining of human behaviour. This method of reasoning makes sense of the social world. These same methods are used in everyday life whereby understandings are the product of a circular process between an event and the background against which it takes place. This process embodies both indexicality and reflexivity because changes in social reality will only make sense against the context in which they appear. The consequences are that individual(s) are required to change their understandings and evaluations. These new meanings structures become, once again, the topics of methodological inquiry. We are now firmly on the original route that Garfinkel was to take ethnomethodology down:

> We have been concerned with the question of how, over the temporal course of their actual engagements, and 'knowing' the society only from within, members produce stable, accountable practical activities, social structures of everyday activities.
>
> (Garfinkel 1967: 185)

The diversity of ethnomethodology

Looking back over its history, the reaction to ethnomethodology among the social scientific community has usually been one of refutation and condemnation to varying degrees (Gellner 1968, 1974; Goldthorpe 1973; Hollis and Lukes 1982; MacIntyre 1973; Mennell 1975; B. Wilson 1970). These critiques have tended to focus upon its refusal to consider history, power and social structure, as well as the relativism engendered by its presuppositions. The result is said to be an idealist and empiricist social theory, which is inevitably conservative in orientation and has achieved little in the way of advancing an understanding and explanation of the dynamics of social relations.

At another level, ethnomethodology has been translated as an offshoot of symbolic interactionism (Meltzer, et al. 1975). Although some ethnomethodologists allude to the works of those such as Mead or Blumer to sustain their arguments, there are important differences in the basis of their understandings of social life (Denzin 1974; Zimmerman and Wieder 1974). However, there are those who self-define as ethnomethodologists and who are closer to interactionism than others. Goffman is sometimes mentioned in these terms, but as the discussion in Chapter 3 and his own writings make clear, he is hardly a convinced ally of this school of thought. For instance, Goffman regarded social reality as more multilayered than these one-dimensional views of social life seem to assume. Yet he was to provide inspiration for the writings of Harvey Sacks.

This state of affairs leaves many social scientists somewhat bewildered in their attempts to situate ethnomethodology. For some, the very choice to have a chapter on this subject will lend credence to a discredited perspective. This view is mistaken because it fails to take account of the history, aims and achievements of ethnomethodological studies of social life.

Given this mixture of misunderstanding and critique, this section will concentrate upon the diversities which exist within this broad tradition of thought. For the sake of brevity, these may be considered as endogenous issues which are raised by those who are more sympathetic to its history and aims than those exogenous critiques noted above. This will enable a measured evaluation of its basis and achievements, as well as its shortcomings.

The seeds of diversity

In its genesis, ethnomethodology contained the seeds of diversity and difference. The phenomenological input, for example, always possessed the potential for reactivation in the face of the assault by ordinary language philosophy. This is particularly manifested in its translation into conversation analysis. The critique of the mind-body duality which ordinary language philosophy brought with it was no friend of phenomenology with its emphasis on consciousness and intentionality. As Jeff Coulter puts it:

> A major corrective ... to the Schutzian programme is to insist upon the relevance of what Wittgenstein termed 'criteria' for practical utilization in everyday life. Criteria are defeasible, conventional

evidences for the constitution of phenomena, and they are inextricably linked to the differential distribution of practical interests in social existence.

(Coulter 1983: 123)

This tension between language as a medium for the expression of intentions, motives or interests and language as a topic for uncovering the methods through which ordered activity is generated, is an important one. While there are overlaps between these approaches, those of the latter persuasion are concerned with the external observation of 'naturally occurring' statements made by individuals. The result is to downplay the phenomenological input of meaning in interaction. While meaning clearly relates to linguistic categories, it is clear that the translation of Wittgenstein into ethnomethodology, in terms of meaning as use and the notion of publicly available linguistic forms, has lent itself to a desire to achieve a presuppositionless form of social inquiry that translates into a descriptive endeavour without a social subject.

Ironically, this lack of reference to a motivated subject who engages in conversation with some purpose or strategy in mind, has led to variants of ethnomethodology sharing its critique of phenomenology with structuralism (Lemert 1979; M. F. Rogers 1984). Conceptually, there exists a general agreement that the basis for understanding social action is environmental in nature, without reference to the mental states of individuals. Empirically, this is manifested in a concern with the sequencing of conversations, as opposed to considerations of their content. The result is that agents appear as decentred mechanics who, in drawing upon the natural attitude, take turns in conversations. The radical reflexivity which was once stressed is then 'all but expunged from the ethnomethodological sensibility' (Pollner 1991: 373).

This abandonment of praxis, despite the parallels between Marx and Wittgenstein (Rubinstein 1981) leads to a displacement of the social 'self' with de-contextualized conversations becoming of prime focus in the study of social relations. Further, the analysis of conversations, without any reference to interest or motive, leads to functionalism. Take, for instance, the following quote from a leading ethnomethodologist:

> we will briefly illustrate a variety of ways in which the design of actions can contribute to the maintenance of social solidarity ... it will be suggested that there is a 'bias' intrinsic to many aspects of the organization of talk which is generally favourable to the maintenance of bonds of solidarity between actors which promotes the avoidance of conflict.

(Heritage 1984: 265)

As suggested, this tension within ethnomethodology is exemplified by conversation analysis. This route here is an empiricist, rather than a hermeneutic one (May 1999a). CA seems to have travelled in two directions. First, through attention to the detail of 'descriptive accounts' in everyday life (Garfinkel and Sacks 1986; Sacks 1972). Here, the idea of 'categorization devices' which people employ in order to make sense of their environments is found. Thus, Roy Turner (1974) documents how people explain and predict the behaviour of formal mental patients in accordance with particular categories generated within interaction.

Second, CA has moved ethnomethodology even further away from its phenomenological input. This route entails a description of the sequential organization of interactions. Of course, it may be argued that such indexical expressions are windows through which the analyst can 'gaze upon the bedrock of social order' (Maynard and Clayman 1991: 399). Within this genre, there are studies on turn-taking in conversations, initiating topics and the starting and finishing of phone calls (Button and Casey 1984; Houtkoop-Steenstra 1993; Wooffitt 2005). Taped, naturally occurring conversations exhibit sequences which lend themselves to a processual mode of social inquiry.

At this point an argument may be employed whereby social settings are not of interest because people use conversational devices to account for what they do, regardless of the situation in which it takes place. The talk itself will then reflect methods of accounting which may even transcend, it is sometimes contended, cultural context. Therefore, these works may omit reference to not only the purposes of conversations, but also the settings in which they take place. What is or is not empirically admissible is then set according to such precepts. This allows the contention that political and economic resources are seen by 'other' social scientists to zoom down on everyday life as if from some 'conceptual ionosphere' (Benson 1974). Conversations are seen to exhibit symmetrical power relations. However, this is highly contentious, particularly with reference to the question of gender and conversational interaction (Tannen 1993); although there exist exceptions to such an approach (West and Zimmerman 1983)

If understanding of the interaction order is said to be more complete by using these methods, two further questions remain. The first has been considered: what happens to the practical creativity, as well as the constraints, in the interaction? This decentring of the strategic subject is manifest in CA reports which refer to 'members'. Members, presumably, who routinely and procedurally draw upon some impersonal interaction order. This desire to see social life from the 'inside' apparently free from presupposition is achieved at a very high cost: 'The radical stress on observable details risks becoming an unprincipled, descriptive recapitulation devoid of significance ... minute descriptive detail is assembled in a hyper-realist profusion, until the reader loses any sense of meaning'. (P. Atkinson 1988: 446).

Second, there is a methodological problem. This concerns the status of investigators who, in ignoring social context, appear to believe themselves capable of floating freely across language games without being fettered by the constraints of their own. This we can characterize as the hermeneutic absence in ethnomethodology. In this way, the analyst ignores the central question of translation between language games.

These problematics have been raised because, in various ways, they are addressed by those who once appeared in ethnomethodological anthologies. Among these we find a concern not only with language, but also with the meanings of interactions for the parties concerned. In addition, we find an attention to the social contexts in which such interactions take place in order that the connections between speech-acts and the forms of life of which they are a part are understood. For this reason we find a reluctance to submit to disembodied and decontextualized studies of the sequencing of conversations.

This 'out-group' of the ethnomethodologically inspired includes Dorothy Smith, Aaron Cicourel, Jack Douglas, Mary Rogers, Alan Blum and Peter McHugh. Their collective works provide for yet more differences within the ethnomethodological perspective which address some of those issues raised above. For instance, a recovery of the phenomenological notions of 'intentionality' and 'inner-time consciousness' and 'horizon' in order to address the limitations of a naturalistic ethnomethodological study of social action (M. F. Rogers 1983).

Aaron Cicourel has been largely responsible for bringing logical insights to a wider audience. Despite this, his attempts to avoid objectivism in interview and survey methods (Cicourel 1964) have, according to some, abandoned ethnomethodology as an alternative paradigm to conventional action theories (Sharrock and Anderson 1986). Yet Cicourel does seek to develop a theory of meaning which is sensitive to social context and is concerned with reflexivity:

> If we hope to construct a theory of meaning that enables us to understand how we assign sense to our everyday worlds and establish reference, then we cannot assume that oral language syntax is the basic ingredient of a theory of meaning. The interactional context, as reflexively experienced over an exchange, or as imagined or invented when the scene is displaced or is known through a text, remains the heart of a general theory of meaning.
>
> (Cicourel 1973: 140)

This search involves an empirical consideration of the sign language of the deaf with conceptual armoury provided for by Schutz and the linguist Noam Chomsky. Chomsky's emphasis on competence by the users of language separates him from the structuralist tradition, but is taken as indicative of a deeper structure of rules which the surface utterances express (Chomsky 1980). In using these insights, Cicourel argues that it is necessary to understand what he calls 'interpretative procedures' which are 'socially relevant cognitive properties' (Cicourel 1973: 168). It is these properties which provide for the competencies which enable people to produce every-day social structures and a sense of social order. These 'typifications' have then been analysed in relation to the processing of juvenile delinquents (Cicourel 1976) and provide the means through which micro events may be linked to macro considerations (Cicourel 1981) through, for example, the interplay between language, socialization and power (Cicourel 2003).

Dorothy Smith's (1988, 1993, 2005) work, which is further considered in Chapter 8, is unusual among the ethnomethodologically inspired. Although once thought of as worthy of inclusion in ethnomethodological anthologies (D. E. Smith 1974), an examination of more recent representations would seem to rule her out (see Coulter 1990). Broadly speaking, Smith sees in ethnomethodology the potential for examining the nature of the ideology which infuses women's everyday lives. At the same time, she is critical of conventional empirical and theoretical routes for getting at social 'reality' which end up sequestrating women's experiences (D. E. Smith 2005). A more critical theory, aware of the 'relations of ruling', is required to understand this process which a descriptive sociology only serves to reproduce:

> Though women are indeed the expert practitioners of their everyday worlds, the notion of the everyday world as problematic assumes that disclosure of the extralocal determinations of our experience does not lie within the scope of everyday practices. We can see only so much without specialized investigation, and the latter should be the sociologist's special business.
>
> (D. E. Smith 1988: 161)

Clearly, she is not in the business of describing the sequencing of alleged symmetrical verbal interactions. Her starting-point is a power imbalance in social relations and this steers her towards the field of critical linguistics (see Fairclough 2001). As John Thompson puts it, the domain of ideology, which is Smith's topic, is the place 'where the construction of meaning intersects with asymmetrical relations of power' (Thompson 1984: 118). What we might refer to as 'mainstream' contemporary ethnomethodological writings seem to view these formulations as a distraction from the goal of accurate descriptions of the orderliness of social reality (Button 1991).

It is this goal of description and its tenuous connection to the anti-positivist strand within the original development of ethnomethodology which concerns Blum and their colleagues (McHugh et al. 1974). To find context-free rules of interaction, as variants of CA seem to suggest, is to reproduce the very generalizing tendencies of positivism which do not exhibit a concern for situated meanings. This form of ethnomethodology has become more concerned with 'endogenous' rather than 'referential' reflexivity (May 1998, 2000; Pollner 1991). The former refers to that which 'members' possess in a social setting, while the latter considers the process of constructing the object or field of analysis.

Here we find a tendency for ethnomethodology to gloss over referential reflexivity in the search for naturally occurring descriptions of social interaction. According to Blum and McHugh, this should be replaced by a relativism which sees truth in terms of time and convention. As McHugh puts it: 'the truth of a statement is not independent of the conditions of its utterance' (McHugh 1974: 329). Yet this is the theme which variants of CA appear to overcome by generalizing about conventions of language free of social context as if reasons for actions were causes of actions. If such practices are submitted to the original canons of referential reflexivity which ethnomethodology had called for, it would clearly fall short of meeting these standards. Instead, what is now produced is a supposed authoritative inquiry which fails to see how its own grounds of thinking are themselves constituted as a product of social relations (McHugh et al. 1974).

In the above manner, the world appears as a fixed entity, rather than a collaborative one involving people working together in an imaginative manner over problems which concern them. This Heideggerian inspired critique expresses the limitations of a form of ethnomethodological analysis which is pessimistic because it fails to see the possibilities which exists for different courses of social action. The result being a social universe which appears as a static, not dynamic phenomena:

> We ... are not interested in terminating our analysis with descriptions of things, or in using our ability to speak about things in an orderly way as criteria of successful analysis. ... Our concern with such productions is reflected in our seeing them as occasions for renewing our own collaboration called analysis, because it is on such occasions that we become engaged with the question of possibility itself.
>
> (McHugh et al. 1974: 17)

In all of these modifications to the ethnomethodological school of thought, it is clear that it is a very broad tradition. Paradoxically, contemporary forms of its practice seem to repeat the very mistakes which were the inspiration for its beginnings: for example, the parallels with structuralism via a critique of the subject and with positivism through an abandonment of referential reflexivity in favour of a narrow form of scientism as apparent in the practice of forms of conversation analysis.

Summary

Ethnomethodology found its inspiration in Heidegger's idea that understanding is the business of life and Wittgenstein's ideas on language. It refuses to be shackled by theory, epistemology and philosophical speculation, in favour of being an empirical, some would say empiricist, programme of investigation. Here, therefore, lies an important change in social thought which many commentators have overlooked in their desire to trivialize and dismiss its implications for social scientific practices.

In general, ethnomethodology requires nothing less than a radical shift in the focus of social scientific inquiries. Sociologists, for example, should no longer assume Durkheim's notion of social reality as *sui generis*, or view human behaviour as following the impersonal and general rules of a role, or the covering laws of cause and effect. Instead, social order is a direct result of people's 'accomplishments' in their everyday lives. Psychologists should cease experiments which are of no relevance to the practical activities of people as they go about their daily lives and anthropologists should stop 'glossing over' the details of people's situated activities (Button 1991).

Ethnomethodology is thus concerned with common-sense understandings in everyday life which are publicly available. These render intelligible the environments which people encounter in their situated activities. These cognitive methods are not derivable in some a priori sense through, for example, a general theory of the dynamics of society, formal rules or the universal properties of the human mind. Instead, in fusing the moral and cognitive aspects of interpretation, Garfinkel and his followers examine the practical and situated ways in which people make sense of their environment and of each other.

Ethnomethodology is believed to be a descriptive, not normative endeavour. There is a continual stress upon indexicality, reflexivity, accomplishment, intelligibility and knowledgeability in everyday life. The result is that the Parsonian problematic of social order is approached from the micro, not macro end of the theoretical spectrum. Conventional questions, such as: 'Where does the natural attitude come from in the first place?' are either reframed or abandoned. The question of rationality, for example, becomes that which is situationally accountable. Questions of epistemology and ontology are transformed. The theory of knowledge becomes a description of the properties of social organization (Layder 2006). Quite simply, questions of 'what?' and 'why?' become those of 'how?' Even when it comes to the relationship between the individual and society or macro versus micro theory, these are 'resolvable in the work of sociological description, which is remorselessly reliant upon the documentary method of reasoning' (Sharrock and Anderson 1986: 54).

In these ways ethnomethodology is enabled to sidestep conventional questions of truth. However, this has a cost in terms of an increased abstraction from the concerns which preoccupy not only social scientists, but also people in their daily lives. Ethnomethodology will remain unattractive to those who still wish to pursue something called 'the truth', or illuminate meaning, or relations of power and modes of oppression which exist within societies and even produce studies in the service of policy makers. The unfortunate consequence is that an ethnomethodological 'ingroup' seems to increasingly refer only to the works of each other and itself becomes a topic for textual analysis (Gubrium and Holstein 2006).

Despite these differences within ethnomethodology and the critiques that have emerged from other social scientists, there is no doubt that it has informed other developments and interesting parallels may be drawn, for example, with the positioning theory of Rom Harré (see Harré and Moghaddam 2004; May and Williams 2002). For the purposes of this journey, however, there is a social theorist who has incorporated the insights of ethnomethodology, but who is not content to permit it the last word on society and social relations. The result is an attempt to fuse the macro and micro by examining the reproduction of society in social relations. It is to the work of Anthony Giddens that we now turn.

5 Reproducing society in social relations

Let us start by returning to discussions on Erving Goffman. He makes three important advances in linking the macro and micro aspects of social life (Manning 1992). First, the interaction order is connected to the production and reproduction of social structures. Second, via this link, it is possible to see how relations of power are implicated in social life and third, the identities of role incumbents are open to general analysis: for example, along race, ethnic, class and gender dimensions.

Manning's inspiration for his observations does not come from Randall Collins (1981) or Aaron Cicourel's (1981) 'aggregation hypothesis' which suggests that: 'macro-phenomena are made up of *aggregations* and *repetitions* of many similar micro-episodes' (Knorr-Cetina 1981: 25–26, original italics) – a point we will pick up with our journey on actor network theory in Chapter 7. The theoretical route that he takes is one of the 'hypothesis of unintended consequences' (Knorr-Cetina 1981) as derived from the work of Anthony Giddens. In this case, micro-events are seen to both produce and reproduce social systems by virtue of the intended and unintended consequences of human actions (Stones 2005). The choice is now no longer between the micro or macro in analysing society and social relations, for the overall intention is to transcend the agency-structure dualism in social thought. The task of the social analyst then becomes, for example, one of charting the connections between social and system integration (Lockwood 1976). For Giddens:

> unintended consequences *condition* social reproduction. ... Social systems appear to exist and to be structured only 'in and through' their reproduction in micro-social situations which are in turn limited and modalized through the unintended consequences of previous and parallel social action.
>
> (Knorr-Cetina 1981: 27, original italics)

To arrive at this position Giddens draws upon an extensive range of ideas, including classical social theory, which is then used to develop a 'hermeneutically informed social theory' (Giddens 1982: vii). He seeks to avoid the problems of the philosophy of consciousness and those of action theories in general, while acknowledging that society is not the creation of individuals, but without resort to structuralist explanations (Giddens 1984: xxi). In order to examine these ideas in more depth, this chapter is divided into two sections. First, an overview of the development of his ideas via an encounter with other schools of thought and his resultant theoretical synthesis (all references to works in this section are by Giddens, unless otherwise stated). Second, an examination of the issues which are then raised in this approach for conducting social analysis.

The intellectual development of structuration theory

The theory of structuration develops from encounter and synthesis. The former stems from a reaction to an 'orthodox consensus' in social science. This is taken as a combination of naturalism and functionalism (Giddens 1987: 24) that is said to render social science impervious to the insights of phenomenology, ordinary language philosophy and hermeneutics. The consequence being that the social sciences have remained in the shadow of the natural sciences long after they should have freed themselves from its shackles. Indeed, those who are waiting for a Newton of the social sciences 'are not only waiting for a train that won't arrive, they're in the wrong station altogether' (1976: 13).

Structuration theory shares with micro-theoretical approaches the view that society is 'the outcome of the consciously applied skills of human subjects' (1976: 15). To sustain this view, without resorting to the limitations of action theories, various theoretical insights are mobilized. For instance, a scientific Marxism is abandoned as symptomatic of a natural science model, as are evolutionary theories of social change. On the other hand, a modified humanist-Marxism, concerned to historically analyse the connections between the objective and subjective features of social life becomes, from an ontological point of view, reconcilable with the aims of structuration theory (1976: 12).

A twist now enters structuration theory. Although Giddens retains a respect for the skilled accomplishments of actors in everyday life, he is also concerned not to abandon the idea of structure as a necessary part of socio-theoretical development (1976: 22). However, how is this achieved without resort to structuralism or structural-functionalism' both of which downplay agency in everyday life? Or, without resorting to micro-theoretical approaches which downplay the role of structure in everyday life? To focus upon these questions, an examination of his encounters with these traditions of thought is required. This will then permit us to consider the synthesis of structure and action within structuration theory.

Encounters: taking aim at dualisms

Action theories are considered by Giddens as: 'Strong on actions, weak on institutions' (1982: 29). For instance, in Schutzian inspired social theory, the question remains as to how, given the reduction of consciousness to an individual ego, an outer reality may be constituted or reproduced. The Husserlian attempt to overcome the subject – object dualism, which Schutz inherited, simply ends up prioritizing the former over the latter. As one extensive study of his work puts it, Giddens' concern in this respect is to examine the reproduction of social practices while also insisting upon the opportunities which exists for innovation in social conduct (I. Cohen 1989).

As noted, ethnomethodology originally substituted the cultural dope approach to social analysis in favour of the skilled and accomplished actor in everyday life. To meet the postulate of subjective adequacy, Garfinkel prioritized situated rationalities over those of scientific rationality. However, while scientific rationalities should be connected to lay accounts, as Schutz (1972) argued, they are not simply illegitimate reifications, for there is still a need to render 'intelligibility intelligible' (Giddens 1976: 40). Mainstream ethnomethodologists, in their mobilization of ordinary language philosophy, do not escape from this requirement. For this reason, Giddens addresses the very issue that was raised in Chapter 4: that is, with an apparent air of indifference, how are ethnomethodological analysts able to both translate between and transcend language games?

To consider this question, Giddens employs hermeneutics. This allows him to tackle the question of the mediation between different frames of meaning in social analysis, as well as the empiricism, indicative of the orthodox consensus, which arises from attempts to provide presupposition-less descriptions. Quite simply one cannot make statements which refer to 'sensory observations' in a theoretically neutral way (1976: 135). The reflexivity which mainstream approaches abandoned is now opened up to hermeneutic scrutiny:

> The process of learning a paradigm or language-game as the expression of a form of life is also a process of learning what a paradigm is not: that is to say, learning to mediate it with other, rejected, alternatives, by contrast to which the claims of the paradigm in question are clarified.
>
> (Giddens 1976: 144)

This scrutiny occurs at two levels. First, both the social and natural sciences are 'forms of life' which have to be learnt by their practitioners. Second, the relationship between lay and technical languages is not, as Schutz (1979) argued, one way. There is what Giddens calls a constant 'slippage' between the two. As such: 'It would not be at all unusual to find a coroner who had read Durkheim' (1990: 42). This is an insight which he seeks to encapsulate in the notion of the 'double hermeneutic'.

In addition to the above, through its reading of ordinary language philosophy, ethnomethodology identifies rationality with accountability. However, the consequence of this is to strip social relations of an analysis of the purposes, motives or interests that routinely inform social conduct. 'Doing' should be viewed as more than making something accountable, it is also a practice and it is this which makes it an accomplishment on the part of actors in everyday life (1976: 44).

For Giddens, macro-theoretical approaches to social life are also deficient: for example, normative functionalism (Parsons), conflict functionalism (Merton) and historical materialism (Giddens 1977, 1981a, 1985). As we saw in Chapter 2, this approach suggests that societies have 'needs' and the manner in which such needs are met is seen as an explanation of the social processes themselves. A number of criticisms of this approach can be made. First, human agency is subsumed under the internalization of societal values, whether for the purposes of social order in Parsonian theory or ideological control in Althusser's Marxism. This is manifest in the attribution of rationality to social systems rather than individuals (Layder 2006).

Second, in the case of normative functionalism, an explanation of power, which is an 'elemental concept' in the social sciences (Giddens 1984: 283), is subsumed under consensually produced norms and values. The result is, as with interpretative social theories, problems in explaining asymmetries of power and the divisions of interests which exist within social relations and societies as a whole (1976: 157). In contrast to these views structuration theory considers norms as the products of differing interpretations based on competing interests. As such, they are not simply enabling (Winch, Schutz) nor constraining (Durkheim, Parsons), but both enabling and constraining.

Third, in the dichotomy between synchronic and diachronic explanation, there is a neglect of history. This is manifested, for instance, in the separation of function (the relations between 'parts' and the 'whole') from 'happenings in time' (1976: 120). The result is a homeostasis in which concern is directed towards the maintenance and equilibrium of social systems that, in turn, structure social relations. Given Giddens' Heideggerian emphasis on an ontology of potentials, both the static and dynamics elements in society require an equal consideration. This results in a contrast between structuration theory and the conservative elements in both structural-functionalism and ethnomethodology as apparent in their preoccupations with social order.

The only legitimate space for teleological explanation in social science is that which can be situated within the bounded conditions of action. Agency is ascribed to agents and is not a property of social systems as exemplified in the form of the explanation: 'the reason that people do X is to furnish the needs of the system Y'. As will be noted, in order to account for continuity in social institutions and relations across time, structuration theory does not resort to functionalist explanation. Similarly, while denying that systems have reasons or needs of their own, Giddens does not deny that systems possess properties which both enable and constrain practices (1979: 113). In sum, functionalism and structuralism fail to see society and social life as the product of active subjects, while action theories consider only the production, but not reproduction, of social systems in social relations. Now to an examination of the synthesis of these positions in structuration theory.

Synthesis: action and structure in structuration theory

In opposition to the dualisms of action and structure, Giddens directs attention towards the reproduction of structures within social relations. In their place we find the duality of structure and the process of structuration. Structure is seen to enter into 'the constitution of the agent and social practices and "exists" in the generating moments of this constitution' (1979: 5). This reproduction is a concrete, not philosophical question, manifested in 'the situatedness of interaction in time and space' (1984: 110). As he puts it:

> According to the notion of the duality of structure, the structural properties of social systems are both medium and outcome of the practices they recursively organize. Structure is not 'external' to individuals: as memory traces, and as instantiated in social practices, it is in a certain sense more 'internal' than exterior to their activities in a Durkheimian sense. Structure is not to be equated with constraint but is always both enabling and constraining. This, of course, does not prevent the structured properties of social systems from stretching away, in time and space, beyond the control of individual actors.
>
> (Giddens 1984: 25)

Structure thus becomes conceptualized as both the medium and outcome of the production and reproduction of social practices. To focus upon the structuration of social practices is to find an explanation for 'how it comes about that structures are constituted through action, and reciprocally how action is constituted structurally' (1976: 11). It follows from this, contrary to the propositions of structural-functionalism and structuralism, that structure is a dynamic, not static, phenomenon. How it is actually manifest, as either constraint or enablement or a combination of these, is held deliberately open and to be decided by empirical investigation. Given this, the duality of structure obtains its explanatory value only when considered against 'real historical situations' (1993: 6).

Giddens' writings exhibit an adherence to an ontology of potentials whereby the opportunities for innovative social conduct are deliberately held open in opposition to the idea of the constraining regularities of systemic forces. This provides for his primary concern to investigate 'the nature of human action, social institutions and the interrelations between action and institutions' (1991a: 201). Quite simply, if the possibility of always being able to 'act otherwise' were not the case, then Giddens would succumb to a structural form of explanation which he sees as a 'futile' and even 'harmful' search in the social sciences (1984: 214). These points noted, a further specification of the details of social reproduction is now required.

To return to an earlier discussion. The post-Wittgensteinian view is that society can be studied as a 'language'. In its ethnomethodological variant, this ended up having parallels with structuralism, while the idea of linking social context and account actually led to a severing of practical consciousness from social practice. In opposition to this, Giddens seeks to fuse these as 'crucial mediating moments between two traditionally-established dualisms in social theory' (1979: 4). The concept of praxis thus becomes mobilized as the connection between language and social practice. Praxis represents neither freedom nor determinism. It is

> an ontological term, expressing a fundamental trait of human social existence. To speak of human social activity as Praxis is to reject every conception of human being as 'determined objects' or as unambiguously 'free subjects'. All human action is carried on by knowledgeable agents who both construct the social world through their action, but whose action is also conditioned or constrained by the very world of their creation.
>
> (Giddens 1981a: 53–54)

The echoes of the 'humanist' Marx are clear. The Constitution of Society, the most systematic exposition of structuration theory, is actually described as a reflection upon famous phrase: 'Men (let us immediately say human beings) make history, but not in circumstances of their own choosing' (1984: xxi). At this point, a particular idea of agency becomes directly linked into the process of structuration.

We may identify two aspects of human conduct: capability and knowledgeability. Capability is taken to mean that someone 'could have acted otherwise'. Unlike the utilitarian influences on social theory, as manifest in rational-choice theories, this is not identified with the 'decisions' or 'choices' which people consciously make between various courses of action open to them, for most of social life is actually routinized. Yet according to the precepts of praxis, agency is identified with the ability to "make a difference" to a pre-existing state of affairs or course of events' (1984: 14). Given this, Giddens sees power as prior to both subjectivity and the agent's reflexive monitoring of their conduct (1984: 15). According to this view, which shares affinities with both Parsons and Foucault, power is not simply a repressive, but also an enabling force in social relations. It is the very means through which agency, defined as 'transformative capacity', is achieved.

Knowledgeability, on the other hand, refers to 'the fact that the members of a society know a great deal about the working of that society, and must do so if that society is recognizably a "human society"' (1981b: 163).

However, this is not to be equated with what is known 'consciously'. Why? Because it is bounded by two aspects: first, the unacknowledged conditions of action and second, the unintended consequences of action (1981a: 19). This is where Giddens' theory of the make-up of individuals enters his formulations. In place of Freud's threefold psychic organization of the individual, Giddens substitutes a basic security system, with its emphasis on ontological security and practical and discursive consciousness.

Practical consciousness is regarded as displaying an 'extraordinary complexity' (1984: 281). It is concerned with the routine monitoring of day-to-day conduct which, at the level of knowledgeability, is bounded by the above two conditions. At the level of capability, it represents what people know in order to get on with their daily lives, but through which the structural properties of social systems are also reproduced. Discursive consciousness, on the other hand, is revealed during times of departure from routine modes of action. It may arise when asking people the reasons for their actions or activities, or from an abrupt change in a person's circumstances. People then reflect upon the reasons and intentions which inform their actions, but not necessarily the motives for their actions. It is in the distinction between practical and discursive consciousness that one derives such insights on everyday life from reading Goffman.

Importantly for our purposes, what Giddens is doing here is making a distinction between the rationalization of action and the motivation for action. Motives play a part in social life only in 'unusual circumstances': for example, they inform what he refers to as 'overall plans or programmes' (1984: 6). These may be considered as a person's 'wants' which underlie the potential for action, but not necessarily the action itself. This distinction permits Giddens to bring into his theoretical frame of reference, with its clear respect for the actions of people in their everyday lives, unconscious elements of motivation: 'Motivational components of action, which I take to refer to the organization of an actor's wants, straddle conscious and unconscious aspects of cognition and emotion' (1979: 58).

Lest this be misinterpreted, it is important to note that although a conception of the unconscious is thought essential to the development of social theory (1979: 58) Giddens is not suggesting conscious manifestations of action can simply be 'read off' against unconscious motivations, a point he makes in an interesting comparison between Goffman and Freud on 'everyday slips' (1984: 98–104). The problem with such psychoanalytic approaches to social life centres upon their downplaying of the influence of social forces on everyday actions (unintended consequences), in favour of viewing conduct as symptomatic of the psychological make-up of individuals (unconscious motivations). At the same time, action theories, influenced by American philosophies of action, have equated 'reasons' with 'motives' and thereby failed to examine the potential for unconscious motivations for actions. Similarly, they do not consider the very social conditions which work to structure activity, but which remain outside of the self-understandings of people in everyday life due to the bounded nature of their knowledgeability. These social conditions are referred to as 'the unintended consequences of intentional conduct' (1979: 59).

The above represent the beginnings of a link between situated practices and the reproduction of social institutions through the unintended consequences of social action and hence, a synthesis between action and structure. To render this understanding more complete, a consideration of the ideas of rules and resources, which make up social structure, is required.

Giddens finds structuralist insights useful in the development of structuration theory, but they are deficient in some important respects (1977: 45–48). Indeed, he starts an essay on structuralist and poststructuralist thought by pronouncing that they are 'dead traditions of thought' (1987: 73). In placing his focus upon praxis, he may have accepted the decentring of the subject, but not its death. Structure, as external to human agency, is rejected because *'there is no such thing as a distinctive category of "structural explanation"'* (1984: 213). However, there is a second sense of 'structure' reflected in the intersection of presence and absence. In this sense, the underlying properties of social systems may be inferred from the surface manifestations of action (1984: 16). This ontological realism has conceptual mileage for structuration theory in terms of understanding and explaining the intentional reproduction of unintended consequences (Stones 2005).

To consider this second sense of structure, Lévi-Strauss's work is found to be useful (Giddens 1979: 63–64). The problem is that Strauss omits time from his considerations with the result that social structure becomes manifested only in the first sense: that is, as a static 'thing', separate from its reproduction in the situated practices of everyday life. To overcome this, Giddens employs the insights of time-geography (1984: 110–119). The idea of social systems as having structuring properties which 'bind' time and space is thereby introduced (1979: 64). History is returned to social theory in a way which makes it possible for social systems to exist across time and space. Continuity, in terms of society displaying a 'systemic form', may then be admitted. This overcomes the limitations of action theories, but without succumbing to structure as separate from the actions of agents in social life.

Despite the existence of systemic forms, the basic ontology of human 'action' and 'doing' must leave open the possibility for innovation in social conduct. Therefore, systems are seen to be reproduced in social relations. The result is that structure is permitted a 'virtual order' because, from a logical point of view, it is not a property of social systems or collectivities:

> To say that structure is a 'virtual order' of transformative relations means that social systems, as reproduced social practices, do not have 'structures' but rather exhibit 'structural properties' and that structure exists, as time-space presence, only in its instantiations in such practices and as memory traces orientating the conduct of knowledgeable human agents.
>
> (Giddens 1984: 17)

Social systems exist only through the process of structuration. This allows for a definition of 'social institutions' as those social totalities which exhibit the greatest 'time-space extension' in social relations (1984: 17). Social systems and the situated activities of human beings are thus connected through structuration: that is, the reproduction of social systems in social practices. Therefore, in the course of their conduct, people draw upon structures, which exists out of time and space, which themselves comprise rules and resources:

> One of the main propositions of structuration theory is that the rules and resources drawn upon in the production and reproduction of social action are at the same time the means of system reproduction (the duality of structure).
>
> (Giddens 1984: 19)

So, action and structure are implicated, but what are the concepts of 'rules' and 'resources' being employed here? Rules exhibit two properties. These may be conceptually distinct, but in actual social practices cannot be separated. First, rules are drawn upon by people in everyday life in skilled and knowledgeable ways. The result is those regularities in language production and exchange that are so carefully described by ethnomethodologists. These rules 'are only tacitly grasped by actors' (1984: 22). As such, although drawn upon and applied, these rules cannot necessarily be formulated. Despite this, actors are dependent upon their 'structuring properties' for making sense of the social world. For this reason, social practices are both enabled and constrained by these rules of signification.

This leaves some problems. If such rules are implicated in social reproduction they could be linked, for example, to the maintenance of social order (ethnomethodology), or be interpreted as causal mechanisms which operate independently of human agency (structuralism). Giddens would then be open to the charge of systemic teleology, structural determination or the conflation of reasons with motives. Given the centrality of power in structuration theory and the capacity of the agent to 'make a difference' in their interventions, structural constraints cannot 'operate independently of the motives and reasons that agents have for what they do' (1984: 181). As such, there must be more to structure than these rules of signification. This is where the idea of rules as 'regulative' enters his formulations.

In the process of 'strategic conduct', actors 'draw upon modes of domination structured into social systems' (1982: 83). Here, the term 'domination' does not carry its usual negative connotations but power is, as noted, also related to the possibility of producing productive outcomes. These modes of domination are divided into 'allocative' and 'authoritative' resources (1984: 259). While these vary with different types of social systems, allocative resources refer, in general, to the domination of nature by human beings. These include, for example, raw materials and technology and those goods which may be produced as a result of an interaction between the two. Authoritative resources, on the other hand, refer to the control of the social world and comprise the organization, in terms of time and space, social relations, plus the production and reproduction of the human body, as well as life chances as they affect the possibilities for self-development and self-expression (1981a: 51–52)

Both allocative and authoritative resources represent forms of asymmetrical power. These are manifest in agency which is defined, as noted, in terms of the capability of 'making things happen' or of 'bringing about particular states of affairs' (1981b: 170). These resources may be mobilized for the purposes of sanctioning the conduct of individuals in relation to the application of rules. Production, power and normative sanctions are thus implicated in social practices; the result being the reproduction of social systems and structures. This is the 'regulative' sense of rule. It follows that, in terms of praxis, the 'correct' use of language (constitutive rules) cannot be separated from the environment in which they take place (regulative rules). To return to the opening paragraph of this chapter, Goffman's interaction order may now be linked to social structure as comprising rules and resources which are routinely drawn upon in social interaction.

In intentionally drawing upon resources, the unintended consequence is to reproduce social systems. However, if this power is a 'built-in' feature of domination within social systems, does this not constrain the actor in a

Marxist sense? In considering this question, Giddens shares Weber's refusal to reduce the operation of power to the forces and relations of production. This places him at odds not only with historical materialism but also with a Nietzschean conception of the 'will to power' as indicative of the continual desire for domination in social relations (Giddens 1982, 1984). Although constraints may work, for example, at the level of a person's life chances (authoritative resource) structure is, to repeat, both enabling and constraining. Quite simply, people possess the capability to recognize objective social conditions which are then incorporated into their social conduct: 'No matter how complete the power of one individual or group might be over others, resources are always available whereby subordinates can reciprocally influence power holders' (1987: 162).

This process expresses a transformative capacity which is equated with the exercise of agency. There is always a dialectic of control tempering domination within social relations. As such, no single person can completely influence the actions of others. Their very freedom of action is dependent upon their ability to perform a range of practices with a high degree of competence. Given that no one person is able to perform every practice as skillfully as their co-actors this, in turn, represents a constraint upon their actions (I. Cohen 1989).

Summary

Action theories have a limited concept of action due to their inability to conceive of social institutions and the role of power in social life. In contrast, structuralist theories are said to submit agency to a systematic determination which gives society a life of its own, separate from the actions of individuals. In its ontological emphasis, structuration theory replaces this dualism by the duality of structure and the process of structuration. Agency is then defined as a 'transformative capacity' which focuses attention upon strategic conduct in everyday life. Power is thereby central to this process.

'Praxis' is the link between practical consciousness which informs actions and the social conditions in which action takes place. In the course of social action, rules and resources, as part of social structure, are drawn upon with the effect of reproducing social systems (the unintended consequences of intentional conduct). Structure is both the medium and outcome of interaction because 'practices are situated within intersecting sets of rules and resources that ultimately express features of the totality' (1982: 82). Further, in order to explain continuity in social relations and overcome the limitations of action theories, the systemic aspect of societies are allowed for in the 'stretching' away of social systems in the dimensions of both time and space. Any systemic determination on localized conduct, however, is tempered by the necessity of systems and structures being reproduced in the situated activities of agents. Therefore, agency implies structure and structure implies agency.

Issues in structuration theory

Anthony Giddens' project is highly ambitious. In the attempt to synthesize the dualisms of action and structure, which is at the heart of social theory, it should come as no surprise that this has resulted in a number of works which criticize, elaborate upon and generally interrogate structuration theory. In this section, attention will first be devoted to matters of interpretation and applicability. We then wish to move on to examine whether action and structure is usefully thought of as a duality or a dualism.

First, there is a question over the accuracy and selection of Giddens' readings of the theoretical traditions which he mobilizes for the development of structuration theory. We can, for example, find authors who question his readings of Marxism (Wright 1989), poststructuralism (Boyne 1991) and postmodernism (Hekman 1990a). In this sense, structuration theory has been viewed as a kind of conceptual raiding party which, in its single-mindedness, often results in the loss of original insights from other theoretical traditions.

Readings of this type are symptomatic of the sheer breadth of Giddens' work. For instance, he draws upon the traditions of Continental thought, via hermeneutics, while also wishing to appeal to the empirical (and empiricist) tendencies in Anglo-American thought. This is exemplified in his preference for an ontologically based social theory, where understanding is seen as part of human existence itself, rather than a method of social investigation *per se*. This is a difficult juggling act. There are those with an eye for the empirical utility of social theory who have described his work more as 'philosophization' (Rex in Mullan 1987: 19) and of lacking empirical applicability (Gregson 1989; Mouzelis 1991; Stinchcombe 1990).

Giddens (1984, 1991a) is clearly concerned to render structuration theory useful for social researchers and there are those who have sought to explicitly utilize his ideas for this purpose (C. W. Smith 1983). Yet he also argues that it represents a body of thought which acts as a corrective to empirical research through its illumination of key areas of social life which are frequently overlooked: for example, the relationship between human knowledgeability and the unintended consequences of social action. In addition, empirical implications should not be the only criterion upon which social theory is judged. The coherency of its formulations, the problems that it generates and the insights it offers, are also of importance

(Giddens in Mullan 1987: 102). In these terms, let us consider one of the problems that it generates and whether it is successful in its insights.

Consider the role of gender and agency in structuration theory. Although the women's movement has clearly identified weaknesses in sociological reasoning (Giddens 1987: 24) is gender domination not structured into social systems? If it is, the possibility of an engendered social structure is not considered by Giddens (Wolffensperger 1991). That said, he is admirably frank in reply to questions of this type raised by Linda Murgatroyd (1989): 'I have simply not accorded questions of gender the attention that they undeniably deserve' (Giddens 1989: 282). This has begun to change in his works on the self and social and political relations (Giddens 1991b, 1992, 1994). However, does this example reveal a more general weakness?

If one thinks of time as a resource which has the power to organize social life, rather than chronologically (Adam 1995) then it has the potential to be mobilized for the purposes of excluding particular groups whose lives are structured according to dominant interpretations of time. If this is considered in terms of the burden of the division of labour between home and work, for example, the very timing of a union meeting or work meeting can act as an impediment to participation, the effect of which would be to force women back into the domestic sphere (Marshall and Witz 2004).

The proliferation in part-time work could, of course, be seen as enabling. However, what happens to the insight when seen against the relationship between low pay and part-time work? It may then only be enabling in terms of the prior constraints of a gendered division of labour within a patriarchal-capitalist society. As people are always able to 'make a difference' in their actions, it is difficult to see how the persistence of such structured inequalities may be explained in the face of attempts, by women's movements, to change these practices. After all, both social systems and social structure are permissible in structuration theory only to the extent that they are instantiated in situated activities. This suggests that there are constraining influences on action, but only in so far as these are invoked in the course of human action. This does not appear to overcome a voluntarist-determinist dualism, because the latter is seen to exist only in the exercise of the former.

The point of this discussion is that structure and action may not be a duality, but a dualism. In the remaining part of this section, we would just like to highlight some of the issues around this question which authors have raised in respect to Giddens' work. Underlying these observations is what Roy Bhaskar (1993: 154) has termed Giddens' 'tendential voluntarism'. It is held that there is an underlying subjectivism in his work which prevents him dislocating structure from agency, as if such a move would automatically imply a surrender of social actions to deterministic social forces.

Giddens' overall attempt to collapse the action-structure dualism in social thought is mediated through particular lenses. These are ontological and provide a focus upon human 'doing' and 'being', which, in turn, gives structuration theory a particular conception of social reality. This is a reality where active subjects and social reality itself are taken as being one and the same. As such, while wishing to avoid the pitfalls of a philosophy of consciousness, any form of structuralist explanation which views social reality as external to social relations is also rejected. However, due to the nature of this separation, structuration theory cannot help but resort to subjectivism:

> It is only Giddens' insistence that a synthetic duality is the only alternative to a false dualism that prevents a realization that a dualism of action and (objective) structure is, in fact, the only way to understand structure and action as implicated in each other in a way that avoids subverting the integrity and influence of either.
>
> (Layder 1987: 31–32)

The duality of social structure views social change as dependent upon instantiated conduct. However, what of the durability of social systems, as in the case of the patriarchy and work example above? Quite simply, different amounts of time and effort may be required to effect change in social conditions. In such instances people might deliberately distance themselves from the very rules which they view as oppressive. The result is that the rules of language, upon which Giddens places so much stress, actually become topics for conflict rather than resources for actions. Subjects and objects are therefore deliberately distanced from each other and so become dualisms, not a duality (Mouzelis 2007). Further, during these times of struggles constraints may continue to operate independently of agency:

> Nations can fall, polities be deposed and economies bankrupted, while efforts are being made to change the factors responsible (for example, birth rates, despotism, illiteracy, ethno-centrism). As a general theoretical proposition this holds good however short the time interval involved. Yet this is what Giddens spirits away by making all cultural properties atemporal and according them only a pale 'virtual existence'.
>
> (Archer 1989: 89)

Another way of considering this issue is to examine the relationship between power and transformative capacity. Giddens does not see power as a property of social structures. Therefore, systemic constraint can never be complete as represented by the concept of the dialectic of control: 'the weak ... always have some capabilities of turning resources back against the strong' (Giddens 1981a: 63). Even in the case of solitary confinement, a 'hunger strike' or 'suicide', as the ultimate refusal of control, is seen as an option. Although this is a limited case and action is taken to be more fluid in social systems, is this link between power and transformative capacity adequate for the purposes of explaining social relations?

Power structures, once products of human actions, can become sedimented in social systems thereby affecting the degree to which agency can mobilize power in subsequent actions – as in the case of the relationship between women and paidwork. Therefore, it is this interplay between the dualisms of agency and structure which needs to be analytically and empirically considered, not the duality of structure. However, by theoretical fiat, structuration theory precludes this possibility: that is, structure is taken to be that which is reproduced in situated conduct, not something which may confront individuals as a durable constraint. Take, for example, the issue of contraception. In some instances, the church and the state become powerful contestants. The result can be a stalemate which actually blocks any transformation in contraceptive practices to the detriment of those who are subject to such relations of ruling (Layder 2006). Power cannot be simply considered in terms of agency, but is also the property of social systems which constrain group and individual actions:

> Do I have an opportunity to vote for my government? Do I have a wide or narrow range of jobs from which to choose? If I want to work, do I have to work in a job where wages keep me on or below the poverty line? These choices are not always my responsibility. They result from something that we can call 'social structure', and the experience we have of these structures is often similar to that we have of the physical world, the constraints of which Giddens *can* recognize.
>
> (Craib 1992: 154, original italics)

Many of these issues stem from conceptualizing structure in terms of rules and resources. To consider constraint in terms of constitutive or regulative rules is highly problematic. When individuals who have not had a job for six months are faced with a reduction in their state benefits because it is said to reflect their personal inability to make themselves 'marketable', are we to consider these constraints as something reducible to the level of their comprehensibility of such sanctions? On the contrary:

> it is the *range of alternatives* which is restricted, and these restrictions do not stem from semantic and moral rules, but from the structural conditions for the persistence (and decline) of productive institutions.
>
> (J. B. Thompson 1984: 168, original italics)

Because of the link between agency and 'options' in terms of strategic conduct, Giddens seems to leave us with the idea that where there is no choice in terms of realizing our wants and desires, we can no longer be conceived of as an agent. As in the case of 'suicide' and imprisonment noted above, options of one are not options! The point is that wants and desires vary. It is the relationship of this variability to the social positions in which people find themselves which is largely unexplicated in structuration theory:

> One of the key tasks of social analysis is to explore this space of possibilities, both in terms of the differential distribution of options according to class, age, sex and so on, but also in terms of the kinds of wants and desires, the interests and needs, which are themselves differentially possessed ... certain individuals or groups of individuals have greater scope for action and choice than other individuals or groups of individuals: freedom, one could say, is enjoyed by different people in varying degrees.
>
> (J. B. Thompson 1984: 170)

An analysis of this type would show that structure and agency are not antinomies. It would demonstrate that they are not implicated in the way that structuration theory argues due to a prioritization of the open-ended nature of praxis and its 'over-assertion' of human freedom (Craib 1992). Yet in recent times, Giddens has espoused a reconfiguration of the relationship between structure and agency in his political analyses of government through the 'third way' (Giddens 1998). This doctrine was about rejecting top-down power (socialism) and bottom-up power (of neoliberalism with its emphasis on individualism).

Giddens claims that 'individuals' are faced with the task of piloting themselves through a changing world in which globalization has transformed time and space and our relations with each other have been transformed by 'risk'. New partnerships are needed between government and civil society where government supports the renewal of community through local initiative, giving an increasing role to the third sector of 'voluntary' organizations, encouraging social entrepreneurship and significantly, supporting the 'democratic' family characterized by 'equality, mutual respect, autonomy, decision-making through communication and freedom of violence' where parents have 'negotiated authority' over children (1998: 93).

An emphasis upon this new contract in which both duties and responsibilities are highlighted, provides for an emphasis upon community building participatory programmes rather than state provided financial benefits. What is needed, he argues, is not an encouragement of the 'moral hazard' of dependence, but a programme of 'positive welfare': that is, an investment in human capital, the promotion of autonomy, active health, lifelong education, well-being and initiative (Giddens 1998: 128). This was very influential to politicians such as Tony Blair when he was UK Prime Minister (1997–2007) and Bill Clinton (1992–2000) when he was US President. More recently, he has explicitly sought to influence Gordon Brown in terms of the direction of government policy (Giddens 2007).

Summary

Despite the above issues, there is no doubt that structuration theory is an innovative approach to tackling the dualisms within social theory. At the level of the subject, structuralist lessons on its 'death' are criticized, yet without recourse to a Cartesian ego given the centrality of 'praxis' and power in social life. Knowledge is not open-ended, but bounded, while capability is circumscribed by unacknowledged conditions and unintended consequences. Although most of the time people just 'get on' with their daily lives, an emphasis on practical consciousness means that individuals are knowledgeable about what they do. In addition, their conduct manifests strategic intentions, but their unintended consequences reproduce social systems.

In these formulations, structuration theory has taken on an enormous intellectual task. The myriad of influences which Anthony Giddens brings to his work provides it with the source of both its strength and weakness. As it stands, it is fruitful to use this work as an inspiration for matters which require further empirical investigation and conceptual specification. Overall, therefore, it stands as a corrective to the grander claims of both action and systems' theories.

In this enterprise, Giddens is not alone. A French social scientist emerged from within the tradition of structuralism and was to become a critic of objectivism. Practice, once again, becomes of central focus. However, the intellectual influences and experiences which inform the development of his ideas are different, while in political terms, he has castigated Giddens for becoming an apologist for globalization utilizing an academic veneer born of a theory that is 'a scholastic synthesis of various sociological and philosophical traditions decisively wrenched out of their context and thus ideally suited to the task of academicized sociodicy' (Bourdieu and Wacquant 2001: 5). There, it appears, any similarity ends! Nevertheless, the result is also a novel and often misunderstood project that illuminates a gap in structuration theory: that is, an understanding of the relationship between social positions, aspirations and actions.

6 Habitus, capital and field: society in social relations

Since the 1950s Pierre Bourdieu has published works covering the areas of social research, science, social theory, pedagogy, kinship, cultural studies, linguistics, economic change, religion, art, museums, literature, photography and philosophy. The resultant ideas have been framed by empirical investigations carried out under the auspices of a reflexive social science.

Bourdieu's work opposes the dichotomy between objectivism and subjectivism as represented by structuralism and phenomenology. Like Giddens, he added his own interpretation to the agency–structure dualism in social thought. This relationship is conceptualized via a 'genetic linking' which is manifested in the relations between social divisions and mental schemata. However, as mental states are the embodiments of social divisions, the social sciences need to exercise a continual 'epistemological vigilance' over the blurring of the boundaries between everyday opinions and social scientific discourse (Bourdieu et al. 1991). At the same time, it follows that: 'An adequate science of society must encompass both objective regularities and the process of internalization of objectivity' (Wacquant 1992: 13), while objectivity 'is a social product of the field which depends on the presuppositions accepted in the field, particularly as regard the legitimate way of settling conflicts' (Bourdieu 2004: 71).

With an emphasis on social divisions, Bourdieu's work can be characterized as 'critical' in three ways. First, although according validity to people's everyday interpretations, they are not taken at face value for this would represent 'the illusion of immediate knowledge' (Bourdieu 1991a: 250). Received social categories are thus subjected to scrutiny in order that the social conditions which structure life chances and reproduce class distinctions may be analysed. Second, a reflexive social science is employed in order to examine the institutional conditions of knowledge production in an overall process of searching for the 'socio-transcendental conditions of knowledge' (2004: 79, original italics). Bourdieu is concerned to supplant not only the first illusion, but also a second: 'the illusion of absolute knowledge'

(1991a: 250). This would suggest that agents are 'in error' and scientists may place themselves in the position of 'all knowing'. Finally, these elements combine in his thought, in Heideggerian fashion, to open up the realms of the 'possible' by his exposing the basis of the 'actual', for: 'Every established order tends to produce ... the naturalization of its own arbitrariness' (Bourdieu 1977: 164). As such, Bourdieu is not content with either Lazars-feld's positivism, or Adorno's theoretical speculations (Bourdieu 1984: Appendix 1).

In the process of his studies, Bourdieu brings a myriad of influences to his work. These include Weber, Marx, Durkheim, Mauss, Lévi-Strauss, Saussure, Heidegger, Wittgenstein and Austin. As with Giddens, this has led to different interpretations of his ideas, frequently stemming from a misunderstanding of the intellectual and cultural traditions in which he works (Bourdieu 1993a; Wacquant 1993). In addition, there is a tendency in Anglo-American circles to overlook Bourdieu's primary concern with empirical studies and focus upon it as another aspect of 'grand theory'.

These points noted, we cannot pretend to be able to satisfactorily counteract these interpretations within this chapter. However, instead of employing pejorative labels of convenience which serve only to alleviate the reader or speaker of the need for constructive encounter, consideration and dialogue, a more positive approach, we hope, will be available through the following format. First, a brief exposition of Bourdieu's ideas via an examination of his engagement with other traditions of thought and the subsequent development of his own ideas. In this section all unattributed references will be to Bourdieu's work. Second, by considering some of the unresolved issues in his work, a more general appreciation might be gained of its strengths and limitations.

Intellectual development

Encounters and utilizations

In Part I, post-1945 French social thought was characterized as being centred on differences between Sartre's existentialism and structuralism. Bourdieu's notion of a 'sociology of social experience' allows his intellectual formation during this period to be turned into an object of investigation. Indeed, this technique forms part of his work, together with colleagues at the Centre for European Sociology, on French intellectual life and the education system (Bourdieu 1988, 2003; Bourdieu and Passeron 1990; Bourdieu et al. 1994).

Following his graduation in philosophy, Bourdieu taught in a provincial school. He was then conscripted to the army in 1956 to serve in Algeria. There he became more aware of the gap in understanding between French intellectuals, his own experiences and the plight of the Algerian people and French settlers. His subsequent research, mostly secondary analysis, was then supplemented by fieldwork (Bourdieu 1962). One of the overall aims of these studies was 'to understand, through my analyses of temporal consciousness, the conditions of the acquisition of the 'capitalist' economic among people brought up in a pre-capitalist world' (Bourdieu 1990: 8).

This fieldwork was to represent a basis for Bourdieu's intellectual development. It formed the beginnings of the methodological considerations which are now a central part of his work, while also providing the empirical bases upon which he was to subject the dominant intellectual trends of his time to critical scrutiny. In this sense, while reading Schutz and Husserl, he found Merleau-Ponty's concerns with the human sciences and the 'everyday', or what he describes above as 'temporal consciousness', was 'one potential way out of the philosophical babble found in academic institutions' (1990: 5).

This period in Bourdieu's career marked his transition from philosophy to sociology culminating, more recently, in a sociological study of Heidegger (Bourdieu 1991b). An impetus for this transition came from the structuralist revolution in social thought. Led by those such as Lévi-Strauss and interpretations of the work of Saussure, structuralism was to enable the social sciences to become more 'respectable' in French academic circles. Nevertheless, the result was an unquestioning incorporation of ideas which were not concerned with establishing the limits of 'pure theory'. For this reason, Bourdieu sought to 'objectify objectivity', with Saussure's prioritization of langue over parole being one of the main targets of this strategy.

For Saussure, it will be recalled, speech is not seen as the medium of communication in human affairs, but an underlying system of objective relations which becomes devoid of reference to sense-experience. The analyst may then lay claim to being some kind of 'stage manager' who can play at will with their objectifying instruments. The result is that they become caught 'in a dream of power' (1992a: 31). The dream is one of congruence between the underlying rules or structures of concrete actions and the rational patterns of analysis used by the social scientist towards their goal of explanation. It is Lévi-Strauss's dream, for instance, of moving from social context to the establishment of some kind of universal human nature. Yet the consequence of this allusion to universal rules is to undermine the freedom of agents:

> To make transcendent entities, which are to practices as essence to existence, out of the constructions that science resorts to in order to give an account of the structure and meaningful products of the accumulation of innumerable historical actions, is to reduce history to a 'process without a subject', simply replacing the 'creative subject' of subjectivism with an automaton driven by the dead laws

of a history of nature. This emanatist vision ... reduces historical agents to the role of 'supports' (Träger) of the structure and reduces their actions to mere epiphenomenal manifestations of the structure's own power to develop itself and to determine and overdetermine other structures.

(Bourdieu 1992a: 41)

In the processes of inquiries of this type hermeneutics is seen as a matter for the subjects of research, not for the process of how they or their activities are created as objects for research. Speech-act theorists, such as John Austin, on the other hand, counter this structuralist method via an 'internalist' approach which links 'connotations' to social context. The result is that, as in mainstream contemporary ethnomethodology, language is viewed as an end point of social analysis. For Bourdieu, however, there is another way to approach the relationship between language and social life: that is, by linking social conditions to language use.

In contrast to the above approaches to the study of language, Bourdieu considers the power of linguistic utterances to reside in the institutional conditions for their production. The analyst may then ask with what power or authority utterances are invested by examining the access that the speaker has 'to the official, orthodox and legitimate speech' (1992b: 109). Institutions are not simply schools, prisons, factories, and so on, but relatively stable sets of social relations which provide their members with certain resources. History becomes returned to the point where it is abandoned by both ethnomethodology and structuralism, for it is under such conditions that utterances are both produced and heard:

> efforts to find, in the specifically linguistic logic of different forms of argumentation, rhetoric and style, the source of their symbolic efficacy are destined to fail as long as they do not establish the relationship between the properties of discourses, the properties of the person who pronounces them and the properties of the institution which authorizes him to pronounce them.
>
> (Bourdieu 1992b: 111)

This concern with 'properties' takes Bourdieu into other intellectual terrains in the quest to illuminate his empirical findings. This requires an encounter with the insights of classical social theory. In Part I, in an attempt to gain a more productive reading than is usually the case, it was suggested that there were some underlying problematics shared by various theorists from within different traditions. Bourdieu puts this in a somewhat different way. To paraphrase him, the ideas of classical theory are seen as a 'space of possible positions', in whose antagonisms the chance of transcendence may be found (1990: 35). With this in mind and to simplify the resulting synthesis, the following is an overview of Bourdieu's utilization of these insights.

Bourdieu employs a concern with the reproduction of social relations, but tempers his economism by employing Durkheim's sociology of symbolism. In turn, Durkheim's ideas on morals and values are tempered by the manner in which symbolic systems are viewed as ideologically structured. Therefore, they are not seen to represent some consensually agreed upon state of affairs, but systems of domination, the form of which change in the transition from traditional to modern societies. In general, this may be expressed in terms of the move from the interpersonal to the institutional as seen in Bourdieu's (1962) work in Algeria right through to his extensive ethnographical and statistical analyses of French taste, where

> the conservation of the social order is decisively reinforced by what Durkheim called 'logical conformity', the orchestration of categories of perception of the social world, which, being adjusted to the divisions of the established order (and thereby to the interests of those who dominate it) and common to all minds structured in accordance with those structures, present every appearance of objective necessity.
>
> (Bourdieu 1984: 471)

It is Marx and Durkheim who represented the objectivist position within the theoretical spectrum, albeit from materialist and idealist vantage points respectively. Bourdieu seeks to avoid such dichotomies. This is where Weber steps in. Using Weber's work, he seeks to analyse the relations that exist between lifestyles, life chances and the material resources which are at the disposal of particular groups. To return to the opening quote of this chapter, subjective views and social positions become related in what are referred to as the 'prereflexive assumptions that social agents engage by the mere fact of taking the world for granted' (Bourdieu in Bourdieu and Wacquant 1992: 168). What is called this 'doxic acceptance' forms the link between cognitive and objective structures. However, the problem with the objectivist position is that it fails to see the importance of practices and strategies; in other words, the role of agency in everyday life.

Bourdieu's stratification analysis holds that agents engage in forms of identification which permit them to distinguish themselves from other groups. Thus, the struggle for recognition is a central part of social life. The relationship between these strategies and social position, where the accumulations of forms of 'capital' are at stake, is understood dialectically:

> on the one hand, the objective structures that the sociologist constructs, in the objectivist moment, by setting aside the subjective representations of the agents, form the basis for these representa-

tions and constitute the structural constraints that bear upon interactions; but, on the other hand, these representations must also be
taken into consideration particularly if one wants to account for the
daily struggles, individual and collective, which purport to transform or preserve these structures.

(Bourdieu 1989: 15)

The resultant 'constructivist structuralism' provides for an empirical examination of the interplay between the subjective and objective features of social
life, without abandoning the major contribution of the structuralist legacy to
social science: that is, 'the relational mode of thinking … which identifies
the real not with substances but with relations' (1989: 15–16).

Tools of analysis: capital, field and strategy

In examining the relationship between agency and social position, there are
four tools of analysis which Bourdieu employs which require our consideration. They are: capital, habitus, field and strategy. His novel approach to the
questions of action and structure will become apparent in this discussion,
while his interest in the multidimensional relations between phenomena, as
opposed to their reduction to one dimension of social life, should be borne
in mind when reading the following account.

Bourdieu speaks of the social world as a 'space' which is constructed
out of a set of properties that are active at any one time. Social relations
within this space exhibit the deployment of various forms of power or capital
which may act singularly, or in accord with each other. The main types of
capital in his work, each of which have their own subtypes, are cultural,
social, symbolic and economic capital. These objective forms of power are
held to be neither reducible to the intentions of agents as such, nor simply
directive of their interactions. Agents are thus defined by their relative
position to one another. The distribution of people within social relations,
therefore, does not vary according to properties, or chains of properties in
terms of their relation to the means of production. Instead, they are
distributed according to the overall volume of capital in their possession, as
well as its composition (1992b: 231).

Given this latter point, Bourdieu opposes substantialism, which holds
that no form of realities exist other than material conditions. This means
that he modifies a Marxist economism that is seen to 'annihilate specificity'
because of its inability to see the 'socially maintained discrepancy between
the 'objective' reality and the social representation of production and
exchange' (1992a: 113). Again, Bourdieu is examining the dialectical relations between the subjective and objective features of social life. This also
enables him to analyse non-material forms of capital in pre-capitalist and

capitalist societies; an analysis which takes place without recourse to an economistic bias which imposes universal analytic categories upon disparate forms of social relations.

Non-material forms of capital include symbolic capital. This represents the power to confer meanings upon social reality while also providing for a social recognition of one's place within social relations. People in possession of such capital in a non-capitalist society may then go to a market, without any money, because the value placed upon them in terms of trust is as great as their wealth itself (1992a: 119–120). Within a capitalist society, the very accumulation of symbolic capital may actually depend upon its 'distance' from economic necessity. We can thus say that a set of macro conditions provides for the existence of non-material forms of capital which relate to micro lifestyles:

> As the objective distance from necessity grows, life style increasingly becomes the product of what Weber calls a 'stylization of life', a systematic commitment which orients and organizes the most diverse practices – the choice of a vintage or a cheese or the decoration of a holiday home in the country.
>
> (Bourdieu 1984: 56)

An aesthetic disposition then involves a set of experiences which are 'freed from urgency' and 'are an end in themselves' (1984: 54). In this sense, one is reminded of Goffman's notion of 'role distance' – a process enabled by the mobilization of resources.

To this conceptualization of social relations, the dimension of time needs to be added. This allows for the incorporation of the dynamic aspects of social life, in which the status ascribed to forms of capital changes over time. Here, Bourdieu is seeking to overcome the weaknesses of a synchronic view of social relations. This is where the habitus enters into his work as the key element in overcoming the 'sterile opposition' (1981: 305) which exists between history and sociology. To this extent, there are parallels between the habitus and Giddens' idea of structure. As Bourdieu writes:

> It is necessary to write a structural history which finds in each state of the structure both the product of previous struggles to transform or conserve the structure, and, through the contradictions, tensions and power relations that constitute that structure, the source of its subsequent transformation.
>
> (Bourdieu 1990: 42)

However, as will be noted, the idea of rules, found in Giddens' idea of structure, is replaced in Bourdieu's work by the notion of strategy.

Bourdieu (1981) divides history into that which is 'embodied' and 'objectified'. The latter, for example, is found in books, machines, buildings, monuments and laws. The word 'habitus' means something similar to the Greek word *hexis* which relates to deportment, manner and style, etc. The habitus itself is viewed as history embodied in human beings. Its existence is apparent in and through social practices as manifested in ways of talking, moving, getting on with people and of making sense of the environment. Bodies may then be analysed from the interactions that take place between taste, social location and the formation of habitus.

The habitus is inculcated as much by experience as by teaching, while its power is seen to derive from the lack of thought which informs its manifestations. Quite simply, competent performances are produced on a routine basis, in the process of which objective meaning is reproduced. The habitus can thus be considered as a form of 'socialized subjectivity' (Bourdieu in Bourdieu and Wacquant 1992: 126) where the re-enactment of history takes place in the dispositions which people acquire over time and bring with them into social situations. It is a way of producing social practices and a way of perceiving and appreciating practices: 'the habitus implies a "sense of one's place" but also a "sense of the other's place"' (1990: 131).

In this linking between the objective and subjective aspects of social life in the attempt to overcome the individual–society dualism, the former appears to be prioritized over the latter. The result is that the habitus may be read as a gun out of which the individual is shot, thereby determining their social trajectory. This, however, would clearly undermine Bourdieu's wish to examine the social conditions which underlie the flux of social life through downplaying the role of agency (Layder 2006). As such:

> Habitus is not the fate that some people read into it. Being the product of history, it is an open system of dispositions that is constantly subjected to experiences, and therefore constantly affected by them in a way that either reinforces or modifies its structures. It is durable but not eternal!
>
> (Bourdieu in Bourdieu and Wacquant 1992: 133)

From this, we may draw out three aspects to the habitus and its relation to practice. First, Bourdieu's concept of action stands close to Dewey's idea, as he acknowledges (in Bourdieu and Wacquant 1992: 122). This shares, along with Heidegger, Merleau-Ponty and Wittgenstein, a critique of the body and subject–object duality which has so preoccupied philosophy and social theory. To be fully understood, therefore, it must be situated within this tradition of thought if its implications are to be adequately grasped.

Second, the habitus is not only a set of dispositions which an agent possesses when faced with the social world, for it also implies a creative capacity. This capacity will depend upon the social situations in which agents find themselves as the condition for its 'fulfilment'. In the absence of these, the habitus may become a 'site of explosive forces (resentment) which may await (and even look for) the opportunity to break out' (1993b: 87). Therefore, a disjuncture may occur between the practices generated by the and the objective conditions required for their outlet. What Bourdieu calls the 'Don Quixote effect' can then arise where practices appear 'ill-adapted because they are attuned to an earlier state of the objective conditions' (1984: 109).

This idea of a 'pre-objective' fit between disposition and position does not rule out the strategic choices which an actor makes in the course of their conduct. That said, Bourdieu is no ally of rational-action theory. As with the ideas of Park, Mead and Thomas, times of crisis will call for an adjustment between objective and subjective structures and at these points, a degree of rational choice may take over. However, this does not imply a methodological individualism which would simply reintroduce the very dichotomy he seeks to overcome. Instead, the individual must always be viewed as socially positioned 'within the limits of the system of categories he owes to his upbringing and training' (Bourdieu in Bourdieu and Wacquant 1992: 126). If the mind is the site of rationality, it is socially bounded, not asocial. Given this, we might characterize Bourdieu as being more interested with what it is to act reasonably rather than rationally.

The third and final point is that they must, as the quote above suggested, be seen in relation to a habitus. Without this it would, once again, prioritize subject over object and lose the centrality of Bourdieu's dialectical method:

> The habitus ... enables an intelligible and necessary relation to be established between practices and a situation, the meanings of which is produced by the habitus through categories of perception and appreciation that are themselves produced by an observable social condition.
>
> (Bourdieu 1984: 101)

Now the habitus represents a 'feel for a game' which is acquired during practical experience. It is the acquisition of technique with the result that practical sense has a 'fuzzy logic' to it (Wacquant 1992). Science seeks to totalize this aspect of social life, with the result that it does not capture its sense. For instance, to ask a person what they are doing is to ask them a question for which they have no need, since the essence of practice is the very suspension of such questioning:

> Practice has a logic which is not that of the logician. This has to be acknowledged in order to avoid asking of it more logic that it can give, thereby condemning oneself either to wring incoherences out of it or to thrust a forced coherence upon it.
>
> (Bourdieu 1992a: 86)

As noted, this 'feel for the game' requires a social situation for its enactment. There are two ways in which the relation between habitus and field may be considered. First, the field structures or conditions the habitus to the extent that it provides for its realization. As such, the roots of a divided habitus may lie in a discrepancy between fields. Second, there is the part that the habitus plays in constituting the field as a place where the agent decides that it is worth investing their energy. It follows that there is a two-way relation between the habitus and field: 'Social reality exists, so to speak, twice, in things and in minds, in fields and in habitus, outside and inside of agents' (Bourdieu in Bourdieu and Wacquant 1992: 127).

Fields vary and are viewed as relatively autonomous from one another: for example, the artistic (Bourdieu 1995) and scientific fields (1988). In general, the field of power informs all other fields and thus constitutes a 'meta-field'. There are also 'game fields'. These are seen by their participants as arbitrary constructs of which they are more or less aware and which contain specific rules where conditions of entry entail a kind of 'quasi-contract' between agents. In locations such as these one will find comments being made like: 'it's only a game'. Social fields, on the other hand, result from long and slow processes of 'autonomization'. These are games 'in themselves' rather than 'for them selves' (1992a: 67). The agent who enters these is equipped with the sets of beliefs which makes them work in the first instance. The earlier a person enters a game and the less aware they are of its learning, the greater is their ignorance of what the field grants them through such investment (1992a: 67). In the two-way relationship between people and field, a congruence is established whereby the social world is understood because it comprises the person and so appears as self-evident. The result is an 'ontological complicity' (Bourdieu in Bourdieu and Wacquant 1992: 128) between a person and the social world of which they are a part. This is where the idea of social reality 'existing twice' provides for the possibility of analysing the field separate from those who comprise it:

> Fields present themselves synchronically as structured spaces of positions (or posts) whose properties depend on their position within these spaces and which can be analysed independently of the characteristics of their occupants (which are partly determined by them).
>
> (Bourdieu 1993b: 72)

A field is thus constituted by the power relations, or distribution of types of capital, which are mobilized in the struggles taking place within them. However, while fields are structured by these relations, the form of the struggles which take place within them will vary. It follows that the dynamics of one field may not be transposed into another, for the habitus within a field implies a knowledge of its laws, stakes and interests. The resultant struggles centre around what Bourdieu calls the 'monopoly of legitimate violence (specific authority) which is characteristic of the field in question' (1993b: 73). What is at stake is the conservation or subversion of the structure of the capital within the field. Those who are inclined towards conserving its power relations are defined as being engaged in orthodoxy, while newcomers to the field are likely to be subversive and engage in strategies of heresy.

The existence of heresy or heterodoxy in a field forces the doxa, or set of prereflexive assumptions, to awake from its slumbers. The dominant agents within the field will then seek to defend orthodoxy, with the overall aim being the restoration of common assent to doxic appearance. Once this is in place, the forms of domination within the field will operate through 'hidden persuasion' in what is taken to be 'the order of things' (Bourdieu in Bourdieu and Wacquant 1992: 168). This is ably assisted by the fact that even where the field exhibits overt antagonisms, there is still an agreement over what it is worth fighting for. 'Partial revolutions' may take place, but the players cannot question the basis of the game itself, otherwise they will be excluded (1993b: 74).

From the above discussion we can say that the following elements appear to be the most significant in considering the constitution of fields. These are the 'interests' of agents in the field; what particular forms of capital are being deployed; the agents 'feel' for what is happening; the strategies adopted and their commitment to the fields' presuppositions, or doxa. Further, there is no mechanical set of laws which govern fields because agents adopt strategies leading to degrees of indeterminacy. To put it in economic terminology, this does not imply a conscious desire on the part of agents to maximize their own utility. In this sense, Bourdieu's use of 'strategy' and 'game' has unfortunate connotations which are rooted in a subjectivist tradition that finds its contemporary representation in rational-action theory (Bourdieu in Bourdieu and Wacquant 1992: 129).

To make this latter point as clear as possible, let us recap on an earlier discussion. First, the habitus as a set of acquired dispositions over time, acts as a generative mechanism, between structure and practice, which constitutes the field as meaningful. Second, the field conditions the through habitus being the place of its embodiment. A less-than-conscious ontological complicity therefore exists between the agent's and the field. This is not indicative of a conscious rationality concerned to maximize self-interest. At the same time, actors are not the mere bearers of structures. The employment of strategies within a field provides for the generation of practices which are not simply reducible to any underlying rules of the field. An argument of this type would prioritize the construction of a macro-theoretical model against which the agent's practices are to be explained, thus countering Bourdieu's reflexive approach to the practice of social science (Bourdieu 2003).

Second and relatedly, there is an ambiguity surrounding the word 'rule' and hence its applicability to the study of social life. As found in previous chapters, it is often employed in a 'quasi-juridical' way to mean its employment in some conscious way by agents. Alternatively, in the structuralist sense, it is held to impose objective regularities on a game (1990: 60). While Bourdieu is not suggesting that rules do not exist within fields, his reservations on this matter are summed up by his paraphrasing of Weber: 'Social agents obey the rule when it is more in their interest to obey it than to disobey it' (1990: 76). From this point of view, rules cannot be automatically invoked to explain social relations and it obliges the analyst to examine the conditions under which a rule operates. A practical mastery of a game is found; one acquired through experience, but which often works outside of the conscious control of agents.

We now return to the relationships between habitus, strategy and practical sense which Bourdieu employs in overcoming objectivism and subjectivism. The unconscious is not said to replace the conscious. Strategy is the means by which he seeks to avoid the structuralist notion of action without an agent, while struggles are those which take place between collectivities. As a result, he seeks to transcend two long-established and entrenched positions in the history of social thought:

The good player, who is so to speak the game incarnate, does at every moment what the game requires. That presupposes a permanent capacity for invention, indispensable if one is to be able to adapt to indefinitely varied and never completely identical situations. This is not ensured by mechanical obedience to the explicit, codified rule (when it exists). Nothing is simultaneously freer and more constrained than the action of the good player (Bourdieu 1990: 63).

Summary

In the intersection between field, habitus and capital lies the dynamics of social relations which, at the same time, allows for the reproduction of society and the production of practices. The notion of habitus for example, is used: 'as a way of escaping from the choice between structuralism without subject and the philosophy of the subject' (Bourdieu 1990: 10). The interplay of each of these is open to empirical examination. This provides for a multiplicity of practices via the formula: ([habitus] [capital]) + field = practice (1984: 101). Capital therefore functions only in relation to a field and there is a two-way relationship between the field and habitus, an apparent diversity often conceals a unity which is the basis for such action: that is, class habitus as a generating and unifying principle (1984: 101). It is these common properties among people of particular classes which produce probable, but not determined, life chances.

Within the relationship between field and habitus lies the potentiality for a 'doxic appearance' enabled by the absence of overt struggles informed by particular interests. Given this: 'the misrecognition of the reality of class relations is an integral part of those relations' (1992a: 136). This is not to suggest the type of ideological determinations associated with Althusser's brand of structuralism. Instead, practices, aimed at transformation, are central to Bourdieu's work. As he puts it: 'The different classes and class factions are engaged in a symbolic struggle properly speaking, one aimed at imposing the definition of the social world that is best suited to their interests' Bourdieu 1992b: 167).

His more recent work before his death extended to the analysis of the 'body'. In his work *Masculine Domination* (2001) Bourdieu highlighted how distinctive bodily forms are reproduced by agents' practices which themselves are an internalization of social structure. This work follows *Distinction* (1984) where Bourdieu focused on the body of social class. For Bourdieu (2001), the body mediates the dialectic between practices and social structures and constitutes a core entity for reproduction of power relations and social order. The body becomes a site of experience in which social structures are internalized.

Issues in the work of Pierre Bourdieu

Pierre Bourdieu's work has been subjected to a number of interpretations. In this section, we wish to draw attention to some of these which critically examine his preoccupation with power and strategy and his desire to generalize across particular social contexts. In the process, attention will be drawn towards possible inconsistencies in his methodological injunctions, as well as raising challenges regarding his substantive findings on the dynamics of social relations.

Sitting within the tradition of French structuralism, and seeking to overcome its limitations, inevitably leads to comparisons between Bourdieu and the tradition of poststructuralism, as represented, for example, by the writings of Gilles Deleuze, Jacques Derrida, Michel Foucault and Julia Kristeva. This interpretation is lent some credence through the manner in which power saturates Bourdieu's work (the question of power and poststructuralism will be considered in Chapter 9). Scott Lash (1990, 1993) argues that the potential for human practices to gain autonomy from the operation of power is conceived to be 'only minimal' in Bourdieu's formulations, leading commentators to focus upon his somewhat one-dimensional view of human action (Alexander et al. 2004).

Scott Lash raises important issues in Bourdieu's work. From a methodological vantage point, this revolves around the possibility for the scientific field to operate independently of 'interests'. This clearly depends at what point interests inform the production of scientific work. There is a Weberian edge to Bourdieu's ideas on this subject, which reveals an ambiguity in his formulations (Dumas and Turner 2006). Interests, as Weber argued, inform the direction of scientific work. Thus, Bourdieu can be found saying:

> This interest may consist, as it does everywhere else, in the desire to be the first to make a discovery and to appropriate all the associated rights, or in a moral indignation or revolt against certain forms of domination and against those who defend them within the scientific world. In short, there is no immaculate conception.
>
> (Bourdieu 1993b: 11)

At this point in Bourdieu's formulations, reason seems to depart in favour of underlying power relations. Questions are then left over his 'invitation to reflexivity' where social scientists

> are instructed to reflect, not on the validity of statements and propositions, but on the social and power position of the producers of these statements. Attention is drawn thus not to the autonomous 'universe of discourse' and its logic of 'true versus false' but to the field of power and its logic of 'friend versus foe'.
>
> (Lash 1990: 264)

Bourdieu thus hovers uneasily between power as the final arbitrator of scientific discourse on one side and the view of a detached and rational scientific observer on the other.

Bourdieu does recognize that for the social sciences to be 'scientific', 'there must be specific, falsifiable, universal claims' (Dreyfus and Rabinow 1993: 40). At the same time, Bourdieu argues that the 'misrecognition' of class relations is an essential part of their functioning. However, does this not privilege the insights of the social scientific observer over the meanings that the lay actor attributes to their social reality? It was in this sense that Marx referred to 'false consciousness', Freud spoke of the 'unconscious', Gramsci spoke of the effects of 'hegemony' and Bourdieu now speaks of 'doxic appearance'. From this point of view, he sits within a tradition of critical theory which extends from Marx to the Frankfurt School (Calhoun 1995). In general, what is postulated here is a 'repressed truth' which claims 'to be able to liberate humanity by revealing it' (Dreyfus and Rabinow 1993: 41).

The substantive 'truth claim' to which Bourdieu can allude in solving this issue of judging the adequacy of his social scientific insights is the ubiquity of class relations as manifested in a universal struggle for symbolic capital. However, concerns are then voiced in relation to the idea that class is used as a universal explanatory principle in Bourdieu's work. The problem is that because it is so all-encompassing, it ceases to designate a particular social group – as it did for Marx and Weber – and thereby loses its explanatory power. Class then becomes

> a metaphor for the total set of social determinants. Class structure is synonymous with social structure; class struggles are assimilated to sexual, generation, regional, ethnic, and occupations struggles; and class theory merges with sociological theory in general.
>
> (Brubaker 1985: 770)

Bourdieu's substantive work thus exhibits the same tensions that are found in his methodological writings. In this case, it is between the richness of his ethnographic descriptions of particular practices and his desire to generalize from these (Brubaker 1985). This leads to the tendency, despite his wish to avoid this very problem, for an ahistorical structuralism to reassert itself. As such, it has been argued that he fails to see how changes over time occur in relation to the ways in which capitalism affects culture (Gartman 1991); how historical changes in 'doxa' are important for an analysis of gender relations (Risseeuw 1991) and how the relations between men and women are more complex and contradictory than his more one-dimensional analysis permits (Moi 1991). At the same time Bourdieu (2001) did attempt to address this thought his analysis of the 'gendered body'.

The issue concerning the ubiquity of his explanatory concepts may also be applied to the relationship between language and institutions. While serving as a corrective to Austin's (1976) idealist concept of speech-acts due to a consideration of the extra-linguistic sources of their power, the theory becomes too general. Here, as noted, Bourdieu establishes a correspondence between utterances and social position such that the power of speech is one which is 'delegated' to the speakers. This observation itself need not be denied. However, Bourdieu then generalizes to the idea that all utterances are those which are 'authorized'. As John Thompson (1984) argues, from whose work these comments are derived, not all instances of everyday speech are authorized in the way that Bourdieu suggests:

> Consider the case of a person who, in the course of a conversation among friends, seeks to embarrass or humiliate another, to silence or subordinate him or her, by commenting on some aspect of that person's appearance or past ... or consider the case of a person who, when faced with the prospect of being left by a lover, threatens to commit suicide or to carry out some other act of self-mutilation. So many cases, it seems to me, in which to speak is to perform an act of power, but which it could hardly be said that the latter was the delegated power of a *porte-parole*.
>
> (J. B. Thompson 1984: 68, original italics)

Bourdieu tends to sever language from reason. The rational force of speech itself, or the conviction with which something is said, becomes explicable only in terms of reference to an outside institution. In other words, an utterance has no 'rational force' of its own (J. B. Thompson 1984: 69) leaving understanding reduced to the operation of power. There is no standard to which one can then allude for the purposes of reaching consensual agreement separate from the institutional authority which is bestowed upon the utterance of the speaker. The possibility that language involves communication which is 'supported by reasons' is absent and this also exposes ambivalence in his methodological edicts:

> The justification of a claim to truth presupposes, not the suspension of power as such, but rather the suspension of systematically asymmetrical relations of power, that is, relations of domination. For it is the power to dominate others and to impose one's will on them that stands opposed to the demands for justification.
>
> (J. B. Thompson 1984: 71)

The link that Bourdieu makes between language, power and rationality could become one between rationality, reason and communication in the absence or suspension of power relations. Language could then exhibit a claim to validity and the desire to communicate in order to reach under-standing. This argument will be raised in Chapter 8, but it is an issue which remains problematic in both Bourdieu's methodological injunctions and substantive writings.

Summary

The formation of Bourdieu's ideas took place within the generation of a considerable body of empirical work. The result is a set of 'tools for thinking' to be used by social theorists. This encompasses the invitation to think with, beyond and even against Bourdieu (Wacquant in Bourdieu and Wacquant 1992: xiv) within an overall programme of a reflexive social science. This is not simply an existential call, but one aimed at the institutional conditions of knowledge production itself. The tools of the social sciences are turned back upon themselves, while also being used to illuminate the social conditions of action in society. This both recognizes and defends the possibilities that are afforded by rational, scientific dialogue without an allusion to some transcendental standard against which its observations might be measured (Dumas and Turner 2006; Wacquant 1992). This exhibits Bourdieu's tendency to turn philosophical problems, such as those con-cerned with 'truth', 'into practical problems of scientific politics' (Bourdieu 1990: 33).

Whatever else may be observed, the result of Bourdieu's social scientific practices create possibilities by uncovering the forms of domination that saturate social life. Reflexive analysis has the potential, therefore, to introduce us 'to the unthought categories of thought which limit the thinkable and predetermine what is actually thought' (Bourdieu 1990: 178). As one study of his work concludes, he wishes to debunk the pretensions of institutions to reflect some fixed reality (Robbins 1991: 176):

> It is through the illusion of freedom from social determinants (an illusion which I have said a hundred times is the specific determination of intellectuals) that social determinations win the freedom to exercise their full power. ... And so, paradoxically, sociology frees us by freeing us from the illusion of freedom, or, more exactly, from the misplaced belief in illusory freedoms. Freedom is not something given: it is something you conquer – collectively.
>
> (Bourdieu 1990: 15)

The tensions inherent in this project have been discussed. In particular, the nature of the relationship between universality and particularity and the connections between language, reason and power. It is at this point that actor network theory can be introduced. This theory attempts to follow a model of analysis looking at relationship of power to positioning of human and non-human elements. Chapter 7 focuses on a different route to overcoming the subject/object dichotomy.

7 Action, networks and intermediaries

Chapters 5 and 6 examined the work of Anthony Giddens and Pierre Bourdieu. Both have generated controversies within social theory. Similarly, the subject matter of actor network theory (ANT) has infuriated as many theorists as it has intoxicated. Whereas Giddens and Bourdieu looked at interrelationship between human agency and social structure, actor network theory incorporates non-human or post-humanist variables into the 'social action' process.

Bruno Latour (2005) claims that actor network theory attempts to overcome what he sees as the major shortfall of social theories of modernity and variations of postmodernism: the slicing of a continuous, 'hybrid' reality into analytical domains. The epistemology of modernity divided nature and society into two incommensurable poles. Nature was only observed, never human-made; whereas society was only made by humans. The two poles were indirectly connected by language that allowed us to make stable references to either one of them (Fuller 2007).

Postmodernism separates the middle ground, language, from both poles by declaring it autonomous. This autonomous domain has been described as free-floating signs via French postmodernism (Baudrillard) or as self-referential texts and language games (Derrida) or discourses (Foucault) via poststructuralism. It is ANT's goal to show that the separation introduced by modernity and extended by postmodernism is artificial. This is because (technological) reality is 'simultaneously real, like nature, narrated, like discourse, and collective, like society' (Latour 2005: 6). Latour does not follow the clean divisions envisioned by modernity (Latour 2005). In order to integrate the three separate domains of 'nature', 'society' and 'language', he highlights how humans and non-humans can both be actors which are integrated into networks and sometimes sealed in black boxes (Latour 1999). These networks can be read through the inscription in the intermediaries, which circulate within those networks (Latour 2005). The intended product of these networks varies: it can be nature in the form of scientific facts

(Latour 1986, 2005); it can be technology (Callon 1991, 1997; Latour 2005; Law and Hassard 1999) and it can also be society. The means and actual products of these enterprises are never purely one or the other; they are always 'hybrids' comprising all three domains simultaneously.

This type of social theory has been referred to as 'translational (Callon 1986; Law 1992) and is concerned with studying the mechanics of power as this occurs through the construction and maintenance of networks made up of both human and non-human actors (Fuller 2007). It is concerned with tracing the transformation of these heterogeneous networks (Law 1991) that are made up of people, organizations, agents, machines and many other 'objects'. ANT explores the following: how networks of relations are composed; how they emerge and come into being; how they are constructed and maintained; how they compete with other networks and how they are made more durable over time. It examines how actors enlist other actors into their world and how they bestow qualities, desires, visions and motivations on these actors (Latour 1996): 'Our object, then, is to trace the interconnections built up by technologists as they propose projects and then seek the resources required to bring these projects to fruition' (Law and Callon 1988: 285).

Actors share an interconnection in the construction of the 'network' of interactions leading to the stabilization of the system. There are then evident overlaps with other theoretical disciplines that explore 'network' analysis. In social theory there are parallels to Parsonian systems theory discussed earlier, as well as 'neo-functionalism' (Alexander et al. 2004) and a commonality with Manual Castells, albeit from a different conceptual vantage point, through use of 'network' as exemplified in *The Rise of the Network Society* (Castells 1996). Niklas Luhmann's (1989) concept of 'autopoiesis' and Callon's (1991) and Latour's (2005) 'actornetwork' also have some overlap in the notion of self-formation and the idea of mutual constitution between actors and networks.

A network is composed of actors that define the network, or, the network forms and maintains itself out of its own components. It is in this sense relevant to Luhmann's (1989) 'autopoietic' concept. The criteria of self-production can be applied to define the limits of a network. It then includes all elements that are necessary to achieve and maintain the objectives of the network and society. The communication, therefore, between the network and society is always indirect and determined by the characteristics of the network itself. Niklas Luhmann (1989) turned it into one of the cornerstones of his influential revision of Parsonian systems theory.

Actor network theory: authors, concepts and trajectory

Before we consider its main theoretical propositions it is important to contextualize actor network theory's emergent influences. Actor network theory evolved from the highly influential work of Callon (1991), Latour (1987, 1992, 2005) and Law (1992). Their analysis of a set of negotiations describes the progressive constitution of a network in which both human and non-human actors assume identities according to prevailing strategies of interaction. Actors' identities and qualities are defined during negotiations between representatives of human and non-human acts. In this perspective, 'representation' is understood in its political dimension, as a process of delegation. The most important of these negotiations is 'translational'; a multifaceted interaction in which actors construct common definitions and meanings, conceptualize representativeness and co-opt each other in the pursuit of individual and collective objectives (Latour 1987).

According to Latour (2005), the modern constitution or worldview uses one-dimensional language operating in the framework of the opposite poles of nature and culture. Knowledge and artefacts are explained either by society (social constructionism) or by nature (realism). In order to transcend this dualism a second dimension is needed. It is the process of nature/society construction that results in the stabilization of a strong network. By selecting this process as a unit of analysis, it is possible to understand the simultaneous construction of culture, society and nature:

> Instead of being opposite causes of our knowledge, the two poles are a single consequence of a common practice that is now the single focus of our analysis. Society (or Subject, Mind or Brain) cannot be used to explain the practice of science, since both are results of the science and technology making.
>
> (Latour 1992: 251)

The rationale that Latour posits for this is:

> The reason why we went to study the laboratories, active controversies, skills, instrument making, and emerging entities was to encounter unstable states of nature/society and to document what happens in those extreme and novel situations.
>
> (Latour 1991: 287)

In the next section, we dissect the conceptual relevance of the main terms of actor network theory to assess its relevance to social theory.

Actor

Actors are 'entities that do things' (Latour 1992: 241). Even in this most minimal definition, the main difference from the more conventional definition of actors as 'social entities' is stressed: what actors are, whether social or technological entities, is less important, whereas the aspect of action, doing things, is clearly emphasized: 'The distinction between humans and non-humans, embodied or disembodied skills, impersonation or "machination", are less interesting than the complete chain along which competences and actions are distributed' (Latour 1992: 243).

Actor is further defined as:

> whatever acts or shifts action, action itself being defined by a list of performances through trials; from these performances are deduced a set of competences with which the actant is endowed ... An actor is an actant endowed with a character.
>
> (Akrich and Latour 1992: 259)

While actant is the thing itself in its unspecified 'nature', actor comprises the thing and competences that are attached to it. The competences are negotiated in processes of trial and error. For example, an object such as a coin as piece of metal is an 'actant'. Within the context of financial-based economy, a valid coin or financial note has an attributed competence, it serves as a standard measure of value and mechanism for exchange and it becomes an actor (Callon 1991).

Latour (1987: 84) extends the conceptualization of actor to 'whoever and whatever is represented as an actant'. Latour (1993) aims at retying the separated categories of language, nature and society. In Latour's work *Science in Action* (1987), the level of observation is scientific texts and what appears in those texts and what is 'represented' there. Actor indicates that the elements represented in texts act-that they do particular things. Outside the text, are actants, entities that have an independent reality. Inside the text, they become actors-entities that do things. They act precisely because they are represented in the text. A text can be understood as a network aligning heterogeneous elements (people, other texts, equipment, procedures, and institutions) to achieve a particular objective, which can be proving a scientific discovery or introducing a new procedure. Each of these aligned elements has a reality outside the text (T. Owen 2007).

This reality outside the text allows enforcement of the meaning and of the strength of the text. For example, if objects do not exist independently of a scientific text, then representing them in such a text would be meaningless. However, it took a Louis Pasteur to align 'microbes' as objects in his texts with all kinds of other elements and turn them into the acknowledged source of infections, thus making them (social) actors (Latour 1987). A coin, for example, is able to mobilize the reputation of a whole national economy to simplify mundane transactions, such as purchasing consumer goods. If the coin cannot mobilize those elements because it is not real or is forged, or if the mobilized elements are weak, because the government is in discredit, the coin loses all of its power, which diminishes its value and existence. A coin is an actor because it can mobilize a network of heterogeneous allies to do things, to store and exchange value. In a valid coin this network of allies is tightly sealed and it is almost impossible to question the connections of those networks for an individual using the coins (and thus becoming a part of the network of exchange). A coin is in this sense a 'black box'.

Black box

'A black box contains that which no longer needs to be considered, those things whose contents have become a matter of indifference' (Callon and Latour 1981: 285).

A black box is any setting that, no matter how complex it is or how contested its history has been, is now so stable and certain that it can be treated as a fact where only the input and output counts. The term itself is derived from cybernetics, where it signifies a piece of machinery or a set of commands that might be very complex but can be substituted by a box because it is regular and stable (Latour 2005). The law, for example, is a collection of black boxes. In its formation stage a law is a contested set of competing sentences around which occasionally large alliances are built to influence their specific shape. During the legislative process they are fluid and open. Once the legislation has been passed, contested sentences turn into a black box, sealing all the elements, however arbitrary they might be, in a fixed and stable relationship that cannot be questioned easily. Similar processes happen with any product once it passes from the development stage to the production stage (Callon 1997).

The stability of a black box is influenced by the costs of reopening it. This is not only determined by the social groups and procedures sealed into the black box, but also by the materials which are included. The media into which such a setting is sealed are a crucial element for understanding its overall dynamics. Turned into a black box, hardware tends to be closed. Bijker and Law (1992) give the example that it took an earthquake to open the black box of the Interstate 880 in California and uncover the corruption and construction errors that it had enclosed (Bijker and Law 1992). Software, on the other hand, is constantly reopened and sealed again because of its fluidity. This is the process of constantly questioning some elements of the box (finding Internet viruses) and trying to seal it again in a new upgrade for example, the constant 'patch upgrades' of Microsoft Windows software for PCs to run without 'malicious attack' from hijackers (Loader 2001).

The more a box appears to be closed, the more are the networks it includes assumed to be reliable and stable themselves: 'The more automatic and the blacker the box is, the more it has to be accompanied by people' (Latour 1987: 137).

To isolate a black box and conceptualize it with a trajectory of its own right means to presuppose as a given all the conditions that keep that box closed. Hence, a black box contains a sealed network of 'people' and 'things' – subjects and objects become intertwined in the process of action.

Network

Besides actor, network is another important conceptual discourse essential to the dynamics of actor network theory. The term network is defined as a 'group of unspecified relationships among entities of which the nature itself is undetermined' (Callon 1993: 263).

The inclusive character of this definition becomes more evident when contrasted with one of the conventional definitions of network where 'a social network consists of a finite set or sets of actors and the relation or relations defined on them' (Wasserman and Faust 1994: 20). An actor-network is not restricted to 'social actors', not even to actors in the theory's broader sense. A network ties together two systems of alliances. First, there are people, a notion of everyone who is involved in the invention, construction, distribution and usage of an artefact. Describing this system leads to a 'sociogram'. Social network analysis focuses on this composition of alliances (Wasserman and Faust 1994). Second, things are the pieces that were already on stage or had to be brought into place in order to connect the people and this leads to a 'technogram' (Latour 2005).

While it is analytically useful for clarification purposes to separate the two levels, it is not appropriate to study these systems separately because they are inter related. A change on one level will simultaneously produce a change in the other. Each modification in one system of alliances is visible in the other. Each modification in the technogram is made to overcome a limitation in the sociogram and vice versa (Latour 1987: 138–139; 2005). Interrelations between the sociogram and the technogram become evident, for example, when its envisioned users do not accept a product. One way to react to this mismatch might be to change the product, to bring a different technological network into place in order to give rise to acceptance by the users and change the sociogram.

Market failure does not lead necessarily to a change in the product. It is possible that the sociogram, the network of people who are associated with a product, is changed by adding more people to an organization's marketing department, for example. In order to understand the dynamics in one level of a network, one has to examine the dynamics in the other part (Latour 1987). Actor and network are mutually inclusive of each other. An actor cannot act without a network and a network consists of actors. This relationship is highlighted in yet another definition of the actor as: 'any element which bends space around itself, makes other elements dependent upon itself and translates their will into a language of its own' (Callon and Latour 1981: 286).

Actor and network constantly redefine each other; one is dependent on the other:

> The actor network is reducible neither to an actor alone nor to a network. Like a network it is composed of a series of heterogeneous elements, animate and inanimate, that have been linked to one another for certain period of time ... An actor network is simultaneously an actor whose activity is networking heterogeneous elements and a network that is able to redefine and transform what it is made of.
>
> (Callon 1987: 93)

The size or importance of an actor is dependent on the size of the networks it can command and the size of the networks depends on the number of actors it can align. Since networks consist of a number of actors that have different possibilities to influence other members of the same network, the specific power of an actor depends on the position within its network (Sibeon 2004). There is no structural difference between large and small actors, or between a major institution or a single individual or even a thing as mundane as a door opener (Latour 2005). This does not suggest that they are all equal. This simply means that the main differences between micro and macro actors is the size of the network they can bring into place for a particular goal: that is, the number of actors they can arrange according to their objectives (Bijker and Law 1991). These objectives can be a strategic choice of options, adaptive necessities or built-in properties of a certain piece of equipment (Callon 1991). Properties of a setting, the fact that it makes certain things possible and others impossible, are called prescriptions.

Inscription/prescription

Several related concepts have been developed to 'read' a setting and to understand the constraints and forces which come to bear through a scientific discovery. The activity of the analyst is called description, which can be understood as the: 'analysis of what the various actors in a setting are doing to one another. The opposite movement, inscription, is the activity of the engineer, inventor or manufacturer who make others do certain things' (Akrich and Latour 1992: 259).

In the process of inscription, the properties of a setting are assembled bearing the mark of the actors aligned in the network that produces that setting. For the process of description a type of inscription is a text (Bijker and Law 1992). Texts explain the object, be it in form of a manual, on the device itself or in a separate brochure, promotional material or the critical reviews or others. The activity of inscriptions materializes in the prescriptions of a given object. Prescription is 'what a device allows or forbids from the actors (humans and non-humans) that it anticipates; it is the morality of a setting both negative (what it prescribes) and positive (what it permits)' (Akrich and Latour 1992: 261).

There is a potential conflict in any type of research that is concerned with the unmasking of present social relations. The status of an artefact can be highly contested and emerge just as the result of complex strategies. For instance, to strengthen the inscriptive force of a text, the author might insist on its descriptive, hence scientific and objective, character (Bijker and Law 1992). Those who want to weaken its authoritative, and hence possibly inscriptive, power will try to cast doubt on its descriptive quality. They may, for example, initiate a counter study to demonstrate a different type of description or the bias of the author (Layder 2006). They are activities, the results of actors doing things, be it assembling a setting, using the setting or the analyst deconstructing the setting, i.e. opening the black box. All these activities shape the form and content of the product. As Callon (1991: 140) points out: 'the social can be read in the inscriptions that mark the intermediaries'.

Intermediary

Intermediaries provide the still missing link that connects actors into a network and defines the network itself (Bijker and Law 1992). Actors form networks by circulating intermediaries among themselves, thus defining the respective position of the actors within the networks and in doing so constituting the actors and the networks themselves (Bijker and Law 1992). An intermediary is anything that 'passes between actors in the course of relatively stable transactions' (Bijker and Law 1992: 25). It can be a text, product, service or financial transaction. Intermediaries are the language of the network. Through intermediaries actors communicate with one another and that is the way actors translate their intentions into other actors. Considering the definition of actors as any element 'which makes other elements dependent upon itself and translates their will into a language of its own' (Callon and Latour 1981: 286), the possibility to command intermediaries lies at the heart of action itself, which is translating an actor's will into other actors (Latour 2005).

With the concept of translation we have arrived at the point when things begin to get dynamic. We now have to use the tools prepared so far to describe some central aspects of the dynamics within actor-networks. Networks are put into place by actors (Latour 2005). However, since there is no actor without a network, new networks emerge out of already existing ones. Sometimes this happens through subtle changes; sometimes as the result of revolutionary developments that might push into the background the element of continuity that is part of every dynamic (Callon 1991). Defining a beginning is a necessary but 'artificial' analytical operation based on the interests of the analyst within his or her particular empirical situation. If the interest is in a product, then the beginning might be found in some form of perceived need or possibility. This could be based on, for example, a new invention, which would then be one of the old networks out of which a new network emerges (Callon 1997).

Other things could serve as a mark for the beginning as well. Callon and Latour (1992) trace the beginning of a failed project for a UK military aircraft back to a policy decision for rationalization of the aircraft industry. This decision, however, is itself contested, functioned only as an intermediary, reconnecting existing networks of industry, labour and government to begin aligning themselves for the development and production of a new aircraft. At the beginning, therefore, stands an intermediary which is brought into circulation by a network in order to align more or different actors for the network's own interest. In other words, the attempt of an existing actor to grow and include new domains can be a good starting point to observe the emergence of a network. Networks allow actors to translate their objectives, be it conscious human choice or prescription of an object, into other actors and adding the other actors' power to their own:

> By translation we understand all the negotiations, intrigues, calculations, acts of persuasion and violence thanks to which an actor or force takes, or causes to be conferred to itself, authority to speak or act on behalf of another actor or force.
>
> (Callon and Latour 1981: 279)

Networks can be so large and stable that they appear to be independent from the actors. This, however, is a misconception. While they can constrain the range of action for certain actors, they always need actors. Any given actor might be replaceable, but only by another actor. There is, therefore, no gap between the individual and the structure that is made up of individuals that are made up of structure which is made up of individuals and so on, endlessly. For Latour 'the two extremes, local and global, are much less interesting than the intermediary arrangements that we are calling networks' (1993: 372).

A network can develop in two different directions, towards convergence or towards divergence of its actors. Adding new actors to a network at first increases their divergence. The process of translation by which the will of one actor is transferred to another actor becomes initially more difficult because each new actor is already included in other networks that might have aligned it for differential objectives. What to do in and how to account for new situations, how to assess the meaning of an intermediary is unclear at the beginning. The divergence of a situation or an element of the network is its 'interpretative flexibility' (Bijker 1994).

For networks to operate successfully, the circulation of intermediaries needs to be co-ordinated. This means the included actors do not, or may only to a limited extent, contest their own translation. Actors thrive toward an internal agreement that allows for an optimal circulation of intermediaries, because their strength depends on the co-ordination within the networks. In networks where the actors have successfully converged they are strongly co-ordinated, the network as a whole stands behind any one of the actors who make it up. The way agreement can be reached, the scope of the translations possible, shapes the form of the network. In other words: 'the network is constructed according to the translation's own logic' (Callon 1992: 84). The stronger the co-ordination of the circulation is, the more the different elements are aligned, the more stable and predictable it becomes. The more stable a network is, the better it defines its components. The possibilities decrease for other networks to untie the connections in order to redefine an actor for its own purposes. The setting turns into a black box.

An actor-network thrives for stabilization because none of the entities that make it up would exist without that network in that form. The promotion of a network is a way to ensure the actor's existence and development. It is, therefore, in the interest of all actors within a particular network to stabilize the network that guarantees their own survival to a higher or lower extent (Latour 2005). The stability of a network depends on the 'impossibility it creates of returning to a situation in which its current form was only one of many possible options among others' (Callon 1992: 89). In other words, stabilization or closure 'means that the interpretive flexibility diminishes. Consensus among the different relevant social groups [or more broadly, actors] about the dominant meaning of an artefact merges and the "pluralism of artefacts" decreases' (Bijker1994: 86).

Coupled with this, social relations that are embedded in artefacts are a stabilizing factor of society:

> Society and technology are not two ontologically distinct entities but more like phases of the same essential action. By replacing those

two arbitrary divisions with syntagm and paradigm, we may draw a few more methodological conclusions. The description of socio-technical networks is often opposed to their explanation, which is supposed to come afterwards ... If we display a socio-technical network – defining trajectories by actants' association and substitution, defining actants by all the trajectories in which they enter, by following translations and, finally, by varying the observer's point of view – we have no need to look for any additional causes. The explanation emerges once the description is saturated ... There is no need to go searching for mysterious or global causes outside networks. If something is missing, it is because something is missing.

(Latour 1991: 129–130)

Heterogeneity is another, central aspect of a stable network. The more the diverse elements are interrelated, the more complex and stable a network becomes. In a heterogeneous network each element is kept in place through a set of heterogeneous ties to other actors and in order to untie multiple determined actors, multiple connections have to be untied (Latour 2005). The size and the heterogeneity of a network are related. The larger it becomes the more heterogeneous it becomes because it develops additional elements just to keep all other elements in place. In the language of systems theory this development is called 'differentiation' (Parsons 1968). The network starts to develop its own trajectory, supported by its elements. A network starts to 'become heavy with norms of all sorts' (Callon 1992: 91) in the course of stabilization. This means, of course, nothing else than that more actors are integrated or created. A network that stabilizes itself does

not only resist competing translations but also restrict[s] the number of possible future translations. This means in order to establish other links and set-up new translations you would first have to undo those which already exist, and change the equivalence in operation, which would in turn mean mobilizing and enrolling new alliances ... Thus non-linearity and path dependence can be seen to be integral to the dynamics of [a network].

(Callon 1992: 92)

Issues in actor network theory

Actor network theory has raised some very interesting questions related to the notion of action in context of human and non-human relations. The problem, however, is that ANT has remained much more interested in the establishment of networks than in their later dynamics. The closure involved in the establishment of a network is real, but how does it help us understand how a network changes and perhaps becomes destabilized? The answer is that it does not without an addition to the theory.

While ANT's bias towards the achievement of actor-networks may be refreshing in its theoretical boldness, the overall result of work in this area is 'to skew the field of analysis towards a narrative of success through a mock-heroic history' (Barnes 2002: 344). Worse, what is celebrated is limited to an account of human agency as extended by technological networks: for all that at one level actor network theory modestly follows the actors and marks no distinction of its own between humans and things, at another level it is a profoundly intrusive monism engaged in the celebration of human agency (Barnes 2002).

ANT is interested in the celebration of human agency in terms of its entanglement with technology and not any other dimensions of human agency – all this in spite of the fact that from other perspectives networks are at most the infrastructure of human action, not its dynamic content (Fuller 2007). One problem, then, of building ANT into a fuller account of social theory is its neglect of time, or rather its concentration on one type of temporal dynamic and historical achievement, at the expense of others (Sibeon 2004). This first limitation is linked to a second: ANT's neglect of the long-term consequences of networks for the distribution of 'power'. ANT offers a precise and non-functionalist account of how actors become established as powerful through the stability of the networks that pass through them (T. Owen 2007).

The actor (human or non-human) that is an obligatory passing point in a network has power and the more networks where that is true, the more power that actor has. As a result, over time, the ability of an actor to act effectively on a larger scale becomes established. For example, there is the basis here for an account of how media institutions feed a global empire that acquires power over large territories through their incremental insertion in an increasingly dense web of communication circuits such as television, Internet, sports, music, news and film. What limits the usefulness of ANT as a research tradition for social theory is its relative lack of interest in the long-term power consequences and its effects on inequality (T. Owen 2007).

For all its intellectual radicalism, it could be argued that ANT comes armed with political conservatism that is linked to a disinterest in human agency (T. Owen 2007). Power differentials between human actors matter in a way that power differentials between non-humans do not: they have social consequences which are linked to how these differences are interpreted and how they affect the various agents' ability to have their interpretations of the world fixed. ANT has much to contribute to understanding the 'how' of such asymmetries, but it is silent when it comes to assessing whether, and 'why', they matter. Its deconstruction of the humanist subject is disabling and is a paradox of value that also lies at the crux of Foucault's work (Best and Kellner

1997). Criticism of neglect of wider power structures and of possibilities of resistance to and contestation in ANT, is therefore well placed.

Sibeon (2004) suggests that ANT is 'ludicrous reductionism'. Objects do not hold causal powers or the ability to formulate, act and implement decisions. For Tim Owen (2006), actor network theory engages in the 'cardinal sinning' of social reification of the concept of actor both in terms of subject and object. Further, Latour claims that, 'power is not something you may possess or hoard', and that power is 'an effect … never a cause' (1986: 265). Sibeon (2004: 136) cogently disagrees with Latour's suggestions, arguing that: 'Latour is wrong; power can be hoarded or stored, and therefore power – though often an effect – can sometimes be a "cause" '.

Summary

Actor network theory originated as a movement within social studies of science. Key developers were Bruno Latour, Michel Callon, Antoine Hennion and John Law. It was sharply critical of earlier historical and other forms of analyses of science, which had drawn a clear divide between the 'inside' of a science (to be analysed in terms of its adherence or not to a unitary scientific method) and its 'outside' (the field of its application).

Actor-network theorists have made three key arguments. First, they have argued for a semiotic, network reading of scientific practice (Latour 2005). Human and non-human actors or what is known as 'actants' were assumed to be subject to the same analytic categories: 'just as a ring or a prince could hold the same structural position in a fairy tale' (T. Owen 2006: 165). They could be enrolled in a network or not, could hold or not hold certain moral positions and so forth. This profound ontological position has been the least understood but the most generative aspect of the social theory.

Second, they argued that in producing their theories, scientists weave together human and non-human actors into relatively stable network nodes, or 'black boxes'. Thus a given astronomer can tie together her telescope, some distant stars and a funding agency into an impregnable fortress and in order to challenge her results you would need to find your own telescope, stars and external funding sources. Practically, this entailed an agnostic position on the 'truth' of science (Fuller 2007). Indeed, they argued for a principle of symmetry according to which the same set of explanatory factors should be used to account for failed and successful scientific theories. There is no ultimate arbiter of right and wrong.

Third, they maintained that in the process of constructing these relatively stable network configurations, scientists produced contingent nature–society divides (T. Owen 2007). Nature and society were not pre-given entities that could be used to explain anything else; they were the outcomes of the work of doing technoscience. Latour (2005) called this the 'Janus face' of science. As it was being produced it was seen as contingent; once produced it was seen as always and already true.

Together, these three issues of ANT made the central analytical unit the work of the intermediary. There is no society out there to which scientists respond as they build their theories, nor is there a nature which constrains them to a single telling of their stories. Rather, the technoscientist stands between nature and society, politics and technology. A person can act as a spokesperson for her array of actants (things in the world) and if successful can black-box these to create the effect of truth.

The theory has given rise to a number of concepts which have proven useful in a wide range of technoscientific analyses. It has remained influential as a methodological tool for amalysing truth-making in all its forms. The call to 'follow the actors' – to see what they do rather than report on what they say they do – has been liberating for those engaged in studying scientists, who frequently hold their own truth and practice as if above the social and political fray (T. Owen 2006). Latour's (2005) work on the distribution of political and social values between the technical world and the social institution has opened up a powerful discourse about the political and moral force of technology.

ANT itself has changed significantly in recent years, including Latour's (1999) self-critical denial of each of its central terms and the hyphen connecting them. This has been in response to a number of critiques that the theory privileged the powerful, technoscientist as world-builder, without giving much opportunity for representing the invisible technicians within the networks and alternative voices from without (Star 1995). Knorr-Cetina (2005) also has tried to formulate new questions set by Callon (1991) and Latour (1993) in a more open way in terms of a rethinking actor network theory and its legacy for understanding social organization (Knorr-Cetina 2005).

The role of technologies, such as information technology, in organizing forms of attachment and belonging can be analysed without abandoning an interest in social interaction and its dynamics. Knorr-Cetina (2005) suggests that social theorists consider computer programmes, investment vehicles and fashion designs as unfolding structures of absences. This captures both the patterned, highly routinized nature of how technologies contribute to the social world. Crucially, Knorr-Cetina (2005) raises the question of interpretation and representation ignored by Callon and Latour. We must think about the pervasiveness of the images themselves in an information society and their contribution to what now passes for social 'order'. This is to take on the challenge that power provides to our understanding of the social and be ready to admit that this challenge remains.

The challenge for social theory is not to just provide an account of object–subject dualism but to provide the intellectual resources to overcome the constraints to communications aimed at understanding and the co-ordination of action. This challenge is addressed head on by the work of Jürgen Habermas.

8 The linguistic turn in critical theory

The theoretical work of Jürgen Habermas occupies a very significant position in western social and political discourse. Some writers regard Habermas's work as the most important attempt to reconstruct critical theory out of the shadows of Marx (Borradori 2003). Habermas deploys Kant and Hegel to revitalize Marxism through developing an emancipatory theory of society. In addition, drawing on the Frankfurt School, he elaborates a far-reaching critique of methods of domination in modern society. Some of the ideas that he has taken on board and utilized include those of Weber, Freud, Mead, Durkheim, Parsons, Piaget, Chomsky, Luhmann and the moral-developmental theory of Kohlberg, as well as the traditions of hermeneutics, pragmatism and ordinary language philosophy.

Habermas has written on the Enlightenment project in a reflexive manner, facing up to Enlightenment thought and its profound legacy via a systematic critical analysis of the present: its historiography, pathologies and future prospects (Habermas 1992c). At the same time, there has been a huge escalation in neo-Nietzschean philosophers under the labels of 'postmodern-ist' and 'poststructuralist' who have castigated the Enlightenment, claiming that its metanarratives of 'progress' and 'freedom' have failed and that western rationality is exhausted (Cooke 2002).

As noted in Part I, the Marx–Hegel connection is important for understanding certain aspects of twentieth-century social theory. There was also the creative tension between Hegel and Kant. For one member of the critical theory tradition, this is 'one of the most productive elements' (Honneth 1993: 37). It is not surprising, therefore, that he has utilized their works in order to understand the relationship between knowledge and human interests (Habermas 1989a) and develop his ideas on 'discourse ethics' (Habermas 1993) and the pragmatics of social interaction (Habermas 2003). Yet this philosophical tradition has provided for misunderstanding when it comes to interpreting the works of Habermas. As Taylor and Montefiore (1980) put it:

Notoriously ... this enterprise has been little appreciated or understood in Anglo-Saxon philosophy of the last half-century or so. ...
This inevitably makes it difficult for someone from within this
culture to gain a familiar sense of the ground plan of the house of
critical theory.

(Taylor and Montefiore 1980: 1)

With the myriad of ideas which are evident in his work and the fact that he
has subjected them all to critique we gain an insight into why his ideas are so
complex and wide-ranging, as well as misunderstood. Despite this, the
exercise of perseverance is more than compensated for by the considerable
insights that it offers into the operation of societies and the dynamics of
social life.

We cannot pretend to be able to redress any imbalance in interpretation within a single chapter and there are those who have performed an
excellent service in this regard in book-length studies of his work (Finlayson
2004; McCarthy 1984; Outhwaite 1994; White 1990). Here we simply wish to
provide some foundations upon which a further exploration of his work
might proceed. First, there is a consideration of the intellectual antecedents
and development of his ideas, paying particular attention to the role of
rationality, language and the relationship between the system and lifeworld.
In the second section of the chapter, some issues which his work raises will
then be outlined in order to assess its strengths and weaknesses.

The domain of communicative reason

There is a core theme that informs much of Habermas's thought. This is
exhibited, to one degree or another, in his earlier work on structural changes
in the public sphere, written in 1962, but which remains influential (Habermas 1989b); his use and criticism of Freudian psychoanalysis (1989b); his
linguistic turn (Habermas 1984, 1987) and his writings on law and democracy (Habermas 1996) and the divided west (Habermas 2006): that is, the
pathologies which arise in the lifeworld which result from systemic imbalances. These imbalances serve to impede the production of meaningful
communication which is aimed at the formation of understanding and a
'democratic will' among peoples. They interfere with the symbolic reproduction of the lifeworld and are exemplified at a macro level via economic crises
and questions over the legitimacy of the state apparatus (Habermas 1993:
148).

In Marx's work, pathologies in the lifeworld were caused by the
capitalist system and represented in the state of alienation. In the case of
Weber, the triumph of formal rationality over substantive rationality was to

form an 'iron cage' of modernity. For Habermas, both of these analyses are limited. While Marx had sought to transcend Hegel's idealism, so Habermas seeks to transcend the limitations of materialism while not abandoning it to idealism. Similarly, he seeks to generate a theory of rationalization using Weber's work but, in so doing, also overcome the pessimism of Nietzschean inspired social theory where reason becomes viewed as the 'will to power'. Therefore, in order to situate Habermas's work, we must consider the nature of these critiques. We shall then be in a position to examine the main elements of the theory of communicative action.

Thinking with and beyond Marx, Weber and the Frankfurt School

Labour was of primary significance for Marx. Alienation was not derived from Hegel's 'mentalist' conception, but from the actual material conditions of capitalist production. However, in his later work or 'mature' work, as encapsulated by Althusser's (1969) notion of an 'epistemological break', Marx appears to reduce ideas to material interests, instead of viewing them in a dialectical fashion. The result is a paradox in 'praxis' philosophy:

> Marx reduces the process of reflection to the level of instrumental action. By reducing the self-positing of the absolute ego to the more tangible productive activity of the species, he eliminates reflection as such as a motive force of history, even though he retains the framework of the philosophy of reflection.
>
> (Habermas 1989a: 44)

Marx thus reduces the potential for reflection to the mode of production and that, in turn, to labour. The social self is then linked to the environment in such a manner that there is no social sphere in which people might reflect upon their situation. Therefore, although Marx acknowledges not only the relationship between production and nature, but also the transformation of societies via class struggle, a mechanical view of history remains apparent. A desire for recognition and the pursuit of understanding in human relations is reduced to instrumental action as represented by labour. Marx ends up giving primacy to the application of knowledge towards particular goals over the achievement of understanding within human relations. The consequence of this dilemma was expressed in a different form in Chapter 1 where the question was posed: where are the resources for spontaneous radical change, within an all-encompassing system such as capitalism, actually derived?

Relatedly, Habermas argues that Marx did not adequately differentiate between natural-scientific knowledge, with its implications for control as manifested through technical knowledge harnessed in the process of production, with that of 'critique'. Instead, in positivistic fashion, Marx argued that the 'objective' conditions of capitalism would, as it evolved over time, create the necessary conditions for 'subjective' proletarian emancipation: 'Marx regarded the productive forces unleashed by capitalism as an objective presupposition for overcoming it' (Habermas 1984: 367). Once again, this is a mechanical view which repeats the subject–object dualism in social thought. It does not allow for human interpretation, reflection and understanding which are, to a degree, independent of the labour process:

> In his empirical analyses Marx comprehends the history of the species under categories of material activity and the critical abolition of ideologies, of instrumental action and revolutionary practice, of labour and reflection at once. But Marx interprets what he does in the more restricted conception of the species' self-reflection through work alone.
>
> (Habermas 1989a: 42)

An analysis of the evolution of human learning and understanding, which is not simply reducible to labour, is absent from work. Of course, a similar problematic preoccupied the Frankfurt theorists for whom he worked in the early stages of his career. Thus, Habermas identifies a need to incorporate the dimensions of labour and interaction in order to develop a more adequate critical theory.

Without this, interaction collapses into labour and is open to manipulation by the sort of 'technical' or instrumental knowledge that is constitutive of a positivistic social science with its consequences for control, not emancipation. Here we can detect the influence of Horkheimer's critique of instrumental reason. Within capitalist societies increasing areas of social life are informed by the logic of a system governed by instrumental action. What Habermas (1989a) refers to as the 'empirical-analytic' sciences, simply add to a purposive-rationality oriented towards the achievement of particular ends. This stands in contrast to those areas of social life which are normatively informed: for example, familial relations. Habermas must now retain the critical edge of Marx within a reconstructed historical materialism that refuses to surrender to instrumentality as the principal mode of characterizing modern societies. A realm of interaction that aims at the achievement of understanding must then be delineated; a realm which contains an evolutionary human-learning process which

> cannot be ascribed exclusively either to society or individuals. Certainly the personality system bears the learning process of ontogenesis and, to a certain extent; only individuals are capable of learning. However, social systems can form new structures by utilizing the learning capacities of their members in order to cope with

problems that threaten system maintenance. In this respect the evolutionary learning process of societies is dependent on the competence of their individual members. These in turn acquire their competence, not as isolated monads, but by growing into the symbolic structure of their social world.

(Habermas 1981: 269)

Society is dependent upon this realm for its reproduction. This allows for a theory of culture that is not simply reducible to labour. Similarly, it permits a reconstruction of historical materialism which recognizes that the wage–labour relationship produces distorting effects within the lifeworld. In the process, the base-superstructure model, with its economistic approach to social and political relations, is abandoned, together with a monocausal analysis of power relations as reducible to wage labour; to say nothing of any direct faith in the proletariat as the instrument of socialist revolution. With these grounds in mind, we can now make more precise links with our previous discussions on reason and rationality.

Adorno, Horkheimer, Marcuse and Lukacs were all, to one degree or another, influenced by Weber's theory of rationalization. As we saw in Part I, instrumental rationality is seen to penetrate the lifeworld to such an extent that modernity represents 'disenchantment'. For Adorno and Horkheimer, in their initial attempts to explain the ideological incorporation of the working classes within capitalism, rationalization and the Enlightenment end up as the prime suspects. Once again, in a similar twist, only from a different starting-point, the idea of progress in the unfolding of human history was destroyed, the result being that they 'surrendered themselves to an uninhibited scepticism regarding reason' (Habermas 1992a: 129).

In charting the development of social theory, history, once again, is seen to offer little hope. Yet each of these theorists is taken to task by Habermas for their failure to diagnose modernity in order to recognize the existence and potential of what he calls 'communicative reason'. A brief examination of his critique of Weber, Adorno and Horkheimer will assist in understanding how he forges this realm in order to argue that a modified Enlightenment project is yet to be completed.

Weber's theory of rationalization views the economy and the state as subsystems of purposive-rationality; the prime cause of capitalism then being the process of rationalization. At the same time, Weber was to abandon any idea of laws in history. Dilthey's historicism urged connections to be made with the meaning-constituting activities of human subjects in order to abandon dialectical and evolutionary theories of history which were viewed as deterministic (Habermas 1984: 153). Yet while Weber urged social scientists to start with the meanings that people attach to their social environments, at another level we find him espousing determinism as exemplified in the idea of the 'iron cage'. This gap in Weber's analysis is filled by a

Nietzschean-style pessimism, accompanied by the call for an ethic of personal responsibility in the face of historical uncertainty and the continual and never ending struggle for power.

This gap in Weber's reasoning may be summed up as follows:

> Weber did not adequately distinguish between the particular value contents of cultural traditions and those universal standards of value under which the cognitive, normative, and expressive components of culture become autonomous value spheres and developed complexes of rationality with their own logics.
>
> (Habermas 1984: 249)

This is symptomatic of the more general problem of viewing society and social relations in terms of a subject–object dualism. The end result is a series of critiques, epitomized by Adorno and Horkheimer, of the contemporary forms of 'subjective' reason from the vantage point of an 'objective' reason which itself has fallen into disrepute (Habermas 1984: 377). From this point of view, it was inevitable that the end result was pessimism, commonly manifested in the idea of a 'reification of consciousness'.

Habermas seeks to avoid such conclusions. Take, for example, Weber's conflation of a particular form of societal rationalization with the entire notion of rationality. For Weber, it was the institutionalization of purposive rationality, beginning with Protestantism and culminating in legal systems, that explains the rise of capitalism. This form of rationality, as noted earlier, involves the selection of means for the attainment of particular ends based upon an interpretation of the intentions of other actors who are, or might be, party to the interaction. However, this does not allow for the possibility that other forms of rationalization exist within modernity. An analysis of these would open up theoretical avenues and lead to the realm of communicative reason.

To develop an adequate critical theory, the need exists to reconsider the possibilities that modernity offers, without succumbing to the same errors that beset previous theorists. This requires that avoid the pitfalls of instrumental rationality via a critique of the underlying philosophy of consciousness upon which these theorists relied. In particular, this is manifest in the inadequacy of their theories of action and systems (Habermas 1984: 145). Expressed in this way, we can return to the conceptualization of the relationship between agency and structure in terms of the forging of the domain of communicative reason which

> refers neither to a subject that preserves itself in relating to objects via representation and action, nor to a self-maintaining system that demarcates itself from an environment, but to a symbolically struc-

tured lifeworld that is constituted in the interpretive accomplishments of its members and only reproduced through communication.

(Habermas 1984: 398)

To achieve this requires not only extensive historical excavations over
the terrain of social theory and philosophy, but also the development of an
entirely new basis for critical theory which does not get trapped in the
philosophy of the subject. For this purpose, Habermas turned his attention
towards the development of the theory of communicative action (TCA) that
is informed by four main themes. First, the construction of a theory of
rationality which seeks to overcome the above problems, which is not
content to let relativism as exemplified, for example, by Winch's (1990)
work, to have the last word on the subject. Second, the development of the
theory of communicative action itself. Third, an examination of the 'dialectic of rationalization' for the purposes of constructing a theory of modernity
which is then able to analyse socio-pathological states in contemporary
society. Finally, the bringing together of action and systems theory within a
new conceptual framework (Habermas in Dews 1992: 104–105). The result is
a highly complicated set of intriguing and challenging ideas. In the next
section, attention is turned to the development of the TCA.

The theory of communicative action

The theory of communication serves to disclose a profound continuity
between human language and the values embedded in the project of
modernity. According to Rasmussen (1990), Ferdinand de Saussure's (1959)
distinction between diachronic and synchronic is fundamental in unravel-
ling Habermas's thought: diachronic historical-evolutionary schemes for
understanding language follow the model of the enlightenment. From this
perspective, Habermas's attempt to reconstitute the project of modernity
through language is consistent with diachronic model of understanding
language. Language is the vehicle for the most fundamental form of social
action, namely his theory of communicative action. We can define communicative action as 'that form of social interaction in which the plans of action
of different actors are co-ordinated through an exchange of communicative
acts, that is, through a use of language orientated towards reaching understanding' (Habermas 1981: 44).

Habermas (1981) fuses micro and macro dimensions and uses Mead
and Durkheim as a theoretical bridge to develop communicative action.
While Mead is important because of symbolically mediated interaction,
Durkheim is important because of his analysis of the 'sacred' and process of

secularization of religion. Therefore, Habermas (1981, 1992b) sees the 'language–communication' framework as a new way of reaffirming the project of modernity. Habermas wants to show how the transformation from traditional society to modernity involved a progressive secularization of normative behaviour reconstructed through communicative action. Drawing on his assessment of communicative competence of social actors, Habermas (1981) distinguishes between 'action orientated to success' and 'action orientated to understanding' and also between the social and non-social contexts of action. Action orientated to success is measured by rules of rational choice, while action orientated to understanding takes place through 'communicative action'. This manifestation of communicative action materializes by mutual and co-operative achievement of understanding among collective participants.

Communicative action is linked to reason embodied in universal pragmatics, since it is guided by a search for intersubjective recognition of validity claims (truth, rightness and sincerity) although this guidance may be only implicitly present in any particular case of social interaction and it is not an instant of an actually existing concept (Habermas 2003: 103). Communicative action is based on an analysis of the conditions necessary for communication to occur in order then to reach a common understanding when action is co-ordinated by the validity claims offered in speech acts (Habermas 1981). Communicative action is internally linked to communicative rationality which is a central plank for Habermas's version of idealized communicative action: a condition he terms 'unconstrained communication'. This involves an attempt to characterize universal features of communication in their structure and consolidation. Similarly, Roderick (1986) interprets communicative rationality as an attempt to identify empirically the historical development of rationality structures as well as an attempt to problematize further rationality to more modern spheres in different spheres of life. These different spheres – such as the economy, the political order, and culture – represent distinct domains whose underlying logic impinges on communicative action and the constitution of lifeworld.

The origins and constitution of the lifeworld

To consider the constitution of the lifeworld, Habermas develops his ideas on intersubjective communication. Following our earlier discussion on Mead, it should be clear that this mode of communication does not denote the coming together of autonomous subjects, but how it is that people are formed in and through their interactions with others. Nevertheless, while Habermas refers to his general attempts at a reconstructive science as 'universal pragmatics', Mead's work is found to be limited in terms of his accounts on the development of the self and the lifeworld. It is at this point that Durkheim, read from the point of view of his theory of evolution, enters Habermas's formulations.

Durkheim's lifelong concern was 'to explain the normative validity of institutions and values' (Habermas 1987: 47). Durkheim's principal legacy regarding society as an active moralizing force enables us to discuss the concept of rationality without succumbing to the trap of instrumentality. As Durkheim argued, norms are held to be valid due to the moral authority which they contain, not simply because their infringement is attached to particular sanctions (Habermas 1992c: 73). From this point of view, Habermas now considers the origins of the lifeworld within a normative framework. Furthermore, Durkheim's focus upon the 'collective consciousness' permits him to correct the ontogenetic emphasis of Mead's ideas and recover them at a phylogenetic level (Habermas 1987: 46). Briefly, how does this take place?

For Mead the moral authority of the group rested upon the internalization of the 'generalized other' within the individual. In turn, this is based upon an initial set of group sanctions for the purposes of maintaining social control. However, there remains an issue: 'groups must have first been constituted as units capable of acting before the sanctions could be imposed in their name' (Habermas 1987: 45). According to Mead's formulations it appears that individuals can become members of a group only once a collective consciousness has formed! With this paradox in mind, Mead resorted to ideas on the personality for his explanatory resource, with the result that he failed to provide an account of the origins of the collective lifeworld itself.

In contrast to Mead, Durkheim rooted his analysis in terms of beliefs which were 'the expression of a collective consciousness rooted deep in tribal history and constitutive of the identity of groups' (Habermas 1987: 46). However, there are gaps in Durkheim's ideas through an absence of the linguistic component of the lifeworld. After all, the everyday world of the profane is channelled through linguistic communication which aims at intersubjective understanding. Instead of seeing the sacred and profane in this way, Durkheim collapsed both normative consensus and the process of reaching understanding through speech acts under the umbrella of the collective consciousness (Habermas 1987: 57). What we are witnessing here is yet another repetition of the subject–object dualism in social thought. In Durkheim's work this is manifest through his duality of human nature in terms of self-interested activity and morality. The result being, in evolutionary terms, he failed to answer the question 'How do institutions draw upon social solidarity in order to maintain their validity?' (Habermas 1987: 57).

> This may be resolved only if we bear in mind that profane everyday practice proceeds by way of linguistically differentiated processes of

reaching understanding and forces us to specify validity claims for actions appropriate to situations in the normative context of roles and institutions.

(Habermas 1987: 57)

Linguistic communication fills the analytic gap between institutional reproduction and normative consensus. It may be characterized as having a 'mediating function' that links individuals to the collective consciousness. Therefore, both normatively grounded symbolism and linguistic communication are fundamental constituents of the lifeworld which, together, account for the origins of the lifeworld. Durkheim's focus upon norms, the sacred and the moral, thus end up as supplements to Mead's theory of intersubjective communication. With a normative background in place, our everyday speech can then be argued to presuppose its basis in consensual validity. Overall, this fusion yields 'the structure of linguistically mediated, normatively guided interaction, which is the starting point for sociocultural development' (Habermas 1987: 46).

To complete this connection we must draw upon one more analytic resource: ordinary language philosophy. As we have noted before, this 'has taken the place of the traditional problem of consciousness' (Habermas 1990: 117). In furtherance of the concept of intersubjective communication, language becomes the medium for reaching understanding, learning and achieving co-operation. As Habermas puts it so eloquently:

> From the structure of language comes the explanation of why the human spirit is condemned to an odyssey. ... Only at the greatest distance from itself does it become conscious of itself in its irreplaceable singularity as an individuated being.
>
> (Habermas 1992b: 153)

At this stage in the development of Habermas's thought the discussion becomes highly technical. For our purposes we can consider this in the following manner. To complete the forging of the potential of communicative reason, Habermas employs Austin's speech-act theory (Austin 1976). If the potential for communicative reason exists in language itself then there exists a scientific, as opposed to a normative basis, for critical theory. He then ends up employing the analytic tradition of philosophy for the purposes of working on a continental problematic which, as noted at the beginning of the chapter, can lead to interpretative misunderstanding. Briefly, how is this achieved?

Austin (1976) divides performatory utterances – speech-acts which are also performances of an action – into locutionary, illocutionary and perlocutionary statements. Simply put, the first involves the act of actually *saying* something; the second refers to what is done *in* the act of an utterance – for example, a promise – and the third produces particular effect in others. From

this Habermas seeks to make a distinction between illocutionary and perlocutionary statements by arguing that the former are oriented towards
understanding and the latter employed in strategic action. In other words,
once again, albeit at a different level, instrumental action in terms of being
oriented towards success is perlocutionary, but this is parasitic upon communicative action as oriented towards reaching understanding as exemplified by
illocutionary speech acts. The latter are therefore primary and speech acts
take place against the background of normative consensus in the world: 'The
illocutionary components express the fact that the speaker is explicitly
raising a claim to propositional truth, normative rightness, or subjective
truthfulness, as well as the particular aspects under which he is doing so'
(Habermas 1987: 72).

As Habermas (1984: 328) recognizes, one might then ask how we can
link this into everyday usages of language. He seeks to use these ideas to
arrive at a general classification of 'linguistically mediated interaction' (1984:
329). The issue here is, if he is not to repeat the mistakes that Weber and
others have made in relation to the general problem of rationality, that what
should be examined is not the motivations for actions, but the relationship
of these to the structures of the lifeworld itself for this is presupposed as the
background to actions:

> Communicative action takes place within a lifeworld that remains at
> the backs of participants in communication. It is present to them
> only in the prereflexive form of taken-for-granted background as-
> sumptions and naively mastered skills.
>
> (Habermas 1984: 335)

While Habermas finds the insights of ordinary language philosophy
important for the development of communication action, it is also limited
for reasons which we have come across before. First, the absence of any
hermeneutic input in terms of the translation between language games.
Second, it shares an idealism along with hermeneutics. Therefore, although
Gadamer (1975) was correct in overcoming Wittgenstein's limitations by
connecting language use with the history through which we inherit our
language, he shares a failure to see the ways in which language 'serves to
legitimate relationships of organized force' (Habermas 1990: 172. Also see
Holub 1991: ch. 3). Third, the analyses of those such as Wittgenstein, Austin
and Searle remain particularistic and hence they fail to develop a general
theory of language games (Habermas 1984: 354).

Recalling Habermas's critique of Durkheim, we can characterize communicative action as a 'switching station for the energies of social solidarity'
(Habermas 1987: 57). We are bound together by the rationally motivating
force of communicative reason that is embedded in the background to our
everyday utterances:

The concept of communicative rationality does not just apply to the processes of intentional consensus formation, but also to the structures of a state of pre-understanding already reached within an intersubjectively shared lifeworld. The latter demarcates in the shape of a context-forming horizon the respective speech situation; at the same time, as an unproblematic and prereflexive background it plays a constitutive role in the achievement directed toward reaching understanding. Lifeworld and communicative action thus relate to one another in a complementary fashion.

(Habermas 1991: 223)

In relation to a theory of rationalization, if communicative reason holds across societies, then it represents a form of rationality that cannot be viewed as a subsystem of purposive rationality (the Weberian problematic). Instead, the point of reference becomes 'the potential for rationality found in the validity basis of speech' (Habermas 1984: 339). Communicative action can also be examined in terms of how it 'mediates between the ritually preserved fund of social solidarity and existing norms and personal identities' (Habermas 1987: 77). This is the very realm upon which the reproduction of society and social relations is dependent.

Despite these arguments we are still left with a fundamental question. If this is the basis for the lifeworld, how is it that its potential has not reached fruition? We witness conflict and misunderstanding as much, if not more, than we see consensus and understanding. Clearly, does Habermas not intend to furnish us with yet another idealist social theory and wishes to retain Marx's critical spirit, if not the substance of his work. This is where the relationship between the system and lifeworld enters his formulations.

The uncoupling of system from lifeworld

From an evolutionary perspective, to chart the space that is now occupied by communicative reason, Habermas poses the following hypothesis: the socially expressive and integrative functions within society which were once part of ritual are now performed by communicative action. A 'linguistification of the sacred' has occurred over time which may be expressed in the following manner:

the authority of the holy is gradually replaced by the authority of an achieved consensus. This means a freeing of communicative action from sacrally protected normative contexts. The disenchantment and disempowering of the domain of the sacred takes place by way of a linguistification of the ritually secured, normative agreement; going along with this is a release of the rationality potential in communicative action. The aura of rapture and terror than emanates from the sacred, the spellbinding power of the holy, is sublimated into the binding/bonding force of criticizable validity claims and at the same time turned into an everyday occurrence.

(Habermas 1987: 77)

Given this, Habermas can maintain that any analyses of modernity in terms of instrumental rationality are bound to be limited. Furthermore, if the use of language involves particular claims to validity which, under given social conditions, may be resolved by a consensus based upon such reason, then the potential exists to reach human understanding under the umbrella of an incomplete, but highly modified, Enlightenment project. At the same time, however, in terms of a theory of human action, we have seen that he must distinguish between communicative and strategic action so that the potential of the former is realized and that he does not commit the error of reducing all human action to the latter.

At this point Habermas emphasizes that there is not, as Weber had maintained, a state of competition between two modes of action in the lifeworld – one being oriented to success and the other to understanding. Instead, the competition exists between

principles of societal integration – between the mechanism of linguistic communication that is oriented to validity claims – a mechanism that emerges in increasing purity from the rationalization of the lifeworld – and those de-linguistified steering media through which systems of success-orientated action are differentiated out.

(Habermas 1984: 342)

Two domains now appear. This is a dualism that views social integration as part of the lifeworld and system integration as part of the system. In order to consider this further, he turns to the ideas of Parsons and Luhmann; although not without criticism (see Habermas, 1987; Holub 1991). In the process he furnishes us with a theory of social change that sees an increasing 'uncoupling' of the system from the lifeworld. System reproduction and the differentiation of more and more autonomous organizations increasingly rely not upon communicative action, but what Habermas (1987: 154) terms the 'delinguistified media of communication'. Normative consensus is replaced by the non-normative regulation of individual decisions which extends beyond the consciousness of individual actors (Habermas 1987: 117).

According to these formulations, society must comprise both system and lifeworld. If accepted, the question is how to connect the two? For Giddens it rests on duality, for Parsons on the system and for those such as Mead, Garfinkel and Schutz, on the lifeworld. For Habermas, we need both in order to explain the evolution of societies. Society becomes a system that has to fulfill conditions for the maintenance of sociocultural lifeworlds. The formula – societies are systematically stabilized complexes of action of socially integrated groups ... may stand for the heuristic proposal that we view society as an entity that, in the course of social evolution, gets differentiated as a system and as a lifeworld.

(Habermas 1987: 152)

The thesis is that as new systems emerge over time, they are increasingly separate from those structures which contribute to social integration. As social systems become more differentiated, they rely less on structures of social integration and more on systemic mechanisms that are not anchored in the lifeworld. The result is norm-free objectified structures. The consequences for the lifeworld and the individuals who comprise it are clear:

in modern societies, economic and bureaucratic spheres emerge in which social relations are regulated only via money and power. Norm-conformative attitudes and identity-forming social memberships are neither necessary nor possible in these spheres; they are made peripheral instead.

(Habermas 1987: 154)

Yet, as noted before, the transmission of culture and socialization relies upon the domain of communicative action. This cannot take place through the mediums of power and money. The result is that the processes of commercialization and bureaucratization generate 'disturbances, pathological side effects in these domains' (Habermas in Dews 1992: 172). Again, the consequences are apparent:

The reproductive constraints that instrumentalize a lifeworld without weakening the illusion of its self-sufficiency have to hide, so to speak, in the pores of communicative action. This gives rise to a structural violence that, without becoming manifest as such, takes hold of the forms of intersubjectivity of possible understanding.

(Habermas 1987: 187)

The reification of consciousness does not then arise, as it does for those trapped in the tradition of Cartesianism, from the forward march of instrumental rationality. Instead, it derives from the ways in which the norm-free and purposively rational co-ordinating mechanisms of system reproduction continually undermine the potential of communicative reason, aimed at social integration, within the lifeworld. The material conditions for undistorted communication therefore remain absent due to the distorting effects of money and power as exemplified by increased state intervention into the operation of capitalist societies – a phenomenon that orthodox Marxism is not able to satisfactorily analyse.

Summary

To return us to Weber's problematic with a Marxist edge, while rescuing the potential of critical theory from the clutches of the subject–object dualism in social thought via an analysis of language use, is a formidable task. Habermas stands as a defender of a foundationalist social theory, via a modified Enlightenment project, in a world which has allegedly become subject to the process of postmodernization.

Habermas reaches back in time to construct an evolutionary social theory which argues for a normative basis in the lifeworld. The result is that our everyday utterances, as a matter of course, raise claims which are open to consensual validation. Communicative reason is then seen to form the bedrock of social relations. As such, there is potential where Weber found only fatalism and the possibility of consensus where Marx found only instrumentality.

Habermas formulates a basis for critical theory in the very structures of language itself. This places him at odds with Adorno. For Adorno under the influence of the literary theorist Walter Benjamin (1991) high art, rather than empirical studies, became 'the last refuge of critical practice in a world completely dominated by total administration' (Aronowitz 1992: 308). He became increasingly anti-scientific and rejected any attempt to grasp social totality in the name of reason. Habermas, through his extensive excavations accompanied by considerable theoretical power, may thus be characterized as having saved critical theory from its retreat into negativism.

Issues in the theory of communicative action

Habermas's work is so rich and wide-ranging that it should come as no surprise that there is a great deal to choose from in the way of critical commentary that stems from a variety of disciplines. In this section we wish to consider a core issue in his work which illuminates our central theme of the relationship between action and structure. More specifically, this concerns his utilization of systems theory.

For Zygmunt Bauman, Habermas provided a source of inspiration, until, that is, he turned to a 'positivistic re-hashing of Parsons' (Bauman 1992: 217). Further, in what is one of the most telling critiques of Habermas's use of systems theory by an otherwise sympathetic critic and translator, Thomas McCarthy concludes:

> Habermas once criticized Marx for succumbing to the illusion of rigorous science, and he traced a number of Marxism's historical problems with political analysis and political practice to this source.

The question I have wanted to pose here is whether in flirting with systems theory he does not run the danger of being seduced by the same illusion in more modern dress.

(McCarthy 1991:139)

Niklas Luhmann has also claimed: 'there are far too many grounds and arguments ... when it has not been very precisely determined in advance what is relevant and what is not ... communication can, in actual fact, not lead to anything' (Luhmann quoted in Brand 1990: 120). Similarly, Brand (1990) rejects Habermas's position because of his hostility to empirical research and deductive logic. Yet Habermas has been successful in using empirical research in linguistics and moral development to explicate his social theory. His 'speculative' epistemology actually retains strong ties to empirical science, which is one reason he cannot follow a strictly Marxist ideology.

The central tenets of the 'project of modernity' are the ideals of rationality and progress which Habermas attempts to formalize as practical achievements. Yet these ideals must be put into a darker context. As the predecessors at the Frankfurt School in 1949 saw and Zygmunt Bauman (1989) powerfully narrates, the Holocaust provides a devastating critique of Enlightenment legacy and thought and highlights the danger of slipping into a barbarism anticipated by Nietzschean nightmares. For example, on one level, Hitler's regime in Germany merely refined and perfected nineteenth century techniques of social discipline. On yet another level, Hitler's regime was a deliberate throwback to an archaic 'society of blood', a society of savagery with a lust for domination, control and power; a society which raises further disturbing questions about the Enlightenment project. We have seen periodic episodes of inhumanity which have ranged from genocide to 'ethnic cleansing'. Habermas (1984) universalizes narratives of communicative action in a world which illuminates many differences between states, cultures and ideologies.

Habermas's work is based on a concern with rethinking the tradition of critical theory and German social philosophy and he has advanced that tradition in distinctive ways. Rationality, freedom and justice are not just theoretical issues to be explored and debated, but they are practical tasks that demand commitment and achievement. Habermas's entire work aims to defend and continue the Enlightenment project against the challenge of instrumental rationality and the 'will to power' (Delanty 2001).

We have seen that Habermas uses the insights of systems theory to make a series of distinctions between communicative and purposive rationality or, expressed in another way, between communication and power. However, this begs questions. First, does the use of systems theory for this purpose actually undermine the aims of critical theory? Second and relatedly, does this distinction fail to see the ways in which the lifeworld itself is regulated by power as opposed to some normative consensus?

It has been argued that if we are to explain macrosocial phenomena, then simple recourse to actors' intentions for explanatory purposes is inadequate. However, as Giddens has argued in recognizing the importance of analysing the unintended consequences of social action, it does not follow that functionalism, in its attribution of teleology to social systems, has a monopoly over this analytic sphere. Nevertheless, in order to maintain his distinction between system and lifeworld, Habermas uses not only Parsonian functionalism, but also the works of Luhmann (1982) who argues that with the increasing complexity of society, it is the 'system' which possesses its own rationality and this is separate from the rationality of the interacting subjects who comprise it.

With the introduction of this distinction, the potentiality of communicative reason is assumed to be preserved against the encroachment of strategic action. However, is this satisfactory? Reason, rooted in the structures of language within the lifeworld, is viewed as a final arbitrator. What we then witness is the increasing encroachment of system rationality upon the lifeworld to such an extent that the societal sphere of the communicative lifeworld shrinks significantly. We are then left wondering how so much might be invested, for the purpose of generating a viable critical social theory, in something which has been so successfully reduced by the forces of systemic power?

For the purpose of analytic illumination, we can approach this issue in another way. The theoretical utilization of systems theory enables us to create a duality between an independent lifeworld and the operation of power. However, for Axel Honneth, writing in the tradition of critical theory, this is a 'fiction' which

> results not only from Habermas's evolution-theoretic explanations of the emergence of modern societies in terms of the uncoupling of system and lifeworld but also from the terminological constraints into which he falls with his distinction between two forms of integration of social action.
>
> (Honneth 1991: 299)

This distinction between two forms of social action – action oriented to success and action oriented to understanding – is highly problematic. Paradoxically, it permits criticisms from two different angles. First, from neo-functionalist approaches to social relations which regard Habermas as still being trapped in Marxist notions of 'contradictions', only this time between the system and lifeworld, while remaining insensitive to cultural influences in the desire to locate a new basis for universal reason (Alexander et al. 2004).

A second basis for critique comes from writers such as McCarthy (1991), Honneth (1991) and Joas (1993) where we find the argument that this dualism cannot be maintained through the utilization of systems theory. The result is that the concrete struggles of groups of people within their everyday lives, against the continuing encroachments of purposive rationality, become surrendered to a domain which is assumed to be separate from the exercise of power. To attribute a self-maintaining purposive-rationality to material reproduction, separate from the activities of those who comprise it, actually loses the very power of insight that Marx possessed: that is, to critique supposed natural systems as human constructions which are symptomatic of a particular mode of production within a given epoch.

McCarthy puts this general argument in a slightly different form. Luhmann's separation between politics and administration permits a distinction to be made between procedural decision-making and the legitimacy which is required to ensure its mass support. One is viewed as goal motivated, the other providing the legitimacy for its effective functioning. In following Habermas's argument, the political system, as the producer of mass loyalty, takes precedence over the communicative process in which values and norms are formed (McCarthy 1991: 127). If we empirically examine the relationship between the informal and formal aspects of an administrative system, the interactions within it cannot be simply explained through reference to the functionally co-ordinated activities of its members which are seen as oriented towards collective goals. This is often found expressed in terms of what is deemed 'functional' for system maintenance.

Recognition of this tension is evident in Habermas's work. Despite this, he still maintains that 'action within organizations falls under the premises of formally regulated domains of action' (1987: 310). However, the achievement of social integration in organizations may equally be achieved through interactional threats or fear of sanctions and the giving and taking of orders (McCarthy 1991: 130). To attribute this role to system integration, by theoretical fiat, fails to see how organizations are co-ordinated in social, as well as system, terms:

> All of this is meant merely to say that system integration and social integration, as they are defined by Habermas, seem to be extremes rather than alternatives that exhaust the field of possibilities: the denial of one does not entail the other ... Moreover, if softened to correspond to the differences in methodological perspectives, it seems clear that most, if not all, domains of social action can be looked at in both ways.
>
> (McCarthy 1991: 130)

A similar critique of the system–lifeworld distinction is made by Nancy Fraser (1989). She argues that the idea of non-normative and non-consensual co-ordination of action through systems is not tenable. Indeed, however dubious the nature of consensus might be or the status of the norms invoked in the course of interaction, 'virtually every human action context involves some form of both of them' (Fraser 1989: 117). From this point of view, strategic action is neither analytically, nor practically, distinct from a horizon of shared meanings and norms. In the workplace, for example, the co-ordination of actions will take place against the presumption of normative consensus: 'Thus, the capitalist economic system has a moral-cultural dimension' (Fraser 1989: 118).

Fraser goes on to argue that we cannot hold human actions as being devoid of a strategic component. The dichotomies – between labour and interaction and the system and lifeworld – while apparently mirroring empirical reality in terms of the lifeworld of familial relations and the systemic domain of paid work are, in fact, highly problematic when it comes to gender relations:

> Feminists have shown through empirical analyses of contemporary familial decision-making, handling of finances, and wife battering that families are thoroughly permeated with, in Habermas's terms, the media of power and money. They are sites of egocentric, strategic, and instrumental calculation as well as sites of usually exploitative exchanges of services, labor, cash, and sex – and, frequently, sites of coercion and violence.
>
> (Fraser 1989: 119–120)

The restriction of power to systemic properties is thereby limited, for it does not capture the operation of power within the lifeworld itself. The distinction between the official economy (system) and family (lifeworld) is incapable of analysing the relationship between women's unpaid labour and the official economy. From this point of view, Habermas repeats the Marxist problematic of reducing reproduction to production.

Summary

Habermas's overall project is to escape from the philosophy of consciousness and ground critical theory in communicative action. In the process he seeks to avoid the idealism that is apparent in approaches to the study of language. Now, as we saw in relation to issues in Bourdieu's work, as soon as one admits of the role of power in language, any notion such as communicative reason departs in favour of viewing action in terms of the employment of the strategic resources at the disposal of actors oriented towards particular ends. Quite simply, it would not be the better argument that wins the day, but the deployment of power.

In view of the centrality of language in social life, we must question, given the above, the possibilities of ever reaching a position where discourse might be free from domination. However, this is not what Habermas actually says: 'People who impute this to me make it a bit too easy for themselves' (Dews 1992: 180). From an historical point of view, he argues that there are trends in world history that are witnessing the erosion of prejudices. That is certainly not to suggest that they do not exist, as a number of tragic events in recent times have made only too clear. What he argues is that the very use of language presupposes an ideal-speech situation as a regulative principle. This is very different from saying that it has a factual existence.

From a socio-theoretical and philosophical point of view, with a political project in mind, Habermas reaches back into the history of social and philosophical thought in order to critique the philosophy of the subject so that he might develop his notion of communicative reason. This also requires that, from the point of view of a 'discourse ethics', he examines the procedures through which this might be achieved. He refers to this as 'practical discourse'. As he so eloquently expresses it in his summary of the works of Albrecht Wellmer on this question:

> Like all argumentation, practical discourses resemble islands threat-ened with inundation in a sea of practice where the pattern of consensual conflict resolution is by no means the dominant one. The means of reaching agreement are repeatedly thrust aside by the instruments of force. Hence, action that is oriented toward ethical principles has to accommodate itself to imperatives that flow not from principles but from strategies necessities.
>
> (Habermas 1992c: 106)

This is a tall order given the saturation of social life by power effects and strategies. However, it is the interpenetration of the distorting effects of the system on the lifeworld that prevents the possibility of reaching such agreement.

We are left with a powerful theory of contemporary social relations. A theory that is a 'reconstructive science' whose aim is to examine our 'pre-theoretical' knowledge by seeking to 'isolate, identify, and clarify the conditions required for human communication' (Bernstein 1985: 16). We are also left with a thinker who argues that consensus might be achieved based on something called communicative reason, but only once the distorting effects of power are removed from everyday discourse; a thinker who argues that human emancipation is attainable only in a society which is rationally organized and that the conditions of such organization is the institutionali-zation of universally valid norms. As such, those social institutions which embody 'norms with a valid claim to universality are a necessary condition of human emancipation' (N. Smith 1993: 42).

The end result is a linguistically based critical social theory that is said to possess the potential to fuse indexicality with a pragmatic emphasis on practicality (McCarthy in Hoy and McCarthy 1994: 72). All of this takes place under the umbrella of a modified project of modernity that stresses the one-sided nature of social theories which concentrate on instrumental rationality to the exclusion of communicative reason. In sum, Habermas refuses to surrender the concept of transcendence, while remaining critical of such a conception, to the relativism of so much recent social and philosophical thought. There is nobility in Habermas's aim. To reconcile the competing claims of reason and the lifeworld, to look realistically yet optimistically at the heritage of modernity, these, in the end, are the great contributions of Habermas not only to the formulation of contemporary social theory, but also practical interventions in world problems.

Despite the undoubted power of Habermas's ideas, issues remain. In particular is Habermas's theorizing built on a conception of the world in which, surreptitiously, essentialist characteristics (e.g., 'middle class', 'white', 'males') dominate? It is a fact that the entire 'project of modernity' and associated discourses of rationality and progress have historically sided with men over women. The Enlightenment philosophizing was a language-based project that presumed women in an inferior position to that of men.

While Habermas's notion of emancipation is influential for feminists seeking a normative theory of consciousness and liberation, they reserve judgement on Habermas's theory of communicative action (McNay 2000; Stanley and Pateman 1991). They see it as gender blind, thereby perpetuating an Enlightenment tradition of male streaming analysis by reconstituting the project of modernity. On the other hand, the feminist philosopher Selya Benhabib (1986) has found in Habermas certain valuable elements that can provide the basis for a wide-ranging normative critique of contemporary society. Similarly, for Nancy Fraser (1989) there is a need to substantially modify his insights in order to be applicable to an analysis of gender relations and both she and Axel Honneth have formulated ideas on recognition in the spirit of critical theory (Fraser and Honneth 2003).

General critiques aimed at social theory for being gender blind are not simply applicable to Habermas. It should also be noted that he has consistently demonstrated his willingness to enter into discussions concerning his ideas, thus translating his own theories into personal practice (Eriksen and Weigard 2004). These are critiques that have been applied to social theory in general. Therefore, it is now necessary to examine the arguments and insights of feminisms.

9 Where did all the women go?

An argument was noted in Part I whereby social practices, and the production of social theory as part of those practices, exhibit a bias by reflecting interests and values associated with a masculine identity and perspective on social life. The result is that mainstream social theory, much of which we have covered so far, is said to represent a partial and incomplete view of society and social relations. Such is the power of this critique that any book which seeks to chart the contemporary terrain of social theory will be incomplete without due consideration being given to its main themes and ideas.

In Chapter 2 it was suggested that feminist theories can be divided into three broad perspectives. First, there are the works of those such as Wollstonecraft, informed by liberalism and individualism, for whom women's nature was rational and gender-neutral. From this point of view, femininity can be viewed as an artificial condition which subordinates women within a patriarchal culture. The implication is that women should become integrated within dominant modes of thought. This may be characterized as the integrationist perspective.

Within the second perspective, feminist theorists examine the basis of society and its social practices. This necessitates subjecting the history of social theory to critical scrutiny in terms of its production being shaped by masculine perspectives and experiences. Shunning liberal individualism, it is the social process of gender construction that becomes the object of its study: that is, the manner in which social relations confer meanings upon sexual differences. Its basis therefore is the ways in which patriarchal practices cause exclusion. As such, they cannot form the basis of an integrative strategy. We may term this perspective one of critique and exposure of bias. Quite simply, women cannot achieve equality on foundations set by men. Instead, what is required is a process of building a more adequate social theory through utilizing studies on women, by women, in order that their perspectives and experiences are recovered from the realms of marginality.

A third broad perspective exists which aims at the heart of the Enlightenment project itself. This does not seek to replace a masculine truth with the equal 'bias' of a feminine truth. Instead, it is argued that differences and diversities among women mean that there cannot be one essential category of woman, but multiple experiences, identities and truths; in other words, there are women. This is the perspective of postmodern feminisms:

> A postmodern feminism would reject the masculinist bias of rationalism but would not replace it with a feminist bias. Rather it would take the position that there is not one (masculine) truth but, rather, many truths, none of which is privileged along gender lines.
>
> (Hekman 1990b: 9)

The purpose of this chapter is to examine the second perspective and in the latter section it will introduce some of the ideas of the third, the basis of which will be clearer as we move on through Chapters 10 and 11. As will become evident, however, feminist theorists, as with social theory in general, do not automatically embrace postmodernism. On the contrary, many are highly critical of its arguments and presuppositions.

The development of feminist social theory

The second phase of feminist theorizing may be characterized in terms of deconstruction and reconstruction. Both of these strategies have profound implications for the ways in which we theorize about agency, structure, society and social relations. Deconstruction is understood to be an examination of the ways in which masculine perspectives inform and produce 'the most fundamental and most formal aspects of systematic thought in philosophy and in the social and natural sciences' (Harding and Hintikka 1983: x). The desired end being to reveal the ways in which such biases shape dominant modes of thought in everyday life. The reconstructive project, on the other hand, involves the identification of women's experiences which can then 'provide resources for the construction of a more representatively human understanding' (Harding and Hintikka 1983: x).

With a combination of the deconstructive and reconstructive modes in mind, we can focus upon an examination of social theory in terms of its biases and provide an account of the reconstruction of a more representative social theory. Therefore, we shall begin with an account of the issues associated with contemporary social theory and then move on to provide an overview of the development of modern feminist thought.

Where did all the women go?

Thus far, questions concerning the applicability of social theory for explaining and understanding the position of women in society have been raised without a detailed exposition of the arguments concerned. In this section, we explore these in more depth. As will become apparent, what we uncover is a systematic exclusion of women from the concerns of social theory due to an over-reliance upon partial modes of thought, that exist within society in general, that place men at the centre of its analytic foci.

The 'engendering of modernity' (Marshall and Witz 2004) is a project that captures the strategies of both deconstruction and reconstruction. At the level of deconstruction, the most influential social theories and theorists find themselves subjected to a number of criticisms; in particular, the manner in which the social world is divided into the realms of the public and the private. This is of significance if we trace it in the following manner.

With the growth of modernity, social theory has placed the socialized individual, as opposed to the pre-social autonomous ego, at the heart of its analysis. As we have seen throughout our journey, the idea of the social self and its relationship to society is central to this development. It is the very tensions between a socialized and pre-social individual and its ramifications for understanding and explanation that provides social theory with much of its dynamism. However, the social self is a gendered concept: that is, the very processes of socialization ascribe particular characteristics and modes of behaviour to individuals on the basis of their sex. This process, in turn, is based upon dominant normative standards. Differences in anatomy, for example, often assumed to be the most physical, as opposed to social aspects of the self, are constituted as meaningful in entirely different ways according to political relationships of male dominance (Millett 1992). The ramifications for gender relations as a whole, as well as the self-conception of women and men in particular, are clear. Yet the causes and effects of these insights are absent from much modern socio-theoretical discourse. Alternatively, when present, they are accounted for in a manner which owes more to dominant presuppositions than to analytic scrutiny.

The attribution of characteristics to social structure follows similar patterns. Take, for instance, an account of women's place in society according to traditional Marxist analysis. Here it is held that gender categories have arisen which may be explained through reference to class oppression. A one-way causal relationship between capitalism and the evolution of the family is thus posited such that the latter serves the needs of the former. However:

> The fact that the family continues to coexist with a capitalist economy does not prove it serves the latter, still less that it serves only the latter. All their coexistence proves is that the prior institution, the family, and the wage labour system, etc., are compatible. What does need to be stressed, however, since it seems not to be

evident to many authors, is that compatibility is necessarily mutual. Coexistence does not imply a hierarchical relationship, still less a one-way causality.

(Delphy and Leonard 1992: 33)

The manner in which the family affects capitalism, in terms of the constituent relations between men and women, is an equally important area of concern. Of course, this does not suggest that the subordination of women is without a material basis, simply that it is limited not to the means of production, but also to that of reproduction (Barrett 1988). Therefore, how social structure is theorized will inevitably affect the content of the theory itself. If social structure is conceived of in the absence of any gendered component then it will limit the analytic power of the theory. Given this, feminist theorists have preferred to conceive of social structure in terms of patriarchy, defined as the manner in which men as a social group exploit, dominate and oppress women as a social group (Walby 1990: 20).

This joint absence of considerations of gender relations – at the levels of the self and social structure and the relations between them – inevitably leads to gaps, or gaping chasms, in social theory. These points have been noted in relation to the works of Giddens, Bourdieu and Habermas, among others. What is argued to be reproduced in the texts of these and other authors are partial versions of society and social relations. To return to the public – private dichotomy, the very areas of social activity in which women participate appear to be absent on grounds which leave more to the realms of common sense than to the type of critical scrutiny that theorists reserve for other spheres of life. This point may be illustrated in relation to the world of work:

> We think of paid work as being work and exclude other kinds of work (housework, DIY and voluntary work) from our definition. We tend also to have a conception of paid work derived from an analysis of manual work in manufacturing industry, which was perhaps more appropriate to nineteenth century conditions than the present day. Workplaces are generally thought of as strictly demarcated from the home and family life. Similarly, we think of workers as people who leave home in the morning to travel to these workplaces and who work for a certain number of hours that has nothing to do with the home.
>
> (Beechey 1986: 77)

The above might well be an accurate characterization of paid work undertaken by men, but it is not useful for the purposes of understanding women's paid work (Beechey 1986: 78). Domestic work is viewed as a peripheral activity which is not directly related to economic issues and this may be traced in analyses relating to time, gender and the development of capitalism (Odih 2007). Giddens, for example, is open to the criticism that far from being peripheral to economic activity, as he has suggested, women are part of the fundamental process of 'producing people' and 'things' (Murgatroyd 1989: 156).

As noted in Chapter 5, while being refreshingly honest in meeting such criticisms, Giddens' suggestion that psychoanalysis is a useful paradigm for understanding the differences between men and women (Giddens 1989: 284) sits somewhat uneasily with his reservations concerning its general explanatory power. Given the centrality of an analysis of gender relations and a recognition of the need to explain the position of women in society in relation to power inequalities through their confinement to domestic contexts (Giddens 1989: 284), why is there an absence of any discussion of the gendering properties of social structure from a general theoretical analysis which places power at its centre?

A similar point can be made in relation to the work of Habermas. His distinction between system and lifeworld fails to account for the patriarchal aspects of both economic and administrative systems and thus the content and effects of the systemic operations of money and power as they apply to women. His 'colonization thesis' thus

> tends to replicate, rather than to problematize, a major institutional support of women's subordination in late capitalism, namely, the gender-based separation of both the masculine public sphere and the state-regulated economy of sex-segmented paid work and social welfare from privatized female childrearing.
>
> (Fraser 1989: 137)

Conceptions of agency and structure within contemporary social theory are found wanting when applied to women. Clearly, the very idea concerning how society is divided into different realms and by what causes and with what consequences, is a central issue for social theory. It requires problematization, as opposed to being bracketed by definitional fiat or even ignored altogether. That noted, the question is now begged as to what an adequate feminist social theory might consist of? The next section is therefore devoted to an outline of the development of feminist ideas with the caveat that the reader should be aware that this is highly selective. In order to commence this thematic overview, we shall start with Shulamith Firestone's (1988) critique of Marx and Engels. This work represents a distinct and radical development in social theory.

Bringing women back in: forging feminist theory

Firestone begins her study by noting that class analysis, particularly in the work of Engels (1942) is a 'beautiful piece of work, but limited' (Firestone

1988: 14). Indeed, the original division of labour between men and women was observed by Engels as based upon child-rearing. As such his 'outstanding achievement' was to see 'women's oppression as a problem of history, not biology' (Delmar 1976: 287).

Despite the potential of Engels' work, Firestone finds it limited because it rests upon the reduction of sexual class to the economic sphere. On the other hand, to concentrate on the psychosexual realm of human behaviour which underlies the economic sphere is also inadequate because it is ahistorical. In this way Firestone rejects both Marxist and Freudian accounts. Yet she also retains an explicit preference for a materialist theory of history in order to account for women's subordination. How does she overcome these apparent limitations? Firestone argues that there is a third way: 'we can attempt to develop a materialist view of history based on sex itself' (Firestone 1988: 15). How is this accomplished? The following is an outline of her argument.

Simone de Beauvoir spoke of women as the 'other'. Femininity is then constructed in terms of being all that the masculine is not:

> One is not born, but rather becomes, a woman. No biological, psychological, or economic fate determines the figure that the human female presents in society; it is civilization as a whole that produces this creature, intermediate between male and eunuch, which is described as feminine.
>
> (de Beauvoir in Humm 1992: 48)

In true existentialist fashion, de Beauvoir argued for a greater role of rationality in the lives of women in order that they might transcend their position in society. The book *The Second Sex* (1972) may thus be characterized as having two targets: one is male institutions and the other, as in Wollstonecraft's work, is women themselves (Crosland 1992).

Firestone's debt to de Beauvoir is apparent in her work. She writes of de Beauvoir's thoughts on representation whereby men describe the world: *'from their own point of view, which they confuse with absolute truth'* (de Beauvoir quoted in Firestone 1988: 148, original italics). However, as Marx and Engels had argued, Hegelian notions of 'transcendence' must be rooted in actual history. As one part of humanity (men) have transcended nature, for Firestone this cannot be the origin of women's oppression. Further, where de Beauvoir was clearly ambivalent concerning the potential of women's unification, Firestone displays fewer uncertainties. The reason is that she locates women's subordination in the power which men exercise over their reproductive potential:

> it was women's reproductive biology that accounted for her original and continued oppression, and not some sudden patriarchal revolution, the origins of which Freud himself was at a loss to explain ...

throughout history, in all stages and types of culture, women have been oppressed due to their biological functions.

(Firestone 1988: 74–75)

Not only is the dominant culture sustained in this way, but also women are alienated because of their reproductive capacity and the historical division of labour which surrounds child-rearing. It follows that women must recover the means over which their bodies are controlled in order to become liberated. New reproductive technologies provide the means as long as its power is utilized by women, for women. The works of Marx and Engels, for whom production, not reproduction, was paramount, is inadequate to this task. Male theories cannot contribute to this task because the basis of women's inequality lies in the control of their biology by men, not in economic relations. Where Marx and Engels spoke of proletarian revolt, Firestone now speaks of sexual revolution:

> not only the full restoration to women of ownership of their own bodies, but also their (temporary) seizure of control of human fertility ... just as the end of the socialist revolution was not only the elimination of the economic class privilege but of the economic class distinction itself, so the end of feminist revolution must be, unlike that of the first feminist movement, not just the elimination of male privilege but of the sex distinction itself.

(Firestone 1988: 19)

Ideas of this type are part of a whole body of radical feminist scholarship. Adrienne Rich (1980), for example, has been a central contributor to the development of lesbian theories. She speaks of 'compulsory heterosexuality' in order to signify how women's history, culture and values are distinct from the dominant patriarchal culture. Her use of the terms 'lesbian existence' and 'lesbian continuum' are not intended to supplant one set of compulsions for another, but to indicate that women lack choices in their sexual predispositions and emotional attachments. Similarly, Andrea Dworkin (1946–2005 focuses upon the exploitative nature of patriarchy where men not only exercise power over women, but also decide 'how women will suffer' (Dworkin 1987: 194). Along with Catharine MacKinnon (1988), Dworkin has been pivotal in the debate on pornography and the representation of women (see Tong 1989: 123).

In terms of Firestone's work, the question of whether an account of women's position within society might be adequately captured by an emphasis on biology has led feminist theorists to seek other explanations, but ones which might equally account for the pervasive nature of gender divisions within societies. Juliet Mitchell (1974), for instance, employs psychoanalysis for the purposes of developing her ideas within a Marxist historical framework. After Freud, Alfred Adler, Karen Horney and Clara

Thompson had all emphasized an environmental component to the growth of personality. In utilizing these insights, together with those of Althusser, Marx, Lacan and Lévi-Strauss, Mitchell aimed to explain the causes of women's oppression. In the process, 'woman' is not seen as a static category, but one which is historically located.

We may recall Althusser's argument that ideology 'flows through' the individual creating social and self-images. In addition, social structures are viewed as both autonomous and contradictory with the economic sphere being 'ultimately determining'. In Mitchell's work, the key structures in society become production, reproduction, sexuality and the socialization of children. Each of these is argued to play an important role in the unfolding of history. The problems of prioritizing any one of these elements is evident from the following quote: 'A modification of any of them can be offset by a reinforcement of another (as increased socialization has made up for decreased reproduction). This means that a mere permutation of the form of exploitation is achieved' (Mitchell 1971: 120).

Mitchell seeks to understand not only the social, political and economic forms of women's oppression, but also the realm of sexual ideology. Although men are exploited by the state and class society, women's oppression centres upon patriarchy and ideology. Freud's insights permit her to see how subjectivity is 'sexed', thereby linking power, identity and social practice within an overall explanation based on social structure. Social reforms, which seek equality of opportunity at a political level, are thus doomed to failure given that women's oppression is part of her collective psyche. The roots of women's inequality are thus seen as more complicated than Firestone's analysis would suggest.

Mitchell's utilization of Freud's work, involving as it does a focus upon the role of the unconscious, aims directly at Cartesian-based theories. Her concentration upon women's psyche is directly concerned with the nature of the mental representations that women carry with them. The emphasis is less upon biology, than the social construction of gender within a capitalist society. In this way, the family comes to occupy a central place on the analytic stage through forming part of the ideological superstructure.

Although the family found its economic function most aligned in peasant-based forms of production, over time a growing dislocation has occurred between the economic and ideological functions. The result is to place a particular burden upon women where the family becomes the centre of contradictions generated by a system that both promotes, yet destroys, individualism and private property: 'The housewife-mother is the guardian and representative of these' (Mitchell 1974: 161). The effects of this pressure upon women are clear and their causes apparent in a dual system of oppression:

It produces a tendency to small-mindedness, petty jealousy, irrational emotionality and random violence, dependency, competitive
selfishness and possessiveness, passivity, a lack of vision and conservatism. These qualities are not the simple produce of male
chauvinism. ... *They are the result of the woman's objective conditions
within the family* – itself embedded in a sexist society.

(Mitchell 1974: 162, original italics)

A psychoanalytic approach to gendering is also apparent in the works
of Nancy Chodorow (1978). However, it is the specific relationship between
the mother and the child in the pre-Oedipal stage that becomes of central
importance to identity formation and from there to cultural formation.
'Mothering', for example, within the family unit is of prime analytic concern
and the root of gender oppression. To put a complex argument as simply as
possible, focusing upon the pre-Oedipal stage, Chodorow contrasts a mother's identification with her daughter with the separation that takes place
between the mother and son, a process that is accompanied by the unconscious sexualization of this relationship by the mother. Despite a 'primary
love' for the mother by the son, at the Oedipus stage, he represses this desire.
The result is to be pushed out of the pre-Oedipal relationship into the realm
where the tie with the mother is severed and his love for her curtailed
through repression. This process is enabled by his being constituted as
'other'.

The overall result of this process for the male is one of individuation.
He achieves a defensive autonomy by the repression of his desires. The
female, on the other hand, continues with the pre-Oedipal phase for a longer
period and the mother experiences her as aligned, rather than differentiated,
from her own sense of self. The female child's experiences of merging and
separation at this stage thereby form an entirely different basis of personality.
Here we find an emphasis upon empathy and less of a differentiation of self
from the object-world.

These gender differences, between what we might term a 'concrete' and
'generalized' 'other', appear in social thought. The latter refers to the means
whereby 'we' consider what individuals have in common from a general set
of normative principles. The former, on the other hand, refers to a reverse of
the commonality-individuality process to 'view each and every rational
being as an individual with a concrete history, identity and affective-emotive
constitution' (Benhabib 1992: 159). With this in mind, alongside Chodorow's theories on personality formation, we have an explanatory resource
with which to approach the differences in perspective which exist between
men and women in relation to the social world. Here we are thinking, in
particular, of gender differences in ethical deliberations and actions as
encapsulated by the debate between Carol Gilligan and Lawrence Kohlberg
whose work, as noted, is utilized by Habermas (see Larrabee 1993).

Given the above, in both her elaboration and critique of the Freudian account, Chodorow develops powerful ideas on gender identification and formation. Her account reveals a sociological component which is informed by 'objects' in the world, including the mother, as opposed to being motivated by the Freudian concept of 'drives' where the idea of 'object' becomes arbitrary. The Freudian ahistorical component of self-formation is thus grounded in a manner that takes account of cultural context:

> This self is intrinsically social, and, because it is constructed in a relational matrix and includes aspects of the other, it can better recognize the other as a self and, ultimately, attain the intersubjectivity that creates society. This self's full historical grounding contrasts with that of the drive-determined individual. The grounding of the object-relational self derives from an appropriation and interpretation of experienced relationships and accordingly varies by individual, culture, period, gender, and so forth.
>
> (Chodorow 1986: 204)

The appeal of Chodorow's work, which has been very influential on the development of psychoanalytic feminisms, appears threefold. First, it offers an explanation of a woman's participation in her own repression without recourse to Freudian ideas on penis-envy, or via the invoking of a male norm. Second, it indicates that the participation of the father in child care may actually assist in the escape from gender-oppression and finally, there are her observations that women seem to gain little in the way of gratification from heterosexual relationships because men are not able to express intimacy due to their lacking the means for meaningful communication (Munck 2002).

The process of gender formation and its consequences for women does not necessitate a resort to psychoanalysis. Here one would turn the feminist gaze upon the process of knowledge production as being as important as that which is produced. If the process of knowledge production is itself exclusionary, so too will be its product or content with a corresponding effect on self-image. As Dorothy Smith puts it:

> The universe of ideas, images, themes – the symbolic modes that are the general currency of thought – have been either produced by men or controlled by them. In so far as women's work and experience have been entered into it, it has been on terms decided by men and because it has been approved by men.
>
> (D. E. Smith 1988: 19)

The exploration of these 'relations of ruling' occurs through a process of social construction (D. E. Smith 2005). The assumed universality of men's standpoint is consequential for the formation of culture, the result of which is the production of partial images, ideas and practices. In order to develop her notion of ruling interests, Smith utilizes ideas, in the process of which she posits a ruling class whose interests are served by this outcome. However, this does not take place on the lines suggested by Marx, for the resulting disjunctures between images, ideas and experiences have particular ramifications for women. These social forms of thought are then argued to be 'made for us by others, which come to us from outside, and which do not arise out of experience, spoken of and shared with others, or out of the need to communicate with others in working contexts' (D. E. Smith 1988: 55).

This, however, is not a model of hegemonic and intended manipulation by a ruling elite. Instead, it is 'a set of positions in the structures that "rule" (manage, administrate, organize, and otherwise control). These constitute the bases of common perspectives' (D. E. Smith 1988: 56). The public-private dichotomy is then viewed in terms of an increasing public sphere dominated by male interests and a diminishing private sphere occupied by women. The sphere in which women have the potential to draw links between their experiences, and the images and ideas through which they can make sense of them, is thereby institutionally limited.

Drawing upon phenomenological, ethnomethodological, Marxist and symbolic interactionist insights, without being constrained by the limitations of each, Smith argues that this whole process creates a 'bifurcated consciousness'. On one side there is the male, rational and neutral world. On the other is the subjective and emotional world of the female. Yet this is a gendered process. Therefore, to accept a phenomenological focus would be to prioritize the subjective side, but this is not conducive to a feminist social theory because it ignores the material and social bases which give rise to this process. Similarly, while Marxist categories are invoked for explanatory purposes these only serve, as with dominant modes of thought in general, to 'subordinate the actualities of the world' (D. E. Smith 1988: 86). For these reasons, the starting-point for analysis must be a woman's standpoint. Her bifurcated consciousness provides the very resources upon which new modes of thought can be constructed. Ontological exclusion is now employed in the service of epistemological correction as a strategy that is central to standpoint feminisms in general (Harding 1986; Hartsock 1983; Jaggar 1983).

If an examination of patriarchal relations of ruling is required to account for woman's location within society and her sense of self, this begs questions concerning the socio-structural composition of patriarchy itself. It is the means through which women are constituted not as subjects, but the 'other'; they are the objects, not the subjects, of discourse. They are not seen as having 'an autonomous source of knowledge, experience, relevance and imagination' (D. E. Smith 1988: 51). Yet if this is an important project for the development of feminist theory, mainstream concepts of structure are, once again, inadequate for this task.

The need to recast ideas on social structure has led those such as Delphy and Leonard (1992), Gibson-Graham (1996) and Walby (2005) to argue that class categories cannot be simply manipulated to incorporate women but must, instead, be subject to major critique and restructuring. Without such a project being undertaken, inequalities within the 'private' world of the family would be overlooked in the conceptual prioritization of the 'public' realm of work. Explanations for women's oppression would then be sought in the realms of sexuality and motherhood, rather than being seen as also rooted in the material advantages that men enjoy over women. Therefore, both the public and private dimensions need to be incorporated in a feminist account of social structure.

In these terms, the family should be seen as an economic system which itself generates inequalities: 'The family as a system in space and in time is a social institution which pre-exists them and sets parameters to their choices' (Delphy and Leonard 1992: 265–266). There exists what may be characterized as a dual system of production which involves both domestic and industrial components. Of central analytic interest is the position that women occupy in both spheres, without the prioritization of one over the other. For instance, one might emphasize the public sphere to the detriment of the private and thereby reduce gender to class relations.

With these arguments in mind, a distinction has to be made between degrees and forms of patriarchy. This dynamic form of analysis would allow for changes over time without committing oneself to the fallacy of uniform progress, the Marxist notions of regress and stasis or the radical-feminist positions of 'no change':

> Degrees of patriarchy refers to the intensity of oppression on a specified dimension, for instance the size of the wages gap between men and women. Forms of patriarchy refers to the overall type of patriarchy, as defined by the specific relations between the different patriarchal structures.
>
> (Walby 1990: 174)

Situating changing relationships in this way, between forms and degrees of patriarchy, allows for a diachronic approach that corrects for the synchronic tendencies of structuralism. The relationship between the public and private may then be analysed without resort to either sexuality or labour as determinant in the last instance. Instead, what we find is an examination of the relationship that occurs between six structures:

> the patriarchal mode of production; patriarchal relations in paid work; patriarchal relations in the state; male violence; patriarchal relations in sexuality; and patriarchal relations in cultural institutions including religions, media, education. In different times and

places some of the structures are more important than others. The elimination of any one does not lead to the demise of the system as a whole.

(Walby 1990: 177)

In this way, it is possible to conceive of forms of resistance to oppression, thereby avoiding the deterministic strands of structuralism. The production and reproduction of women's subordination is also historically understood and explained according to two main forms of patriarchy: the public and the private. The former views women's subordination as based upon structures which lie outside of the household unit and these take a collective form. Private patriarchy, on the other hand, has the analytic potential to view an individual man as the main beneficiary of the direct control of women within the household (Marshall and Witz 2004). At the same time, however, the maintenance of private patriarchy is enabled by the exclusion of women from the public arena: 'Patriarchal relations outside the household are crucial in shaping patriarchal relations within it. However, the effect is to make women's experience of patriarchy privatized, and the immediate beneficiaries are also located there' (Walby 1990: 178).

Structures, rationales, strategies and outcomes of actions are thus infused with male power. In addition, the means through which society and social relations, as well as science in general, conducts its studies and justifies its findings, are themselves part of the same process (Harding 2004). Therefore, when it comes to the conduct and products of social theory, it requires nothing less than deconstruction, followed by reconstruction. The next section illustrates, through example, how deconstructing gender can lead to new modes of analysis of reconstructing women's experiences based on the ageing body.

The body, gender and identity

There has been a critique of feminism which suggests that gender has missed articulating with other elements of social identity: for example, ageing. There has been an increase in body politics (Twigg 2000, 2006) but a lack of work relating gender to micro/macro, inside/outside, subject/object (McNay 2004). We do recognize that discussions of gender sometimes fall prey to the philosophical error of essentialism: that is, an appeal to meta-narratives that claim to capture universal processes underlying essential differences between men and women which are insensitive to local knowledge and diversity (Harper 1997). Rather, the body is like a hinge, a pivot point, between two realities. Grosz (1994) asserts that the body is neither, while being both. Some of these categories are inside/outside, subject/object, and active/

passive. It is not that older women are one way, while older men are the opposite. Bodies, whether of men or women, are both ways. It is primarily their relationship to power that makes them different. According to Shilling (1993), women are more likely than men to develop their bodies as objects of perception for others. The downside of this conscious embodiment of women is that as they age, they tend to lose a key asset, and thus come to think of themselves as invisible (Gilleard and Higgs 2005). Beauty and sexual allure are perishable values. The impact on negative identity of these diminished assets of female identity is undeniable.

Women may lose an asset in sexual politics as they age, but that eventuality does not necessarily mean that women are increasingly discontent with their bodies. Oberg and Tornstam (1999) tested the notion that women become more discontented with their body images as they grow older, as compared with men. When asked to agree or disagree with the statement 'I am satisfied with my body', they found that about 80 per cent of men agreed with that statement regardless of their age. Only about 65 per cent of young women agreed, however, and women in succeeding older decades of age tended to agree more with the statement until there was essentially no difference between men and women after age 65. It is younger women, not the older ones, who are the most dissatisfied with their bodies. These findings challenge the double marginality notion: that is, the interaction of gender and age.

There are theoretical models other than hierarchical and explicitly structural ones that are relevant for the study of ageing and gender. There can be insufficient attention, for example, to the ways in which gendered bodies have always enjoyed varying degrees of absence or presence in old age – in the guise of female corporeality and male embodiment. Indeed, there are discursive strategies whereby 'the body' and 'the social' are dissociated in the first place. In this framework, woman is saturated with, while man is divested of, corporeality. Older women have higher rates of chronic illnesses than do men and their bodies outlast those of men. In clinical settings, in old age, women outnumber men in nearly all waiting rooms. Male bodies animate the social: they appear for a fleeting moment, only to disappear immediately, in the space between 'corporeality' and 'sociality'. Thus, it is not simply a case of recuperating bodies into the social, but of excavating the gendered discourses whereby bodies are differently inscribed into and out of the social in the first place as highlighted above in general terms by such theorists as Firestone and Millet.

Feminists have underlined the limits of Cartesian thought which considered the subject as disembodied and, above all, asexual (Braidotti 1994; Longino and Powell, 2004). In the representation of the female body, the dichotomy between body and mind has been used to emphasize sexual difference. On the one hand, we have masculinity, which is defined in relation to the mind and the 'logos,' while the feminine is defined in relation to the body and its procreative function in an essentialist construction (Twigg 2006). As Adrienne Rich reminds us, women have had to deconstruct the patriarchal stereotype which links the female body with its procreative function: 'I am really asking whether women cannot begin, at last, to think through the body, to connect what has been so cruelly disorganized' (Rich 1976: 184).

With this incisive sentence, Rich (1976) stresses that women have to overcome the damning dichotomy between soul and body, in order to reappropriate their bodies and to create a female subject in which the two entities are complementary. Contrary to androcentric and Eurocentric philosophical traditions, feminist philosophical studies have emphasized that the body is a symbolic construct, located in a specific historical and cultural context. Women often find themselves defined as 'the other' (the residual category) against men, just as black people do so against white people and gay people do so against heterosexual people (Longino and Powell 2004).

Contemporary cultural representations of ageing focus on the body because this provides the clearest evidence of the historical inequality in gender differentiation. The body of woman is inscribed with oppressive ideological mystifications (Friedan 1965; Sontag 1991). Western literature and iconography are full of representations of old age as a woman with 'grey hair', 'withered', 'faded', 'pale and wan face', 'foul and obscene' (Friedan 1965). The old woman becomes a symbol of 'evil' and an allegory of time that completely corrupts everything. In *Portrait of an Old Woman* by Giorgione (1508–10), the devastation impressed on the curved figure, balding with few teeth and deep lines on her face, her eyes pervaded by sadness, acts as a reminder of the transience of beauty. It provides a terrible warning of what is to come, hence the scroll laid on one of her hands reads: 'with time' (Greenblatt 1980).

Summary

The practice of feminist theory may be characterized in the following manner. In the first place it necessitates an uncovering of the ways in which ideas contain, both overtly and covertly, misogynist perspectives. These may take subtle forms, but the strategy involves exposing how male values come to predominate and perpetuate particular views of the social and natural worlds. In the process it uncovers how silences and absences also structure ways of thinking about women.

From these deconstructive modes, we move on to its reconstructive elements. It is not sufficient to simply explain the relations of dominant modes of thought, but to then develop understandings of the ways in which partial representations of women suppress alternative identities that may be available to them. This strategy provides for women to be able to see themselves in a different way to the dominant conceptions that exist of their roles and places within social relations. Here, in particular, because feminist theories will not countenance a simple separation of the public from the private and questions the demarcation between nature and culture on a gendered basis, it possesses the power to threaten identities, as well as to create new ones.

From the above, feminist social theory develops the means to move beyond patriarchal thought. However, this requires the formation of alternative research programmes which recover women's perspectives in order to inform social, political and economic changes. In sum, as Elizabeth Grosz (1992) puts it, from whose work these characteristics are derived, feminist theory involves both a refusal of the props upon which patriarchal theory and practices sustain themselves, as well as a positive affirmation of the alternatives that are made available through such critiques.

Issues in feminist theory

In this section we wish to outline some of the issues which have informed debates within feminist theory. Our intention is to provide a further basis upon which to consider the insights of this very broad body of scholarship and to demonstrate that many of these not only mirror but also add a new dimension to our ways of thinking about the social world. Here we shall focus upon two aspects to these debates which are not mutually exclusive topics. First, the concept of patriarchy, and second, debates concerning essentialism in feminist theory.

Feminist theory is a project for positive change. If patriarchy is to be employed towards this end, it has to avoid the problems of structuralism where deterministic concepts have a tendency to rule the day. Within the development of feminist theory this concept has, as with structural ideas in social theory, been subjected to criticism for being ahistorical, deterministic and of little analytic utility by virtue of its abstraction (Barrett 1988). The result is that it is 'too specific an expression to describe very diffuse and changing forms of male domination' (Cockburn 1990: 98).

Patriarchy has the potential to be employed in feminist theory as a 'catch-all' to describe what is a diverse set of social relations. From its early use by Millett (1969) via the work of Spender (1980) through to Dworkin (1987) it may be read as an analytic monolith against which social 'reality' is not only to be explored, but then explained. For instance, take the work of Dale Spender. She holds that language creates reality and that language is produced by males, for males, as the dominant group within society. This is seen as an intentional process whereby the use of 'he' to refer to both sexes is regarded as a deliberate policy of exclusion and dominance. Clearly, language of this type can and does act in this way, but to consider this as intentional according to dominant and absolute criterion of patriarchy is highly problematic:

> Though the effect of the use of language may be to subjugate the female sex, it is ludicrous to suppose that every man who has ever used such language intended to do that by his use of it. Many men may have had every intention of not doing women down, yet they may still have done so, precisely because their language has an effect that is not apparent to them.
>
> (Assister 1983: 27)

This thesis does not adequately distinguish between the use of language and the utterance of particular words, while it is infused with idealism in the form: 'language makes reality'. The materialist version of this would be: 'reality makes language'. In this sense, patriarchal ideology would be held as either unconnected to economic conditions, or as directly reducible to them; the former taking no account of the material basis of women's oppression. The latter, on the other hand, opens up the issue of the 'unhappy' relationship between Marxism and feminism.

At this point Juliet Mitchell's work becomes of central importance in the development of feminist theory; in particular, her emphasis upon the psychic aspects of gender relations while, at the same time, exposing their historical and material constitution and potential for revision and change. This use of psychoanalysis and its relationship to women's self-image is of clear importance through allowing for the investigation of the representation of women in relation to the public organization of sexual structures (Coward 1982).

The fusion of Marxism and psychoanalysis to generate a theory of patriarchy is, however, problematic. Are its explanations context bound or universal? Quite simply, is psychoanalysis predicated on law-like generalizations, or is it sensitive to historical context? In contrast to Mitchell, if the former reading of Freud is taken, then it is incompatible with a theory that seeks to understand how particular historical structures limit women's potential. In this way, an unhappy relationship between psychoanalysis and feminism appears for two reasons. First, there is a tendency to repeat a determinism, only this time it takes a psychic form such that social relations are held to mirror their structure. Second, Mitchell's dual systems of ideology and capitalism views feminist struggles as taking place in the realm of ideology and a socialist struggle as taking place against capitalism.

The separation of these two spheres is highly problematic. Mitchell employs it in order to argue that the arrival of socialism will not end women's subordination and thus not to repeat the reductive trap of Marxism. However, to use Freud specifically, or in terms of a modified psychoanalysis in general, is still to risk 'psychic essentialism' (Segal 1987). What is then witnessed is a repeat of the structuralist tendencies of patriarchy, only this time in the unconscious, not the economy.

Issues such as these have opened up a debate in feminist theory over the utility of psychoanalysis (J. Rose 1990; E. Wilson 1990). As Elizabeth Wilson puts it:

> The last thing feminists need is a theory that reaches them only to marvel anew at the constant recreation of the subjective reality of subordination. ... Psychoanalysis is of interest in its account of sexual identity and its construction – indeed, in many ways it is fascinating. More useful to contemporary feminists may be theories of social change that speak to aspects of the self not harnessed to the Phallic taskmaster. To change the conditions of work – in the world and in the home – might do more for our psyches as well as for our pockets than an endless contemplation of how we came to be chained.
>
> (E. Wilson 1990: 224)

The debate over patriarchy has also taken another route with essentialist consequences. Take, for example, the work of Firestone (1988). She sought to replace the centrality of class as the motor of a materialist history. However, there are those who have taken this to the conclusion that 'sexuality is to feminism what work is to marxism' (MacKinnon 1988: 106). Accompanying radical feminist explanations of women's subordination, therefore, is a tendency towards biological determination such that the two sexes appear fundamentally incompatible. This can translate into the call for all women to become political lesbians (Leeds Revolutionary Feminist Group 1982).

Importantly, when it comes to political lesbianism as a variant of radical feminism, it should be noted that this does not necessarily mean alluding to biological essentialism to sustain its arguments. However, there is a clear tendency within aspects of feminist discourse to base arguments upon a particular view of the origins of women's oppression which is not only seen as universal, but determining. The problems of being ahistorical and taking no account of cultural differences within and between societies becomes, once again, apparent. The form of argument is reductionist whereby social and cultural factors are provided with biological causes (Grosz 1990). Quite simply, if biology is destiny, then perhaps we should abandon social explanations to physiology and anatomy?

Concerns of this type have led feminist theory to examine relations between men and women without recourse to the formulation of theoretical bases which have an absolute ontology, a series of indispensable attributes, or objective properties upon which all others depend (de Lauretis 1990). This is precisely the fault that has been found in mainstream theory; for it also resorts to so-called 'essences' in its working assumptions. We thus move from an 'old' essentialism whereby women were seen as inferior to men, to a 'new' essentialism that asserts the superiority of women (Martin 1994).

On these and other grounds radical feminism has been subjected to criticism. These critiques, however, also come from within this perspective. Audre Lorde, for example, criticized Mary Daly for her presentation of black women as victims, rather than seeing them as making a positive cultural contribution to their own history. Lorde's theoretical position is a fusion of Enlightenment rationality with an understanding of emotion derived from the experiences of African women. As this quote illustrates, women may share particular experiences, but this should not be placed at the service of a 'white' lesbian theory encompassing all experiences:

> The oppression of women knows no ethnic nor racial boundaries, true, but that does not mean it is identical within those differences. Nor do the reservoirs of our ancient power know these boundaries. To deal with one without even alluding to the other is to distort our commonality as well as our difference.
>
> (Lorde in Humm 1992: 139)

If biological explanations suffer from essentialism, so social explanations might fail to account for the ways in which people remain so firmly attached to their gender-identities. For Brenner and Ramas (1990) the relationship between the social and the natural must be incorporated into feminist theory in order to account for this ubiquity. Nevertheless, questions are still begged as to the idea of 'woman'. It is here that one detects a clear movement in feminist theory towards rethinking ideas on the 'self'. This has consequences for the formulation of patriarchy as a useful explanatory device; to say nothing of the direction and nature of feminist politics.

According to Andrea Dworkin, men's violence at physical and symbolic levels is a key determinant of the inequities and inequalities of gender relations, both disempowering and impoverishing women. Yet, men's 'natural aggression' is often invoked as a defining characteristic of an essential gender difference and as an explanation for the gendered hierarchical arrangements in the political and economic lives of richer and poorer countries alike. Gender inequality is responsible for, and expressed in, the different articulations of the global 'feminization of poverty' (F. Williams 1993). Women represent approximately 70 per cent of the 1.3 billion poor people in the world (Beneria and Bisnath 1996: 6). Compared with men, girls and women are most likely to be undernourished, and girls and women are most likely to be receiving less health care. Out of approximately 900 million illiterate adults in the world, 66 per cent are female (Powell 2007). The solution is to challenge patriarchal power, violence and control; a struggle to gain female control over their bodies, sexuality and intellectual ideas.

Both patriarchy and capitalism are the source of women's problems. The approach places a strong emphasis on the historical nature of female oppression and the way it changes over time and between social classes. Men as a group gain real and large advantages from current system of gender relations; the scale of this 'patriarchal dividend' is indicated by the fact that men's earned incomes, world-wide, are about 180 per cent of women's (Connell 2007). The solution is a critique of and challenge to patriarchal capitalism that reinforces women's role as 'dependent' unpaid carer and low-paid workers. 'Caring' should be socialized and the sexual division of labour challenged.

The self in feminist theory has travelled through periods of autonomy, selfhood and determinism and provided a basis upon which to evaluate patriarchal practices according to women's latent potential. This has witnessed a movement through the agency–structure debate which, in the terms presented above, has travelled through patriarchal concepts based on sex, gender, psychoanalysis and the economy, in order to make sense of the public–private divide. New ideas then enter the terrain of feminism because analyses of this type are seen to take place against the backdrop of modernity with its fixed ideas of the self: for example, power belongs to a class (men) and is exercised by them over women as a class. However, if we see individuals as the vehicles of power and as constituted by its effects, this whole edifice begins to crumble:

> The individual is not to be conceived as a sort of elementary nucleus, a primitive atom, a multiple and inert material on which power comes to fasten or against which it happens to strike, and in so doing subdues or crushes individuals. In fact, it is already one of the prime effects of power that certain bodies, certain gestures, certain discourses, certain desires, come to be identified and constituted as individuals. The individual, that is, is not the vis-à-vis of power; it is, I believe, one of its prime effects.
>
> (Foucault 1980: 98)

As with some developments in social theory, there are feminisms which have moved into these realms in the pursuit of explanations. If the techniques of power are not attributable to a particular group and are transmitted and exercised throughout the social body, any idea of essential subjectivity is called into question. The projects of deconstruction and reconstruction, as part of Enlightenment thought itself, may then be jettisoned, leaving the critical gaze of a new feminism to be turned against what is seen as outmoded forms of thought. Nevertheless, this is not a linear progression; far from it. As a result, debates exist within feminist thought between what we have characterized as the second perspective and postmodern feminisms, with contributions by those who seek to move beyond the political paralysis implied by the latter (Landry and MacLean 1993). Black feminists have, however, criticized historical problems of globalization, racism, imperialism and international division of labour as alongside gender and social class (Williams, 1994). Social theory is very much bound up as reinforcing racism and imperialism as many feminisms ignore and do not include the experiences of black women.

Summary

Ideas of the self, agency and social structure have been criticized and reconstructed in order to provide for an adequate explanation of the position of women in society. The result is an extraordinary growth in feminist scholarship since the mid 1960s. This journey has witnessed an array of ideas through its encounters with Marxism, psychoanalysis and phenomenology – to name but a few.

The response to this intellectual journey, by women and men, often takes a reactionary form, including from people who consider themselves broad-minded. This appears to be an inevitable feature of any body of ideas which question the status quo. However, feminisms add an important dimension to this process: they also aim at intimacy and what are assumed to be the most 'personal' aspects of people's lives. This derives from their focus upon the public–private divide not as some commonsensical manifestation of a natural process, but a socially constructed topic to be investigated in terms of its ramifications for women's places and identities within society. Ideas on selfhood and identity, thereby fuse with power, social structure and sexuality.

At the same time this may be evaluated as a project within modernity. This, as noted before, is seen to possess the potential not simply to liberate, but also to stifle. First-wave feminism was to be informed by the liberal individualism of the Enlightenment and second-wave feminism was to turn its analytic tools into those which could be used by women, for women. However, a new perspective was to develop which found their underlying ideas on the self, culture and body to be problematic.

These changes are mirrored within mainstream social theory with a turn towards new ideas. For many, these ideas represent a negation, not a celebration, of the aims of feminism. In light of these arguments and insights, therefore, Chapters 10 and 11 are devoted to an examination of poststucturalism, with reference to the work of Michel Foucault and postmodernism. In each of these, issues will be raised with regard to agency and structure and both will contain references to the ways in which these ideas have been utilized by feminist theorists.

10   The making of the modern subject

The thematic continuity for understanding contemporary social theory in this book has been the relationship between agency and structure in the unfolding of modernity. For some, modernity is an 'attitude' which orientates thinkers in particular ways. Yet in one way or another, all contemporary social theories have challenged aspects of these background assumptions; in particular, the concept of the autonomous ego who stands at the core of the social universe. In the history of ideas presented here, this tendency has been traced back to Hume.

Despite modifications to the idea of the self, it is argued that from the Enlightenment onwards social thought has exhibited a movement away from an analysis of representations towards an analytic: 'From Kant on, an analytic is an attempt to show on what grounds representation and analysis of representations are possible and to what extent they are legitimate' (Dreyfus and Rabinow 1982: 28).

Michel Foucault (1992) characterizes this as the desire to achieve a correspondence between reality and the language which describes that reality, from whose propositions an ahistorical and normative basis for ways of life may be derived. In practice, differences between cultures can then be judged according to reason and the authenticity of any dialogue is based upon the participants' abilities to reach a particular standard. However, as has been noted, the power of reason is double-edged: in its judgements it can also exclude on the basis, for example, of race and gender.

The end result of this desire is that we have become both the subjects and objects of knowledge. According to this view the beginnings of the human sciences are not seen to be the result of a need to address some 'scientific' problem which demanded analysis, or some 'pressing rationalism', but the decision to include people among the objects of science occurred 'when man constituted himself in Western culture as both that which must be conceived of and that which is to be known' (Foucault 1992: 345). We should look upon this as 'an event in the order of knowledge' (Foucault 1992: 345).

As abstract as this may at first appear, it is of central importance for understanding contemporary ideas and practices. Therefore, it is for good reason that Habermas (1986) entitles one essay on Foucault's thought 'Taking Aim at the Heart of the Present'. Suspending, for the moment, a discussion of the relative merits of these arguments, the point is that Foucault has offered us a new perspective on society and social relations. For this reason, his work is worthy of inclusion in this tour of modern social theory. Given this, we shall first consider the intellectual influences on his ideas and the development of his thought and then outline some of the issues which his work raises for understanding social life.

Michel Foucault: against (and in) modernity

From our discussions in Part I, we can take two broad positions in relation to 'truth'. First, truth is ahistorical, and second, truth is constituted in history. If we take the second, however, we often attribute the history of ideas, discoveries and inventions to individuals. The idea of the 'individual' is then 'fixed', while the individual's actions are understood and explained within the flux of history. The result is that the individual appears to transgress historical context. In this way we can read work in terms of the 'true' subject in history eventually revealing itself in an historical ending: communism. In the mean time, the potential of the individual is stifled due to the exploitative effects of capitalism. The humanist and structuralist elements in Marx's work are thereby juxtaposed in an uneasy tension. For Weber, on the other hand, history had no laws and the subject was simply enjoined to act responsibly in the face of historical uncertainty.

With this theme in mind, we have another approach to the history of social theory through the conceptualization of the subject. On the one hand, there stands the isolated individual whose excavations over history will eventually reveal a truth lying within it. On the other hand, knowledge is regarded as historically located. Attempted resolutions to this paradox, aside from that of Marx, have also been considered in relation to Husserlian phenomenology and Saussure's structuralism. The latter 'dissolved' the subject as the rules of language gained analytic and ontological primacy over a phenomenological emphasis upon the attribution of meaning to social reality on the part of a transcendent individual.

In essence, it was within the analytic space of this problematic that Foucault worked: 'my problem has always been ... the problem of the relationship between the subject and truth' (Foucault 1991b: 9). Nevertheless, we find a very different emphasis from previous perspectives and it is this that causes difficulty in situating Foucault. For instance, consider his approach to the work of Kant. Foucault historically situates Kant in terms of his ideas being a response to a particular problem at a point in time. Kant then derived an elaborate defence of the critical capacity of reason, as well as a formulation of its limits, in the face of uncertainty. Yet despite this, it results in a mode of thought which is assumed to be universally applicable. We need to ask what are the major works that impinged on Foucault's understanding of modernity and reflexive shaping over the period of his early and latter theorizations about self, subjectivity and power. This provides the contextual backdrop to the conceptual tools for social theory that Foucault provides. With this historical legacy in place, what we should then examine is an

> analysis of ourselves as beings who are historically determined, to a certain extent, by the Enlightenment. Such an analysis implies a series of historical inquiries that are as precise as possible; and these inquiries will not be oriented retrospectively toward the 'essential kernel of rationality' that can be found in the Enlightenment in any event; they will be oriented toward the 'contemporary limits of the necessary,' that is, towards what is not or is no longer indispensable for the constitution of ourselves as autonomous subjects.
>
> (Foucault 1984: 43)

What analytic tools does Foucault use for this purpose? Once we have examined these, we can then consider his arguments on power and the subject. Unless otherwise stated, all references in the following two sections are to works by Foucault.

Beyond structuralism and hermeneutics

In order to situate Foucault's thinking, we need to understand the background against which he formulated his views. If we return to an earlier discussion on the intellectual climate in post-1945 France, two views emerge in relation to Husserlian phenomenology. First, structuralism, and second, a hermeneutics which did not resort to the transcendental subject, but argued that the source of meaning production should be sought in the social practices and texts which are fundamental to human activity. For the purposes of this section, we may trace this latter intellectual lineage from Heidegger. In the process, we shall be required to consider the generation of meaning without reference to an autonomous subject and to utilize the idea of discourses without allusion to underlying rules of structure. In other words, we have to move beyond the limitations of structuralism and hermeneutics in order to develop an 'interpretive analytics' (Dreyfus and Rabinow 1982).

The fusion of these different ideas in Foucault's work results in an approach to the history of thought that is freed 'from its subjection to transcendence' (1989: 203). In this journey we are also required to take two further steps. First, the relationship between the subject and truth should be viewed as an effect of knowledge itself. As Foucault put it:

> what if understanding the relation of the subject to the truth, were just an effect of knowledge? What if understanding were a complex, multiple, non-individual formation, not 'subjected to the subject', which produced effects of truth?
>
> (Foucault in Elders 1974: 149)

Knowledge should not, therefore, be viewed as 'theoretical' separate from the realm of 'practice'. Instead, knowledge becomes a practice which has the effect of constituting particular objects – non-theoretical elements – which are part of practice itself. Similarly, the theory of knowledge and the subject of knowledge become fused and the subject and truth are not related in the ways suggested earlier, but are seen as part of a relationship between knowledge and power that is socially constructed (Gutting 2003):

> The important thing here, I believe, is that truth isn't outside power, or lacking in power: contrary to a myth whose history and functions would repay further study, truth isn't the reward of free spirits, the child of protracted solitude, nor the privilege of those who have succeeded in liberating themselves. Truth is a thing of this world: it is produced only by virtue of multiple forms of constraint. And it induces regular effects of power. Each society has its of truth, its 'general politics' of truth.
>
> (Foucault 1980: 131)

What Foucault is doing here is rejecting certainty in social and political life and arguing that there is no universal understanding beyond history and society. In the process a 'history of the present' is written, according to which history is not excavated to reveal a deeper meaning but, instead, is viewed as a 'battleground' between relations of power. Now this begins, albeit in a different guise, to look like structuralism: that is, to view events as manifestations of a deeper, underlying reality. How is this issue tackled in his work?

In commentating on those who have labelled him a structuralist, Foucault writes: 'I have been unable to get it into their tiny minds that I have used none of the methods, concepts, or key terms that characterize structural analysis' (1989: xiv). Fine! Beyond assertion, however, what are his justifications for this position? After all, the opening for the type of analysis we have considered so far occurred in Althusserian structuralism. Ideologies are seen as ways of constructing subjects and their perspectives on the world, all of which takes place against the backdrop of a Marxist model of social reality.

The first point we might observe here is that Foucault eschews grand theoretical projects of the Althusserian type. Perhaps the most simple way to view his relationship with structuralism is by examining his analysis of historical 'events'. What we find here is a refusal to read historical 'events' as manifestations of deeper social structures, or as located on particular levels, accompanied by a focus upon the seemingly marginal as indicative of relations of power. Events are thereby seen to differ in their capacity to produce effects:

> The problem is at once to distinguish among events, to differentiate the networks and levels to which they belong, and to reconstitute the lines along which they are connected and engender one another. From this follows a refusal of analyses couched in terms of the symbolic field or the domain of signifying structures, and a recourse to analyses in terms of the genealogy of relations of force, strategic development, and tactics. Here I believe one's point of reference should not be to the great model of language (langue) and signs, but to that of war and battle.
>
> (Foucault 1980: 114)

If Foucault does not reach for structuralism, neither does he resort to grounds in the universal preconditions of human understanding (Heidegger). What he calls genealogy, following Nietzsche, is an analysis of cultural practices without a reference point outside of history itself. The motivating question underlying this approach is: 'What are we today?' (Foucault 1988a: 145). For it is history which makes us what we are and what we think of ourselves as being. This is a very different starting-point from, say, an analysis of the limits which are continually placed upon what is seen as our 'hidden' creativity as found in a critical social theory based in philosophical anthropology (Honneth and Joas 1988). The manifestations of such a project we have covered in relation to a 'dialectic of freedom' whose aim is to determine the good and bad elements in the Enlightenment. Genealogy, in contrast, does not involve a search for any 'origin':

> On the contrary, it will cultivate the details and accidents that accompany every beginning; it will be scrupulously attentive to their petty malice; it will await their emergence, once unmasked, as the face of the other. The genealogist needs history to dispel the chimeras of the origin.
>
> (Foucault 1984: 80)

We have come across other universal grounds for analysis through the employment of modified forms of reason; none more powerfully argued than by Jürgen Habermas. Yet the issues motivated by such an approach are still couched in terms of the ability to provide grounds for distinguishing between the true and the false, not in terms of the formation of truth itself. It is via this focus in Foucault's work that we uncover the legacy of Nietzsche.

Unlike Kant, Nietzsche did not ask what the grounds or basis for our knowledge was, but why knowledge was necessary in the first place. He argued that it was the belief we have in knowledge that is of importance, not whether it is true or false. This belief is seen to be indicative of a 'will to truth' which, as part of the 'will to power', involves the desire to affirm life as it appears to us. Truth now becomes inverted to be a fiction that is 'invented':

> What urges you on and arouses your ardour, you wisest of men, do you call it 'will to truth'? Will to the conceivability of all being: that is what I call your will! You first want to make all being conceivable: for, with a healthy mistrust, you doubt whether it is in fact conceivable. But it must bend and accommodate itself to you! Thus will your will have it. It must become smooth and subject to the mind as the mind's mirror and reflection. This is your entire will, you wisest men; it is a will to power; and that is so even when you talk of good and evil and of the assessment of values.
>
> (Nietzsche in Hollingdale 1977: 224)

With the Nietzschean turn in place, the object of Foucault's analyses became the production of discourses that provide justifications for actions: 'my problem is to see how men govern (themselves and others) by the production of truth' (1991c: 79). With a focus upon how the truth is constructed in a manner that permits, from the point of view of practice, a distinction to be made between the true and the false, Foucault's use of language as an analytic resource becomes distinct from any we have come across before.

Thus far we have considered the role of language in social life in a number of ways: de Saussure's structuralism; as a 'form of life' (Wittgenstein) analysed in terms of speech-acts (Austin, Searle); a fusion of speech-act theory onto the problematic of rationalization (Habermas) and the relationship between utterance and institutional authority (Bourdieu). We could undertake genealogical analysis by, for example, examining the rules of language governing an utterance and then derive a set of rules which produced the utterance in the first place. Our results may then be transposed from context to context. Once again, however, Foucault throws a spanner into the works of these approaches.

Foucault's analysis of discourse does not contain the idea of knowledge production via a meaning-producing subject, or rules that govern speech-acts, nor an allusion to rationality that poses some absolute value in reason

(1991c). Given this, his approach cannot be situated within any of the above positions. Nevertheless, he sees discourses as a unity of statements in what is termed a 'discursive formation'. The question is: what provides their unity? Foucault rejects four possible answers to this question. First, that there is a well-defined field of objects to which they refer; second, that they possess a clear normative basis; third, that they possess what he calls an 'alphabet of notions'; and finally, that they are characterized by 'the permanence of a thematic' (1989: 37).

With these possibilities rejected, what we uncover is the existence of possibilities and differences in structures and rules. Where it does become possible to describe these 'systems of dispersion' in terms of objects, statements, concepts or themes that make up a 'regularity' then we may say:

> for the sake of convenience, that we are dealing with a discursive formation. ... The conditions to which the elements of this division (objects, mode of statement, concepts, thematic choices) are subjected we shall call the rules of formation. The rules of formation are conditions of existence (but also of coexistence, maintenance, modification and disappearance) in a given discursive formation.
>
> (Foucault 1989: 38)

In a description of the events of discourse the question then becomes 'How is it that one particular statement appeared rather than another?' (1989: 27). However, there exists the potential for terminological confusion in Foucault's idea of 'statements'. Dreyfus and Rabinow (1982: 48) thus propose the term 'serious speech acts'. This neatly encapsulates Foucault's adherence to the study of relations between speech acts and their continual formation and transformation where they are validated by particular procedures and the increasing army of 'experts' which characterize modern societies. It also takes account of Foucault's acceptance of the idea we have come across before to the effect that speech-acts are formulated against a background of everyday assumptions, while the idea of 'serious' retains his emphasis upon the generation of meaning within discourses.

With these themes and arguments in mind, we can now say that Foucault did not resort to a depth-hermeneutics whereby, via an excavation of the background assumptions which inform everyday interpretations, a 'truth' is revealed to exist. Further, that he was not content to view meaning as ultimately residing in a transcendental subject, nor to eliminate meaning through the employment of structuralist insights (May and Powell 2007). His concerns were to empirically examine the effects of social practices without recourse to some idea of their intrinsic homogeneity. It is to an understanding of this project in relation to power and the subject that we now turn.

Power and the modern subject

The above situates Foucault's approach to analysing social phenomena in terms of the politics of truth, but it says little of the effects of these discursive regimes. For this purpose, Foucault turned towards analyses of the exercise of power in contrast to a consideration of the forms of knowledge which create a sense of social order. In more specific terms, his objective became 'to create a history of the different modes by which, in our culture, human beings are made subjects' (1982: 208).

To return to our earlier discussion. The position which the analyst occupies in this process of inquiry is still not that of the 'bearer of universal values' (1980: 132). It is, however, as someone who is situated within society and does not speak for the truth, but engages in a 'battle' regarding its status and the political and economic role that it plays in social relations (1980: 132). In other words, what is taken as being self-evident in the present, is viewed as part of an historical process. From this point of view Foucault's (1991d) study on imprisonment and punishment aimed

> to write a history not of the prison as an institution, but of the practice of imprisonment: to show its origin or, more exactly, to show how this way of doing things – ancient enough in itself – was capable of being accepted at a certain moment as a principal component of the penal system, thus coming to seem an altogether natural self-evident and indispensable part of it.
>
> (Foucault 1991c: 75)

Three lines of inquiry are required in order to understand how the subject is objectified. First, how particular sciences contribute to this process. Second, a study of the 'practices' that divide people from others, as well as within themselves: for example, the mad and sane, the sick and healthy and the criminal and non-criminal. Third, in what ways people then turn themselves into subjects (Foucault 1982: 208). Just to reiterate: the form of this analysis is opposed to the search for origins and ideal significations, as well as the notion that we possess an intrinsically rational and coherent sense of self.

At this point we find another central aspect to Foucault's work which causes interpretative confusion. Quite simply, it is the tension which exists between his approach to the study of social relations and a deep-seated idea within western cultures: that is, the belief that the condition of freedom is the absence of power and thus power is always repressive. To commit oneself to this tradition would be to fall into the trap that Foucault's inspired genealogies seek to avoid. For instance, when it comes to the individual in relation to the means of production, or as involved in relations of significa-tion, we turn to economic history, linguistics and semiotics to shed light on these matters. When it comes to power all we ever ask is: 'What legitimates power?' (1982: 209). However, with the individual implicated in these relations, this approach cannot suffice. In order to understand how the subject is objectified, this idea of power needs total revision. This is where Foucault's 'reconceptualization' of power is of central importance and we need to understand what he means by this before we continue with our discussion.

Power is not inevitably vested in the state, nor localized in, say, relations between the citizen and state. Instead, the effects of the domination of power are attributable to various 'dispositions, manoeuvres, tactics, techniques, functionings' (1991d: 26). Its properties are invested in those over whom it is exercised, so it not only exerts pressures upon people, but is also transmitted by them: 'Power comes from below; that is, there is no binary and all-encompassing opposition between rulers and ruled' (1979: 94). Power is part of the social body as a whole – in the machinery of production, families, limited groups, and institutions (1979: 94). Thus, power is not a property of capitalism, patriarchy, or the bourgeoisie – it is a strategy that has evolved as part of the characteristics of modern society. Nor should power be identified with an individual who possesses or exercises it by right of birth:

> Not the domination of the King in his central position, therefore, but that of his subjects in their mutual relations: not the uniform edifice of sovereignty, but the multiple forms of subjugation that have a place and function within the social organism.
> (Foucault in Kelly 1994: 34)

Given this, if we conceive of power as emanating from one source, we will not understand its effects. When it comes to politics and power, the sovereign's head must be cut off. Further, to think of power as repressive (the repressive hypothesis) is to neglect its positive aspects. In this sense, power becomes 'a machine in which everyone is caught' (Foucault 1980: 156).

Yet a question still remains: if power is transmitted in this way, where does it come from in the first place? This is one of the most difficult concepts to grasp. After all, if knowledge and power are linked, one thinks of Marx and the idea that those who are in charge of the means of production are, at the same time, in charge of the means of mental production. An illuminating discussion of this issue can be found in an interview with Foucault, conducted by Jean-Pierre Barou and Michelle Perrot (Foucault 1980: 156).

Let us take the example of a factory: here, relations of power may be seen in terms of how 'individuals try to conduct, to determine the behavior of others' (1991b: 18) The system of power is pyramidal and it occurs between the managers and the managed. However, the strategic apex (the managers) is not the source of power, nor is a principle or goal which organizational members are expected to invest with legitimacy in terms of their practices. Power and its techniques are used throughout the factory. Therefore, it cannot be simply identified with a particular group:

> These tactics were invented and organized from the starting points of local conditions and particular needs. They took shape in piecemeal fashion, prior to any class strategy designed to weld them into vast, coherent ensembles. It should also be noted that these ensembles don't consist in a homogenization, but rather a complex play of supports in mutual engagement, different mechanisms of power which retain all their specific character.
>
> (Foucault 1980: 159)

We can draw three points from this quote. First, in his analysis of power Foucault is concentrating on the local and contingent. Therefore, as noted before, he is not prepared to 'read off' practices against some universal idea of rationality. Rather, he is concerned to examine the ways in which particular rationalities are deployed, leaving the connections to be established among them open to investigation. Second, power should not be seen, from this point of view, as existing above, but alongside developments in the forces and relations of production. Power is transformed along with, but not by these changes and may be found in both socialist and capitalist societies (1980: 160). Third, the workings of this form of power can be traced far back into history.

In terms of tracing the history of this form of power, it was during the seventeenth, eighteenth and nineteenth centuries that a new form of political rationality found its target. When faced with the issue of population growth, political economists examined it in terms of wealth accumulation and the productive capabilities of labour, with the causes of poverty being conceived of in terms of disease, idleness, etc. The social reformer and philosopher Jeremy Bentham (1748–1832) on the other hand 'poses the question in terms of power – population as object of relations of domination' (Foucault 1980: 151). It was the economic changes occurring in the eighteenth century that

> made it necessary to ensure the circulation of effects of power through progressively finer channels, gaining access to individuals themselves, to their bodies, their gestures and all their daily actions. By such means power, even when faced with ruling a multiplicity of men, could be as efficacious as if it were being exercised over a single one.
>
> (Foucault 1980: 151–152)

The differentiation of the population thus required this new form of power. The simple domination of one group by another was no longer a feasible technique given the increasing complexity of society. Contrary to simple ideas of coercion, power has both a political and economic cost. If you are too violent in controlling a population, you risk revolt. If you intervene too frequently, then resistance and disobedience may result. Disciplinary technologies and regulatory procedures must inform and produce a normative basis which spreads throughout the social body, while masking the operation of power that underlies this process (Katz 2007). In this way, the modern subject becomes inextricably linked to the society of which they are a part through turning themselves into an object:

> There is no need for arms, physical violence, material constraints. Just a gaze. An inspecting gaze, a gaze which each individual under its weight will end up interiorizing to the point that he is his own overseer, each individual thus exercising this surveillance over, and against, himself. A superb formula: power exercised continuously and for what turns out to be a minimal cost.
>
> (Foucault 1980: 155)

The body, space and time are routinely controlled (Dumas and Turner 2006). What Foucault calls 'bio-power' relies upon the scientific categorization of the population, in terms of being an object of systematic and sustained political intervention, as well as encompassing a focus upon the human body as an object of control and manipulation. Collectively, these 'technologies' centre around the 'objectification' of the body. They form a 'disciplinary technology' whose aim is to forge the individual, with 'normalization' being one technique (Foucault 1977). This is best exemplified in enclosed situations, such as a prison, school, and hospital or, as above, the factory, where the control of space and time is more readily apparent. It is here that we find

> a whole micro penality of time (lateness, absences, interruptions of tasks), of activity (inattention, negligence, lack of zeal), of behaviour (impoliteness, disobedience), of speech (idle chatter, insolence), of the body ('incorrect' attitudes, irregular gestures, lack of cleanliness), of sexuality (impurity, indecency).
>
> (Foucault 1991d: 178)

This disciplinary technology permits supervision and control with interiorization being the most effective deployment of power. In this respect, Foucault suggests that there are three ways in which 'self-examination' has developed over time. First, the Cartesian form such that thoughts are considered in relation to their correspondence with reality. Second, the ways in which our thoughts correspond with, or relate to, rules. Third, the relationship between a thought which is 'hidden' and some inner impurity:

> At this moment begins the Christian hermeneutics of the self with its deciphering of inner thoughts. It implies that there is something hidden in ourselves and that we are always in a self-illusion which hides the secret.
>
> (Foucault 1988b: 46)

The discourse of constituting the subject as object thereby also requires the discourse of the subject and this too, has changed over the course of history. The means of exposing the truth of ourselves in Christianity involved being subjugated to a master. This model of obedience means that once the confession was verbalized, it was accompanied by a renunciation of the sense of self and 'will' as part of a continual process of self-renunciation: that is, disclosing oneself to an authority. This is a 'permanent verbalization'. However, what then occurs is that the interpretative sciences come to play this central role. After all, it is they who 'claim to be able to reveal the truth about our psyches, our culture, our society – truths that can only be understood by expert practitioners' (Dreyfus and Rabinow 1982: 180):

> From the eighteenth century to the present, the techniques of verbalization have been reinserted in a different context by the so-called human sciences in order to use them without renunciation of the self but to constitute, positively, a new self. To use these techniques without renouncing oneself constitutes a decisive break.
>
> (Foucault 1988b: 49)

This is accompanied by the state performing 'a modern matrix of individualization' (1982: 215). Together, these are the new forms of 'pastoral power'. Nevertheless, while claiming to speak the truth, these interpretative sciences are actually part of the rationalities which inform a political technology that saturates everyday life. Importantly, however, this should not be conceived of as being a deterministic relationship.

To illuminate the indeterminacy of these practices and hence the possibilities for their transformation, the focus of Foucault's investigations change. He now considers not so much the ways in which we are constituted as both subjects and objects, but the effects of this on our relations with others and the implications for the relationship between power, truth and the self. Now these are not discrete topics, but ultimately complementary strategies of historical investigation (Foucault 1988c: 15). The body then becomes not only the object or target of power, but also the centre for resistance and opposition. After all, contemporary society is increasingly characterized by struggles against the exercise of power 'opposition to the power of men over women, of parents over children, of psychiatry over the mentally ill, of medicine over the population, of administration over the ways people live' (Foucault 1982: 211).

Foucault asks the empirical question 'what happens?' when power is exercised as opposed to becoming involved in endless debates over what power 'is' and where it comes from (1982: 217). Resistance to forms of power is the starting-point for this investigation. These are struggles for new subjectivities which encompass the right to be different and distinguish oneself from the ways in which the effects of particular 'technologies of the self' routinely constitute people: 'These struggles are not exactly for or against the "individual", but rather they are struggles against the "government of individualization"' (1982: 212). This makes sense if we remember that the individual is not constituted before the effects of power because 'it is already one of the prime effects of power that certain bodies, certain gestures, certain discourses, certain desires, come to be identified and constituted as individuals' (Foucault 1980: 98).

There is a clear tension between struggles for new identities and the totalizing forms of power characteristic of modern society. These forms are considered to be more rational and economic, but this does not imply that people are more obedient. Nor does the exercise of power imply that people are not capable of acting in the first place. Indeed, its very exercise presupposes the condition of freedom:

> It is a total structure of actions brought to bear upon possible actions; it incites, it induces, it seduces, it makes easier or more difficult; in the extreme it constrains or forbids absolutely; it is nevertheless always a way of acting upon an acting subject or acting subjects by virtue of their acting or being capable of action.
>
> (Foucault 1982: 220)

Summary

We are now in a position to summarize the ways in which Foucault gives us a new perspective on social relations. In particular, if we think of structure as determining and action as freedom, we simply replicate the determinist duality in social thought. This stems from seeing the individual as the centre of social relations through invoking the idea of a transcendent subject. In so doing, we will not understand the dynamics of modern society. In these terms, we should not view power and freedom as opposites. Instead, they exist in antagonism or, as Foucault characterizes it, an 'agonism' or 'permanent provocation' (1982: 222). The connection between Foucault's writings and the Frankfurt School were noted in Part I. However, we should not over-extend such parallels. As Barry Hindness (1996: 149) notes, for this tradition of critical theory the autonomous agent provides the 'postulated ideal' against which a real state of affairs is then evaluated. For Foucault, there are no such utopias. Yet there are similarities between Foucault's characterizations of modernity and the writings of Weber. Although Foucault did not regard himself as a Weberian, if that is seen in terms of viewing rationality as an 'anthropological invariant' (Foucault 1991c: 79) interesting comparisons can be made between these thinkers (Gordon 1987; D. Owen 1997; Warren 1992). In both we can trace the influence of Nietzsche's idea of the 'will to truth' which is exercised in the name of reason so that order might be achieved out of what would otherwise be a chaotic and unstable world.

Despite these observations, given the particular influences and directions of his thought, Foucault's questions were of a different order to those we have come across before. As he puts it:

> *What* is this Reason that we use? What are its historical effects? What are its limits, and what are its dangers? How can we exist as rational beings, fortunately committed to practicing a rationality that is unfortunately crisscrossed by intrinsic dangers?
>
> (Foucault 1984: 249, original italics)

This does not suggest that he is in favour of irrationality, simply that his approach to understanding our contemporary practices has the effect of questioning the rationale upon which they are based.

Finally, we should note that Foucault's methods for these inquiries did not follow Schutz's postulate of subjective interpretation, nor a depth-hermeneutics such that an underlying truth may eventually be revealed to the actor. Both positions force one into a regime of truth which then stands as the final arbitrator, whereas it actually serves to hide yet another meaning and so forth. We can thus summarize Foucault's interpretation of current practices as 'interpretative analytics' which is

> a pragmatically guided reading of the coherence of the practices of the society. It does not claim to correspond either to the everyday meanings shared by the actors or, in any simple sense, to reveal the intrinsic meanings of the practices. This is the sense in which Foucault's method is interpretative but not hermeneutic.
>
> (Dreyfus and Rabinow 1982: 124)

Issues in the work of Michel Foucault

Foucault's studies have proved to be both highly influential and controversial. Much of his influence is explained by the failure of 'conventional' accounts to explain the ubiquity of power and the struggles in contemporary societies for new forms of identity. Power is frequently evaluated against and reduced to a series of conceptual monoliths: the state, class, 'race' and gender relations. This is not to suggest that his work does not illuminate the dynamics of these relations. On the contrary, when it comes to understanding the dynamics of race and ethnicity (Gilroy 2001), sex and gender (Jones 2006), geography, space and power (Crampton and Elden 2007) and politics (Dean 2007), it is clear that his works have been of considerable use. That noted, his studies are not without their conceptual flaws. In this section, we wish to bring your attention to some of these.

We have seen that Foucault offers a new approach to the relationship between agency and structure, as expressed in terms of an 'agonism' between power and freedom. However, he simply asserts that we should resist power, but does not provide the grounds upon which such a resistance can take place. As one theorist, who also employed a relational theory of power, put it:

> no kind of resistance is possible if we follow Foucault's analyses. For if power is always already there, if every power situation is immanent in itself, why should there ever be resistance? From where would resistance come, and how would it even be possible?
>
> (Poulantzas 1978: 149)

We end up with mixed messages. At one level, 'power is a machine that no-one owns'. At this point, Foucault reads as a structuralist bidding yet another farewell to the subject. At another level, he recognizes struggles for new subjectivities but in abandoning the idea of the subject to 'discursive formation', it is difficult to conceive of any basis upon which to build change. We can develop this point further in relation to the centrality of a normative basis upon which to conduct feminist-inspired critiques.

The attraction of Foucault's work for some feminist researchers is clear in terms, for example, of its avoidance of essentialism through supplanting naturalism in favour of cultural constructionism. He thus brings our attention to the ways in which we experience ourselves not in some state of nature, but in a symbolically mediated fashion, thereby shedding light on the gendered nature of the self and social relations. Nevertheless, while he is correct in questioning the idea of a 'natural' body, it is also argued that 'the body exists as a physical entity prior to any cultural work' (Soper 1993: 32). Yet he refused such ideas on the basis of being epistemologically sceptic regarding the status of acultural explanations, while his studies analysed the effects of political rationalities as the routine denial of differences via tactics of incorporation and neutralization.

If feminism takes these kinds of insights too far, it risks losing its basis for critique; hence the clear 'tensions' between feminism and Foucault (Ramazanoglu 1993). If everything, including desire, is up for discursive grabs, then what may be viewed as 'authentic' in social life? A feminist social theory built on this basis risks nothing less than a negation of feminist politics which, necessarily, requires some common interest or cause as a unifying principle upon which to base change. The underlying reason for this is a central issue in the use of Foucault's work. It may be further illuminated through a consideration of his concept of power.

There are a variety of interpretations that may be applied to Foucault's work. His pluralist concept of power, for example, lends itself to an American liberal political science tradition, as well as having parallels with Weber and the Frankfurt School in terms of analysing the effects of instrumental rationality under conditions of modernity. The basis for these multiple interpretations may be understood if we take the requirements of genealogical critique to be politically engaged, in order to take power effects seriously and hence retain the domain of human meaning, while also remaining normatively neutral. However, the result is that Foucault;

> adopts a concept of power that permits him no condemnation of any objectionable features of modern societies. But at the same time, and on the other hand, his rhetoric betrays the conviction that modern societies are utterly without redeeming features. Clearly, what Foucault needs, and needs desperately, are normative criteria for distinguishing accept-able from unacceptable forms of power.
>
> (Fraser 1989: 33)

Foucault's rejection of humanism, in order to avoid the problems of intellectual traditions built upon Cartesian philosophy, seems to imply that values do not require justification. How, therefore, can Foucault claim that 'discipline' is a bad thing as part of the routine political judgements which he makes in the course of his inquiries (Fraser 1989: 42)? His refusal to engage in these debates is perhaps a strategy of resistance to the premises of humanism which, of course, he sought to avoid. However, when we act, do we simply do so strategically in order to gain the upper hand in a never ending game of power relations? As we have seen, explanations of human agency as being motivated by the desire to gain some strategic advantage over one's 'adversaries' are limited.

Foucault's price for analysing the processes of objectification and subjectivism of the subject is therefore high. It is, without doubt, illuminating to question the belief that the production and operation of norms takes place in the absence of the exercise of power. However, does power saturate our lives to the extent that Foucault suggests? If it does, then we are caught in endless games of power with strategic action being the only dimension to all human actions. While Foucault (1984: 351) spoke of 'creating oneself' in his discussion of a genealogy of ethics, this stands in clear tension with his idea of power which rules out, by fiat, the possibility of reaching consensual agreement. We should not be surprised to find levelling this critique at Foucault and poststructuralist thought in general:

in passing through structuralism, this movement of thought has made transcendental subjectivity disappear without a trace, and indeed in such a way that one also loses sight of the system of world relations, speaker perspectives, and validity claims that is inherent in linguistic communication itself. Without this reference system, however, the distinction between levels of reality, between fiction and reality, between everyday practice and extra-ordinary experience, and between the corresponding kinds of texts and genres becomes impossible and even pointless. The house of 'being' is itself sucked into the maelstrom of an undirected linguistic current.

(Habermas 1992b: 210)

Social relations are manifested in Foucault's work as a continuous battleground and given that power has no origin and is seen as the multifaceted play of social forces, conflict is endemic. The possibility that power might be institutionally stabilized is supplanted by 'the possibility of interpreting the institutionalization of positions of power as a process of the constant use of force' (Honneth 1991: 174). We then become but spectators of discourses that are seen to possess their own constitutive power: that is, they have the ability to define objects in particular ways through warranting some statements and thereby excluding others. Of course, in order not to surrender to structuralism and to retain the role of meaning in the analysis of discourses, Foucault focuses upon the 'serious speech acts' of professionals and experts. His concern being to explain the conditions under which particular speech acts are validated.

Here, again, he runs the danger of removing the realm of human agency for these discourses define 'positions' which any subject might occupy. Given this, it is the rules of the discourse which define these positions and what the subject may, or may not say, as a result. Yet Foucault also speaks of 'strategies' and 'choices'. However, how can such things be spoken of without a theory of human agency (May and Powell 2007)? Even in his later work on 'technologies of the self', where he examines how we fashion ourselves, we are not granted much in the way of self-determination (Freundlieb 1994). Instead, it is the structure of discourses which define the conditions of the subject. Despite his attempts to avoid the trap of structuralism, determinism seems to reassert itself.

Foucault's concepts and ideas have also become significantly influential in a variety of 'disciplines'. To those noted earlier, we can add: criminology (Garland 2002), feminism (McNay 2001), social gerontology (Katz 1996 Powell 2005), accounting (Chua 1999) and human geography (Sibley 2006). These writers have been influenced by Foucault's interest in the way in which individuals are constructed as social subjects, knowable through disciplines and discourses. Foucault's work on governmentality has also been of huge influence in recent years. For Dean (2007) modernity itself requires a new discourse of governmentality that comprises the ensemble formed by institutions and reflections, the tacit and esoteric tactics of subjectification that allows the operationalization of forms of power.

Summary

In asking the question 'What are we today?' Foucault asks a central question that informs our everyday existences. He does so on grounds that link what we are to the regimes of truth that pronounce on the nature of our being. Here is the rub. Notions of autonomy and transcendence, dear to the liberal position and to our self-conceptions, are analysed by an approach which views the social body as infused with politics. In the process, Foucault shows us that there is critique and life after Cartesianism (Fraser 1989).

It has been argued that to see the operation of power in Foucault's method is problematic. Are our lives so saturated in this way? His own answer to this question suffices. Asked why he was so interested in politics, he replied:

> what blindness, what deafness, what density of ideology would have to weigh me down to prevent me from being interested in what is probably the most crucial subject to our existence, that is to say the society in which we live, the economic relations within which it functions, and the system of power which defines the regular forms and the regular permissions and prohibitions of our conduct. The essence of our life consists, after all, of the political functioning of the society in which we find ourselves.
>
> (Foucault in Elders 1974: 168)

Although Foucault was interested in what makes the truth 'true', it does not follow that he denied the concept of validity (Visker 1995) nor does the absence of a normative basis in his work mean that it cannot be used in examining contemporary social relations. His concerns were with the basis of forms of life, or the lifeworld. This did not involve the celebration of relativism, but an investigation of the conditions under which truth is produced. Critical theory with guarantees may be abandoned, but it is replaced by a critical research programme with possibilities. Therefore, at the end of his life, Foucault could not help but face 'the fact that the understanding of social and historical processes is, if not a component of our self-understanding, at the very least a contribution to our liberation from self-misunderstanding' (Dews 1989: 40).

Further, his refusal of humanism does not necessarily imply a rejection of the values of modernity (Hoy 1986). However, there are forms of thought which seek to do just that. Here it is argued that we have entered a new epoch. Foucault was sceptical not only regarding there being any solid foundations for modernity, but also over the idea that history possesses such 'breaks'. To that extent, his work cannot be subsumed under the subject of the next chapter.

11 Beyond modernity?

The formulation of concepts and theories which may be employed for the purpose of analysing social relations is the essential ingredient of an adequate social theory. The attribution of some form of rationality to human conduct, social relations or to social systems as a whole, is the means through which the basis for such an endeavour is often formulated. This tendency is evident in rational action theory, ethnomethodology, through to Habermas's idea of communicative reason and Parsons's and Luhmann's variants of systems theory. Wherever they start and finish, however, they can be viewed as expressing the same underlying characteristic: that is, the desire to move beyond an analysis of the particular in order to derive principles for the understanding and explanation of human relations in general.

For Descartes, the mind was the site of reason which found an order in the world. Then, with Kant, came the tempering of Cartesian certainties. With the external world a less certain place for Kant than it was for Descartes, the ordering powers of the mind were placed at its centre. Then there was the empiricist-minded Hume. For him, it was impressions which gave rise to ideas. The mind is then viewed as more of a reflection of the world, than a coherent entity which sits at its centre. Nevertheless, despite these differences between Kant and Hume, with one stressing reason and the other custom, both held that

> they could prove that the mind is so constructed that it must bring forth from within itself such a tidy, cognizable, Newtonian world. So we were, after all, rationally entitled to believe in it; but the considerations enabling us to do so were henceforth to be based on qualities of our mind alone.
>
> (Gellner 1992: 29)

In contrast to this route, which laid the basis for society to become an object of study, let us take another route. This route will not seek to uncover something called 'social reality', whether by measuring the external world through 'neutral' instruments, or by generalizing on the basis of rules informing language games that construct the object world. Instead, the task now changes and the role of the social theorist should be to invent

> allusions to the conceivable which cannot be presented. And it is not to be expected that this task will effect the last reconciliation between language-games (which, under the name of faculties, Kant knew to be separated by a chasm), and that only the transcendental illusion (that of Hegel) can hope to totalize them into a real unity. ... We have paid a high enough price for the nostalgia of the whole and the one, for the reconciliation of the concept and the sensible, of the transparent and the communicable experience. ... The answer is: Let us wage war on totality; let us be witnesses to the unpresentable; let us activate the differences and save the honor of the name.
>
> (Lyotard 1993: 46)

What is this argument? Why is it invoked? How we get there and the reasons for doing so are the subjects of this chapter. In the process, we will find an argument that we have entered a new epoch and further, that to adequately understand what this consists of requires something called a 'postmodern social theory'. This epoch, called postmodernity, is characterized by heterogeneity, indeterminacy, fragmentation and flexibility. Given this state of affairs, a postmodern social theory necessitates that we relinquish the quest for foundations or the search for the grounded set of premises, conceptual strategy and explanation (Seidman 2004). If 'modernism', as a term applied to culture, is characterized by the rise in avant-garde forms of literature, art and so on in the early twentieth century and the rejection of previous restrictive styles and structures (Ritzer and Ryan 2007) then it can argued also that 'postmodernism' in culture came about in the 1970s, signalling an erosion of boundaries and a destabilizing of high/low cultural barriers. Postmodernism brought with it an 'anything goes' policy 'which renounces purity, mastery of form and elitism and is more playful, ironic and eclectic in style' (Powell 2005: 9).

Postmodernism not only affects culture as a whole but a new social epoch emerged due to a range of developments in all areas of society such as politics, industry, media and the rise of social movements (Layder 2006). This has ultimately led to the development of a postmodern world characterized by 'fragmentation, multiplicity, plurality and indeterminacy' (K. Thompson 1992: 223). If this characterization is correct, it has had strong implications for the Enlightenment aims and values. Within social theory, Zygmunt Bauman claims that postmodernity is, above all, a state of mind (Bauman 1992: vii). He suggests that the term 'modernity' has come about only through the postmodern vantage point. The labelling of modernity is merely a re-evaluation of the past and is not a term which is simply descriptive of a certain period in the logical progression of history (Lemert

2006). This is equally true of postmodernity in that it is not merely a label for a set period in time. Postmodernism represents a shift of focus from universalism to pluralism. It is the acceptance that the aims of universalism are futile and a recognition of 'pluralism of cultures, communal traditions, ideologies, forms of life or language games' (Bauman 1992: 102).

The emergence and analysis of the postmodern

The rise of the postmodern

Certainty and progress is assumed to characterize the epoch known as modernity. In Part I, an emerging attitude became apparent. This may be called the 'attitude of the modernists'. These were and are the people who celebrate the potentiality which is said to exist in history, art, science and politics and the achievements of the human race. Yet they also

> deplore modernization's betrayal of its own human promise. Modernists demand deeper and more radical renewals: modern men and women must become the subjects as well as the objects of modernization; they must learn to change the world that is changing them, and to make it their own.
>
> (Berman 1993: 33)

This attitude, therefore, is one of ambivalence in its viewing of broken promises and celebrations (Bauman 2001). We have found those who approached their analyses of social relations in this manner: for example, Simmel and Weber. Their writings can be contrasted with the relative optimism of Marx and Durkheim. Weber regarded western societies as exhibiting an increased potential for control in the name of instrumental rationality. A fatalism was then apparent in his reflections via a recognition that the realm of human meaning was being trammelled by vast impersonal forces. Weber was not prepared to overcome such observations through an allusion to the external by the freezing of time and all of its 'fleeting qualities' (Harvey 1990: 21). From this point of view, we can read both Weber and Simmel as writers who were straddling a chasm that was opening up between two epochs.

A recognition of this state of affairs was apparent in the writings of Charles Wright Mills, who sits within the broad tradition of American pragmatism. He wrote of the changing ideas of 'reason' and 'freedom' and the collapse of liberalism and socialism as explanations of ourselves and the relations into which we enter (there are echoes here of Weber's brittle synthesis of Nietzsche and Marx). The social sciences are seen to have inherited terms which, although outdated, are still part of its practices. If generalized to contemporary situations, they 'become unwieldy, irrelevant, not convincing' (Mills 1970: 184). He thus argues that the Modern Age is being superseded by a 'Fourth Epoch'. He refers to this as the 'postmodern period':

> The ending of one epoch and the beginning of another is, to be sure, a matter of definition. But definitions, like everything social, are historically specific. And now our basic definitions of society and self are being overtaken by new realities ... I mean that when we try to orient ourselves – if we do try – we find that many of our old expectations and images are, after all, tied down historically.
>
> (Mills 1970: 184)

In particular, it is the role of reason and the idea of the free individual which he argues are the prime legacies that twentieth-century social scientists have inherited from the Enlightenment (Mills 1970: 186). In the face of change, the central issues that now face us are concerned with our very nature and our limits and possibilities. After all, is our destiny to become what may be called 'the Cheerful Robot' (Mills 1970: 189)?

We may characterize this tension as one which exists between two elements of the process of modernization: specialization and rationalization. Specialization, as Durkheim noted, necessitates a complex division of labour which, for the purposes of social cohesion, requires a new form of social integration. This time, of course, it was with society taking the transcendent role, not the autonomous subject. Authority and freedom, therefore, were not opposites. For Weber, the same process was charted but he then wrote of 'specialists without spirit and sensualists without heart'. This was symptomatic of the process of increasing societal complexity running alongside greater centralization and control.

Habermas (1992b) claims that the process of societal evolution depends upon a normative basis which exists in the lifeworld, but in the forward march of modernity the 'steering media of power and money' evolve which have no basis in the lifeworld. As we have seen, there is a way out of this 'iron cage' through a modified Enlightenment project which finds the possibility for a consensus that is not imposed upon the lifeworld, but emerges from within it. However, is this quest for consensus yet another version of the modernists' attitude which is doomed to failure? Do metanarratives of this type, in their desire to universalize, render violence to heterogeneity? This is clearly the case for Jean-François Lyotard (1924–98) who, in reference to Habermas, plays on the same themes that the earlier quote indicated:

> Is legitimacy to be found in consensus obtained through discussion, as Jurgen Habermas thinks? Such consensus does violence to the heterogeneity of language games. And invention is always born of

dissension. Postmodern knowledge is not simply a tool of the authorities; it refines our sensitivity to differences and reinforces our ability to tolerate the incommensurable. Its principle is not the expert's homology, but the inventor's paralogy.

(Lyotard 1984: xxv)

A recognition of heterogeneity is not the monopoly of postmodernist perspectives (Ritzer and Goodman 2001). That noted, what seems to have changed in socio-theoretical discourse is that those who are the bearers of the dream of universalism now have to defend themselves against the relativists (Mouzelis 2007). In considering these issues we have to ask if this is symptomatic of a changing set of social conditions such that there can no longer be any unifying principles of co-ordination or communication that are available to us?

In considering this question, we might first recall the arguments of Kroker and Cook that Augustine, while signalling the beginning of the modern age, also possessed a discourse on the will that commenced the 'arc of a dead power which will not come fully into light until the nineteenth century in Nietzsche's nightmarish vision of the "will to power" (Kroker and Cook 1988: 72). In these terms, they can then go on to characterize the postmodern condition as

a coming home to the 'perfect nihilism' (Nietzsche) which has always been at work in Western consciousness and which only now, in the fully realized technological society, reveals itself in the fateful meeting of power and the sign.

(Kroker and Cook 1988: 73)

Nihilism may be viewed as the celebration of the relativism of values such that there is no absolute good, or the refusal to create ultimate values, or an absolute subjectivity that accompanies a 'loss of the world' (Glucksmann 1992: 336). Nevertheless, from whatever vantage point it is viewed, if the postmodern condition is that which gives rise to its celebration, then attempts at delineating a new basis for reason are not moving against some trendy intellectual movement, but 'real' historical changes that are taking place in the organization of societies as a whole. If this is the case, then consensus would, as part of the modernists' dream of a better future, indeed become 'a horizon that is never reached' (Lyotard 1984: 61).

As noted, the forward march of modernity came to witness the increasingly complicated nature of the social world being compensated for by mechanisms of communication and control. These functions were taken over by systems which came to represent the need for specialization and co-ordination. These systems are argued to reduce the complexity of the social world. However, does their legitimacy then come to supersede that of the realm of human values? For instance, even matters of risk, as part of both the excitement and tragedy of the human condition, are now open to their calculations:

> In binary coding, modern society possesses a highly specific form for heightening, normalizing and contextualizing risky behaviour. By attributing observations to certain coded systems, we can recognize which risk network we are operating within – and which one we are not operating within. Whenever a matter is dealt with in the context of a binary code, the implication is that not only the positive value but also the countervalue could be assigned validity.
>
> (Luhmann 1993: 76)

These systems come to represent the site of reason and it is from these that Habermas seeks to recover its critical capacity in order to restore the power of rational argumentation. Despite these differences, both systemic and critical modernism represent a celebration of the potentiality of reason to achieve regularity and understanding. Yet there is an historical process that might be argued to counter these attempts.

One such process is that of 'de-differentiation' (Lash 1990). The implications of this process are that a differentiation between the aesthetic, cultural, social, economic and political realms, as a characteristic feature of modernity, is no longer a feasible option for analytic purposes. Instead, from a cultural vantage point, we now have a colonization of the moral-political and theoretical spheres by the aesthetic; a collapse of the social into the cultural, accompanied by a breakdown of the barriers between high and low culture, and finally, in terms of 'cultural economy', the 'death' of the distinction that was once made between the author and their text and, for instance, the distinction that is made between the production of a play and its reception by its audience who now form part of its cultural production (Butler 2003).

If we extend this process, beyond the cultural sphere (Lash and Urry 1987, 1994), it follows that we can no longer divide the social world into autonomous units. In this sense, there are those who are willing to engage in this embrace via the argument that differentiation extends to all spheres of social life. Whereas the process of modernization, as series of socio-economic changes, bore witness to the specialization of subsystems by function such that those systems with similar functions possess similar structures, we are now said to be witnessing 'an extension of this process in which social units are differentiating at the level of structure as well as of function' (Crook et al. 1992: 33). In these terms:

> Patterns of economic production may be said to be hyperdifferenti-ating, providing a multiplicity of directions in the absence of a

unifying structural principle. Such hyperdifferentiation of structure is, we argue, a generalized and widespread pattern.

(Crook et al. 1992: 33)

Durkheim wrote: 'A discipline may be called a 'science' only if it has a definite field to explore. Science is concerned with things, realities' (in Giddens 1972b: 57). The basis upon which this was to proceed is the correspondence between the language of representation (theory) and reality. Yet the process of de-differentiation renders this strategy obsolete. There is no 'reality' to represent, only realities. There is no reason to base analysis upon, only reasons.

A tension between the forces of centralization and dispersion under postmodernity now manifests itself in various ways. First, the media of control change. Second, as noted above, the ability to control the object world is lessened. Third, there is a collapse of the boundaries between the different spheres of social life: for example, the public and private. In relation to the first aspect, specialization is seen to be superseded by hyperdifferentiation whereby control is no longer the province of specific spheres of life, nor specialized disciplines for their study. This all results in the generation of a 'limitless range of media types' within society:

> for example, TV churches can generate money as well as value-commitment and influence, and businesses which professionalize their employees and offer them lifetime security can be a source of value-commitments as well as money. In other words there is no longer an oligopolistic set of sources for money and power and they thus lose their effectivity as sources of control.
>
> (Crook et al. 1992: 34–35)

Similarly, the breakdown of the correspondence between structure and function, in turn, leads to a breakdown of the potential for prediction and control: 'States become ungovernable, economies unmanageable, and worlds anarchistic' (Crook et al. 1992: 35). The result is that postmodernization is characterized by unpredictability and chaos, not homogeneity and control. However, not only is system de-differentiation a characteristic of this process, but also when it comes to an analysis of social action, this is seen to be

> divorced from underlying material constraints (or rather these constraints disappear) and enters the voluntaristic realm of taste, choice and preference. As it does so the boundaries between determined social groups disappear. So class, gender and ethnicity decline in social significance and so also do some of their characteristic forms of expression, including class-based political action and the distinction between high and popular culture.
>
> (Crook et al. 1992: 35)

With this breakdown of divisions in social space, the cultural realm of signs and symbols comes to penetrate the socio-structural realm of social relations to such an extent that individual and multiple realities come to predominate (Layder 2006). Therefore, the potential for individual distinctiveness is heightened. At this point in our journey, it is the ideas of Jean Baudrillard which become of central importance.

Postmodern social theory

Baudrillard (2005) argues that we have moved from societies which are characterized by production, to those of consumption. His ideas have been charted as moving from a development of Marxism, through a transitory phase, before finally becoming a critique of Marxism itself. For instance, in relation to the object world, Baudrillard was to argue that the things we consume form systems of signs. These systems, to recall our earlier discussions on Saussure, are self-referential and precede the individual. Now, during the earlier stages of his work, while seeing consumption as determined by production in a classical Marxist manner, the influences of Barthes and Mauss also provided the basis for a structuralist analysis of symbolic exchange. Ultimately, this was to render distinction between use-value and exchange-value untenable. Briefly, what form did this transition take?

In Marxist terms, a commodity is seen as having a basis in a reality through the meeting of some specific human need. Adding the insights of French structuralism to this leads one to see commodities as objects of desire that then enable the individual to relate to the social order via their consumption. In this way, people may be said to be both ordered and differentiated. However, Baudrillard now starts the process of bringing that which is considered to be marginal in Marxist thought, to having analytic primacy. In order to understand this we need to note the distinction that Marx made between exchange-value and use-value in relation to commodities (Ritzer and Ryan 2007).

Use-value is said to relate to the utility that a commodity has in relation to satisfying a human want. Exchange-value, on the other hand, possesses value due to its ability to be exchanged for other goods or services. Therefore:

> The use-value and the exchange-value of a commodity are not just two different determinations, or aspects; they are contradictory determinations. A commodity is a use-value only if it is immediately useful to whoever has it. It is an exchange-value only if it is not immediately useful but is used for exchange to get something else.
>
> (Cleaver 1979: 90)

Exchange-value is the opposite of use-value. From a political vantage point, use-value may be related to working-class commodity consumption which is utilized for the satisfaction of needs. Capitalism, on the other hand, is concerned with exchange-values for the extraction of surplus value and profit. Despite this, each depends upon the other, for example: 'It is exactly because labor-power is a use-value for capital that it is an exchange-value for labor' (Cleaver 1979: 92). Nevertheless, for Marx, use-value still functions as a basis for the objective assessment of needs that are assumed to exist independently of relations of capital (Lavalette and Pratt 2007). Yet how can one evaluate and compare in this manner separate from the social context of consumption?

In contrast to this approach Baudrillard argues that use-value should be viewed in terms of structures of symbolic exchange:

> consumption does not arise from an objective need of the consumer, a final intention of the subject towards the object; rather, there is social production, in a system of exchange, of a material of differences, a code of significations and invidious (statuaire) values.
>
> (Baudrillard 1993: 75)

This is not a system of consumption whereby the individual subject makes a rational choice, through calculation, in terms of what to consume. Instead, meaning is located within a structure of differences that are conferred upon objects. Take, for example, the consumption of leisure. Is this about the need of the autonomous subject to enjoy 'free time'? No! It is the 'consumption of unproductive time' (Baudrillard 1981: 76). What does this mean? Consider the man [sic] of leisure:

> Outside of the competitive sphere there are no autonomous needs. Spontaneous motivation doesn't exist. But for all that, he can't permit himself to do nothing. At a loss for something to do with his free time, he nevertheless urgently 'needs' to do nothing (or nothing useful), since this has distinctive social value.
>
> (Baudrillard 1981: 77)

Analytic primacy is afforded to the relationship between value and symbolic exchange, not use- and exchange-value. Use-value has now disappeared within a system of sign values: 'This must be recognized today as the truth of the sphere of "consumption" and the cultural system in general' (Baudrillard 1981: 87). Indeed, science, artistic and intellectual work and even transgression and innovation are part of the same process.

Baudrillard could choose to analyse the relationship between the workings of the system and the cultural processes that inform it – as had Marx before him. However, having asserted primacy to the system of symbolic exchange, he then hovers between seeing the system from the point of view of an oppressed class or group and as a system of signs of consumption which refer only to each other and have no external referent. In arguing for the latter, production is to give way to consumption with its vortex of symbols. As such, any hint of a humanist legacy with respect to a state of 'alienation' is abandoned. At this stage in his thought, he thus exhibits a curious blend of Marx, Durkheim, Nietzsche and Freud in the development of what Mike Gane (1991: 95) characterizes as a 'non-humanist idea of alienation'.

All of this was taking place in the era of the 1970s. It was then possible to believe in the theoretical and political possibilities that came with a fusion of Freud and Marx: 'it was in their copulation that things could be saved' (Baudrillard in Gane 1993: 59). This was not to last long with Nietzsche hovering in the background. Here was a thinker who Baudrillard acknowledges is the most influential figure in relation to his thought: 'but not as a point of reference ... but as a spirit (esprit), as a stimulus (impulsion), or inspiration' (Baudrillard in Gane 1993: 203).

With Nietzsche in place, Baudrillard will now take us into the condition where models of reality, and not reality itself, predominate. No longer is reality to be measured against the sign, nor are they seen to exist in a dialectical relationship. There is now only the sign:

> Now the sign seems to me to posit what I have called the 'principle of hyper-reality'. That is, what we have now is the disappearance of the referent – and it is in relation to this disappearance of the referent that there is a sort of omnipresence of the sign.
>
> (Baudrillard in Gane 1993: 142)

The system now comprises the consumption of signs without an external referent. Critical theory, for example, cannot allude to a dialectic of the Enlightenment to discover the truth with an existing state of affairs. The negation of reality and reality itself are now one: 'In short, what we now have is a principle of non-reality based on "reality" – a principle of hyper-reality as I call it' (Baudrillard in Gane 1993: 143). This is the era of postmodernity: nothing real exists, but only 'codes' of the original and it is these that enable simulation to predominate over production.

This is Baudrillard's final rejection of Marxism. The real and its representation have become erased to such an extent that everything is either, or has the potential to become, simulacra: that is, we only have models of reality and it is no longer possible to represent things as they are. The ability to decide, for example, between ideas, aesthetics and political persuasions, collapses. This is the era in which information is predominant. Computers, cyberspace, the media and information technological processing systems in general add to a 'politics of seduction' which are part of the signs that are a routine feature of our everyday lives:

> life is conducted in a ceaseless circulation of signs about what is
> happening in the world (signs about news), about what sort of
> identity one wishes to project (signs about self), about one's stand-
> ing (signs of status and esteem), about what purposes buildings serve
> (architectural signs), about aesthetic preferences (signs on walls,
> tables, side-boards), and so on.
>
> (Webster 1995: 177)

There is no transcendental position from which one may view this
process and pronounce upon its 'truth'. The best we might achieve is to be a
spectator in the process of seduction. The sign is no longer to refer to the
'real' as a semiological strategy might seek. The steering media of modernity
is now the media in postmodernity. What Weber referred to as 'disenchantment' is the irreversible postmodern condition in which meaning has
'imploded'. There is nothing beyond appearance, for appearance is all we
have: 'The screen, the image, the sign, the modern message, the media
require profusion, proliferation; there must be plenty for everyone' (Baudrillard in Gane 1993: 148). This is the end to history that leaves rationalism in
its wake:

> We tend to forget that our reality, including the tragic events of the
> past, has been swallowed up by the media. That means that it is too
> late to verify events and understand them historically, for what
> characterizes our era and our fin de siecle is precisely the disappear-
> ance of the instruments of this intelligibility. It was necessary to
> understand history when there was still history.
>
> (Baudrillard in Gane 1993: 160)

The political realm may no longer be viewed of as autonomous, while
the social realm is now so saturated with media images that is has become
'anonymous'. It follows that those meaningful referents invoked during the
course of social inquiries – class, gender, age, disability, 'race', ethnicity –
disappear in the collapse of the 'social' (Ritzer and Ryan 2007). These
concepts are no longer tenable because the real has been overrun by the
'hyperreal'. Allusions to characteristics of the 'masses' are fatally flawed:

> The mass is born short-circuited in 'total circularity'. What seems to
> occur he argues is a circulation around simulation models, and a
> collapse of the complex system into itself. ... For no-one, no organi-
> zation as has been the case previously can any longer speak with
> confidence 'for' the mass.
>
> (M. Gane 1991: 136)

Baudrillard takes this into America. Here is the postmodern condition where
culture and social life are not distinct. Europeans are said to locate them-

selves in terms of their past and their destiny. However, America is a 'fiction' where the notion of the 'authentic' which accompanies a sense of history disappears in a perpetual simulation in the 'present'. We find cities which are 'exponential', not 'referential'. Las Vegas is Disneyland. This is not a referential city: that is, one with a past, a defined territory and a sense of history. Instead, it is a city whose 'total superficiality ... is bound up with superficiality of gambling and speculation itself' (Baudrillard 1993: 246). This is the imaginary of the real that is to be found in Disneyland:

> In both Disneyland and Disney World, it is clear that everything that can be derived from the imaginary has been caught, represented, made representable, put on display, made visual. Literally putting on a show for consumption without any metaphors is obviously a radical deterrent to the imaginary. Once again, utopia becomes reality.
>
> (Baudrillard 1993 : 246)

Baudrillard focuses then on the transcendental nature of society through the concept of hyperreality. He argued that in today's society there is no distinction between reality and illusion (Rojek 2004), and that individuals live their lives through a simulation of reality. Nothing has any true origin or authenticity and lived experience is itself a mere construction, made of a series of depthless signs and representations (Smart 1993: 52). In this way Baudrillard argues that not just consumer society but social sciences as disciplines of study can serve no political purpose any more as power relations have been dispersed through the hyperreal nature of society (Smart 1993: 55). The 'neat divisions', 'hierarchies' and 'foundational premises' of both modernity and social science (Seidman 2004) are no longer relevant. In particular, Baudrillard (2005) rejects the economic determinism of Marxism (as is true of all the first wave postmodernists) and states that there are no longer such fundamental systems of exploitation, only superficial simulations and exchanges:

> Like the philosopher Nietzsche, Baudrillard criticizes such claims to truth and favours a model based on what he calls seduction. Seduction plays on the surface: it is the surface appearance that is effective in determining action, not some latent or hidden structure as claimed by Marxism or Freudianism.
>
> (K. Thompson 1992: 244)

With the obliteration of the ability to allude to those processes, products, effects, forms of rational argumentation, rules, or relations of cause and effect which might enable us to explain and decide between truth and falsehood, we have entered the postmodern condition. This is the end of metanarratives of explanation that accompanies 'an internal erosion of the legitimacy principle of knowledge' (Lyotard 1984: 39). This is yet another vantage point through which we can illuminate Lyotard's antagonism for any search for consensus within social life. Lyotard found it necessary to distinguish between what constituted pre-modern, modern and postmodern thought and he then set out to deconstruct the way in which bodies of knowledge are created in order to legitimize hierarchical structures in society.

In his influential work *The Postmodern Condition* (1984, first published in French in 1979) Lyotard looked at the changes that have occurred to the nature of 'knowledge' throughout history. He pointed to how premodern society was based on narratives that were made up of religion and myth (Seidman 2004). Knowledge was a body of stories that were thought to explain the way society was and determine that which was 'good' or 'evil'. In this way such narratives legitimated the social rules of behaviour that determined how society was structured and who had authority (Seidman 2004). In contrast modernity, Lyotard argued, was thought to be based on 'true' knowledge that rejected the 'narratives' of premodernity. However in *The Postmodern Condition*, Lyotard asserts that in actual fact supposedly 'pure', 'real' scientific knowledge is also self-legitimizing so is itself merely another 'narrative' (McLennan 1995: 332). Lyotard argues that scientific thought and knowledge has political and philosophical agendas and is therefore value laden and not totally objective (Harrington 2005).

An ideal that underpinned the beginnings of Enlightenment thought was the attainment of absolute knowledge towards freedom for all (Calhoun et al. 2006). It was thought that knowledge was the key to breaking down power structures that had existed during the domination of premodern narratives. Lyotard pointed to the contradictions within modern scientific bodies of knowledge and argued that they are themselves still made up of hierarchical power structures. Just as in earlier society narratives served to determine who had the right to speak and who did not, Lyotard states that this is still the case. Hierarchies still operate and serve to give the decision making elite the power to decide what gets defined as legitimate knowledge. 'Countless scientists have seen their "move" ignored or repressed, sometimes for decades, because it too abruptly destabilized the accepted positions, not only in the university and scientific hierarchy, but also in the problematic' (Lyotard 1984: 63).

Lyotard argues therefore that science can no longer be seen as a unified body working towards the emancipation of humanity (Connor 1989: 31). His ideas can be linked to those of Nietzsche who believes that 'truth' and 'knowledge' are merely a 'matter of conventions that falsify and dissimulate to promote human survival' (Hollinger 1994: 105). Rather than being a grand quest for universal laws, Lyotard argues that knowledge is sought in order to keep human society functioning efficiently (Steuerman 1992: 108). The assertion by science that it is constantly objectively striving for truth and progress is called into question by the fact that the search for knowledge is inextricably linked to achieving economic growth in society (McLennan 1995: 332). That is not to say that these two things are incompatible but rather to question if the search for truth and progress can ever be totally objective when there is a financial incentive. Lyotard argues that those involved in striving for progress 'allocate our lives for the growth of power. In matters of social justice and of scientific truth alike, the legitimation of that power is based on its optimizing the system's performance – efficiency' (Lyotard 1984: xxiv).

Since, as Lyotard (1984) points out, the legitimation of science can be called into question, knowledge as a unified, overarching metanarrative (such as the Enlightenment narrative that knowledge = liberation) as was key in modernity, breaks down into a wide range of 'micronarratives' (Lyotard 1984: xxiv). Each separate specialism has a different discourse and play different 'language games' in an attempt to gain accreditation from their specific audience (Harrington 2005). This to Lyotard is what ultimately characterizes the 'postmodern condition': 'Simplifying to the extreme, I define postmodern as incredulity toward metanarratives' (Lyotard 1984: xxiv).

Lyotard's rejection of grand narratives obviously has strong implications for social theory. By rejecting the belief in the ability to universalize, philosophical thought loses its authority to make any suggestions as to what action can be taken in order to make changes in society (Best and Kellner 2001). In response to the criticisms of the Enlightenment made by Lyotard, Habermas wishes to consolidate the 'project of modernity' and further argues that we should not completely abandon the possibility of a rational pursuit of truth. He defends modernity and argues that what is needed is more philosophical discussion, not less. Habermas states that through the use of communicative action, language and rational dialogue, the Enlightenment aims of truth, justice and freedom are still attainable alongside social consensus. However, Lyotard argues that Habermas ignores the fact that communication cannot simply take the form of consensual, rational dialogue, it will always take place in the context of power struggles (Bertens 1995: 128).

Rather than holding on to the ideals of Enlightenment scientific thought, Lyotard suggests that we attempt to 'restructure' social theory in a postmodern vein so that we might find a democratic, pluralistic solution (Seidman 2004). He argued that while grand narratives, such as the Marxian narrative of class conflict, were well intentioned and essential to modernist sociology, to continue to utilize such concepts failed adequately to challenge the hierarchical structures in society (even though such hierarchies have become less steep over time) and therefore continued to marginalize and repress issues of difference: 'Postmodern science abandons absolute standards, universal categories and grand theories in favour of local, contextual-ized, and pragmatic conceptual strategies' (Seidman 1998: 207).

Seidman outlines the postmodern idea that the splintering of meta-narratives has occurred to such an extent that society has become decen-tered. That is to say that there is no longer a common unifying culture in existence. Individuals experience their lives at constantly shifting intersec-tions of different discourses and language games. Instances of oppression, therefore, occur in many different contexts as individuals constantly con-struct, deconstruct and reconstruct themselves in terms of these 'fractured identities' (Bradley 1996: 211).

Where this could not be explained utilizing modern grand narratives which centred on one concept such as class conflict, Lyotard argues that a postmodern analysis does offer a way of explaining issues of multiplicity and difference (Lyotard 1984: 81). Employing Wittgenstein's idea of language games, Lyotard calls for the abandonment of any search for 'hidden' meanings along the lines, for example, of a depth hermeneutic approach to the study of social life, in favour of the 'play' of language games about which he makes three observations. First, the rules of such games do not contain their own legitimation, but are part of a contract between players who do not, necessarily, formulate those rules. Second, in the absence of rules, there is no game. In this way, an alteration in rules leads to an alteration in the nature of the game itself. Third, it follows that 'utterances' should be seen as moves within a game.

The third point may be given particular emphasis if we consider it in relation to Habermas's ideas, for 'to speak is to fight, in the sense of playing, and speech acts fall within the domain of a general agonistics' (Lyotard 1984: 10). This is not to suggest that people then 'play to win', simply that there is joy and pleasure to be gained in 'the endless invention of turns of phrase, of words and meanings, the process behind the evolution of language on the level of parole' (1984: 10). This pleasure, however, is still derived from the achievement of success over one's adversary. Underlying this process being the rules of the language game which provide for an 'observable common bond'.

Lyotard divides the normal methodological representation of the 'com-mon bond' into two approaches. First, the functional holism of Parsons, and second, the conflict model of Marxism. The former is seen to chart an optimism in the faith of the system to adjust itself to the demands of stabilization in the age of globalization. The latter, on the other hand, as it evolved over time through the Frankfurt School, came to represent less of a theoretical model of critique based upon an analysis of social divisions, but acquired the status of 'utopia' or 'hope'. In the face of such contrasts we appear to be left with the choice between a technocratic positivism which feeds the system and a critical, hermeneutic or reflexive social theory

(Lyotard 1984: 14); the point being, however, that this choice is no longer relevant to the society in which we live. In the postmodern condition, the functions of regulation and reproduction are no longer the province of particular groups or institutions. Instead, it is machines who hold information. While those who have access to that information will continue to make decisions,

> What is new in all of this is that the old poles of attraction represented by nation states, parties, professions, institutions, and historical traditions are losing their attraction. And it does not look as though they will be replaced, at least not on their former scale.
>
> (Lyotard 1984: 14)

The implication is that if these sources of the social bond are absent from our current social condition, then they should be sought elsewhere: for example, in social origins, or in some authentic history that requires decoding. However, it cannot be uncovered in a single lifeworld and then used to explain or understand other lifeworlds. Given the necessity for the activation of differences within language games, there is no principle or general rules that enable us to establish meaningful connections. Indeed, the very attempt renders violence to heterogeneity.

In contrast to these strategies, we should understand the ways in which we are part of narratives. It is these language games that position 'the person who asks, as well as the addressee and the referent asked about: it is already the social bond' (Lyotard 1984: 15). In the age of information, these narratives flow through society and participation does not require justification in terms of reference to some grand, legitimizing narrative. As such, any person may occupy the place of the 'speaker'. These narratives are part of a communities relationship to itself and in their transmission we find 'the set of pragmatic rules that constitutes the social bond' (Lyotard 1984: 21).

As Baudrillard said of exponential cities, the meaning of narratives is not derived in relation to a past, but in the immediate act of their telling. This does not require 'science'. Nor does it require legitimation through allusions to humanism: that is, a referent to the autonomy of the will based in reason. The self is now part of the narrative society. As with the systems of rational co-ordination, the autonomous individual is part of a bygone era that is remembered only in the narratives of utopian radicals. In the dissemination of numerous language games without a common thread: 'The social subject itself seems to dissolve' (Lyotard 1984: 40). Systemic and critical modernism is thereby left in its wake.

As for Baudrillard, Lyotard argues that modernity contained the seeds of its own destruction. The desire for freedom, which is said to come with the greater accumulation of knowledge, is seen as symptomatic of Nietzsche's will to power. Scientific narratives, in the service of reason and progress, are no longer legitimate. Instead, they are part of a self-serving game, symptomatic of the forward march of delegitimation. What is now at stake is the optimal relationship between inputs and outputs. This is not knowledge in the service of truth, but 'performativity'. Therefore, when it comes to research:

> The State and/or company must abandon the idealist and humanist narratives of legitimation in order to justify the new goal: in the discourse of today's backers of research, the only credible goal is power. Scientists, technicians, and instruments are purchased not to find truth, but to augment power.
>
> (Lyotard 1984: 46)

This system may not be overcome through the allusion to metanarratives of explanation. It exists alongside narratives whose heterogeneity and dispersion is a cause for celebration. Given this, social theory should tell alternative stories in order to activate these differences and place its 'nostalgia' for 'the whole and the one' finally to rest.

Summary

A new condition requires a new social theory that represent an abrupt disjuncture with its entire history. Therefore, we have entered a new era which stands as the negation of all that went before. In addition, to adequately grasp the implications of this, we also need a radical break from past conceptions of agency and structure and their corresponding relationships.

The postmodern condition turns rational systems and the rational subject into fictions. The quest for any sense of consensus among peoples is seen to deny the differences upon which society relies for its dynamism via the agonisms that are a fundamental and necessary part of language games. Steering media of co-ordination and control are now part of the information society. Those referents which served as the conceptual monoliths against which the modernist could demarcate the true and the false and the emancipatory and the hegemonic, no longer exist. What we now have are self-serving systems of which the self is a part and not distinct as the discourse of humanism would argue.

Whether or not Mills might have subscribed to the views of Lyotard and Baudrillard, among others, is almost an aside, for there are those who have translated his arguments in particular ways. After all, for those in search of a postmodern social theory, he may be employed via a contrast with Parsons's grand theoretical schema that marks out the terrain of social inquiry in the name of conceptual transcendence. This pragmatist-based social theory, recalling Baudrillard's remarks on the United States, is argued to resonate with American emphasis on utility, social consequences and diversity (Seidman 2004).

This social theory would not appeal to standards of knowledge as the judge of progress. Knowledge, therefore, is no longer the path to liberation separated from the moral and political realms and the general exercise of power within society. Social theory should now invent new narratives as part of the field of symbolism which now saturates our lives. Groups can then draw upon these: 'in order to define themselves, their social situation, and their possible future' (Seidman 1994a: 130). The ghosts of Descartes, Kant and Hume are finally put to rest:

> Today, knowledge – scientific, Western reasons bears the scars of its many wars. Its dreams are tattered and its confidence irrevocably shaken. In generations past, science and Western reason triumphed grandly by means of a relentless assault on its competitors: religion, myth, narrative, moral philosophy, folk knowledge. Today, it is as if those repressed rivals have returned to take their revenge.
>
> (Seidman 1994b: 327)

Issues in postmodern social theory

To claim that postmodernism has met with criticism, as well as embrace, would be an understatement. Critiques have been brought to bear on its presuppositions, insights and consequences for the study of social life (Callinicos 2000; Ritzer and Ryan 2007). In this section we wish to draw your attention to two issues which are not mutually exclusive. First, whether our current age may be characterized as postmodern, and second, if it does exist, whether its analysis requires a postmodern social theory.

Postmodernism is argued to be a cultural phenomenon. To this extent, in reaction to the ideas associated with social, political and economic conditions as being in some way determinant, it serves as a corrective. However, this has been over-extended in the hands of those cultural theorists for whom the consumption of signs is assumed to be separate from the conditions and relations under which this takes place. In this sense, postmodernism can be read, in its celebration of the fragmentation of the self and social structure, as a form of cultural imperialism (Layder 2006).

A number of commentators have noted that this new conservatism heralds an age in which self-consciousness, reflexivity, self-realization – characteristics of the age of modernity – are now part of the reaction of an intelligentsia to the failure of the revolutionary hopes of the late 1960s. Adherents of postmodernism are the very people who have 'turned their backs' on the potential for human emancipation (Callinicos 2000). The idea of a collapse between low and high culture, in a whirlpool of self-referential models of signification, should therefore be resisted in order to maintain a vision. Baudrillard's pronouncements on the death of the social should be subjected to critical scrutiny in order that the postmodernization thesis becomes a topic, not an assumption. Although, postmodern narratives of difference and multiplicity maybe a refreshing theorization of the social, such an argument suggests that the fragmentation and pluralization of society has occurred to such an extent that it is impossible for the individual woman to identify any strict loyalties (Marshall and Witz 2004). Radical feminists have argued that postmodern theory is both confused and self-contradictory.

Anthony Giddens argues that, for example, Lyotardian postmodernism is merely an off-shoot of developments occurring within modernist sociology. What we should be aiming for instead is a 'radicalized' form of modernity (Giddens 1990: 3). Giddens states that 'Modernity no longer equals Enlightenment: such is clear to almost everyone. The task now is to grasp the implications of this severance without relapsing into the aporias of postmodernism' (Giddens 1992: 174).

A main criticism of postmodernism is that the belief that there is no fixed 'truth' or meaning to anything is ultimately nihilistic and undermines any possibility of moral action (Ritzer 2004). However, Lyotard argued that by taking a localized approach postmodernism was more adaptable than any grand narrative to address issues of power and oppression (Ritzer and Ryan 2007).

This is a view consolidated by Bauman (2006), who points to the way that society has become increasingly individualized. All individuals' lives are affected by localized conditions and narratives, and what is needed is an analysis of to what extent the individual is governed by external conditions in terms of their life choices (Bauman 2001). Power has progressed to a state which is not set or easily determined and can shift quickly and easily between situations. This is ultimately linked to the highly developed nature of what it is that is bought and sold as Capital (Bauman 2001: 26). Bauman argues that postmodern culture is effectively a competitive market trading in 'life meanings' (Bauman 2001: 4) and this can be linked to Lyotard's suggestion that knowledge has become the product of different 'specialisms' to be bought and sold for profit (Lyotard 1984: 5). Hence, Lyotard appears to acknowledge the relevance of a Marxist analysis (Ritzer and Ryan 2007). Theorists such as Bauman, therefore, do not advocate that the process of restructuring should abandon 'all the values of the Enlightenment' and so it is not necessary to even construct a choice between the modern and postmodern (May 2002).

Fredric Jameson (1991) understands postmodernism as an extension of the 'logic of late capitalism'. Jameson argues that globalization and multinational capitalism had resulted in mass consumerism and the total commodification of culture where 'images, styles and representations ... are the products themselves' (Connor 1989: 46). However, such theories which focus on the 'global postmodern' have been criticized. Stuart Hall argues that the postmodern idea of cultural homogenization is too simplistic (Hall et al. 1992: 304). He says that in our restructuring of theory we should acknowledge how the 'global' and the 'local' articulate and recognize that globalization is unevenly distributed and is also a western phenomenon indicative of unequal power relations between the 'west and the rest'.

One of the compelling criticisms of an aspirational postmodern social theory is that it offers no vehicle for social transformation (Sibeon 2007). To abandon all the values of Enlightenment ultimately means there would be no pursuit of generalizable knowledge and beyond mere assertion. This is a view held by Alex Callinicos (2000), who offers a Marxist critique of postmodernism. He states that postmodernity 'is merely a theoretical construct' (Callinicos 2000: 65) and that we should in no way move away from grand narratives. Only through the utilization of theories such as Marx's concept of class conflict and the possibility of revolution will social theory retain its ability to transform the world. To abandon modernist theorizing, Callinicos states, would mean 'there is little left for us to do, except, like Lyotard and Baudrillard, to fiddle while Rome burns' (Callinicos 1989: 174).

The criticisms levelled at postmodernism make the case that if a restructured social theory takes place, it must simultaneously acknowledge the power structures that still exist in society. Therefore, in this process, it is still necessary to preserve some Enlightenment values such as 'autonomy, tolerance, equality, and democracy' (Seidman 1998: 347). It could be argued that while postmodernism does offer a way to dismantle the foundations of Enlightenment, there is no offer of any ultimate resolution (Jameson 1991: xiii). Yet Lyotard himself firmly states that he is a philosopher and in no way an 'expert' (Lyotard 1984: xxv). In any case, to offer any sort of ultimate 'answer' to the problems posed by the breakdown of Enlightenment thought would indeed go against the postmodern claim that there is no ultimate answer to be found.

Harvey (1990) argues that postmodernism is purely based on aesthetics and has no ethical basis. However, Lyotard believed that the aesthetic nature of postmodern thought could and should be combined with a firm grounding in political practice (Lash 1990: 79). Hollinger argues that in this way Lyotard 'develops a richer and more positive conception of politics, justice and community' (Hollinger 1994: 129) and it could be said that this should form the basis of any restructuring of social theory. Lyotard's acknowledgement of prevailing power struggles alongside his attempts to define the nature of the postmodern world arguably highlights the possibility of a vision of knowledge as 'permanent revolution' (Seidman 2004: 207).

Bauman states that postmodern social theory 'can legitimize its right to exist ... only if it does exactly this: if it generates a social-scientific discourse which theorizes different aspects of contemporary experience, or theorizes them in a different way' (Bauman 1992: 93). Seidman agrees and predicts that 'postmodern paradigms of human studies' will take the place of 'modern social science' (Seidman 1994b: 348). In modern social science, the social scientist is considered capable of complete impartiality and able to relay pure, objective knowledge. The modern view was that the social scientist was striving to discover scientific knowledge in a detached way in the pursuit of public enlightenment and social progress. However, the postmodern social scientist takes on the role of interpretive social analyst and public educator. The social knowledge that they produce is recognized as having moral and political significance in terms of the potential it has to mould and influence public life, social identities and social norms (Seidman 2004).

As Habermas (1992a) points out, within intellectual debate postmodernism is too often seen as purely an attack on the values of Enlightenment and modernity without offering anything with which to move forward. He claims that the 'project of modernity' must not only be viewed as a theoretical necessity but also one which requires utter commitment and practical implementation and realization. Habermas castigates Lyotard as representative of the 'young conservatives' because of neo-Nietzschean discourse of irrationality and pessimism. Habermas (1981) claims that the project of modernity is 'unfinished' and contains unlimited capacity for emancipatory potential. Such potential draws on the specialization of culture for the enrichment of daily life and simultaneously the rational organizational of everyday life and experience. The project of modernity has unlimited potential to increase social rationality, justice and morality; this can be realized by cognitive progression and moral boundaries of rationality.

This issue here may be traced back to Chapter 2. Three of the traditions considered there – hermeneutics, phenomenology and pragmatism – placed in everyday action, speech and forms of life an epistemological status. With the postmodernist abandonment of those insights comes also the absence of a place for everyday practices. They are now consumed by vast impersonal forces. This strategy of rejection should come as no surprise given that the ghost of Nietzsche dances in the lines of their texts. It was Nietzsche who directed the attention of his disciples to the extraordinary. However, the result is that 'they contemptuously glide over the practice of everyday life as something derivative or inauthentic' (Habermas 1992a: 339). With the 'edifice of culture' masking everything: 'These lives do not matter – the text does not invite the reader to share their living, nor their dying' (Billig 1994: 164).

Habermas is concerned with the link between theory and practice. This is severed by postmodernist discourses in the assumption that the lifeworld has now disappeared (Baudrillard 2005), or that the heterogeneity of language games necessarily implies a denial of the universal properties of validity claims in speech (Lyotard). On the other hand, we might give some analytic mileage to its arguments in relation to everyday life and cultural consumption. Nevertheless, it would be the object of our analysis that changes, not the means of analysis. This strategy entails a qualified acceptance of some of its insights regarding consumer society (Rojek 2004).

It is not necessary, as those not always familiar with the history of social theory appear to do, to embrace postmodern social theory as the necessary corollary to postmodernity. Both Harvey and Jameson accept that, to some degree, qualitative changes have taken place in western societies, although both retain more of a Marxist spirit in their writings than this strategy might imply. From this point of view we can read Baudrillard as one who directs our attention to the ways in which the realities of production are increasingly informed by symbolism. This does not mean accepting the destruction of the lifeworld where anger against injustices remain, together with the desire for change (Kellner 2002).

We are now in a position to consider the ways in which abstract systems are becoming an increasing part of our everyday lives. In the age of globalization we do not have to follow a path forged by Lyotard (Spybey 1995). Instead, we are recognizing that 'the geo-historicization of social theory is long overdue' (Bhaskar 1993: 146). As Giddens puts it in his analysis of what he calls the state of 'high modernity':

> The globalizing tendencies of modernity are simultaneously extensional and intensional – they connect individuals to large-scale systems as part of complex dialectics of change at both local and global poles ... Yet this is not primarily an expression of cultural fragmentation or of the dissolution of the subject into a 'world of signs' with no centre. It is a process of the simultaneous transformation of subjectivity and global social organization, against a troubling backdrop of high-consequence risks.
>
> (Giddens 1990: 177)

Earlier tendencies within modernity are now seen to reach their height and spread through to all parts of social life. The postmodern pill is broken up and only partly swallowed. The transition is not from modern to postmodern societies, but from 'classical' to 'reflexive modernization' or, to express it another way, from 'industrial' to 'risk' societies (Beck 2006). This is the place where systems theory meets a 'green consciousness'. Wealth production, distribution and its consequences – the concerns of Marx and

Weber – meet a new paradigm, for we are now more aware of those processes which Weber analysed and found only humanity's fate:

> We are therefore concerned no longer exclusively with making nature useful, or with releasing mankind from traditional constraints, but also and essentially with problems resulting from techno-economic development itself. Modernization is becoming reflexive; it is becoming its own theme.
>
> (Beck 1992: 19)

Postmodernism is replaced by the potential that comes with 'reflexive modernization'. Here, the critical gaze is increasingly turned towards those systems which were once legitimized, but are now undergoing transformation (Beck et al. 1994). With the collapse of abstract systems into daily life comes an increasing awareness of the dual-nature of the forward march of modernity: for example, both empowerment and powerlessness; the fragmentation of identity, together with the possibilities that are created for new identities and the need to act globally, as well as locally (McGrew 2007). In this sense, there is a process of increasing politicization within everyday life as manifested in the growth of new social movements (Delanty 1999).

Summary

The idea of postmodernization as an epoch and postmodernism as a cultural movement, which includes social theory, has been an attractive one; judging, that is, by the numerous texts that have appeared on the subject. Whether by charting this journey through Baudrillard's modification, critique and subsequent abandonment of the Marxist tradition, or via Lyotard's information society and the heterogeneity of language games, the message to the modernists has been clear: abandon your dreams. The postmodern condition now celebrates chaos, diversity and fragmentation.

The reaction to this state of affairs is often either full embrace or total refutation. However, another way has been suggested whereby some of the insights are taken to be indicative of real historical trends. From this point of view, we should see Baudrillard as a kind of sounding board against which social theory might be tested. Indeed, he noted that his writings contain 'an element of provocation ... It is a sort of challenge to the intellectual and the reader that starts a kind of game' (Baudrillard in Gane 1993: 153–154). Perhaps this, in part, explains why he refused the label 'postmodernist' (M. Gane 1990). At the same time, Lyotard's call for the invention of new narratives sounds like a familiar call for resistance in the face of increased commodity fetishism. In this sense, it may be more constructive to see postmodernists as calling upon social theory to awake from any dogmatic slumbers that it may still possess.

Postmodernist writings appear to pick up on the ambivalence that was evident in the works of Simmel and Weber and take it in the direction of fatalism. Another route is available. This is not the route of the assumed complacency of the modernist but, on the contrary, taking the effects of high modernity and applying them to our current malaise. The assumed collapse of the cultural into the social is then tempered, as is the collapse of the aesthetic into the ethical realm whereby moral judgements are simply seen as matters of taste. This strategy is not complacent for it seeks to know and understand the negative, while also seeing the potential in new moral discourses that have emerged within lifeworlds in recent times.

PART III

Theories in action

12 Emotion in social relations

This book has illustrated how situating social theory analyses the ways in which social life is shaped, organized, sustained, experienced and transformed. It has examined the assumptions which shape individual and collective lives and reflected on such issues as power, identity, structure, agency and rationality and experiences as subjects. It is not only important to highlight what social theories say, but also how they can be deployed in understanding and applied for clarification. For this purpose we wish to examine a fundamental element in social life: 'emotion'. Although analysis of emotions has been developed, it does not tend to be at the centre of social theorizing (Barbalet 2002).

Tracking emotion in social theory

By using 'emotion' as a key theme, we hope to illuminate a central issue in all of our lives: that is, how we make our own history, while also being made by it. This relates to the beauty of the 'sociological imagination' (Mills 1970), or ways of thinking that celebrate the individual through an understanding that is relational and not in isolation from the world (Bauman and May 2001). What this refers to is an orientation to analysis that takes questions of our lives and the way we live them and places those in social contexts in order to understand how they are informed, manifest in our actions and hopes and enabled and constrained by particular conditions. It refers to a form of consciousness for understanding social processes (Mills 1970: 76) and unfolds as a lens through which to examine our lives.

Here we can speak of biography, but one placed within a wider social context that includes the history and tradition of a society. Mills suggests that a useful way of understanding this imagination is to deploy a distinction between 'personal troubles' and 'public issues' (Mills 1970: 14). All too often there is a common misperception to perceive biographies as just personal and private. As a result there is a celebration of an individualism which is isolating, rather than one of individual characters whose uniqueness is bound up with their contexts. Biographies are interwoven and interrelated to the wider public and political 'stage' of society. Thus, while emotion can be a 'private trouble', it is not unrelated to wider social forces of public issue. For Norbert Elias (1994), therefore, individual control as well as public regulation of emotions is interpreted as central to the civilizing process.

If we examine our theoretical journey from the point of view of understanding emotions, we can find strong threads throughout the development of social theory: for example, in the rise of the Enlightenment and ideas of rationality. Here we find the idea of controlling irrational emotions in order to enable a superior rationality to take place which then informs scientific reasoning and the idea of mastering nature. Emotions do play a central role in social development. We find this in Weber's concerns for legitimation, status, tradition and rationality in which an iron cage subsumes the emotions; in Durkheim's theory of social solidarity, moral force and symbolism there tends to be an emphasis upon a moral individualism in which emotions are held in check, but he was only too aware of their importance; in Marx's ideas on class consciousness and conflict mobilization there is a clear sense in which emotional attachment is ripped apart by the impersonal forces of capitalism and in Freud's work on the mind and its relationship to the repression of memory and the formation of civilization.

Moving into the terrain of more contemporary theory, there exists a body of knowledge that can revisited to make sense of emotion. We can find this in Goffman's ideas on the presentation of the self, as well as Parsons' (1951) structural functionalism and Luhmann's (1989) systems theory which examines emotions in terms of their congruence with the structural needs of the social systems. Emotions also feature in Giddens' (1990) theorizing on ontological insecurity and risk and Bourdieu's (2000) ideas on how individuals are constantly seeking to shape the world around them according to emotional contingencies. In feminist theorizing emotion is seen as gendered and shaped by ideas and forces of patriarchy (Marshall and Witz 2004), while governmentality also relates to the management of emotion (Dean 2007; Foucault 1977), or is seen as 'simulated' in hyper-reality (Baudrillard 2005).

There is much debate as to how to conceptualize emotion. It has been seen as a form of behaviour, or as an aspect of bodily physiology (Harré 1986). Emotions are also linked to role identities through their common affective representation and quality. In this way the emotional lives of people are part of a confirmation of their identity-situated selves in social interaction which may be manifest in collective forms: for example, in 1997 when Princess Diana died the mass media suggested that the British population were 'weepers' and 'traumatised' (Layder 2004). The media played a key role in defining the expression of 'public issues' through normative means. Expressions of emotion such as 'distress', 'passion' and 'desire' have marked out a territory that is alien to the terrain of rationalization. Emotions may be seen to be integral in everyday life as they play a role in communication, commitment and co-operation with others (Giddens 1992: 202). Within some traditional societies, the coding and regulation of powerful emotions were closely linked to spiritual belief and religious practice. Such forms of emotionality may be seen to have fragmented within the transition to modernity. As rationality replaced organized spirituality as a guarantor of social order, an emotionality that was no longer tied to social constructions of spirituality then presented itself as a threat: a powerful force which sought to scandalize reason and undermine the running of modern society (Layder 2006). Not only was emotion potentially disruptive to the sway of rationality, it had the capacity to carry messages about the operation of injustice and discrimination. It is clear, therefore, that: 'A very large class of human emotions results from real, anticipated, recollected or imagined outcomes of power and status relations' (Kemper 1984: 371).

If we are to see emotion as having a relational component, we need to consider the links between human action and social structure. Bendelow and Williams (1998) argue that there is a need to 'bring emotions back in' to social theory in a more concrete way, as they have always been implicit in the work of theorists. Simon Williams (2000) believes that emotions have a 'deep sociality' in that they are embedded in and constitutive of social interactions, and following Bourdieu (1984), he suggests that possessing the right sort of 'emotional capital' can help us to distinguish between different groups in society. Thus if a person appears to be highly anxious, tense and embarrassed around others, we might interpret their emotional state as being 'shy', and this can have significant implications for our reactions to them, in terms of social inclusion or exclusion. The capacity of the individual to position themselves will relate to how they are accommodated within cultural views with respect to belonging. Positioned as dependent, a person's 'cry of pain is hearable as a plea of help'. Yet, if positioned as dominant: 'a similar cry can be heard as a protest or even as a reprimand' (Harré and van Langenhove 1991: 396). At an individual level this, in turn, will relate to the attributes that a person possesses within given constellations of social relations or, in Bourdieu's terminology, 'fields'. We are therefore dealing with the relations that exist between self-identifying activities, positioning and belonging (May 2000).

Emotions are 'embodied': we do not simply have feelings that are 'all in the mind', but rather we express our emotions through bodily signs and 'symptoms', which in the case of existential characteristics such as being 'shy' or 'embarrassed', for example, might include 'blushing', 'shaking' and 'gaze aversion' (Layder 2006). As Denzin (1984) argues, emotions are temporarily embodied, situated self-feelings that are highly dependent on our perceptions of others and their (imagined) perceptions of us. Therefore, emotional practices can be seen as social acts that are significant in revealing the complex interrelationships between the individual and society via the body (Layder 2004).

These issues are reflected in the culture of late modernity, in which talk about emotions is almost as important as the emotions themselves, with those such as Meštrović (1993) claiming that we are living in a 'post-emotional society' and seeking a different understanding of Durkheim through an interrogation of the 'emotional enlightenment' (Meštrović 1992). It is also argued that discourses concerning emotion are extremely powerful in shaping our understandings of what certain emotions are deployed as linguistic categories to differentiate between different social groups (Lupton 1999).

Structure, emotion and rationality

In this section we discuss attempts to understand emotion by looking at three broad approaches that capture the ideas of those we have already discussed. First, we examine rationality, emotionalism and social structure and here include the work of Durkheim, Marx, Freud, Weber, critical theory and feminism. We then look at the social works of Garfinkel, Goffman and Mead and, finally, Foucault, Bourdieu and Baudrillard. During the course of these discussions we will find that emotion is a vehicle that can be used to shed light on how social theory constitutes its gaze on social life. A number of questions will guide this discussion. Is emotion regulated through structure? How relevant is micro-analysis to its explanation? Can we articulate discourse, embodiment and hyper-reality as conceptual tools to illuminate its complexity? The answers to these questions illustrate the relationship between micro levels of interaction among people (interpersonal troubles) and structures (public issues). We begin our discussion with emphasis on how emotion can be theorized by social structural approaches.

Social structural approaches assess the interpenetration of emotions and socio-cultural phenomena by understanding that emotions emerge from the operative social structure in a situation and emotions allow people to sense that structure, as well as the social consequences of actions. Moreover, because displays of emotion broadcast a person's subjective appraisals to others, they contribute tacitly to sharing views about social structure and to synchronization of rational action and feeling within a group.

Durkheim proposed that rituals hold society together by producing sacred objects and moral constraints. This has been expanded upon by proposing that a common emotional mood generated in rituals creates social solidarity and diffuses charismatic emotional energies that preserve and disseminate normative group patterns. Profaning a symbol usually will elicit anger and conflict between groups or between group factions, but reaffirming symbols generates positive emotion and synchronization within the group. The inherent emotionality of even commonplace interaction rituals is the glue that holds society such that it may be argued that the 'transcendental' of religion itself involves the worship of society as the pre-condition of group life and individuality.

Karl Marx saw society in terms of a conflict between economic classes that created what has been described as an 'alienated' condition. A dominant class (the bourgeoisie or 'capitalist' class) owns and controls the means of production, while an industrial working class, the 'proletariat', is exploited by them. For Durkheim, those members of modern society who did not manifest a degree of moral individualism could fall into a state of anomie, or normlessness. For Marx to prevent alienation is to call upon an 'emotional consciousness' to unite against the capitalist system. Although they did not explicitly speak about emotion, both Durkheim and Marx saw the problem of modernity as a recognition of alienation and normlessness that impinges on the regulation of individual behaviour. Nevertheless, for Marx, capitalist society was a denial of human freedom, while for Durkheim there was a tendency to emphasize society as a precondition. However, that is not to suggest that Durkheim was an apologist for inequality and injustice – far from it (Pearce 1989).

Rationality was a major concern for Sigmund Freud. Freud was struck by the way that people could be more or less rational most of the time but, on occasion, would behave in very irrational ways. For Freud this was very much to do with the tensions between, on the one hand, culture and on the other, instinct. For Freud the condition of humankind is in part a product of the fact that we live in a modern 'civilized' world. Freud believed that 'civilization' was a modern phenomenon and involved the development of control over individual emotions. A Freudian viewpoint would see the emotional content of the unconscious as not easily available to consciousness due to repression caused by painful and, in some cases dangerous, thoughts and feelings. This unconscious is dynamic – containing memories, perceptions, fantasies, impulses and conflicts – and must be pushed back or repressed in order to make life less conflictual. For some people this leads to the development of 'neuroses': 'Freudian theory is more than a theory of dualism, it is a theory of contradiction and struggle' (Kristeva 1999: 327).

Following Freud, Lacan developed a concept of 'desire' that originated in processes of emotional identification with significant others and then becomes encoded within systems of symbolic representations as infants become inducted into the world of language and discourse. At the point when a child is able to speak and think as 'I', he or she is cut off from all of the flows of his or her emotional experience. Lacan (1992) presents a stark choice: the price to be paid for entering into the world of language is also having to submit to the rules of operation of the symbolic order and hence to lose touch with the experience of desire.

We can say that rationalization is the process by which rational action becomes predominant in the social action of individuals and rationality becomes predominant in the patterns of action which are institutionalized in groups, organizations and other collectivities. Max Weber was particularly interested in the rise of instrumental rational action among individuals and formal rationality in organizations that crushed any form of human emotionalism in western modernity.

When we talk about rational-legal authority and bureaucracy, we are talking about instrumental rational action as institutionalized in the formal rationality of modern social organizations. The rationalization of social life involves ever-greater developments of technical means and a progressive relegation of the ends towards which these means are supposed to lead. As Weber argued in *The Protestant Ethic and the Spirit of Capitalism* (1930), the consequences of Calvinist religion were to lead to a rationalization of human behaviour that focused attention on the relationship between everyday activity and hopes for salvation. There is no guarantee of election to eternal life, but there are ways in which one should not behave if the possibility is to remain open. Therefore, an obsession with making the most of each minute gradually came to take complete precedence over the intended goal: that is, demonstrating to oneself that one is doing all that is possible to be destined for salvation.

Weber's analysis of the development of bureaucracy is similar. Bureaucracy, for Weber, is simply the most technically efficient means of organizing according to the tenets of rationalization. Increasingly, bureaucracy takes on a life and a logic of its own which may engender an 'iron cage of rationality' (rules, routines and regulations) from which there is no escape. Weber held a view where humans are seen as pursuing a variety of ends, not always in a rational manner.

Adorrno and Horkheimer (1979) believed that reason had been instrumentalized and incorporated into the structure of society. Thus reason was being used to strengthen rather than transform the system. Enlightenment had turned into its opposite and turned from being an instrument of liberation to domination. Enlightenment had always been infused with myth and the project of dominating nature, of using reason to control and dominate the world, was being applied to humans in oppressive ways (Adorno and Horkheimer 1979; Bauman 1989). The Nazi rationalization of death in the concentration camps and the experiences during war raised deep questions concerning the progressive force of reason and the efficacy of immanent critique in the light of such powerful social systems.

In linking the individual and their emotions to social structure, there is a rich tradition of work that has utilized the insights of Marx and Freud and this includes such figures as Eric Fromm, Wilhelm Reich and Bertell Ollman. Wilhelm Reich published a study in 1933 entitled *The Mass Psychology of Fascism*. In linking such a mass movement to elements of psychoanalysis, he sought to show how social orders create the characters they need for their preservation. Thus, in terms of Horkheimer's interests in the mechanisms through which the working class were increasingly integrated into advanced capitalist systems, Reich's approach went right through to an individual's psyche and the origins of sexual repression and its consequences for a given society. His theory of personality was thus conceived of as a 'specific way of being of an individual' and an expression of their total past (Ollman 1979: 182). Broadly speaking, non-capitalist and non-patriarchal relations are then theorized as being the only types of human relations which would not repress people's natural instinct for industry, honesty and co-operation. However, in other societies, Reich argued, the conscious ego predominates along with the unconscious governed by cruel instincts. Sexual repression is then linked to social and economic circumstances:

> Within capitalist society, the fight against extramarital relations, prostitution, venereal disease, and abortion is fought in the name of abstinence. Yet, it is this very abstinence, with its attendant igno-rance, that is responsible for these ills.
>
> (Ollman 1979: 187)

There are those who link emotional states to systems needs and relate that to environmental issues (Luhmann 1989). Here, the foremost patterns of anxiety concern the individual dimension. Moral communication is then related to insecurity about consequences on the individual level, which finally expresses itself in terms of anxiety. In risk communication the special characteristics of angst communication is understood as communication that cannot be reduced by rational argumentation or scientific analysis. Even attempts to reduce angst by information strategies tend to amplify the effects (Luhmann 1989). The emotional impact of angst communication seems to be self-evident contrary to the functional systems (economics, science, justice) and cannot be reduced by the logics of economics, science or law itself. Angst communication narrows the societal perspective on negative aspects of risks and therefore fades out the positive gains. Such negative emotional communication is understood as being risky as far as it blocks necessary societal decisions and the development of knowledge.

Here we can link emotion to issues associated with trust. However, maintaining emotions is not necessary for trusting, which could be detached from the original emotions. Trust as linked to emotion is understood as rational irrationality (Luhmann 1989). Where learning by trial and error is not possible – for example, in the case of nuclear power and genetically modified food – progress and decisions are only possible on the basis of constituting trust (Powell et al. 2007). Therefore, a modern society, character-ized by a higher degrees of change, is 'endangered by emotions' (Luhmann 1982: 365).

Issues associated with emotions are also brought under the general category of 'ontological security' (Giddens 1990). This, in turn, is linked to routine in everyday life:

> Ontological security and routine are intimately connected, via the pervasive influence of habit. ... The predictability of the (apparently) minor routines of day-to-day life is deeply involved with a sense of psychological security. When such routines are shattered – for whatever reason – anxieties come flooding in, and even very firmly founded aspects of the personality of the individual may become stripped away and altered.
>
> (Giddens 1990: 98)

Growing risks in modernity lead to a sense of fate within what is a secularized world that manages it problems in rational-instrumental ways (Giddens 1990: 133). New risks then strain an emotional basis in late modernity and thereby the personality or identity of people. Because new risks and uncertainties cannot be simply solved, they are managed in different ways. Four strategies are identified (Giddens 1990). They are pragmatic acceptance, sustained optimism, cynical pessimism and radical engagement. Pragmatic acceptance is a response to the insight that many things in the outside world cannot be controlled individually. Therefore in this perspective there is a priority to manage everyday problems. The life-threatening dangers of nuclear power or terrorism are suppressed. Sus-tained optimism represents a faith in science that things can still be managed. Religious concepts of the world can come close to this kind of belief that things will be improved in time. In contrast to pragmatic acceptance, cynical pessimism manages the lack of control regarding the future and its attendant anxieties with the help of 'dark humour'. Radical engagement then encompasses the necessity to do something actively in relation to sources of danger in order that they are alleviated.

The 'McDonaldization' thesis picks some of these points, but takes them in a different direction. This is an influential approach to the analysis of social relations influenced by Weber. The thesis has several characteristics (Ritzer 2004). First, modern society is characterized by the pursuit of efficiency expressed in terms of the means to achieve specified ends. This includes, for example, the assembly-line philosophy of Macs, drive-throughs and making the customers work to assemble their own burgers, dispose of the resultant waste and even operate their own check-outs after buying food and goods. Second, calculability in respect to process and product expressed in terms of quantifying meals, portion and average times. Third, the pursuit of predictability, where we find standardized meals and Mcworkers all over the world trained in generalized ways. Fourth, the deployment of non-human technology in the process of production and consumption: for example, factory farms, microwaves, computerization and stock control through cash tills, as well as drinks dispensers and robot workers (Ritzer 2004; Ritzer and Ryan 2007). Clearly, what is efficient for the interests of a company is not necessarily so efficient for consumers or the environment of which we are all a part. Emotion then becomes detached from any connection with the experience of real emotions and become McDonalized within contemporary experiences whose exemplars include theme parks and heritage centres (Ritzer 2004).

The dichotomy in modernity between rationality and emotion is a common feature in accounts concerning how feelings relate to contemporary existence. We can see this in the public/private split that constructed the family, for example, as an oasis of emotionality, or what has been characterized as 'a haven in a harsh world' (Watson 2001). In this picture, emotions are seen as central to the rationalization of family life whereby women are situated, discursively and economically, in positions where they may be given a 'duty' to care emotionally for others – children, older relatives and men. However, as Marshall and Witz (2004) point out, this emotion bargain may actually be more complex than it appears. Women and men may enter 'partnerships' on an unequal basis in terms of material relations and this can serve to reinforce gendered inequalities in emotional relations:

> Women have been put in a position of being economically dependent within patriarchy but the relationship between economic dependency and emotional dependency is not straightforward. Although this is not usually made explicit within the relationship, men's dependency needs are most often met within marriage and their emotional worries by their wives. No equivalent place exists for women.
>
> (Eichenbaum and Orbach 1985: 86–87).

The unequal social position of women may place them in the contradictory position of feeling dependent on men but actually being depended on by men for the servicing of their emotional needs.

Interaction, symbolism and embodiment

In this section we examine the interpenetration of emotions and social phenomena by understanding that emotions are both constructed and determined. This approach points to a certain paradox: that is, a feeling is what happens to us in terms of private troubles, yet it is also what we do to make it happen (Goffman 1959). Emotions thus can erupt during social interaction. The result is that they become judged for suitability according to cultural and ideological standards and managed to effect culturally acceptable displays that yield social acceptance.

Emotion is more than a biological act of procreation, or a physiological response to pleasure or pain (N. Gane 2005). It is a complex social interaction between two or more people. It is a dynamic interaction not only between one's own personal values, attitudes, dispositions, cognitions, wants, desires and behaviours, but, more importantly, the interaction between these entities and those of others (Layder 2004). For example, sexual behaviours, including acts of 'courtship' can be interpreted not simply as means to ends, but as acts invested with meanings that are interpreted differently by different people (Layder 2004). Both Mead and Goffman propose that people construct and understand social action so as to have important symbolic meanings affirmed by impressions generated in behaviour. People credit themselves and others with specific identities during social encounters. They then engage in physical and mental work so that events create impressions that maintain sentiments attached to their identities, as well as to other categories of action (behaviours, settings and emotions included).

What then happens to the emotions in the context of social interaction? Freund (1988) argues that individuals try to regulate their feelings to fit in with the norms of the situation and that if there are conflicting demands, a 'dramaturgical stress' is then apparent. So people may feel 'sad' or 'happy' because a particular social situation requires that they act in one way, while feeling a different way. Put together, these two oppositional motivations can leave people feeling ambivalent and uncertain (Layder 2004), as well as ill equipped to deal with the situation and this in turn leads to greater self-consciousness:

> we all believe that everyone else knows and understands the 'rules' governing social interaction, even though nobody ever talks about them explicitly, and so we might be forgiven for thinking that we 'ought' to disguise our ignorance with a show of confidence.
>
> (Hochschild 1983: 87

Emotion work (Hochschild 2003) thereby forms part of everyday lives, both in the private world of the self and in the public spheres of interaction where individuals learn socially appropriate ways of acting and expression management. Hochschild referred to these codes as 'feeling rules' and argues that they are historically and culturally specific. In contemporary western societies, emotions have become commercialized and 'sold' in the form of marketable services.

The personal and normative systems unite when members are deeply committed to their group identities; in that case, people spontaneously emote and act according to group norms in order to experience affirmation of self through the reflected appraisals of others (Burke and Reitzes 1991). The two systems diverge when a person maintains multiple definitions of a situation simultaneously, and the actor's deepest commitment is to an identity other than the public identity. In that case, emotion management is required to prevent the display of emotions appropriate to the private identity, and to authenticate one's supposed commitment to the public identity as a public issue.

A social constructionist literature on emotions has been embedded in the Cartesian tradition which treats emotions as an awkward mix of physical and physiological processes, on the one hand, and personal experiences on the other, with the bulk of attention given over to an analysis of the latter (Layder 2004). More recently, social constructionist theory has more plausibly tried to minimize the experiential element in emotion and emphasize the construction of the social setting and role that discourses play in the social construction of emotions.

Within early modernity, emotions could be interpreted as romance, sentiment, or spiritualism. In late modernity, emotions have become commodities that may be consumed, induced or traded within an emotional industrial complex. Foucault's (1967, 1977) approach to emotions focuses on the role of discourses in effecting outcomes. In this perspective, displays of emotion are not uncivilized eruptions coming from deep within individual psyches (Foucault 1977). Discourses are a set of statements, labels and assumptions that operate to 'pin' 'true' definitions on what is or what is not the case: for example, the power of psychiatry in defining 'mental illness' (Foucault 1967). The power to label an individual as 'mad', 'psychotic', 'anxious', 'phobic', 'schizophrenic' and 'neurotic' and the process of pinning such discourses to people reveals an historical unfolding of knowledge and power in psychiatric development. The birth of the medical profession brought with it a different way of seeing illness and well-being related to structural and personal spaces. Most notably, the sick 'other' became an object to be modified (Powell and Biggs 2004). Under the 'medical gaze', a process of normalization is engendered in that people become their bodies; disaggregated into a series of dysfunctional parts (Foucault 1982).

It is typical in neo-liberal societies to deploy statistical risk calculation (as in epidemiology and (social) insurance) and ascribe risks to individual's decision making in order to govern populations (Foucault 1991a). Individuals become object of governmental strategies not as a person, but as a bearer of indicators or factors (Dean 2007). As this relates to governmental, institutional and medial constructions of social reality, emotions become a key component. Yet emotion and affect are subordinated under a moral technology in which subjectivity comes in sight as far as it is addressed and constituted by particular discourses. Governmental strategies use people's enthusiasm by opening opportunities and stressing how much better their life would be if they took up the supports offered to them (N. Rose 2006).

As was noted earlier in the book, there is stress in Foucualt's work on the body. Similarly, Bourdieu's interpretation of emotions rests on the assumption that there is a continuous process of embodiment, whereby individuals are constantly in a relation to the world in order to strive, cope and carry on with life's daily emotional contingencies. Experiences of embodiment then differ because people are situated in a different place in the world (Bourdieu 2000). These differences are apparent in gender, social class, sexuality, ethnicity and age. Social positions – defined by forms of capital – are then associated with a distinctive view-of-the-world that regulates emotional spaces (Bourdieu 1984, 1998).

Although reason has had a bumpy ride under the philosophical gaze of Derrida, or the more culturally inspired and historical works of Foucault, to say nothing of the army of thinkers who occupy the terrain of postmodern-ism, references to reason are often a rhetorical device upon which the power effects that lay beneath the surface of such utterances depend for their continuation and success. In analysing these power effects, aspects of feminist theory offer a corrective to the many assumptions men commonly make in our thinking: for example, by challenging the presumed difference between feelings and emotion (read women) and reason (read men) as essentialist. In terms of everyday organizational life, we can then link the idea of change, substantiated by reason, with identity.

The very commitment that arises from within practice and provides for self-identifying narratives of, for example, professional experience and pur-pose can become marginalized in processes of transformation that allude to narrow concepts of reason for their justification. At this point the gendered components of professional knowledge are at their most apparent. Expres-sions of anger, born of this commitment and directed against the conse-quences and rationale of transformative practices that represent the supposed logic of the market, are then readily dismissed as being symptomatic of 'emotional outbursts'. Displays of episodic power (May 1999b) are individu-alized and co-participants to these encounters are relieved of the need to consider the reasons *why* someone expressed such feelings in the first place. The conditions of practice which give rise to commitment are then bracketed via a concentration on the inappropriateness of behaviour in terms of *how* it is manifested by the individual concerned. This process has its parallels in the presuppositions of performance measures as the triumph of method over purpose (May 2006). What we see here is the expression of a rationale that takes an understanding of the relationship between knowledge and the context of action as heightening professional discretion: that is, the very target of transformation. Measures are then introduced that have no bearing upon that context and so lead to abstracted understandings of organizational actions. It is the pursuit of 'how' through 'what' (May 2001). Emotion and organization then meet (Fineman 2000) in a world in which 'emotional intelligence' becomes a resource into which managers are urged to tap to promote the effectiveness of their organizations (Knights and McCabe 2003).

These disembodied practices meet with the embodied practices of social agents who are in a relation to the world that is accorded with meaning, while that world also accords their actions with meaning (Bourdieu 2000). The habitus provides for a practical sense that refers to an adjustment of social agents' practices to the constraints and opportunities imposed or offered by their emotions (Bourdieu 1990). The emotional body then becomes a way of being-in-the-world: 'the body is in the world but the social world is in the body' (Bourdieu 2000: 152). It is as much a social construction, where social structures are internalized, as the site of experience, desire and creativity. Similarly to Merleau-Ponty's phenomenological bodily schema, which showed how the body adapts to its environment through a system of sensory and motor relations, Bourdieu contends that 'we learn bodily'. Often unconsciously, the body becomes attuned to the world by being exposed to its regularities (Bourdieu 2000).

The symbols that we draw upon in order to make sense of the world around us and of our emotions are clearly changed under conditions that are supposed to represent the 'death of the real'. In this case emotions are seen to exist in a hyperreality that is simulated, connecting more and more deeply to things like television sitcoms, music videos, virtual reality games, or Disneyland. Yet what of the most intimate experiences? Tracing the social construction of love, Baudrillard (2005) suggests that seduction is artificial and symbolic, involves flirtations, double entendres, sly looks and whispered promises. It involves the manipulation of signs like make-up, fashion, perfumes, aftershaves and gestures to achieve control over a symbolic order. On top of each of these modes is now layered the 'cool' seduction of media images disseminated by television, radio and film.

Similarly, when it comes to the emotional content and crises and death, Baudrillard (1993) has claimed that the first Gulf War did not happen, as such, but became a media representation of reality. A resultant manipulation leads in television to emotional clues as to appropriate responses: for example, canned laughter and routine cues to applause. In western culture these 'maps' of reality become more real than our actual lives. Consumerism and emotion are then taken to new lengths. Individuals drive to out-of-town shopping malls full of identical chain stores and products; they watch television shows about film directors and actors and go to films about television production and even vote for former Hollywood actors as president or state governor (Lemert 2006).

Summary

We have provided an overview of how different social theories can be applied to understand emotion. We highlighted how emotion shifts the focus of our attention away from the idea of individual, private worlds, to the wider context of social relations and the way in which symbolism and position are implicated in emotional work and the meanings that are attached to actions. Emotions are inextricably linked to 'private troubles' and 'public issues' in both classic and contemporary social theories. We can see through Weber's concerns for legitimation, status, charisma, tradition and rationality; in Durkheim's theory of social solidarity, moral force and symbolism; in Marx's analysis of consciousness and class alienation; in Mead's work on taking the role of the other; in Bourdieu's work on habitus, capital and field and the so-called hyper-real of the postmodern condition.

If this chapter is about examining the ways different approaches could be mobilized to illuminate what is often taken to be an individual, or private matter, but is in fact social, the next chapter examines what is taken to be a more abstract process but one which shapes all of our lives.

13   Globalization

Introduction

In Chapter 12, we examined the different ways that traditional and contemporary social theories could provide analytical frameworks for understanding the role of emotion in social life. This chapter focuses on a second important theme: globalization. In Parts I and II of the book, we have explored how the Enlightenment and its legacy have impinged upon the emergence and creation of social theories that have attempted to explain social, economic, political and cultural transformations in modernity.

A key component to this unfolding is the development of the nation state and levels of human relations within it (Ritzer 2004). This has also been to define and understand the power of the state and its effects on individual biographies and population groups characterized by social differentiation. The world is now changing at a rapid pace and the scope and impact of these transformations have multiple dimensions and implications that transcend geographic and cultural boundaries (B. S. Turner 2006). Developed and developing countries alike are acknowledging this phenomenon in their attempts to deal with the complex relations of correspondence and contradiction emerging from the 'new world disorder' (Shaw 1994). Globalization is no longer one topic among many, but a central one, being regarded as the way to read world dynamics and the process of world history (Korany 1994).

Globalization is contributing to major challenges and changes at the level of the state. The role of the state has been transformed to that of promoting and funding market solutions and placing greater responsibility upon the individual. Hence globalization has transformed the way individuals see themselves in the world. Individuals must now reflexively accept the common predicament of living in one world (Dean 2007). This provokes the formulation of contending worldviews. In a compressed world, the comparison and confrontation of worldviews are bound to produce new cultural conflicts. In such conflict old traditions and new ideas play a key symbolic role, since they can be mobilized to provide an ultimate justification for one's view of the world: two cases in point being the resurgence of Islamic fundamentalist groups that combine traditionalism with a global agenda and neo-conservative groups who promote 'democracy' and 'freedom' through a 'War on Terror' (Sands 2006). A globalized world is thus connected but not harmonious. It is diverse and prone to multiplicity and fragmentation. In that context it is highly pertinent that social theory steps up to the challenge and rethinks how we 'unmask' the implications of globalization.

We may approach globalization in terms of being 'the present as history' (Mills 1970: 146) and consider its implications at three levels: economic, political and cultural. The economic refers to processes of the global dominance of transnational corporations, global finance, flexible production and assembly and the rise of information and service economies (Smart 2007). Political globalization can be understood in terms of the growth of international organizations, sub-national regional autonomy, the spread of post-welfare public policies and global social movements (Ritzer 2004). Globalization relates to the effectiveness and cohesion of the nation state as its traditional functions are hollowed out and transferred 'upwards' to international organizations and 'downwards' to regional bodies through the exercise of regional governance (Brenner 2004; McGrew 2007). Cultural globalization is a process indicated by the growth of global consumption cultures, tourism, media and information flows and transnational migration and identities. The latter half of the twentieth century has seen the growth of global brands and media that carry both cultural and economic significance (Estes et al. 2003). A globalized world is one where events are experienced instantly even by people in spatially distant locations through access to digital communicative technologies:

> Today, virtually all nation states have gradually become enmeshed in and functionally part of a larger pattern of global transformations and global flows. ... Transnational networks and relations have developed across virtually all areas of human activity. Goods, capital, people, knowledge, communications and weapons, as well as crime, pollutants, fashions and beliefs, rapidly move across territorial boundaries. ... Far from this being a world of 'discrete civilizations' or simply an international order of states, it has become a fundamentally interconnected global order, marked by intense patterns of exchange as well as by clear patterns of power, hierarchy and unevenness.
>
> (Held 2000: 49)

This creates a complex range of social interconnections governed by the speed of communications, thereby creating a partial collapse of boundaries within national, cultural and political space (Bauman 2001).

Situating globalization

Globalization has become one of the central but contested concepts of contemporary social science (Ritzer 2004). The term has further entered everyday commentary and analysis and features in many political, cultural and economic debates. The contemporary globalized world order originates in the international organizations and regulatory systems set up after the Second World War – including the United Nations, General Agreement on Tariffs and Trade (now the World Trade Organization), the International Monetary Fund (IMF) and the World Bank (Smart 2007).

The end of the Cold War was the prelude to the maturity of the concept of globalization. From 1989 to the present, it is possible at least to imagine a 'borderless' world in which people, goods, ideas and images would flow with relative ease and the major global division between East and West had diminished significantly. A world divided by competing ideologies of capitalism and socialism has given way to a more uncertain world in which capitalism became the dominant economic and social system. Coinciding with these changes, a major impetus to globalization was the development and availability of digital communication technologies from the late 1980s with dramatic consequences for the way economic and personal behaviour were conducted (Castells 2005) – this has transcended to mass communication from the Internet in 1990s to mobile phones from 2000 onwards (McGrew 2007). The collapse of communism and growth of digital technologies further coincided with a global restructuring of the state, finance, production and consumption associated with neo-liberalism. Coupled with this, in a post 9/11 world, there has been the 'War on Terror' and its implications for the reordering of the geopolitical global agenda.

Since the advent of industrial capitalism as a feature of the development of modernity, intellectual discourse has been replete with allusions to phenomena strikingly akin to those that have gathered the attention of recent theorists of globalization (Bauman 2001). Nineteenth- and twentieth-century philosophy and social commentary include numerous references to an unclear yet widely shared awareness that experiences of distance and space are inevitably transformed by the emergence of new forms of technological transportation (for example, rail and air travel) and communication (the telephone). These developments dramatically heightened the possibilities for human interaction across existing geographical and political divides (Smart 2007). Bauman has proposed nothing less than a rewriting of human history based on what he called 'the retrospective discovery' of the centrality of spatial distance and speed of communication in the constitution of all societies (Bauman 1998: 15).

Long before the introduction of the term globalization, the appearance of novel high-speed forms of social activity generated extensive commentary about the compression of space. Indeed, Karl Marx formulated the first theoretical explanation of the sense of territorial compression. The imperatives of capitalist production drove the bourgeoisie to nestle

> everywhere, settle everywhere, and establish connections everywhere. The juggernaut of industrial capitalism constituted the most basic source of technologies resulting in the annihilation of space, helping to pave the way for intercourse in every direction, universal interdependence of nations.
>
> (Marx 1980: 476)

Marx identified an ever-rising scope and volume of transnational relations, along with technologically orchestrated process of deepening spatio-temporal integration, as central to the very 'laws of motion' of capitalist development.

Because they were rooted in its core relations, private property and wage labour, they would keep 'reasserting themselves' and on an ever-greater scale, so long as those relations were reproduced over time. The consequence is that globalization as a spatial process has facilitated the emergence of a new kind of global city based on highly specialized service economies that serve specific, particularized functions in the economic system at the expense of former logics of organization tied to manufacturing-based economies. To enable global markets to function effectively, they need to be underpinned by local managerial work that is concentrated in cities. Further, privatization and deregulation during the 1980s and 1990s shifted various governance functions to the corporate world, again centralizing these activities in urban spaces. In post-industrial cities there is a concentration of command functions that serve as production sites for finance and the other leading industries and provide marketplaces where firms and governments can buy financial instruments and services.

Global cities have become strategic sites for the acceleration of capital and information flows and at the same time spaces of increasing socio-economic polarization. One effect of this has been that such cities have gained in importance and power relative to nation states. There have emerged new corridors and zones around nodal cities with increasingly relative independence from surrounding areas. Globalization simultaneously brings home and exports the processes of privatization, competition, rationalization and deregulation as well as the transformation of all sectors of society through technology and the flexibility and deregulation of employment.

The consequences of globalization have led to what has been termed the 'death of distance' or the 'end of geography' (Morgan 2001). An increasing globalization and internationalization of markets, economies, societies and environments is seen to break down the boundaries of time and space. Yet far from being an end to human interaction, there has been an increasing emphasis on regions, localities and cities as engines for economic growth (Cooke et al. 1997; May and Perry 2006; Savitch 2002). The so-called 'knowledge economy' is now seen to be based on economies of scale and a critical mass of complementary expertise leading to innovation and wealth creation (Florida 2002). Successful firms are thus seen to draw upon location-specific factors within their local environments (Perry and May 2007; Porter 1990; Simmie 2002).

We are therefore dealing with both scale and intensity (Sassen 2001). Urban and regional scholars are taking more interdisciplinary approaches to understanding the relationship between the global and local as processes that rely upon each other (Storper 1997). In other words, global success is based on local strengths and vice versa. Cities provide critical mass, vibrant environments, connectivity, highly paid jobs and concentrations of cultural and leisure activities. Regions, on the other hand, provide space for the development of projects, wider choices of housing, a workforce and skills base, as well as leisure opportunities. These socio-economic and spatial shifts have profound consequences for matters of social inclusion and economic benefit to cities and regions.

At this point the uses of globalization as the rationale and means by which corporate capital may transnationally pursue new low wage strategies and weaken the power of labour, women and ethnic minority populations, becomes a key issue. Globalization greatly extends the corporate capacity of capital to 'exit' a nation and thereby to escape corporate responsibility and taxation in the course of struggles with labour (Klein 2001). Global financial markets also challenge traditional attempts by liberal democratic nation states to rein in the activities of bankers, spawning insecurity about the growing power and influence of financial markets over democratically elected representative institutions. An important element in the 'global cultural economy' (Appadurai 1996) concerns perils of monetary globalization, defined as 'cross-border movements' of loans, equities, direct and indirect investments and currencies. He describes a key process of globalization as the 'imperialism of finance' in which uncontrolled and rapid movements of capital may quickly destabilize national economies. Following this, Susan Strange (1986) has characterized the international financial sector to a 'casino' in which assets are traded increasingly by private financial institutions, entirely for profit.

Two oppositional views on globalization have been described (Giddens 1990). First, that of 'sceptics', which sees globalization as a myth and not altogether different from earlier transformational changes in society. Second, there are the 'radicals' who understands globalization as real and with consequences that are indifferent to national borders. Giddens takes the view of the 'radicals', noting that globalization is revolutionary on multiple economic, political, cultural and social levels. He argues that globalization is characterized by a complex set of forces, embodied by contradictory, oppositional processes that both pull away power and influence from the local and nation state level, while also creating new pressures for local autonomy and cultural identity.

In relation to globalization Giddens examines the relationship between abstract systems (for example, 'symbolic tokens' and 'expert systems') and the relations of trust which exist between people that are established in what he calls, following Goffman (1983), situations of 'co-presence'. The analytic focus is on how 'disembedded' systems are 're-embedded' in social relations whereby the former may act to sustain or undermine the latter. However, these should not be analytically separated as per Giddens arguments for a duality, rather than dualism, between actions and structure (Giddens 1984): 'Personal life and the social ties it involves are deeply intertwined with the most far-reaching of abstract systems. It has long been the case, for example, that Western diets reflect global economic interchange' (Giddens 1990: 120).

The nature of personal trust then becomes a central preoccupation. Trust needs to be 'won' which involves *a 'mutual process of self-disclosure'* (Giddens 1990: 121, original italics). This is seen to be derived through a process of self-enquiry that is inextricably linked with the 'reflexivity of modernity'. However, this is not to suggest that the lifeworld and abstract systems are symbiotically linked via the exercise of trust. Opting out of those systems which are regarded as unacceptable can still lead to their persistence. The example Giddens uses here are Jehovah's Witnesses rejecting much of electronic technology. However, the collapse of trust in a bank has very different consequences and from this point of view the world economy is seen to be 'subject to the vagaries of generalized trust' (Giddens 1994: 90).

When it comes to a consideration of this melting of abstract systems into everyday life, Giddens theorizes the self as a humanist heroine or hero. The individual is a defender of the last rights of the autonomous subject; hence a preoccupation with 'ontological security' and pronouncements on the death of poststructuralism (Giddens 1987). Yet this characterization is problematic in the sense that it is not individuals, as such, who face the 'external world', but an external world mediated by social relations with significant others. Paradoxically, ontological insecurity becomes 'de-socialized' (Burkitt 1992).

As Sibeon (2004) has suggested, a general point arising out of Giddens' work on globalization concerns: 'the importance of avoiding either/or dichotomies that emphasise localism and particularity or globalism and homogenising tendencies'. To compound this are the 'disjunctures' between the economy, culture and politics (Appadurai 2000). These occur around five dimensions of global cultural flows: ethnoscapes (the shifting landscape of people moving around the globe); technoscapes (the global configuration of technology); financescapes (the movement of global capital); mediascapes (media images of the world); and ideoscapes (ideologies and counter-ideologies relating to state power). The suffix of 'scape' is used to refer to the

> fluid, irregular shapes of these landscapes, shapes that characterize international capital as deeply as they do international clothing styles. These terms ... also indicate that these are not objectively given relations that look the same from every angle of vision but, rather, that they are deeply perspectival constructs, inflected by the historical, linguistic, and political situatedness of different sorts of actors: nation states, multi-nationals, diasporic communities, as well as sub national groupings and movements ... and even intimate face-to-face groups. ... The individual actor is the last locus of this perspectival set of landscapes [that are] navigated by agents who both experience and constitute larger formations.
>
> (Appadurai 1996: 33)

Whether globalization is imagined or real requires conceptual analysis. The next section examines competing arguments relating to globalization.

Global consequences

As with the phenomena itself, the understanding of globalization is complex. Roland Robertson refers to the concept of a 'global consciousness' in terms of 'the compression of the world and the intensification of consciousness of the world as a whole' (Robertson 1992: 8). Via thought and action, global consciousness makes the world a single place. What it means to live in this place and how it must be ordered, become universal questions. These questions receive different answers from individuals and societies that define their position in relation to both a system of societies and the shared properties of humankind from very different perspectives. This confrontation of worldviews means that globalization involves 'comparative interaction of different forms of life' (Robertson 1992: 27). Unlike theorists who identify globalization with late (capitalist) modernity, Robertson sees global interdependence and consciousness preceding the advent of capitalist modernity.

European expansion and state formation have boosted globalization since the seventeenth century and the contemporary shape of the world in the nineteenth century, when international communications, transportation and conflict dramatically intensified relationships across societal boundaries (Mann 2006). In that period, the main reference points of a globalized order took shape: nation state, world-system, societies and humanity. These elements of the global situation became 'relativised' since national societies and individuals, in particular, must interpret their very existence as parts of a larger whole. To some extent, a common framework has guided that work: for example, states can appeal to a universal doctrine of nationalism to legitimate their particularizing claims to sovereignty and cultural distinction (Delanty and Isin 2003). Nevertheless, such limited common principles do not provide a basis for world order.

The concept of time-space is seen as central to globalization (Giddens 1991a). This is a process in which locales are shaped by events far away and vice versa, while social relations are disembedded, or 'lifted out' from locales. For example, peasant households in traditional societies largely produced their own means of subsistence, a tithe was often paid in kind (goods, animals, or labour), money was of limited value and economic exchange was local and particularistic. 'Reflexive modernization' replaced local exchange with universal exchange of money, which simplifies otherwise impossibly complex transitions and enables the circulation of highly complex forms of information and value in increasingly abstract and symbolic forms. The exchange of money establishes social relations across time and space, which under globalization is speeded up. Similarly, expert cultures arise as a result of the scientific revolutions, which bring an increase in technical knowledge and specialization. Specialists claim 'universal' and scientific forms of knowledge, which enable the establishment of social relations across vast expanses of time and space.

Social distance is created between professionals and their clients as in the modern medical model, which is based upon the universal claims of science. As expert knowledge dominates across the globe, local perspectives become devalued and modern societies are reliant on expert systems (Beck 1992). Trust is increasingly the key to the relationship between the individual and expert systems and is the glue that holds modern societies together. Yet where trust is undermined, individuals experience 'ontological insecurity' and a sense of insecurity with regard to effects of social reality (Giddens 1991a).

The concept of a 'borderless world' epitomises enthusiasm and the belief that globalization brings improvement in human conditions (Ohmae 2005). Ohmae describes an 'invisible continent' – a moving, unbounded world in which the primary linkages are now less between nations than between regions that are able to operate effectively in a global economy without being closely networked with host regions. The invisible continent can be dated to 1985 when Microsoft released its first version of Windows; CNN as a 24 hours a day news channel was launched; Cisco Systems began; the first Gateway 2000 computers were shipped and corporations such as Sun Microsystems and Dell expanded into the market. Nowadays there has been an explosion of corporations that affect social, economic and political relationships. Transnational corporations increasingly do not treat nation states as single entities and region states make effective points of entry into the global economy. For example, when Nestlé moved into Japan, it chose the Kansai region round Osaka and Kobe rather than Tokyo as a regional doorway (Smart 2007). This fluidity of capital is creating a borderless world in which capital moves around, chasing the best products and the highest investment returns regardless of national origin, leaving questions over the future of the state (Jessop 2002).

The Internet has changed not only the way business works, but also the way people interact on a personal level – from buying and selling online to planning for retirement, managing investment and online bank accounts. Although, in recent times, the dark side of the Internet has revealed the illegitimate ways that groups and individuals use 'hyper borderless worlds' with data espionage, data theft, credit card fraud, child pornography, extremism and terrorism – it is estimated that up to £40 billion a year is made by international organized crime syndicates on the web.

The Internet is a global system and decisions made on virtual 'platforms' (that are created by corporations rather than governments) determine how money moves around the globe. The emergence of around-the-world 24/7 financial markets, where major cross-border financial transactions are made in cyberspace represents a familiar example of the economic face of globalization (Schneider 2007). The definition and social construction of 'the problem' of state power is transferring from the state and its citizenry to private sector global finance. Looking ahead, the race is on for 'global custody' through the 'Ticking of the Pensions Time Bomb', as described by the *Financial Times* with Europe as a 'battleground' for the US Banks (The Bank of New York, State Street Bank, JP Morgan and Citibank) competing against the European Deutsche, BNP Paribas and HSBC for custody of the growing pensions market and the highly lucrative financial services supporting it. In less developed countries, women especially have been among those most affected by the privatization of pensions and health care and the burden of debt repayments to agencies such as the World Bank and the IMF (Walker and Naegelhe 1999).

David Harvey (2006) emphasizes the ways in which globalization revolutionizes the qualities of space and time. As space appears to shrink to what Marshall McLuhan (1975) refers to as a 'global village' of telecommunications and ecological interdependencies and as time horizons shorten to the point where the present is all there is, so we have to learn how to cope with an overwhelming sense of compression of spatial and temporal worlds (Harvey 1990: 240). Time-space compression 'annihilates' space and creates 'timeless time' through flexible accumulation and new technologies, the production of signs and images, just-in-time delivery, reduced turnover times and speeding up and both de- and re-skilling workforces. Harvey (1990) points to the ephemerality of fashions, products, production techniques, speedup and vertical disintegration, financial markets and computerized trading, instantaneity and disposability and regional competitiveness as consequences of these transformations.

It could be argued that an exclusive focus on time-space compression would be misleading. Interpersonal exchanges involving individual agency [to negotiate, discuss, interpret and act upon the data) are still of considerable importance and a similar point can be made in relation to socio-economic development and urban spaces (Sassen 2006). Since the vast majority of human activities are still tied to a concrete geographical location, the more decisive facet of globalization concerns the manner in which distant events, cities and forces impact on local or 'glocal' spaces and relations (Tomlinson 1999: 9).

At the same time, globalization refers to those processes whereby geographically distant events and decisions impact to a growing degree on 'glocal' education (Loader 2001). For example, the insistence by powerful political leaders such as George W. Bush and Tony Blair in the western world that the IMF should require that Latin and South American countries commit themselves to a particular set of economic policies might result in poorly paid teachers and researchers as well as large, understaffed lecture classes in São Paulo or Lima. While this is happening the latest innovations in information technology from a computer research laboratory in India could quickly change the classroom experience of students in Tokyo.

There are those who would argue that the changes associated with globalization are so far-reaching that we should now talk of a 'theory beyond societies' (Urry 2005). This position is informed by the alleged decline of the nation state in a globalized world, which has led to wider questioning of the idea of 'society' as a territorially bounded entity. This, in turn, prepares the ground for claims to the effect that since 'society' was a core theoretical concept, the very foundations of social science disciplines have now been undermined as a result of its demise. The central concepts of the new socialities are space (social topologies), regions (interregional competition), networks (new social morphology) and fluidity (global enterprises). Mobility is central to this thesis since globalization is the complex movement of people, images, goods, finances and so on that constitutes a process across regions in faster and unpredictable shapes; all with no clear point of arrival or departure.

Despite the contrasting theoretical understandings of globalization, there is agreement that it creates new opportunities: for example, globalization offers a new form of cosmopolitanism (Delanty 2006) and economic growth (Smart 2007). Yet is also constitutes new threats and global risks such as the ecological crises of global warming, climate change and environmental pollution; global health pandemics such as 'bird flu' and international crime and terrorism (Mythen 2007). Globalization may be seen as encroachment and colonization as global corporations and technologies erode local customs and ways of life, which in turn engenders new forms of protest to counter its negative effects.

The effects of globalization may be argued to be positive in terms of integration into a global economy that increases economic activity and raises living standards (Giddens 1991a). It has been claimed that in 2000 the per capita income of citizens was four times greater than that in 1950 (Legrain 2006). Between 1870 and 1979, production per worker became 26 times greater in Japan and 22 times greater in Sweden. In the whole world in 2000 it was double the figures from 1962. Even more significantly, Legrain (2006) argues that those nation states isolated from the global capitalist economy have done less well than those that have engaged with it. Poor countries that are open to international trade grew over six times faster in the 1970s and 1980s than those that shut themselves off from it: growth of 4.5 per cent a year, rather than 0.7 per cent.

At the same time global patterns of inequality have become even more polarized (Estes et al. 2003). According to United Nations, the richest 20 per cent in the world 'own' 80 per cent of the wealth; the second 20 per cent own 10 per cent ; the third 20 per cent own 6 per cent; the fourth 20 per cent own 3 per cent and the poorest 20 per cent own only 1 per cent. Throughout the world, 2.7 billion people live on less than $2 per day. These global inequalities predate globalization, of course, but there are global processes that are maintaining a highly unequal social system (Phillipson 2005). Equally, there are those who argue that a 'new poor' has emerged whose existence is necessary for the new forms of unbridled capitalism which now exist (Bauman 2001).

Contradictions in global society are illustrated in other ways. The globalization of capital may not have driven costs down in developed countries where few workers are prepared to tolerate the conditions this new model creates. Flexible global ordering systems need not just produce flexible labour, but flexible labour in excess, because to manage the supply of labour it is necessary to have a surplus. Migrants have met this need (Miles and Miles 2004). Yet in the wake of hostility manifest in many developed countries, especially following threats of terrorist attack in The United States and Europe, migrants now face tightening border controls and the deportation of those who are not in areas where there is a shortage of skills.

Globalization has been the focus of extensive social movement activism and 'resistance'; especially against a neoliberal ethos represented by bodies such as the World Trade Organization. This has seen the emergence of a 'global civil society': for example, in the growth of 'parallel summits' such as the 2001 Porto Alegre meeting in Brazil attended by 11,000 people to protest against the Davos (Switzerland) World Economic Forum (Glasius et al. 2003). These are organized through multiple networks of social actors and non-governmental organizations (NGOs) operating on local and international levels. It is perhaps an irony that internationally organized or linked social movements use globalized forms of communication (the Internet) and operate transnationally in order to mobilize a consciousness and solidarity on global issues.

The major contentious claim is that globalization is a new form of imperialism imposing US political and economic dominance over the rest of the world (Estes et al. 2003). The United States represents the most signifi-cant case of privatization as an element in the globalization agenda and a glimpse of what may come to pass for the broader community of nations. Pressures for more and more privatization mount on the US state, as exemplified by the growth of the $1.2 trillion dollar largely private medical industrial complex, which more than tripled in size during Ronald Reagan's two presidential terms during the 1980s alone. Indeed, this comprises nearly 15 per cent of the American economy under the Bush Administration from 2000 to 2007 even though 16 per cent (44 million) of US citizens are uninsured for health care.

Is this an example of market efficiency? The US federal government actually finances around 40 per cent of US health care, while the state limits its own activities to supporting and complementing the market (Estes and Phillipson 2003). Multinational health enterprises are an increasingly impor-tant component of the US medical industrial complex. As early as 1990, 97 US companies reported ownership of 100 hospitals with 11,974 beds in foreign countries. Pharmaceutical firms are also major global corporate players, with the total value of exported and imported pharmaceuticals estimated in excess of $110 billion in 1998 (Estes and Phillipson 2003). Added to this:

> After three decades devoted to market rhetoric, cost containment, and stunning organizational rationalization, the net result is the complete failure of any of these efforts to stem the swelling tide of problems of access and cost. Moreover, there are alarming increases in the uninsured populations among ethnic minority groups.
>
> (Held 2000: 183)

The neo-liberal ideology of globalization pushes the limitations on the role of the state with respect to its citizens. As privatization is financed by governments, there is an equal rhetoric that they can do little to stem the tide of globalization. Yet research has found there is a relationship between social policies and the amelioration of inequality and social exclusion (Byrne 2005). Despite this, the neo-liberal ideology of globalization bolsters the more restrictive limitations on the role of the state with respect to its citizens. David Held and his colleagues make the point that a distinctive feature of current times is the extent to which 'financial globalization has imposed an external financial discipline on governments that has contributed to both the emergence of a more market-friendly state and a shift in the balance of power between the state and financial markets' (Held 2000: 232).

In this respect, the political agenda of advanced capitalist states reflects in part the constraints of global finance, even though the specific impact of financial globalization will vary greatly among states. A tangible conse-quence is the insertion of the operatives and 'requisites' of global finance into state policy-making in ways that frame, if not dictate, the parameters of state power. In the process, responsibility for this state of affairs is denied in terms of the potential for action to ameliorate its worst effects. Indeed, it seems at times that error in the financial sector is the subject of reward as chief executives leave with large remunerations and the sector rewards itself with huge financial bonuses.

Despite what is said, governments do matter and the fatalism that is attributed to this state of affairs by many is false (Byrne 2005; Hirst and Thompson 2000; Sibeon 2004). Here we must recognize subnational govern-ance in addition to transnational and policy processes. A renewed emphasis upon local and subnational governance is reflected in work focusing on the significance of regions in the policy process. Amin and Thrift (1995), for example, have outlined a focus upon mezo-level governance/policy networks within European regions. Charting these trends in regional policy leaves lessons for central governments in ensuring that there are effective voices in the democratic process in the face of globalization (May and Marvin 2008). In the case of Canada, for example, it has been suggested that regional governance can be both utilized as a way of asserting regional and ethnic autonomy (as in Quebec), or exercised reluctantly (as in New Democrat-led Ontario) where subnational governments have identified a tendency for central governments to neglect or even abdicate responsibilities for main-taining standards of national economic management (Jenson 1995).

These developments can be viewed as part of a new global process of shaping the lives of present and future generations of populations in western and non-western states. The change has been variously analysed as a move from 'organized' to 'disorganized capitalism', to a shift from 'simple' to 'reflexive modernity', and to the transformation from 'Fordist' to 'post-Fordist economies'. Given this, we now look ahead in the final section of this chapter and ask to what extent the calls for the development of a 'global social theory' are warranted.

Summary

There can be little doubt that our lives are changing due to what may be termed global forces. Equally, however, to overemphasize rapid transforma-tions at the expense of understanding history is an error. All too often what is called innovation is nothing more than ignoring what has been before us. Culturally speaking, globalization can also lead to the most extreme of reactions born of prejudice. This can be undertaken as if we live in a culturally homogenous world where the threat is assumed to come from those who are apparently different. Power then enters the terrain of understanding to ensure the preservation of something assumed to be an 'essence' to a group which should not be 'contaminated' by those who do not share the assumed 'sameness'.

These forms of politics have been with us for a long time and are continually played out in different ways with varying consequences. Particular ways of life are attributed to whole nations and groups of people as if everyone shared in the participation of extreme views, while there are those who are happy to perpetuate their prejudices in the guise of reason. Mass, global media tend to seek the spectacular and emphasize these differences in the process. Knowledge by these forms of description takes precedence over knowledge by acquaintance whose opportunities are restricted as we hear more of what happens in places all over the world. It is this distance and the forms through which understandings are generated and populated that then becomes of importance for how we live our lives together.

As time and space are no longer assumed to be impediments to the transactions of business and the production and supply of goods, particular consequences then follow for individuals, groups, countries and continents as a whole. Globalization brings with it new experiences and knowledge and also, as we have noted, new forms of resistance to the encroachment of capital which can be so indifferent to its consequences in a continual pursuit of profit. Inequalities then persist and along with the effects of climate change and resource constraint, lead to new challenges. Having looked back over our journey, it is to these that we turn in the next chapter when we look forward in the development of social theory.

Conclusion   Looking back and looking forward

In this final chapter, we wish to do two things. First, to reflect on the journey we have undertaken through the history and contemporary forms of social theory. Second, to examine some of the challenges that lie ahead for its development. In the process we will note how social theory reflects the conditions under and through which it is produced. To that extent it has to be situated to be understood. In this way it gains its relevance and power of insight by reflecting upon the issues that inform the social milieu of which it is a part.

Looking back

We began our journey with a brief examination of the work of Descartes, Kant and Hume, for reasons that we drew attention to in subsequent discussions. This discussion also serves to demonstrate the argument that the validation of science, in general, often proceeds to a large degree on grounds informed by philosophical discourse. Equally, the practice of science can take it into philosophical terrains concerning the basis for knowing what we do and what we assume to exist in our observations on the effects of phenomena. Take, for example, ideas concerning the capacities and limits of reason. These translated into a series of methodological and theoretical proposals that provided for an examination of the social world. In one direction this was to travel towards an attitude of complacency. This was either represented by assumptions regarding the object world and/or the intrinsic validity of the instruments that are used for its measurement. Its ultimate expression is found in the positivist tradition.

Although universal laws were being sought under the broad umbrella of positivism, history became of central importance in the study of social life and our understandings of scientific practice. For Vico, Hume and others, people were viewed as social creatures, not metaphysical entities. Here was a tension between the idea of the autonomous individual 'will' based on reason and the historically situated nature of human activities. These issues, together with the practical and political questions which social theorists faced in their social contexts, provided for a rich history in social thought.

It was Marx, taking up and criticizing Hegel's historicist critique of Kant, who questioned reason, unmasked it, grounded it materially and then offered a way out of the increased commodification that governs daily life under capitalism. Human potentiality is stifled by capitalism. Durkheim then socialized reason, located it within the societies of which people were a part and then formulated the idea of moral individualism with an emphasis upon the symbolic elements in social life. Such issues are a prerequisite for social solidarity and were clearly important in relation to the changes he was witnessing in France when he was writing. Weber then entered the terrain to analyse the unintended effects of a particular form of rationality, despite the intentions that provided for its genesis. We are left in its wake, but accompanied by the injunction to act responsibly. In the process all of these thinkers illuminated tensions that persist in contemporary societies.

Our journey of modification, critique and illumination continued into the twentieth century. The importance of studying the interpretative life-world emerged in the writings of phenomenology, hermeneutics and pragmatism. While possessing differences, a new epistemological self-assurance for the social sciences emerged in the works of both Dilthey and Husserl. Mead and the pragmatists, on the other hand, were to travel in a more explicit anti-Cartesian direction. They formed a basis for social thought in which the self and the lifeworld were inseparable. The result is a clear challenge to the ideologically predominant idea of possessive individualism because the self and community rely upon each other for their existence.

The analytic power of these approaches comes from their prioritization of the lifeworld of meanings, interactions, values and beliefs. At the same time the future of this world of meaning informed Weber's more Nietzschean-inspired fatalistic pronouncements. Marx, on the other hand, retained an optimism through praxis, while Durkheim's holistic structuralism had not focused upon this in any depth given his preoccupations with social solidarity. Yet in all these writings are insights that need to be taken seriously if wishing to explain the dynamics of social life and structural transformations.

The intellectual armoury for the endeavour to put experience and structure together did not come from social action theories in our unfolding journey, for they were seen to reproduce that which was distorted in the first instance. Instead, it was to come from Freud whose work represented yet another critique of the Cartesian tradition. A fusion of the structures of the mind with the process of socialization under capitalism provided for a powerful critique. Nevertheless, while the Frankfurt theorists granted Hegelian historicism a place in its formulations, this was not the case when it came to a form of Marxism in the tradition of French structuralism.

Within structuralism the actions of the individual and the role of the historical in social life are both down-played. Saussure held the structure of language to be predominant over its utterances by individuals, while Lévi-Strauss held that he found in his study of myths, universal features of the human mind. A Marxist expression of this tradition was then apparent in the work of Althusser, for whom structures were ideological state apparatuses which provided for self-conceptions, as well as governing relations in general. Returning to Marx and Engels' idea of economic structures as determinant 'in the last instance', he linked psychoanalysis and Marxism in a manner that was designed to rescue its scientific promise.

Talcott Parsons then stepped onto the socio-theoretical stage. He, as with Lévi-Strauss, operated within a neo-Kantian framework. Nevertheless, in employing the ideas of Freud, Weber, Durkheim and Pareto, he was more interested in the formulation of a theory of action that linked people to the society of which they are a part. As with Durkheim, he could not conceive of how society would be possible on the basis of utilitarian concepts of action. Moving from an earlier formulation to a theory of interaction within a society of functionally interrelated systems, he arrived at a model of society which many found to be attractive, despite the criticisms of the absence of the lifeworld in his formulations.

Running alongside these developments, women were constructing ideas from the margins of societies. Positioned by social structures and a series of unexamined presuppositions and biases within society that social theory itself had drawn upon, the development of important ideas was taking place that utilized this marginalization to great effect. Arguing that the role of reason has been attributed along gender lines provided, once again, for the social tempering of what is so often conceived of as an individualistic concept enacted within some kind of social vacuum. These critiques provided the basis for a recovery of women's voices from history and the central place of women in making our history.

Armed with this history, we proceeded through the book with an underlying issue that was concerned with the relationship between action and structure against the backdrop of modernity. Pragmatism was a first port of call in terms of its translation into social theory. The placing of the development of the self within social relations in terms of a dialectical relationship between subject and object is George Herbert Mead's great achievement. A refusal to countenance a subject–object dualism, however, was thought to be lost in the hands of Herbert Blumer. A subjectivist interpretation of Mead, via the attribution of meanings to a social world on the part of the subject, led to differences within the development of symbolic interactionism.

Erving Goffman then played his part. Influenced by a number of different traditions, the self was to become situated firmly within the lifeworld. A fusion of intentionality, performance and role theory provided the grounds for a fascinating examination of social life within the dramaturgical tradition of social thought. Yet Goffman recognized the role of power in social life and the constraining nature of the role in relation to its performance. Between role expectations, the individual and actual performance lies a reflexive relation to the world of which we are a part.

From here our journey led us in two different directions. First, to an examination of the lifeworld through a fusion of Schutz and linguistic philosophy and second, to a critique of dualism in social thought. In relation to the first of these it is Harold Garfinkel who knocks rationality from its transcendental status and instead views it as an ongoing accomplishment within the lifeworld. Issues of ontology and epistemology were then constituted as issues with methodological solutions. Nevertheless, having situated it, he and his followers then wavered between relativism and generalization in their desire to find rules informing social interaction. A split is then apparent within this tradition between those who wish to retain the role of meaning within the lifeworld and those who, in the spirit of a new scientism, resorted to conversational analysis as if that could eradicate concerns with the meaning of context. Criticisms of variants of ethnomethodology focused on its abandonment of a radical critique of social science through the fusion of endogenous and exogenous reflexivity. In abandoning a hermeneutic dimension to inquiries, an ontology of the lifeworld is missing. Paradoxically, parallels are then evident with structuralism.

Despite criticisms of variants of ethnomethodology, it provides for an important part of the investigation of social life which other socio-theoretical approaches often overlook. This much is recognized by Anthony Giddens. It is he who employed its insights to construct an ontologically based social theory in which history is not bracketed. History, structure, action and power fuse in the process of an argument that action implies structure and structure implies action. Another critique of Cartesianism then emerges, but one that does not imply a structuralist dissolving of the subject. Issues concerning this hermeneutically inspired social theory, however, revolve around whether social life may be actually a dualism between action and structure, rather than a duality.

Our next chapter was devoted to the ideas of a leading French social scientist. Pierre Bourdieu's 'genetic structuralism' represents a rich fusion of ideas, but those gained in the light of a very different history to that of Giddens. With existentialism, phenomenology and structuralism informing the terrain of post-1945 French social thought, Bourdieu formulated an ontological basis for his ideas, but without a refusal to engage in epistemological considerations. Bourdieu remained concerned with the scientific status of his work and its methodological translation in order to illuminate the dynamics of the social world and contribute to its betterment via a 'realpolitik of reason'. In the process, history and social location are examined alongside the strategies of agents in terms of the types of power that inform social relations. We are left with an understanding of how and why certain types of capital inform and are acquired via human agency. However, issues did remain in terms of the role of reason appearing to be left in the wake of strategically oriented actions.

Our focus then moved to actor network theory. This necessitated mapping out the interrelationship between humans and non-human actors and how they play a central role in networks. A vocabulary has been developed that does not seem to take the distinction between subjects and objects, the subjective and the objective, into consideration. What is termed an 'actant' is more than a human actor because both humans and nonhumans may be actants. In the process an actant may be 'enrolled' as 'allied' to give strength to a position. When someone argues for the existence of a particular phenomenon and its effects, data that are held to prove its existence are enrolled actants. In networks of humans, machines, animals and matter in general, humans are not the only beings with agency and not the only ones to act. Thus 'matter' matters! Despite intriguing insights, it may be suggested that by attributing agency to objects the result is an ontological flattening that sanitizes the role of human agency and diminishes human potentiality.

In steps Jürgen Habermas. The sheer range and extraordinary output of this social theorist seeks to recover the critical capacities of reason. Those such as Marx, the Frankfurt theorists and Weber, among others, were found to have built their ideas upon a subject–object dualism. For those with a critical intent to their writings, this could not be sustained for it so often led to fatalism and retreat from its original purpose: the transformation of society to a more free and equitable state. Towards this end Habermas seeks to recover the promise of reason from within the lifeworld itself. He has constructed an elaborate and complex evolutionary theory that holds there is an increasing disjuncture in the unfolding of modernity between the lifeworld and the steering systems of money and power. Social life is then characterized as a dualism, with modernity being an incomplete project, not one in terminal decline.

At this point, the issue that emerged in our discussions is whether Habermas's use of systems theory did not actually undermine his project. Power, for example, exists within the lifeworld, not just systems. Here, as throughout our journey, feminist social theory has much to offer our understanding of social life. In the case of conceptions of both action and systems, their gendered nature is an important matter. The basis for such a project, however, is often the idea of 'woman' and a separation between the private and public worlds. Such a difference sustains particular systems in society and enables an exploitation of the private realm. A continual emphasis upon production as a basis for society, clearly leaves out reproduction and associated relations. As a basis for critique and positive change, issues of essentialism and determinism are of central importance. We then found that some feminist theorists were to discover an inspiration in the content of our next two chapters.

Michel Foucault situated the self within discourses of power and knowledge and these provided conceptions of the subject and object. Overall, this is a highly distinct conceptualization of the action–structure relationship. Foucault's grasp of the history of ideas, combined with historical excavations in particular areas, gave a new perspective on the subject. History makes us what we are. However, when it came to opportunities for positive change, Foucault remained silent and preferred instead to allude to contingency not being destiny and being 'against' non-consensus, rather than 'for' consensus. Yet his works were also said to provide the basis for critical reflection after the apparent death of Cartesianism. Such a characteristic cannot be so easily applied to the subject of our next chapter.

Postmodernism celebrates the absence of reason within current times. In its denouncements of subject-centred reason, it celebrates difference and diversity and holds reason to be totalitarian. The world had become a vortex of symbolism in which the subject is decentred and absorbed into an orgy of consumption. For Baudrillard, indifference became critique and the weapons of the modernists are turned against themselves. Everything is culture. However, as Bourdieu noted, few ask questions about the conditions under which they are able to pursue their own interests. If postmodernism is reflexive, it is highly limited given that the lifeworld is held to have dissolved into the clutches of culture. Poverty is that which is represented in the cinema. Baudrillard is thus found to work at the extremes of an indulgent commodity fetishism. While refusing the nostalgia of the modernists, it was perhaps for this reason that he did not wish to claim the label 'postmodernist' during his lifetime.

Our journey, like social life, is not one of progressive linearity. This is often a matter of surprise to those who look to social theory for simple answers and find only a series of questions, often accompanied by a challenge to their assumptions. By attempting to 'look back' on the social theories identified in the book, social theory illuminated its relevance and power of insight to examine two apparent opposite elements to social life. Emotions are often taken to be personal, while globalization refers to an abstract and general process.

In the chapter on emotions we found that social theories sought not only to reflect upon the conditions under which 'emotion' takes place and its dynamics, but also to transform our understandings of those processes attached to its construction, deconstruction and reconstruction. Without a reflexive and 'applied' feature to its practice, we run the risk of complacency in the particularities of our worldviews.

Emotion is related to morality. In terms of contemplation on their role in social life this goes back to Aristotle. It is also a core part of how we judge ourselves and others (Sabini and Silver 1982). In discussing issues associated with how others are judged according to their professional status, emotion plays its role with its connotations of commitment, but without succumbing to prejudicial judgements. To appear flustered is often assumed to be a sign of weakness in interaction that leads to evaluations of status and character. We are dealing here with the role of emotion is projecting a sense of the self and its acceptability in different contexts (Goffman 1972). Yet this is not simply an intersubjective domain. Emotion play a core role in public evaluations, as is clear in analyses of corporate scandals (Parrott 2003).

Social theory is a discourse in which ideas and events meet and shape one another. It is for this reason that globalization is key. As we experience time and space in different ways, so the apparent certainties of old evaporate before our eyes. Yet as we noted, we should be cautious in applying nostalgia as the means of historical explanation. Judgement given by a present context is not the same as one derived from a different and past context. What has changed is mobility, but this should not be exaggerated, for it is necessary to ask: mobility for whom or what? Mobility for some is gained at the expense of others. Power moves without regard for territory or consequences, but our lives are experienced in those ways. Linking this to our discussion on emotion leads to a tension between what is seen as conditioned in a spatial sense and that which is apparently unconditional in its indifference to context. As Zygmunt Bauman (2001) has put it:

> There is a new asymmetry emerging between the extraterritorial nature of power and the continuing territoriality of the 'whole life' – which the now unanchored powers, able to move at short notice or without warning, are free to exploit and abandon to the consequences of that exploitation. Shedding responsibility for consequences is the most coveted and cherished gain that the new mobility brings to free-floating, locally unbound capital. The costs of coping with consequences need not now be counted in the calculation of the 'effectiveness' of investment.
>
> (Bauman 2001: 188–189)

Despite this trend, emotion can be mobilized to bring such indifference to account through public expression of outrage and while the undoubted power of capital is all around us, there is also a relationship with place that acts as a check upon such indifference: trust matters and interactions still count. When it does evaporate, however, there are differing consequences for people. Apparent failure is often rewarded if one is positioned as a chief executive. This is a paradoxical outcome given we are so often told that such persons are not only exceptional and so should be rewarded accordingly, but also supposed to be responsible given their positions in the first instance.

Looking forward

In the face of contemporary transformations, what are the challenges for social theory and so for understandings of our landscapes and our potentiality? Our geographical, cultural, political and economic terrains are altering. We hear of necessity when faced with global logics, but also how important politics is for achieving our goals. The global world seems to be characterized by a tension in viewpoints between necessity and choice. Such tensions are perhaps not surprising given that debates are constantly informed by power relations which themselves need contesting, not reproducing.

Social theory can provide us with ways of understanding relations between one another and to our environments. In terms of our present era the certitude that once characterized differences between disciplines is showing its cracks and our search for solutions has borne witness to the breaking down of the barriers between science and philosophy. When it comes to the world of theoretical discourse, a substantive theory is now argued to have given way to a philosophically preoccupied one (Mouzelis 2007). As a result we have calls for a return to more 'applied' endeavours, accompanied by suggestions as to how this might proceed (Stones 2005).

A social theory that develops concepts amenable to empirical illumination is an essential part of the practice of the social sciences. The reasons why gaps have appeared between what we might term empirically oriented and philosophically reflexive social theories is because of the changing times through which we are living. We are seeking not only to illuminate these changes, for which empirical work is indispensable, but also to reach back into the history of social thought to ask if the presuppositions upon which practices are based are still relevant to modern times.

Conflicts such as these were evident in the works of Marx, Durkheim and Weber. Weber's methodology, for example, called for a grounding in the subjective meanings that people attach to their social relations. Yet in his historical writings he was fatalistic about the future of that very sphere of human meaning in the unfolding of modernity. The tension was so beautifully captured in his concepts of substantive and formal rationality. However, these are not simply 'theoretical' ideas, for in the clash between these elements in our current age we can hear the call for freedom. Freedom is a philosophically and politically contested term and empirically speaking, the freedom of one group or country, is often bought at the expense of others.

At this point in the twenty-first century, an array of opportunities and challenges present themselves. There is a need to develop a clearer perspective on the pressures facing social groups as a result of global change. A significant issue is how globalization and its impingement on local governance is transforming the everyday texture of day-to-day living. All too often this is driven by narrow economic criteria in an age of diminishing resources and climate change which has consequences for us all. In this context, the need for a framework to respond to the challenge associated with globalization is warranted. The key dimensions here are the changing and contested form of the nation state, citizenship and nationalism; the enhanced role of supra-national bodies; climate change and natural resource depletion; the increased power of multi-national corporations and the emergence and retrenching of social inequalities across the globe.

Social theory should provide us with the means to examine realities and question the extent to which these are not only constructed, but also subject to transformation: that is, that they are not naturalized processes beyond human agency to alter, but the product of particular conditions and circumstances. However, there is no suggestion that they are not real in their consequences. A core task, then, is to examine the structural inequalities and power dynamics that perpetuate current understandings and practices. An analysis that accepts enlightenment assumptions about, for example, 'equality', can fail to ask the key questions about why this state of affairs holds true for some rather than for others. Equally, simple allusions to freedom, without due concern for the actual effects of current conditions upon particular populations, is an empty reference. Crucially, power relations, social processes and structures must be examined as they appear in everyday relations. Links must be made between the traditional and contemporary and between macro, micro and mezzo levels of analysis, so what are challenging explanations have the potential to become a part of everyday considerations.

A key issue here concerns the place and nature of 'society'. The ideas of society as a bounded self-sufficient entity has become taken for granted within certain quarters. Such a formulation assumes there is a coherent and bounded entity into which social integration is attainable. This view has become prominent among a small group of western societies; especially those associated with the recent 'War on Terror' who have aggressively promoted nation statehood and particular expressions of freedom (Walklate and Mythen 2007). Looking out to the deficiencies of others, however, is also a way of not looking within to deficiencies that are more proximate and so uncomfortable. It is not just a way of seeking to provide protection to populations, but also a means of heightened surveillance with serious consequences for our liberties (Lyon 2001).

The idea of society as a sovereign entity is changing with the intensifying social forces of globalization:

there are exceptional levels of global interdependence, unpredictable shock waves spill out 'chaotically' from one part to the system as a whole; there are not just societies but massively powerful empires roaming around the globe; and there is a mass mobility of people, objects and dangerous human wastes.

(Urry 2000:13)

Therefore the traditional formulation of 'society' is being challenged from global forces that impinge on new technology that transforms the experience of social relations (Whyte 2007). In a networked world, everyday life is becoming detached from what was seen as the protective nation state. Steering a path between Giddens' (1991b) 'global optimists' and 'global pessimists', it may be suggested that a new formulation is required that recognizes diverse and unequal networks in and through the way people interact throughout their lives across national, transnational and sub-cultural contexts.

A major dimension of inequalities relate to debates on climate change and their relation to the power of multinational corporations and third world countries and debt repayment (Mythen 2007; Phillipson 2005). The phenomenon of globalization has transformed debates within social theory to the extent that it has reordered concepts typically used by social theorists across the micro–macro continuum (Bauman 1998). Ideas associated with modernity, the state, gender, class relations, ageing and ethnicity retain their importance but their collective and individualized meaning is different and fragmented in the context of the influence of global institutions (Mythen 2007).

Accepting the importance of globalization strengthens the case for rethinking the macro dimensions of social theory. There are those who regard the costs of micro analysis as significant in holding back the ability to address what we mean by society in the context of global economic and technological change (Hagestad and Dannefer 2001: 66). Nevertheless, given the explanatory role of social theory, globalization is setting major new challenges in terms of interaction between individuals, communities and nation states and the global structure within which these are constructed, contested, negotiated and nested. To this extent it is not just one level of analysis that is required, but a more sensitive and nuanced understanding between them.

Traditional attachments may be maintained, but also re-contextualized and re-embedded with the influence of transnational communities, corporations and international governmental organizations producing new agendas and challenges for how we understand 'modern society' (B. S. Turner 2006). The nature of 'citizenship' and 'rights', influenced by Enlightenment philosophy and its conceptions of the individual, are contested under the lead of complex and commanding influences of powerful non-democratic inter-governmental structures such as the World Bank and IMF, plus private multinational corporations such as banks. A situation is then created that contrasts with the idea of rights as independently defined and negotiated through various manifestations of British, European and American nation building and sovereign state power.

The forms of knowledge deployed to analyse these changes will be key. There are many who are only too happy to peddle their solutions to problems not yet identified. Reality then becomes that which is amenable to technical control and manipulation. Its purpose in not aimed at understanding or critique conducted in the name of constituting improvement, but the reproduction of an existing states of affairs. Technocratic applications that inform the formulation of public policy take for granted existing systems as justifications work within definitions that are framed by classical economic theories, including assumptions and models of cost-effectiveness and individual level preferences and outcomes. What is then assured is limited incremental changes that do little to transform the underlying problems facing societies.

Democratic rights may be argued to have become more fragmented and individualized. The duty and necessity to cope with these underlying problems are being increasingly transferred to families (Gilleard and Higgs 2005). The issues affecting everyday life may be defined as global, but the social reconstruction of experience is being cast as a personal, rather than collective, responsibility. Here we find uncertainty reflected in nostalgia and exemplified in allusions to situatedness (Simpson 2002). At one level this is taken to be an objective fact in relation to the position that one occupies in the social world. At another, saying where one is coming from appears as an intention by stating a commitment to a position. The cost is a refusal to engage in reflection that admits of a relation to others.

Oscillations between these senses are part of how we try to construct a narrative about ourselves that we and others can accept. We are both constructed by objective circumstances and yet we also have agency to effect change. In the face of this we have seen a resurgence in ethical considerations, but even these reflect an individualism as a result of ripping people from the contexts in which they find themselves. Empathy vanishes to be replaced by rules assumed to be part of the abstract, individualistic societies characteristic of our current stage of capitalist development. Amelioration of the effects of global warming then become a matter of individual consumption, rather than collective action.

Of course this is not to suggest that changes can result from that level of action, but the provision of a sufficient infrastructure and tackling perverse incentives to off-set carbon emissions takes collective political will. The spaces and places we occupy are relational and real and not amenable to abstract generalizations (Massey 2005). Ethics needs to translate into politics:

> When a society shies away from what is sees as purely destructive transformations, it denies itself the means to overcome or use them. A society which believes it can overcome its own blockages and weaknesses by going with the flow is in serious danger of being torn apart.
>
> (Touraine 2000: 305)

One task must be to understand the nature of individualization and its consequences (Beck and Beck-Gernsheim 2002), but that must relate to practical-philosophical questions concerning the subject (Ferrara 1998; Ricouer 1994; Taylor 1992). Important questions concern why and how people, who are socially differentiated, are enabled or constrained by transformations. Climate change, depleting natural resources, cultural, social and economic transformations and a recovery of the political are all central to our futures.

We have found in our journey that freedom is not something which is inherent in the individual in isolation from their contexts. The idea of the individual cannot be held to be separate from the social world of which they are a part. This is not because it is the latest trend in an enclosed universe of theoretical discourse, but because the struggles for new identities and ways of life are a part of our contemporary landscapes. In this sense Foucault's idea of the agonism between power and freedom hits its mark (Simons 1995):

> I want to say about the task of a diagnosis of today that it does not consist only of a description of who we are, rather a line of fragility of today to follow and understand, if and how what is, can no longer be what it is. In this sense, the description must be formulated in a kind of virtual break, which opens up room, understood as a room of concrete freedom, that is possible transformation.
>
> (Foucault 1996: 359)

A striving for identity through difference is a common act. Yet this also provides fertile ground for the seeds of oppression. If one can become something only via a continual contrast with something that one is not, then this seems an inevitable consequence. It is tolerance, not threat, that should be the partner of difference. If we look in this direction, any common ground upon which we might speak to each other is an essential part of the endeavour. With this in mind, it is the ideas of Habermas to whom we have turned. He is concerned, as was Foucault, with practical matters.

Habermas's reconstructive social science is abstract. We are enabled by this to be sensitive to the ambivalences that characterize our development while he tries, without resorting to a single explanatory framework, to analyse the conditions which are necessary to reach understanding (Habermas 1994: 112). Ideal speech situations are not held to be reflective of a form of life which has existed, but are taken to be a constitutive condition of speech (Habermas 2003: 103). In the face of conflict, therefore, his work informs a practical-political project that allows us 'to confront honestly the challenges, critiques, the unmasking of illusions; to work through these, and still responsibly reconstruct an informed comprehensive perspective on modernity and its pathologies' (Bernstein 1985: 25).

When we approach social theory with these concerns in mind, we can see that Foucault and Habermas speak to the wishes and struggles of modern times – as had many of their intellectual predecessors. Their differences and the implications of these should, of course, be carefully examined, but it leads us to employ their insights in the service of greater understanding. To this extent, we need to make theory work for us and not us work for theory. Theoretical exegesis has its place, but it should never be over-extended so as to undermine the importance of clarification.

Theoretical development from a critical perspective is needed to illuminate alternative understandings alongside a vision of what is possible. This also means social theory, as with all forms of knowledge, acknowledging not just its strengths, but recognizing its limitations. The pursuit of so-called excellence in its mirroring of the universal and abstract must be tempered by a relevance to inform action and so the places of its own production must be open to reflexive scrutiny (May 2005; Perry and May 2006). Other forms of knowledge will play their role in transformations which are about practical-political endeavours in the worlds of which we are a part. Knowledge can, as Cornelius Castoriadis put it, help us both a little and a lot. Little in the sense that transformation is not a matter of such things as theory, philosophy or knowledge. A great deal in the sense that it can 'destroy the rationalistic ideology, the illusion of omnipotence, the supremacy of the economic "calculus" ' (Castoriadis 1991: 197). We need, as he notes, to exercise thought and responsibility alongside seeing reason and rationality as historical creations of our making. After all, we have changed many times in our history before and possibilities remain open to us for how we organize our social relations in a world faced with the depletion of natural resources alongside vast inequalities.

To contribute to this possibility we need a clarifying social theory. Clarification takes place through an examination of the presuppositions that are embedded in world views. It is not content to take appearance at face value and so it challenges us. At the same time it does not seek to denounce or simply align itself with social movements as if resistance were automatically to be encouraged without reference to content and effects. It does not seek abstract generalizations as if that guarantees its authors their expertise and recognition among a small community, nor does it leave its recipients wondering 'how do we now proceed?' It is context-sensitive, but not context-dependent and so it has the potential to be context-revising. It has a willingness to engage in dialogue in the face of practical experiences. Because of these features, it resonates with the hopes, wishes and aspirations for a better way of living in and relating to the world around us.

Bibliography

Adam, B. (1995) *Timewatch: The Social Analysis of Time*. Cambridge: Polity.

Adorno, T. and Horkheimer, M. (1979) *Dialectic of Enlightenment*. Originally published in 1944. Translated by J. Cumming. London: Verso.

Adorno, T., Frankel-Brunswik, E., Levinson, D. and Sanford, R. (1950) *The Authoritarian Personality*. New York: Harper & Row.

Adorno, T., Albert, H., Dahrendorf, R., Habermas, J., Pilot, H. and Popper, K. R. (1976) *The Positivist Dispute in German Sociology*. Translated by G. Adey and D. Frisby. London: Heinemann.

Akrich, M. and Latour, B. (1992) 'A Summary of a Convenient Vocabulary for the Semiotics of Human and Nonhuman Assemblies'. In W. Bijker and J. Law (eds) *Shaping Technology, Building Society: Studies in Sociotechnical Change*. Cambridge, MA: MIT Press.

Albrow, M. (1987) 'The Application of the Weberian Concept of Rationalization to Contemporary Conditions'. In S. Lash and S. Whimster (eds) *Max Weber, Rationality and Modernity*. London: Allen & Unwin.

Albrow, M. (1990) *Max Weber's Construction of Social Theory*. London: Macmillan.

Alexander, J. C. (1984) 'The Parsons Revival in German Sociology'. *Sociological Theory* 2: 394–412.

Alexander, J. C. (2006) *The Civil Sphere*. Oxford: Oxford University Press.

Alexandar, J. C., Eyerman. R., Giesen, B., Smelser, N. J. and Sztompka, P. (2004) *Cultural Trauma and Collective Indentity*. Berkeley, CA: University of California Press.

Almquist, E. M. (1979) 'Black Women and the Pursuit of Equality'. In J. Freeman (ed.) *Women: A Feminist Perspective*, 2nd edn. Palo Alto, CA: Mayfield.

Althusser, L. (1969) *For Marx*. Translated by B. Brewster. Harmondsworth: Penguin.

Amin, A. and Thrift, N. (1995) 'Institutional Issues for the European Regions: From Markets and Plans to Socioeconomics and Powers of Association'. *Economy and Society* 24(1): 41–66.

Anderson, R., Hughes, J. and Sharrock, W. (1986) *Philosophy and the Human Sciences*. London: Routledge.

Appadurai, A. (1996) *Modernity at Large*. Minneapolis, MN: University of Minnesota Press.

Appadurai, A. (2000) 'The Grounds of the Nation-State: Identity, Violence and Territory'. In K. Goldmann, U. Hannerz and C. Westin (eds) *Nationalism and Internationalism in the Post-Cold War Era*. London: Routledge.

Archer, M. S. (1989) *Culture and Agency: The Place of Culture in Social Theory*. Cambridge: Cambridge University Press.

Archer, M. S. (1995) *Realist Social Theory: The Morphogenetic Approach*. Cambridge: Cambridge University Press.

Archer, M. (1998) 'Social Theory and the Analysis of Society'. In T. May and M. Williams (eds) *Knowing the Social World*. Buckingham: Open University Press.

Archer, M. S. (2003) *Structure, Agency and the Internal Conversation*. Cambridge: Cambridge University Press.

Aronowitz, S. (1992) 'The Tensions of Critical Theory: Is Negative Dialectics All There Is?' In S. Seidman and D. Wagner (eds) *Postmodernism and Social Theory*. Oxford: Blackwell.

Assister, A. (1983) 'Did Man Make Language?' *Radical Philosophy* 34: 25–29.

Atkinson, J. M. (1978) *Discovering Suicide: Studies in the Social Organization of Sudden Death*. London: Macmillan.

Atkinson, J. M. and Heritage, J. C. (eds) (1984) *Structures of Social Action: Studies in Conversation Analysis*. Cambridge: Cambridge University Press.

Atkinson, P. (1988) 'Ethnomethodology: A Critical Review'. *Annual Review of Sociology* 14: 441–465.

Austin, J. (1976) *How to Do Things with Words*. Oxford: Oxford University Press.

Barbalet, J. (2002) 'Secret Voting and Political Emotions'. *Mobilization: An International Journal* 7(2): 129–140.

Barber, W. J. (1981) *A History of Economic Thought*. Harmondsworth: Penguin.

Barnes, B. (2002) 'The Macro/micro Problem and the Problem of Structure and Agency.' In G. Ritzer and B. Smart (eds) *Handbook of Social Theory*. London: Sage.

Barrett, M. (1988) *Women's Oppression Today: The Marxist/Feminist Encounter*, revised edn. London: Verso.

Baudrillard, J. (1981) *For a Critique of the Political Economy of the Sign*. Originally published in 1972. St Louis, MO: Telos.

Baudrillard, J. (1983) *Simulations*. New York: Semiotext(e).

Baudrillard, J. (1993) 'Hyperreal America'. Translated by D. Macey. *Economy and Society* 22(2): 243–252.

Baudrillard, J. (2005) *The Conspiracy of Art*. New York: Semiotext(e).

Bauman, Z. (1978) *Hermeneutics and Social Science: Approaches to Understanding*. London: Hutchinson.

Bauman, Z. (1987) *Legislators and Interpreters: On Modernity, Post-Modernity and Intellectuals*. Cambridge: Polity.

Bauman, Z. (1989) *Modernity and the Holocaust*. Cambridge: Polity.

Bauman, Z. (1991) *Modernity and Ambivalence*. Cambridge: Polity.

Bauman, Z. (1992) *Intimations of Postmodernity*. London: Routledge.

Bauman, Z. (1998) *Globalization: The Human Consequences*. Cambridge: Polity.

Bauman, Z. (2001) *The Individualized Society*. Cambridge: Polity.

Bauman, Z. (2006) *Liquid Fear*. Cambridge: Cambridge University Press.

Bauman, Z. and May, T. (2001) *Thinking Sociologically*, 2nd edn. Oxford: Blackwell.

Beck, U. (1992) *Risk Society: Towards a New Modernity*. London: Sage.

Beck, U. (2006) *The Cosmopolitan Village*. Cambridge: Polity.

Beck, U. and Beck-Gernsheim, E. (2002) *Individualization: Institutionalized Individualism and its Social and Political Consequences*. London: Sage.

Beck, U., Giddens, A. and Lash, S. (1994) *Reflexive Modernization: Politics, Tradition and Aesthetics in the Modern Social Order*. Cambridge: Polity.

Becker, H. (1963) *Outsiders: Studies in the Sociology of Deviance*. New York: Free Press.

Beechey, V. (1986) 'Women and Employment in Contemporary Britain'. In V. Beechey and E. Whitelegg (eds) *Women in Britain Today*. Milton Keynes: Open University Press.

Beetham, D. (1974) *Max Weber and the Theory of Modern Politics*. London: Allen & Unwin.

Bell, D. (1960) *The End of Ideology*. New York: Collier.

Beloff, M. (1954) *The Age of Absolutism*: 1660–1815. London: Hutchinson.

Bendelow, G. and Williams, S. (1998) *The Lived Body: Sociological Themes, Embodied Issues*. London: Routledge.

Bendix, R. (1977) *Max Weber: An Intellectual Portrait*. Berkeley, CA: University of California Press.

Beneria, L. and Bisnath, S. (1996) *Gender and Poverty: An Analysis or Action*. Gender in Development Monograph Series 2. New York: United Nations Development Programme.

Benhabib, S. (1986) *Critique, Norm and Utopia: A Study of the Foundations of Critical Theory*. New York: Columbia University Press.

Benhabib, S. (1992) *Situating the Self: Gender, Community and Postmodernism in Contemporary Ethics*. Cambridge: Polity.

Benjamin, A. (ed.) (1991) *The Problems of Modernity: Adorno and Benjamin*. London: Routledge.

Benson, D. (1974) 'Critical Note: A Revolution in Sociology'. Sociology 8: 125–129.

Benton, T. (1977) *Philosophical Foundations of the Three Sociologies*. London: Routledge & Kegan Paul.

Berger, P. L. and Luckmann, T. (1967) *The Social Construction of Reality: A Treatise in the Sociology of Knowledge*. New York: Anchor.

Berman, M. (1993) 'Why Modernism Still Matters'. In S. Lash and J. Friedman (eds) *Modernity and Identity*. Oxford: Blackwell.

Bernstein, R. (1983) *Beyond Objectivism and Relativism: Science, Hermeneutics and Praxis*. Oxford: Basil Blackwell.

Bernstein, R. (1985) 'Introduction'. In R. Bernstein (ed.) *Habermas and Modernity*. Cambridge: Polity.

Bershady, H. J. (1991) 'Practice against Theory in American Sociology: An Exercise in the Sociology of Knowledge'. In R. Robertson and B. S. Turner (eds) *Talcott Parsons: Theorist of Modernity*. London: Sage.

Bertens, H. (1995) *The Idea of the Postmodern: A history*. London: Routledge.

Best, S. and Kellner, D. (1997) *The Postmodern Turn*. New York: Guilford Press.

Bhaskar, R. (1993) *Dialectic: The Pulse of Freedom*. London: Verso.

Bierstedt, R. (1979) 'Sociological Thought in the Eighteenth Century'. In T. Bottomore and R. Nisbet (eds) *A History of Sociological Analysis*. London: Heinemann.

Bijker, W. (1994) 'Sociotechnical Technology Studies'. In S. Jasanoff, G. E. Markle, J. C. Peterson and T. Pinch (eds) *Handbook of Science and Technology*. London: Routledge.

Bijker, W. and Law, J. (eds) (1992) *Shaping Technology, Building Society: Studies in Sociotechnical Change*. Cambridge, MA: MIT Press.

Billig, M. (1994) 'Sod Baudrillard! Or Ideology Critique in Disney World'. In H. W. Simons and M. Billig (eds) *After Postmodernism: Reconstructing Ideology Critique*. London: Sage.

Bittner, E. (1974) 'The Concept of Organization'. Originally published in 1965. Reprinted in R. Turner (ed.) *Ethnomethodology*. Harmondsworth: Penguin.

Blackman, H. J. (ed.) (1967) *Objections to Humanism*. Harmondsworth: Penguin.

Blackman, H. J. (1968) *Humanism*. Harmondsworth: Penguin.

Bloor, D. (1983) *Wittgenstein: A Social Theory of Knowledge*. London: Macmillan.

Blumer, H. (1937) 'Social Psychology'. In E. P. Schmidt (ed.) *Man and Society*. New York: Prentice-Hall.

Blumer, H. (1969) *Symbolic Interactionism: Perspective and Method*. Englewood Cliffs, NJ: Prentice-Hall.

Blumer, H. (1972) 'Society as Symbolic Interaction'. In A. Rose (ed.) *Human Behaviour and Social Processes: An Interactionist Approach*. London: Routledge & Kegan Paul.

Blumer, H. (1983) 'Going Astray with a Logical Scheme'. Reprinted in K. Plummer (ed.) *Symbolic Interactionism*, Volume 1, *Foundations and History*. Aldershot: Edward Elgar.

Boden, D. and Zimmerman, D. H. (eds) (1993) *Talk and Social Structure: Studies in Ethnomethodology and Conversation Analysis*. Cambridge: Polity.

Borradori, G. (2003) *Philosophy in a Time of Terror: Dialogues with Jürgen Habermas and Jacques Derrida.* Chicago, IL: University of Chicago Press.

Bosanquet, T. (1967) 'Auguste Comte and the Positive Philosophers'. In F. J. C. Hearnshaw (ed.) *The Social and Political Ideas of Some Representative Thinkers of the Age of Reaction and Reconstruction: 1815–1865.* Originally published in 1932. London: Dawsons.

Bottomore, T. (1979) 'Marxism and Sociology'. In T. Bottomore and R. Nisbet (eds) *A History of Sociological Analysis.* London: Heinemann.

Bottomore, T. and Nisbet, R. (1979) 'Structuralism'. In T. Bottomore and R. Nisbet (eds) *A History of Sociological Analysis.* London: Heinemann.

Bourdieu, P. (1962) *The Algerians.* Boston, MA: Beacon.

Bourdieu, P. (1977) *Outline of a Theory of Practice.* Translated by R. Nice. Cambridge: Cambridge University Press.

Bourdieu, P. (1981) 'Men and Machines'. In K. Knorr-Cetina and A. Cicourel (eds) *Advances in Social Theory and Methodology: Towards an Integration of Micro and Macro Theories.* London: Routledge & Kegan Paul.

Bourdieu, P. (1984) *Distinction: A Social Critique of the Judgement of Taste.* Translated by R. Nice. London: Routledge & Kegan Paul.

Bourdieu, P. (1988) *Homo Academicus.* Translated by P. Collier. Cambridge: Polity.

Bourdieu, P. (1989) 'Social Space and Symbolic Power'. *Sociological Theory* 7(1): 14–25.

Bourdieu, P. (1990) *In Other Words: Essays towards a Reflexive Sociology.* Translated by M. Adamson. Cambridge: Polity.

Bourdieu, P. (1991a) 'Meanwhile, I Have Come to Know All the Diseases of Sociological Understanding: An Interview'. Conducted by B. Krais. In P. Bourdieu, J.-C. Passeron and M. de Saint Martin, with contributions by C. Baudelot and G. Vincent (1994) *Academic Discourse: Linguistic Misunderstanding and Professorial Power.* Translated by R. Teese. Cambridge: Polity.

Bourdieu, P. (1991b) *The Political Ontology of Martin Heidegger.* Translated by P. Collier. Cambridge: Polity.

Bourdieu, P. (1992a) *The Logic of Practice.* Translated by R. Nice. Originally published in 1980 as *Le Sens pratique.* Cambridge: Polity.

Bourdieu, P. (1992b) *Language and Symbolic Power.* Edited and introduced by J. B. Thompson. Translated by G. Raymond and M. Adamson. Cambridge: Polity.

Bourdieu, P. (1993a) 'Concluding Remarks: For a Sociogenetic Understanding of Intellectual Works'. In C. Calhoun, E. LiPuma and M. Postone (eds) *Bourdieu: Critical Perspectives*. Cambridge: Polity.

Bourdieu, P. (1993b) *Sociology in Question*. Translated by R. Nice. London: Sage.

Bourdieu, P. (1995) *The Rules of Art: Genesis and Structure of the Literary Field*. Translated by S. Emanuel. Cambridge: Polity.

Bourdieu, P. (1998) *Practical Reason: On the Theory of Action*. Cambridge: Polity.

Bourdieu, P. (2000) *Pascalian Meditations*. Cambridge: Polity.

Bourdieu, P. (2001) *Masculine Domination*, Cambridge: Polity.

Bourdieu, P. (2003) *Firing Back: Against the Tyranny of the Market*. London: Verso.

Bourdieu, P. (2004) *Science of Science and Reflexivity*. Cambridge: Polity.

Bourdieu, P. (2005) *The Social Structures of the Economy*. Cambridge: Polity.

Bourdieu, P. and Passeron, J.-C. (1990) *Reproduction in Education, Society and Culture*, 2nd edn. London: Sage.

Bourdieu, P. and Wacquant, L. J. (1992) *An Invitation to Reflexive Sociology*. Cambridge: Polity.

Bourdieu, P. and Wacquant, L. J. (2001) 'NewLiberalSpeak: Notes on the New Planetary Vulgate'. *Radical Philosophy*. 105: 2–5.

Bourdieu, P., Chamboredon, J.-C. and Passeron, J.-C. (1991) *The Craft of Sociology: Epistemological Preliminaries*. Edited by B. Krais. Translated by R. Nice. New York: Walter de Gruyter.

Bourdieu, P., Passeron, J.-C. and de Saint Martin, M., with contributions by Baudelot, C. and Vincent, G. (1994) *Academic Discourse: Linguistic Misunderstanding and Professorial Power*. Translated by R. Teese. Cambridge: Polity.

Boyne, R. (1991) 'Power-Knowledge and Social Theory: The Systematic Misrepresentation of Contemporary French Social Theory in the Work of Anthony Giddens'. In C. Bryant and D. Jary (eds) *Giddens' Theory of Structuration: A Critical Appreciation*. London: Routledge.

Bradley, H. (1996) *Fractured Identities: Changing Patterns of Inequality*. London: Blackwell.

Braidotti, R. (1994) *Nomadic Subjects: Embodiment and Sexual Difference in Contemporary Feminist Theory*. New York: Columbia University Press.

Brand, A. (1990) *The Force of Reason*. London: Allen & Unwin.

Brenner, N. (2004) *New State Spaces: Urban Governance and the Rescaling of Statehood*. Oxford: Oxford University Press.

Brenner, J. and Ramas, M. (1990) 'Rethinking Women's Oppression'. In T. Lovell (ed.) *British Feminist Thought: A Reader*. Oxford: Blackwell.

Bronner, S. (1994) *Of Critical Theory and its Theorists*. Oxford: Blackwell.

Bronner, S. and Kellner, D. (eds) (1989) *Critical Theory and Society: A Reader*. London: Routledge.

Bronowski, J. and Mazlish, B. (1970) *The Western Intellectual Tradition*. Harmondsworth: Penguin.

Brown, P. and Jordanova, L. J. (1981) 'Oppressive Dichotomies: The Nature/ Culture Debate'. In Cambridge Women's Studies Group (eds) *Women in Society: Interdisciplinary Essays*. London: Virago.

Brubaker, R. (1985) 'Rethinking Classical Theory: The Sociological Vision of Pierre Bourdieu'. *Theory and Society* 14(6): 745–775.

Brunkhorst, H. (1992) 'Culture and Bourgeois Society: The Unity of Reason in a Divided Society'. In A. Honneth, M. McCarthy, C. Offe and A. Wellmer (eds) *Cultural-Political Interventions in the Unfinished Project of Enlightenment*. Cambridge, MA: MIT Press.

Bulmer, M. (1984) *The Chicago School of Sociology: Institutionalization, Diversity, and the Rise of Sociological Research*. Chicago, IL: University of Chicago Press.

Burke, K. (1969) *A Grammar of Motives*. Originally published in 1945. Berkeley, CA: University of California Press.

Burke, P. (1980) *Sociology and History*. London: Allen & Unwin.

Burke, P. J. and Reitzes, D. C. (1991) 'An Identity Theory Approach to Commitment'. *Social Psychology Quarterly* 54(3): 239–251.

Burkitt, I. (1992) 'Beyond the "Iron Cage": Anthony Giddens on Modernity and the Self'. *History of the Human Sciences*, special issue on Politics and Modernity, 5(3): 71–79.

Burns, T. (1992) *Erving Goffman*. London: Routledge.

Butler, J. (2003) *Precarious Life*. London: Verso

Button, G. (1991) 'Introduction: Ethnomethodology and the Foundational Respecification of the Human Sciences'. In G. Button (ed.) *Ethnomethodology and the Human Sciences*. Cambridge: Cambridge University Press.

Button, G. and Casey, N. (1984) 'Generating Topic: The Use of Topic Initial Elicitors'. In J. M. Atkinson and J. C. Heritage (eds) *Structures of Social Action: Studies in Conversation Analysis*. Cambridge: Cambridge University Press.

Byrne, D. (2005) *Social Exclusion*, 2nd edn. Maidenhead: Open University Press.

Calhoun, C. (1995) *Critical Social Theory: Culture, History, and the Challenge of Difference*. Oxford: Blackwell.

Calhoun, C. (2000) 'The Specificity of American Higher Education'. *Comparative Social Research* 19: 47–81.

Calhoun, C., Rojek, C. and Turner, B. S. (eds) (2006) *Handbook of Social Theory*. London: Sage.

Callinicos, A. (1989) *Against Postmodernism: A Marxist Critique*. Cambridge: Polity.

Callinicos, A. (2000) *Equality: Themes for the 21st Century*. Cambridge: Polity.

Callon, M. (1986) 'Some Elements of a Sociology of Translation: Domestication of the Scallops and the Fishermen of St. Brieuc Bay'. In J. Law (ed.) *Power, Action and Belief*. London: Routledge & Kegan Paul.

Callon, M. (1987) 'Society in the Making: The Study of Technology as a Tool for Sociological Analysis'. In W. Bijker, T. Hughes and T. Pinch (eds) *The Social Construction of Technological Systems*. London: MIT Press.

Callon, M. (1991) 'Techno-economic Networks and Irreversability'. In J. Law (ed.) *A Sociology of Monsters: Essays on Power, Technology and Domination*. London: Routledge.

Callon, M. (1992) 'The Dynamics of Techno-economic Networks'. In R. Loombs, P. Saviotti and V. Walsh (eds) *Technical Change and Company Strategies*. London: Academy Press.

Callon, M. (1993) 'Variety and Irreversibility in Networks of Technique Conception and Adoption'. In D. Foray and C. Freeman (eds) *Technology and the Wealth of Nations: The Dynamics of Constructed Advantage*. London: Pinter.

Callon, M. (1997) *Representing Nature, Representing Culture*. Paris: CSI.

Callon, M. and Latour, B. (1981) 'Unscrewing the Big Leviathan: How Actors Macrostructure Reality and How Sociologists Help Them to Do so'. In K. D. Knorr-Cetina and A. V. Cicourel (eds) *Advances in Social Theory and Methodology: Toward an Integration of Micro- and Macro-Sociologies*. Boston, MA: Routledge & Kegan Paul.

Callon, M. and Latour, B. (1992) 'Don't Throw the Baby Out with the Bath School! A Reply to Collins and Yearley'. In E. Pickering (ed.) *Science as Practice and Culture*. Chicago, IL: University of Chicago Press.

Castells, M. (1996) *The Rise of the Network Society*, Volume 1, *The Information Age: Economy, Society and Culture*. Oxford: Blackwell.

Castells, M. (2005) 'Global Governance and Global Politics'. *Political Science and Politics* 38(1): 9–16.

Castoriadis, C. (1991) *Philosophy, Politics, Autonomy: Essays in Political Philosophy*. Edited by D. A. Curtis. Oxford: Oxford University Press.

Chappell, V. C. (ed.) (1968) *Hume*. London: Macmillan.

Chodorow, N. J. (1978) *The Reproduction of Mothering: Psychoanalysis and the Sociology of Gender*. Berkeley, CA: University of California Press.

Chodorow, N. J. (1986) 'Towards a Relational Individualism: The Mediation of Self through Psychoanalysis'. In T. Heller, M. Sosna and D. Wellbery with A. Davidson, A. Swidler and I. Watt (eds) *Reconstructing Individualism: Autonomy, Individuality, and the Self in Western Thought*. Stanford, CA: Stanford University Press.

Chomsky, N. (1980) *Rules and Representation*. Oxford: Blackwell.

Chua, W.F. (1999) 'Experts, Networks and Inscriptions in the Fabrication of accounting Images.' *Accounting Organizations and Society* 20, (2/3): 111–145.

Cicourel, A. V. (1964) *Method and Measurement in Sociology*. London: Macmillan.

Cicourel, A. V. (1973) *Cognitive Sociology: Language and Meaning in Social Interaction*. Harmondsworth: Penguin.

Cicourel, A. V. (1976) *The Social Organization of Juvenile Justice*, 2nd edn. London: Heinemann.

Cicourel, A. V. (1981) 'Notes on the Integration of Micro- and Macro-Levels of Analysis'. In K. Knorr-Cetina and A. Cicourel (eds) *Advances in Social Theory and Methodology: Towards an Integration of Micro and Macro Theories*. London: Routledge & Kegan Paul.

Cicourel, A. V. (2003) 'On Contextualizing Applied Linguistic Research in the Workplace'. *Journal of Applied Linguistics* 10(3): 22–43.

Clammer, J. (1976) 'Wittgensteinianism and the Social Sciences'. *Sociological Review* 24(4): 775–791.

Clark, S. (1991) 'The *Annales* Historians'. In Q. Skinner (ed.) *The Return of Grand Theory in the Human Sciences*. Cambridge: Cambridge University Press.

Cleaver, H. (1979) *Reading 'Capital' Politically.* Brighton: Harvester.

Cockburn, C. (1990) 'The Material of Male Power'. In T. Lovell (ed.) *British Feminist Thought: A Reader.* Oxford: Blackwell.

Cohen, G. A. (1984) *Karl Marx's Theory of History: A Defence.* Oxford: Oxford University Press.

Cohen, I. (1989) *Structuration Theory: Anthony Giddens and the Constitution of Social Life.* London: Macmillan.

Coleman, J. S. (1990) *Foundations of Social Theory.* Cambridge, MA: Belknap.

Collins, R. (1981) 'Micro-Translation as a Theory Building Strategy'. In K. Knorr-Cetina and A. Cicourel (eds) *Advances in Social Theory and Methodology: Towards an Integration of Micro and Macro Theories.* London: Routledge & Kegan Paul.

Connell, R. W. (2000) *Men and Boys.* Oxford: Blackwell

Connell, R. (2007) *Education, Change and Society.* Oxford: Oxford University Press.

Connor, S. (1989) *Postmodernist Culture.* Oxford: Blackwell.

Cooke, M. (1994) *Language and Reason: A Study of Habermas's Pragmatics.* Cambridge, MA: MIT Press.

Cooke, M. (2002) 'Five Arguments for Deliberative Democracy'. In M. P. d'Entreves (ed.) *Democracy as Public Deliberation.* Manchester: Manchester University Press.

Cooke, P., Gomez Uranga, M. and Etxebarria, G. (1997) 'Regional Innovation Systems: Institutional and Organizational Dimensions'. *Research Policy* 26: 475–491.

Cooley, C. H. (1902) *Human Nature and the Social Order.* New York: Free Press.

Coser, L. (1979) 'American Trends'. In T. Bottomore and R. Nisbet (eds) *A History of Sociological Analysis.* London: Heinemann.

Coulter, J. (1979) *The Social Construction of Mind: Studies in Ethnomethodology and Linguistic Philosophy.* London: Macmillan.

Coulter, J. (1983) *Rethinking Cognitive Theory.* London: Macmillan.

Coulter, J. (ed.) (1990) *Ethnomethodological Sociology.* Aldershot: Edward Elgar.

Coward, R. (1982) 'Sexual Politics and Psychoanalysis'. In R. Brunt and C. Rowan (eds) *Feminism, Culture and Politics.* London: Lawrence & Wishart.

Craib, I. (1992) *Anthony Giddens.* London: Routledge.

Crampton, J. W. and Elden, S. (eds) (2007) *Space, Knowledge and Power: Foucault and Geography.* Aldershot: Ashgate.

Crook, S., Pakulski, J. and Waters, M. (1992) *Postmodernization: Change in Advanced Society.* London: Sage.

Crosland, M. (1992) *Simone de Beauvoir: The Woman and her Work.* London: Heinemann.

Dahrendorf, R. (1959) *Class and Class Conflict in Industrial Society.* London: Routledge & Kegan Paul.

Dawe, A. (1970) 'The Two Sociologies'. *British Journal of Sociology* 21: 207–218.

Dean, M. (2007) *Governing Societies: Political Perspectives on Domestic and International Rule.* Maidenhead: Open University Press.

de Beauvoir, S. (1972) *The Second Sex.* Originally published in 1949. Harmondsworth: Penguin.

Delanty, G. (1999) *Social Science: Beyond Constructivism and Realism.* Minneapolis, MN: University of Minnesota Press.

Delanty, G. (2001) *Challenging Knowledge: The University in the Knowledge Society.* Buckingham: Open University Press

Delanty, G. (ed.) (2006) *Europe Beyond East and West.* London: Routledge.

Delanty, G. and Isin, E. (eds) (2003) *Handbook of Historical Sociology.* London: Sage.

de Lauretis, T. (1990) 'Upping the Anti [*sic*] in Feminist Theory'. In M. Hirsch and E. Fox Keller (eds) *Conflicts in Feminism.* London: Routledge.

Delmar, R. (1976) 'Looking Again at Engels' "Origin of the Family, Private Property and the State"'. In A. Oakley and J. Mitchell (eds) *The Rights and Wrongs of Women.* Harmondsworth: Penguin.

Delphy, C. and Leonard, D. (1992) *Familiar Exploitation: A New Analysis of Marriage in Contemporary Western Society.* Cambridge: Polity.

Denzin, N. K. (1974) 'Symbolic Interactionism and Ethnomethodology'. In J. D. Douglas (ed.) *Understanding Everyday Life: Towards the Reconstruction of Sociological Knowledge.* London: Routledge & Kegan Paul.

Denzin, N. (1984) *On Understanding Emotion.* San Francisco, CA: Jossey-Bass.

Denzin, N. K. (2007) *Symbolic Interactionism and Cultural Studies: The Politics of Interpretation.* Oxford: Blackwell.

Derrida, J. (1978) *Writing and Difference.* London: Routledge.

Dewey, J. (1896) 'The Reflexive Arc Concept in Psychology'. *Psychological Review* 3: 357–370.

Dews, P. (1989) 'The Return of the Subject in the Late Foucault'. *Radical Philosophy* 51: 37–41.

Dews, P. (ed.) (1992) *Autonomy and Solidarity: Interviews with Jürgen Habermas,* revised edn. London: Verso.

Dore, R. P. (1973) 'Function and Cause'. In A. Ryan (ed.) *The Philosophy of Social Explanation.* Oxford: Oxford University Press.

Douglas, M. (1970) *Purity and Danger: An Analysis of the Concepts of Pollution and Taboo.* New York: Pantheon.

Douglas, M. (1978) *Implicit Meanings: Essays in Anthropology.* London: Routledge & Kegan Paul.

Dreyfus, H. and Rabinow, P. (eds) (1982) *Michel Foucault: Beyond Structuralism and Hermeneutics.* Chicago, IL: University of Chicago Press.

Dreyfus, H. and Rabinow, P. (1993) 'Can There be a Science of Existential Structure and Social Meaning?' In C. Calhoun, E. LiPuma and M. Postone (eds) *Bourdieu: Critical Perspectives.* Cambridge: Polity.

Du Bois, W. (1989) *The Souls of Black Folk.* Originally published in 1903. New York: Bantam.

Dumas, A and Turner, B. S. (2006) 'Age and Ageing: The Social World of Foucault and Bourdieu.' In J. L. Powell and A. Wahidin (eds) *Foucault and Aging.* New York: Nova Science.

Durkheim, E. (1964) *The Division of Labour in Society.* Originally published in 1893. Translated by G. Simpson. New York: Free Press.

Durkheim, E. (1983) *Pragmatism and Sociology.* Originally published in 1955. Edited by J. B. Allcock. Translated by J. C. Whitehouse. Cambridge: Cambridge University Press.

Durkheim, E. (1992) 'Review Article on F. S. Merlino's "Formes et essences du socialisme"'. Originally published in 1899. In M. Gane (ed.) *The Radical Sociology of Durkheim and Mauss.* London: Routledge.

Dworkin, A. (1987) *Intercourse.* London: Secker & Warburg.

Easthope, A. and McGowan, K. (eds) (1992) *A Critical and Cultural Theory Reader.* Buckingham: Open University Press.

Eichenbaum, L. and Orbach, S. (1985) *Understanding Women.* Harmondsworth: Penguin.

Elders, F. (ed.) (1974) *Reflexive Waters: The Basic Concerns of Mankind*. London: Souvenir.

Elias, N. (1991) *The Symbol Theory*. London: Sage.

Elias, N. (1994) *Reflections on a Life*. Cambridge: Polity.

Elliott, A. (1992) *Social Theory and Psychoanalysis in Transition: Self and Society from Freud to Kristeva*. Oxford: Blackwell.

Engels, F. (1942) *The Origin of the Family, Private Property and the State*. Originally published in 1884. New York: International Publishers.

Eriksen, E. O. and Weigard, J: (2004) *Understanding Habermas: Communicative action and Deliberative Democracy*. London: Continuum.

Estes, C. and Phillipson, C. (2003) 'The Globalization of Capital, the Welfare State and Old Age Policy'. *International Journal of Health Services* 32(2): 279–297.

Estes, C., Biggs, S. and Phillipson, C. (2003) *Social Theory, Social Policy and Ageing*. Maidenhead: Open University Press.

Faberman, H. A. (1985) 'The Foundations of Symbolic Interactionism: James, Cooley and Mead'. Reprinted in K. Plummer (ed.) *Symbolic Interactionism, Volume 1, Foundations and History*. Aldershot: Edward Elgar.

Fairclough, N. (2001) *Language and Power*, 2nd edn. London: Longman.

Farganis, S. (1994) *Situating Feminism: From Thought to Action*. London: Sage.

Ferrara, A. (1998) *Reflective Authenticity: Rethinking the Project of Modernity*. London: Routledge.

Figes, E. (1978) *Patriarchal Attitudes: Women in Society*. Originally published in 1970. London: Virago.

Fineman, S. (ed.) (2000) *Emotion in Organizations*, 2nd edn. London: Sage.

Finlayson, G. (2004) 'Theory of Ideology and the Ideology of Theory: Habermas contra Adorno' *Historical Materialism* 11: 169–187.

Firestone, S. (1988) *The Dialectic of Sex: The Case for Feminist Revolution*. Originally published 1970. London: Women's Press.

Fisher, B. M. and Strauss, A. L. (1978) 'The Chicago Tradition and Social Change: Thomas, Park and their Successors'. Reprinted in K. Plummer (ed.) *Symbolic Interactionism*, Volume 1, *Foundations and History*. Aldershot: Edward Elgar.

Fisher, B. M. and Strauss, A. L. (1979) 'Interactionism'. In T. Bottomore and R. Nisbet (eds) *A History of Sociological Analysis*. London: Heinemann.

Florida, R. (2002) *The Rise of the Creative Class and How It's Transforming Work, Leisure, Community and Everyday Life*. New York: Basic Books.

Foucault, M. (1967) *Madness and Civilisation: A History of Insanity in the Age of Reason*. London: Tavistock.

Foucault, M. (1977) *Discipline and Punish: The Birth of the Prison*. London: Tavistock.

Foucault, M. (1979) *The History of Sexuality, Volume 1, An Introduction*. Translated by R. Hurley. Harmondsworth: Penguin.

Foucault, M. (1980) *Power/Knowledge: Selected Interviews and Other Writings 1972–1977*. Edited by C. Gordon. Brighton: Harvester.

Foucault, M. (1982) 'The Subject and Power'. In H. Dreyfus and P. Rabinow (eds) *Michel Foucault: Beyond Structuralism and Hermeneutics*. Chicago, IL: University of Chicago Press.

Foucault, M. (1984) *The Foucault Reader*. Edited by P. Rabinow. Harmondsworth: Penguin.

Foucault, M. (1988a) 'The Political Technology of Individuals'. In L. H. Martin, H. Gutman and P. H. Hutton (eds) *Technologies of the Self: A Seminar with Michel Foucault*. London: Tavistock.

Foucault, M. (1988b) 'Technologies of the Self'. In L. H. Martin, H. Gutman and P. H. Hutton (eds) *Technologies of the Self: A Seminar with Michel Foucault*. London: Tavistock.

Foucault, M. (1988c) 'Truth, Power, Self: An Interview'. In L. H. Martin, H. Gutman and P. H. Hutton (eds) *Technologies of the Self: A Seminar with Michel Foucault*. London: Tavistock.

Foucault, M. (1989) *The Archaeology of Knowledge*. Originally published in 1969. London: Routledge.

Foucault, M. (1991a) *Remarks on Marx: Conversations with Duccio Trombadori*. Translated by R. J. Goldstein and J. Cascaito. New York: Semiotext(e).

Foucault, M. (1991b) 'The Ethic of Care for the Self as a Practice of Freedom: An Interview with Fornet-Betancourt, R., Becker, H. and Gomez-Müller, A.' Translated by J. D. Gauthier Snr. In J. Bernauer and D. Rasmussen (eds) *The Final Foucault*. Cambridge, MA: MIT Press.

Foucault, M. (1991c) 'Questions of Method'. In G. Burchell, C. Gordon and P. Miller (eds) *The Foucault Effect: Studies in Governmentality*. London: Harvester Wheatsheaf.

Foucault, M. (1991d) *Discipline and Punish: The Birth of the Prison.* Originally published in 1977. Translated by A. Sheridan. Harmondsworth: Penguin.

Foucault, M. (1992) *The Order of Things: An Archaeology of the Human Sciences.* Originally published in 1970. London: Routledge.

Foucault, M. (1996) *Foucault Live: Collected Interviews 1961–1894.* Edited by S. Lotringer. New York: Semiotext(e).

Fraser, N. (1989) *Unruly Practices: Power, Discourse and Gender in Contemporary Social Theory.* Cambridge: Polity.

Fraser, N. and Honneth, A. (2003) *Redistribution or Recognition: A Political-Philosophical Exchange.* London: Verso.

Freud, S. (1938) *Psychopathology of Everday Life.* Harmondsworth: Penguin.

Freud, S. (1969) *Civilization and its Discontents.* Translated by J. Riviere. Edited by J. Strachey. London: Hogarth.

Freund, J. (1979) 'German Sociology in the Time of Max Weber'. In T. Bottomore and R. Nisbet (eds) *A History of Sociological Analysis.* London: Heinemann.

Freund, P. E. S. (1988) 'Bringing Society into the Body: Understanding Socialized Human Nature'. *Theory and Society* 17(6): 839–864.

Freundlieb, D. (1994) 'Foucault's Theory of Discourse and Human Agency'. In C. Jones and R. Porter (eds) *Reassessing Foucault: Power, Medicine and the Body.* London: Routledge.

Friedan, B. (1965) *The Feminine Mystique.* Harmondsworth: Penguin.

Frisby, D. (1991) 'The Aesthetics of Modern Life: Simmel's Interpretation'. In M. Featherstone (ed.) *Consumer Culture and Postmodernism.* London: Sage.

Frisby, D. (1992a) *Sociological Impressionism: A Reassessment of Georg Simmel's Social Theory,* 2nd edn. London: Routledge.

Frisby, D. (1992b) *Simmel and Since: Essays on Georg Simmel's Social Theory.* London: Routledge.

Fromm, E. (1969) *Escape from Freedom.* Originally published in 1941. New York: Avon.

Fukuyama, F. (1995) *Trust: The Social Virtues and the Creation of Prosperity.* London: Hamish Hamilton.

Fuller, S. (2007) *New Frontiers in Science and Technology Studies.* Cambridge: Polity.

Gadamer, H. G. (1975) *Truth and Method*. Originally published in 1960. London: Sheed & Ward.

Gane, M. (1990) 'Ironies of Postmodernism: Fate of Baudrillard's Fatalism'. *Economy and Society* 19(3): 314–334.

Gane, M. (1991) *Baudrillard: Critical and Fatal Theory*. London: Routledge.

Gane, M. (ed.) (1992) *The Radical Sociology of Durkheim and Mauss*. London: Routledge.

Gane, M. (ed.) (1993) *Baudrillard Live: Selected Interviews*. London: Routledge.

Gane, N. (ed.) (2005) *The Future of Social Theory*. London: Continuum.

Garfinkel, H. (1967) *Studies in Ethnomethodology*. Englewood Cliffs, NJ: Prentice-Hall.

Garfinkel, H. (1974) 'The Origins of the Term "Ethnomethodology"'. Originally published in 1968. Reprinted in R. Turner (ed.) *Ethnomethodology*. Harmondsworth: Penguin.

Garfinkel, H. (1991) 'Respecification: Evidence for Locally Produced, Naturally Accountable Phenomena of Order, Logic, Reason, Meaning, Method, etc. In and as of the Essential Haecceity of Immortal Ordinary Society, (1) – An Announcement of Studies'. In G. Button (ed.) *Ethnomethodology and the Human Sciences*. Cambridge: Cambridge University Press.

Garfinkel, H. and Sacks, H. (1986) 'On Formal Structures of Practical Actions'. In H. Garfinkel (ed.) *Ethnomethodological Studies of Work*. London: Routledge & Kegan Paul.

Garland, D. (2002) *The Culture of Control: Crime and Social Order in Contemporary Society*. London: Sage.

Gartman, D. (1991) 'Culture as Class Symbolization or Mass Reification? A Critique of Bourdieu's *Distinction*'. *American Journal of Sociology* 97(2): 421–447.

Gellner, E. (1968) *Words and Things*. Harmondsworth: Penguin.

Gellner, E. (1974) 'The New Idealism: Cause and Meaning in the Social Sciences'. In A. Giddens (ed.) *Positivism and Sociology*. London: Heinemann.

Gellner, E. (1988) *Culture, Identity and Politics*. Cambridge: Cambridge University Press.

Gellner, E. (1992) *Reason and Culture: The Historic Role of Rationality and Rationalism*. Oxford: Blackwell.

Gerth, H. and Mills, C. W. (eds) (1970) *From Max Weber: Essays in Sociology* Originally published in 1948. London: Routledge & Kegan Paul.

Gibson-Graham, J. K. (1996) *The End of Capitalism (As we Knew It): A Feminist Critique of Political Economy.* Oxford: Blackwell.

Giddens, A. (1971) *Capitalism and Modern Social Theory: An Analysis of the Writings of Marx, Durkheim and Max Weber.* Cambridge: Cambridge University Press.

Giddens, A. (1972a) *Politics and Sociology in the Thought of Max Weber.* London: Macmillan.

Giddens, A. (ed.) (1972b) *Emile Durkheim: Selected Writings.* Cambridge: Cambridge University Press.

Giddens, A. (1976) *New Rules of Sociological Method: A Positive Critique of Interpretive Sociologies.* London: Hutchinson.

Giddens, A. (1977) *Studies in Social and Political Theory.* London: Hutchinson.

Giddens, A. (1979) *Central Problems in Social Theory: Action, Structure and Contradiction in Social Analysis.* London: Macmillan.

Giddens, A. (1981a). *A Contemporary Critique of Historical Materialism, Volume 1, Power, Property and the State.* London: Macmillan.

Giddens, A. (1981b) 'Agency, Institution, and Time-Space Analysis'. In K. Knorr-Cetina and A. Cicourel (eds) *Advances in Social Theory and Methodology: Towards an Integration of Micro and Macro Theories.* London: Routledge & Kegan Paul.

Giddens, A. (1982) *Profiles and Critiques in Social Theory.* Berkeley, CA: University of California Press.

Giddens, A. (1984) *The Constitution of Society: Outline of the Theory of Structuration.* Cambridge: Polity.

Giddens, A. (1985) *The Nation-State and Violence,* Volume 2, *A Contemporary Critique of Historical Materialism.* Cambridge: Polity.

Giddens, A. (1987) *Social Theory and Modern Sociology.* Cambridge: Polity.

Giddens, A. (1989) 'A Reply to my Critics'. In D. Held and J. Thompson (eds) *Social Theory of Modern Societies: Anthony Giddens and his Critics.* Cambridge: Cambridge University Press.

Giddens, A. (1990) *The Consequences of Modernity.* Cambridge: Polity.

Giddens, A. (1991a) 'Structuration Theory: Past, Present and Future'. In C. Bryant and D. Jary (eds) *Giddens' Theory of Structuration: A Critical Appreciation.* London: Routledge.

Giddens, A. (1991b) *Modernity and Self-Identity*. Cambridge: Polity.

Giddens, A. (1992) *The Transformation of Intimacy: Sexuality, Love and Eroticism in Modern Societies*. Cambridge: Polity.

Giddens, A. (1993) *New Rules of Sociological Method: A Positive Critique of Interpretive Sociologies*, 2nd edn. Cambridge: Polity.

Giddens, A. (1994) *Beyond Left and Right: The Future of Radical Politics*. Cambridge: Polity.

Giddens, A. (1998) *The Third Way: The Renewal of Social Democracy*. Cambridge: Polity.

Giddens, A. (2007) *Over To You, Mr Brown: How Labour Can Win Again*. Cambridge: Polity.

Gilleard, C. and Higgs, P. (2005) *Cohorts of Ageing*. London: Routledge.

Gilroy, P. (2001) 'Driving While Black'. In D. Miller (ed). *Car Cultures*. Oxford: Berg.

Glasius, M. Kaldor, M. and Anheier, H. K. (2003) 'Social Forums, the Anti-War Movement and Regressive Globalizers.' www.opendemocracy.net.

Glücksmann, A. (1992) 'Michel Foucault's Nihilism'. In T. J. Armstrong (ed.) *Michel Foucault: Philosopher*. Translated by T. J. Armstrong. London: Harvester Wheatsheaf.

Goffman, E. (1959) *The Presentation of Self in Everyday Life*. London: Penguin.

Goffman, E. (1961) *Encounters: Two Studies in the Sociology of Interaction*. Harmondsworth: Penguin.

Goffman, E. (1968) *Asylums: Essays on the Social Situation of Mental Patients and Other Inmates*. Originally published in 1961. Harmondsworth: Penguin.

Goffman, E. (1971) *Relations in Public: Microstudies of the Public Order*. Harmondsworth: Penguin.

Goffman, E. (1972) *Interaction Ritual: Essays on Face-to-Face Behaviour*. Harmondsworth: Penguin.

Goffman, E. (1974) *Frame Analysis: An Essay on the Organization of Experience*. New York: Harper & Row.

Goffman, E. (1979) *Gender Advertisements*. London: Macmillan.

Goffman, E. (1981) *Forms of Talk*. Philadelphia, PA: University of Pennsylvania Press.

Goffman, E. (1983) 'The Interaction Order'. The 1982 American Sociological Association Presidential Address. Reprinted in K. Plummer (ed.) *Symbolic Interactionism*, Volume 2, *Contemporary Issues*. Aldershot: Edward Elgar..

Goffman, E. (1984) *The Presentation of Self in Everyday Life*. Originally published in 1959. Harmondsworth: Penguin.

Goldthorpe, J. H. (1973) 'A Revolution in Sociology?' *Sociology* 7: 449–462.

Goldthorpe, J. H. and Marshall, G. (1992) 'The Promising Future of Class Analysis'. *Sociology* 26(3): 381–400.

Gordon, C. (1987) 'The Soul of the Citizen: Max Weber and Michel Foucault on Rationality and Government'. In S. Lash and S. Whimster (eds) *Max Weber, Rationality and Modernity*. London: Allen & Unwin.

Gouldner, A. (1971) *The Coming Crisis in Western Sociology*. London: Heinemann.

Gramsci, A. (1971) *Prison Notebooks: Selections*. Translated by Q. Hoare and G. N. Smith. New York: International Publishers.

Greenblatt, S. (1980) *Renaissance Self-Fashioning: From More to Shakespeare*, Chicago, IL: University of Chicago Press.

Greer, G. (1970) *The Female Eunuch*. London: MacGibbon & Kee.

Gregson, N. (1989) 'On the (Ir)relevance of Structuration Theory to Empirical Research'. In D. Held and J. Thompson (eds) *Social Theory of Modern Societies: Anthony Giddens and his Critics*. Cambridge: Cambridge University Press.

Griffiths, M. (1988) 'Feminism, Feelings and Philosophy'. In M. Griffiths and M. Whitford (eds) *Feminist Perspectives in Philosophy*. London: Macmillan.

Griffiths, M. and Whitford, M. (eds) (1988) *Feminist Perspectives in Philosophy*. London: Macmillan.

Grosz, E. (1990) 'A Note on Essentialism and Difference'. In S. Gunew (ed.) *Feminist Knowledge: Critique and Construct*. London: Routledge.

Grosz, E. (1992) 'What is Feminist Theory?' In H. Crowley and S. Himmelweit (eds) *Knowing Women: Feminism and Knowledge*. Cambridge: Polity.

Grosz, E. (1994) *Volatile Bodies: Toward a Corporeal Feminism*. Bloomington, IN: Indiana University Press.

Gubrium, J. and Holstein, J. (2006) *Couples, Kids, and Family Life*. New York: Oxford University Press.

Gutting, G. (2003) *Foucault: A Very Short Introduction*. Oxford: Oxford University Press.

Habermas, J. (1975) *Legitimation Crisis*. Translated by T. McCarthy. Boston, MA: Beacon.

Habermas, J. (1981) 'Towards a Reconstruction of Historical Materialism'. In K. Knorr-Cetina and A. Cicourel (eds) *Advances in Social Theory and Methodology: Towards an Integration of Micro and Macro Theories*. London: Routledge & Kegan Paul.

Habermas, J. (1984) *Theory of Communicative Action. Volume 1: Reason and the Rationalization of Society*. Translated by T. McCarthy. London: Heinemann.

Habermas, J. (1986) 'Taking Aim at the Heart of the Present'. In D. C. Hoy (ed.) *Foucault: A Critical Reader*. Oxford: Blackwell.

Habermas, J. (1987) *Theory of Communicative Action. Volume 2: Lifeworld and System: A Critique of Functionalist Reason*. Translated by T. McCarthy. Cambridge: Polity.

Habermas, J. (1989a) *Knowledge and Human Interests*. Originally published in 1968. Translated by J. J. Shapiro. Cambridge: Polity.

Habermas, J. (1989b) *The Structural Transformation of the Public Sphere*. Translated by T. Berger and F. Lawrence. Cambridge, MA: MIT Press.

Habermas, J. (1990) *On the Logic of the Social Sciences*. Originally published in 1970. Translated by S. S. W. Nicholsen and J. A. Stark. Cambridge: Polity.

Habermas, J. (1991) 'A Reply'. In A. Honneth and H. Joas (eds) *Communicative Action: Essays on Jürgen Habermas's 'The Theory of Communicative Action'*. Translated by J. Gains and D. L. Jones. Cambridge, MA: MIT Press.

Habermas, J. (1992a) *The Philosophical Discourse of Modernity: Twelve Lectures*. Cambridge: Polity.

Habermas, J. (1992b) *Postmetaphysical Thinking: Philosophical Essays*. Translated by W. M. Hohengarten. Cambridge, MA: MIT Press.

Habermas, J. (1992c) *Moral Consciousness and Communicative Action*. Translated by C. Lenhardt and S. Nicholsen. Introduction by T. McCarthy. Cambridge: Polity.

Habermas, J. (1993) *Justification and Application: Remarks on Discourse Ethics*. Translated by C. Cronin. Cambridge: Polity.

Habermas, J. (1994) *The Past as Future*. Interviewed by M. Haller. Translated and edited by M. Pensky. Cambridge: Polity.

Habermas, J. (1996) *Between Facts and Norms: Contributions to a Discourse Theory of Law and Democracy*. Cambridge: Polity.

Habermas, J. (2003) *On the Pragmatics of Social Interaction: Preliminary Studies in the Theory of Communicative Action.* Cambridge: Polity.

Habermas, J. (2006) *The Divided West.* Cambridge: Polity.

Hagestad, G. and Dannefer, D. (2001) 'Concepts and Theories of Aging'. In R. Binstock and L. George (eds) *Handbook of Aging and Social Sciences.* San Diego, CA: Academic Press.

Hall, P. M. (1987) 'Interactionism and the Study of Social Organization'. Reprinted in K. Plummer (ed.) *Symbolic Interactionism, Volume 2, Contemporary Issues.* Aldershot: Edward Elgar.

Hamilton, P. (1983) *Talcott Parsons.* London: Tavistock.

Hamilton, P. (ed.) (1985) *Readings from Talcott Parsons.* London: Tavistock.

Hamilton, P. (1992) 'The Enlightenment and the Birth of Social Science'. In S. Hall and B. Gieben (eds) *Formations of Modernity.* Cambridge: Polity.

Haraway, D. (1991) *Simians, Cyborgs, and Women: The Reinvention of Nature.* New York: Routledge.

Harding, S. (1986) *The Science Question in Feminism.* Milton Keynes: Open University Press.

Harding, S. (ed.) (2004) *The Feminist Standpoint Theory Reader: Intellectual and Political Controversies.* New York: Routledge.

Harding, S. (2006) *Science and Social Inequality.* Urbana, IL: University of Illinois Press.

Harding, S. and Hintikka, M. B. (1983) 'Introduction'. In S. Harding and M. B. Hintikka, (eds) *Discovering Reality: Feminist Perspectives on Epistemology, Metaphysics, Methodology, and Philosophy of Science.* London: Reidel.

Harper, S. (1997) 'Constructing Later Life/Constructing the Body: Some Thoughts from Feminist Theory'. In A. Jamieson, S. Harper and C. Victor (eds) *Critical Approaches to Ageing and Later Life.* Buckingham: Open University Press.

Harré, R (ed.) (1986) *The Social Construction of Emotions.* Oxford: Blackwell.

Harré, R. and van Langenhove, L. (1991) 'Varieties of Positioning'. *Journal for the Theory of Social Behaviour.* 21(4): 393–407.

Harré, R. and Moghaddam, F. M. (eds) (2003) *The Self and Others: Positioning Individuals and Groups in Personal, Organizational, Political and Cultural Contexts.* Westport, CT: Praeger/Greenwood.

Harrington, A. (ed.) (2005) *Contemporary Social Theory.* London: Blackwell.

Hartsock, N. (1983) 'The Feminist Standpoint: Developing the Ground for a Specifically Feminist Historical Materialism'. In S. Harding and M. B. Hintikka (eds) *Discovering Reality: Feminist Perspectives on Epistemology, Metaphysics, Methodology, and Philosophy of Science*. London: Reidel.

Harvey, D. (1990) *The Condition of Postmodernity: An Enquiry into the Origins of Cultural Change*. Oxford: Blackwell.

Harvey, D. (2006) *Spaces of Global Capitalism: Towards a Theory of Uneven Geographical Development*. London: Verso.

Hawthorn, G. (1976) *Enlightenment and Despair: A History of Sociology*. Cambridge: Cambridge University Press.

Hegel, G. W. F. (1967a) *The Phenomenology of Mind*. Translated by J. B. Baillie. Oxford: Oxford University Press.

Hegel, G. W. F. (1967b) *Hegel's Philosophy of Right*. Translated by T. M. Knox. Oxford: Oxford University Press.

Heilbron, J. (1995) *The Rise of Social Theory*. Translated by S. Gogol. Cambridge: Polity.

Hekman, S. (1990a) 'Hermeneutics and the Crisis of Social Theory: A Critique of Giddens' Epistemology'. In J. Clark, C. Modgil and S. Modgil (eds) *Anthony Giddens: Consensus and Controversy*. Brighton: Falmer.

Hekman, S. (1990b) *Gender and Knowledge: Elements of a Postmodern Feminism*. Cambridge: Polity.

Held, D. (1990) *Introduction to Critical Theory: Horkheimer to Habermas*. Cambridge: Polity.

Held, D. (2000) *Global Transformations*. Cambridge: Polity.

Heller, A. (1984) *Everyday Life*. Translated by G. Campbell. London: Routledge & Kegan Paul.

Heritage, J. (1984) *Garfinkel and Ethnomethodology*. Cambridge: Polity.

Heritage, J. (1990) 'Ethnomethodology'. In A. Giddens and J. Turner (eds) *Social Theory Today*. Cambridge: Polity.

Hill, R. J. and Stones Crittenden, K. (eds) (1968) *Proceedings of the Purdue Symposium on Ethnomethodology*. Department of Sociology, Institute for the Study of Social Change, Purdue University, West Lafayette, IN.

Hindness, B. (1996) *Discourses of Power: From Hobbes to Foucault*. Oxford: Blackwell.

Hirst, P. Q. and Thompson, G. (2000) *Globalization in Question: The International Economy and the Possibilities of Governance*, 2nd edn. Cambridge: Polity.

Hochschild, A. E. (1983) *The Managed Heart: Commercialization of Human Feeling.* Berkeley, CA: University of California Press.

Hochschild, A. E. (2003) *The Commercialization of Intimate Life: Notes from Home and Work.* Berkeley, CA: University of California Press.

Hole, J. and Lévine, E. (1979) 'The First Feminists'. In J. Freeman (ed.) *Women: A Feminist Perspective*, 2nd edn. Palo Alto, CA: Mayfield..

Hollingdale, R. J. (ed.) (1977) *A Nietzsche Reader.* Translated by R. J. Hollingdale. Harmondsworth: Penguin.

Hollinger, R. (1994) *Postmodernism and the Social Sciences: A Thematic Approach.* London: Sage.

Hollis, M. and Lukes, S. (eds) (1982) *Rationality and Relativism.* Oxford: Blackwell.

Holton, R. and Turner, B. (1989) *Max Weber on Economy and Society.* London: Routledge.

Holtzman, S. and Leich, C. (eds) (1981) *Wittgenstein: To Follow a Rule.* London: Routledge & Kegan Paul.

Holub, R. C. (1991) *Jürgen Habermas: Critic in the Public Sphere.* London: Routledge.

Homans, G. (1961) *Social Behaviour: Its Elementary Forms.* New York: Harcourt Brace Jovanovich.

Homans, G. (1973) 'Bringing Men Back In'. In A. Ryan (ed.) *The Philosophy of Social Explanation.* Oxford: Oxford University Press.

Honneth, A. (1991) *The Critique of Power: Reflective Stages in a Critical Social Theory.* Translated by K. Baynes. Cambridge, MA: MIT Press.

Honneth, A. (1993) 'Critical Theory in Germany Today: An Interview'. *Radical Philosophy* 65 : 33–41.

Honneth, A. and Joas, H. (1988) *Social Action and Human Nature.* Cambridge: Cambridge University Press.

Horkheimer, M. (1993) *Between Philosophy and Social Science: Selected Early Writings.* Translated by G. F. Hunter, M. S. Kramer and J. Torpey. Cambridge, MA: MIT Press.

Houtkoop-Steenstra, H. (1993) 'Opening Sequences in Dutch Telephone Conversations'. In D. Boden and D. H. Zimmerman (eds) *Talk and Social Structure: Studies in Ethnomethodology and Conversation Analysis*. Cambridge: Polity.

Hoy, D. C. (1986) 'Power, Repression, Progress: Foucault, Lukes, and the Frankfurt School'. In D. C. Hoy (ed.) *Foucault: A Critical Reader*. Oxford: Blackwell.

Hoy, D. C. and McCarthy, T. (1994) *Critical Theory*. Oxford: Blackwell.

Hughes, E. (1971) *The Sociological Eye: Selected Papers*. Chicago, IL: Aldine-Atherton.

Hughes, S. H. (1979) *Consciousness and Society: The Reorientation of European Social Thought 1890–1930*. Brighton: Harvester.

Humm, M. (ed.) (1992) *Feminisms: A Reader*. London: Harvester Wheatsheaf.

Jaggar, A. (1983) *Feminist Politics and Human Nature*. London: Harvester.

James, W. (1890) *Principles of Psychology*, 2 volumes. New York: Holt.

Jameson, F. (1991) *Postmodernism, or, The Cultural Logic of Late Capitalism*. London: Verso.

Jay, M. (1973) *The Dialectical Imagination: A History of the Frankfurt School and the Institute of Social Research 1923–1950*. London: Heinemann.

Jenson, J. (1995) 'Mapping, Naming and Remembering: Globalization at the End of the Twentieth Century'. *Review of International Political Economy* 2(1): 96–116.

Jessop, B. (2002) *The Future of the Capitalist State in its Place*. Cambridge: Polity.

Joas, H. (1985) *G. H. Mead: A Contemporary Re-Examination of his Thought*. Translated by R. Meyer. Cambridge: Polity.

Joas, H. (1993) *Pragmatism and Social Theory*. Chicago, IL: University of Chicago Press.

Johnson, L. C. (1990) 'Socialist Feminisms'. In S. Gunew (ed.) *Feminist Knowledge: Critique and Construct*. London: Routledge.

Johnson, P. (1993) 'Feminism and the Enlightenment'. *Radical Philosophy* 63: 3–12.

Johnson, T., Dandeker, C. and Ashworth, C. (1984) *The Structure of Social Theory: Dilemmas and Strategies*. London: Macmillan.

Jones, C. (2006) 'Olwen Hufton's "Poor", Richard Cobb's "People" and the French Revolution'. In R. Harris and L. Roper (eds) *The Art of Survival: Essays in Honour of Olwen Hufton: Gender and History in Europe 1450–2000*. Oxford: Oxford University Press

Kamuf, P. (ed.) (1991) *A Derrida Reader: Between the Blinds*. London: Harvester Wheatsheaf.

Katz, S. (1996) *Disciplining Old Age*. Charlottesville, VA: University Press of Virginia.

Katz, S. (2007) *Cultural Aging*. Peterborough, Ont.: Broadview Press

Keat, R. and Urry, J. (1975) *Social Theory as Science*. London: Routledge & Kegan Paul.

Kellner, D. (1993) 'Popular Culture and the Construction of Postmodern Identities'. In S. Lash and J. Friedman (eds) *Modernity and Identity*. Oxford: Blackwell.

Kellner, D. (2002) 'Technological Revolution, Multiple Literacies, and the Restructuring of Education'. In I. Snyder (ed.) *Silicon Literacies*. London: Routledge.

Kelly, M. (ed.) (1994) *Critique and Power: Recasting the Foucault/Habermas Debate*. Cambridge, MA: MIT Press.

Kemper, T. (1984) 'Power, Status and Emotions'. In E. Scherer and P. Ekman (eds) *Approaches to Emotion*. Hillsdale, NJ: Lawrence Erilbaum

Kinnaird, J. K. (1983) 'Mary Astell: Inspired by Ideas'. In D. Spender (ed.) *Feminist Theorists: Three Centuries of Women's Intellectual Traditions*. London: Women's Press.

Klein, N. (2001) *No Logo*. London: Flamingo.

Knights, D. and McCabe, D. (2003). *Organization and Innovation: Guru Schemes and American Dreams*. Maidenhead: Open University Press.

Knorr-Cetina, K. (1981) 'The Micro-Sociological Challenge of Macro-Sociology: Towards a Reconstruction of Social Theory and Methodology'. In K. Knorr-Cetina and A. Cicourel (eds) *Advances in Social Theory and Methodology: Towards an Integration of Micro and Macro Theories*. London: Routledge & Kegan Paul.

Knorr-Cetina, K. (2005) 'From Pipes to Scopes: The Flow Architecture of Financial Markets'. In A. Barry (ed.) *The Technological Economy*. London: Routledge.

Kolakowski, L. (1978a) *Main Currents of Marxism, Volume 1*. Oxford: Oxford University Press.

Kolakowski, L. (1978b) *Main Currents of Marxism, Volume 2*. Oxford: Oxford University Press.

Korany, B. (1994) 'End of History, or its Continuation and Accentuation? The Global South and the "New Transformation" Literature.' *Third World Quarterly* 15(1): 7–15.

Kristeva, J. (1999) 'Women's Time'. In C. Belsey and J. Moore (eds) *The Feminist Reader*. London: Blackwell.

Kroker, A. and Cook, D. (1988) *The Postmodern Scene: Excremental Culture and Hyper-Aesthetics*. London: Macmillan.

Kurtz, L. (1984) Evaluating Chicago Sociology: A Guide to the Literature with an Annotated Bibliography. Chicago, IL: University of Chicago Press.

Lacan, J. (1992) *The Ethics of Psychoanalysis 1959–1960*. New York: Norton.

Laclau, E. and Mouffe, C. (2001) *Hegemony and Socialist Strategy: Towards a Radical Democratic Politics*, 2nd edn. London: Verso.

Landry, D. and MacLean, G. (1993) Materialist Feminisms. Oxford: Blackwell.

Larrabee, M. J. (ed.) (1993) An Ethic of Care: Feminist and Interdisciplinary Perspectives. London: Routledge.

Lash, S. (1990) The Sociology of Postmodernism. London: Routledge.

Lash, S. (1993) 'Pierre Bourdieu: Cultural Economy and Social Change'. In C. Calhoun, E. LiPuma and M. Postone (eds) *Bourdieu: Critical Perspectives*. Cambridge: Polity.

Lash, S. and Urry, J. (1987) The End of Organized Capitalism. Cambridge: Polity.

Lash, S. and Urry, J. (1994) *Economies of Signs and Space*. London: Sage.

Lash, S. and Whimster, S. (eds) (1987) *Max Weber, Rationality and Modernity*. London: Allen & Unwin.

Latour, B (1986) 'Visualization and Cognition: Thinking with the Eyes and the Hands'. In H. Kuklick and E. Long (eds) *Knowledge and Society: Studies in the Sociology of Culture Past and Present* Volume 6. London: Routledge.

Latour, B. (1987) *Science in Action: How to Follow Scientists and Engineers through Society*. Milton Keynes: Open University Press.

Latour, B. (1991) 'Technology is Society Made Durable'. In J. Law (ed.) *A Sociology of Monsters? Essays on Power, Technology and Domination*. London: Routledge.

Latour, B. (1992) 'Where are the Missing Masses? Sociology of a Few Mundane Artefacts'. In W. Bijker and J. Law (eds) *Shaping Technology, Building Society: Studies in Sociotechnical Change*. Cambridge, MA: MIT Press.

Latour, B. (1993) 'Ethnography of a "high-tech" Case: About Aramis'. In P. Lemonnier (ed.) *Technological Choices: Transformation in Material Cultures since the Neolithic*. London: Routledge.

Latour, B. (1996) 'Social Theory and the Study of Computerized Work Sites'. In W. J. Orlikowski, G. Walsham, M. R. Jones and J. DeGros (eds) *Information Technology and Changes in Organizational Work*. London: Chapman & Hall.

Latour, B. (1999) *Pandora's Hope: Essays on the Reality of Science Studies*. Cambridge, MA: Harvard University Press.

Latour, B. (2005) *Reassembling the Social: An Introduction to Actor-Network-Theory*. New York: Oxford University Press.

Lavallette, M. and Pratt, A. (2007) Social Policy: *A Conceptual, Theoretical and Methodological Analysis*. London: Sage.

Law, J. (ed.) (1991) *A Sociology of Monsters*. London: Routledge.

Law, J. (1992) 'Notes on the Theory of the Actor-Network: Ordering, Strategy and Heterogeneity'. *Systems Practice* 5: 379–393.

Law, J. and Callon M. (1988) 'Engineering and Sociology in a Military Aircraft Project: A Network Analysis of Technical Change'. *Social Problems* 35: 284–297.

Law, J. and Hassard, J. (1999) *Actor Network Theory and After*. Malden, MA: Blackwell.

Layder, D. (1987) 'Key Issues in Structuration Theory: Some Critical Remarks'. *Current Perspectives in Social Theory* 8: 25–46.

Layder, D. (2004) *Social and Personal Identity*. London: Sage.

Layder, D. (2006) *Understanding Social Theory*, 2nd edn. London: Sage.

Leeds Revolutionary Feminist Group (1982) 'Political Lesbianism: The Case against Heterosexuality'. In M. Evans (ed.) *The Woman Question: Readings on the Subordination of Women*. London: Fontana.

Legrain, P (2006) 'Why NAMA Liberalization is Good for Developing Countries'. *The World Economy* 29(10): 1349–1362.

Lemert, C. (1979) 'De-Centred Analysis: Ethnomethodology and Structuralism'. *Theory and Society* 7: 289–306.

Lemert, C. (ed.) (1993) Social Theory: *The Multicultural and Classic Readings*. Oxford: Westview.

Lemert, C. (2006) *Social Things*. New York: Rowman & Littlefield.

Lerner, G. (2004) *Conversation Analysis: Studies from the First Generation*. New York: John Benjamins.

Lévi-Strauss, C. (1963) *Structural Anthropology*. New York: Basic Books.

Lewis, J. D. and Smith, R. L. (1980) *American Sociology and Pragmatism*: Mead, Chicago Sociology and Symbolic Interactionism. Chicago, IL: University of Chicago Press.

Lincourt, J. M. and Hare, P. H. (1973) 'Neglected American Philosophers in the History of Symbolic Interactionism'. In K. Plummer (ed.) *Symbolic Interactionism*, Volume 1, *Foundations and History*. Aldershot: Edward Elgar.

Lindsay, A. D. (1967) 'Hegel the German Idealist'. In F. J. C. Hearnshaw (ed.) *The Social and Political Ideas of Some Representative Thinkers of the Age of Reaction and Reconstruction: 1815–1865*. Originally published in 1932. London: Dawsons.

Loader, B. (2001) *Community Informatics: Shaping Computer-Mediated Social Networks*. London: Routledge.

Lockwood, D. (1976) 'Social Integration and System Integration'. In G. K. Zollschan and W. Hirsch (eds) *Social Change: Explorations, Diagnoses and Conjectures*. New York: Wiley.

Lofland, J. (1976) *Doing Social Life*. New York: Wiley.

Longino, C. F., Jr. and Powell, J. L. (2004) 'Embodiment and the Study of Aging'. In V. Berdayes, L. Esposito and J. W. Murphy (eds) *The Body in Human Inquiry: Interdisciplinary Explorations of Embodiment*. Cresskill, NJ: Hampton Press.

López, J. and Scott, J. (2000) *Social Structure*. Buckingham: Open University Press.

Lowith, K. (1993) *Max Weber and Karl Marx*. Preface by B. S. Turner. Edited with an introduction by T. Bottomore and W. Outhwaite. London: Routledge.

Luhmann, N. (1982) *The Differentiation of Society*. Translated by S. Holmes and C. Larmore. New York: Columbia University Press.

Luhmann, N. (1986) 'The Individuality of the Individual'. In T. Heller, M. Sosna and D. Wellbery with A. Davidson, A. Swidler and I. Watt (eds)

Reconstructing Individualism: Autonomy, Individuality, and the Self in Western Thought. Stanford, CA: Stanford University Press.

Luhmann, N. (1989) *Ecological Communication.* Chicago, IL: University of Chicago Press.

Luhmann, N. (1993) *Risk: A Sociological Theory.* Translated by R. Barrett. New York: Walter de Gruyter.

Lukács, G. (1971) *History and Class Consciousness: Studies in Marxist Dialectics.* Originally published in 1923. London: Merlin.

Lukes, S. (1967) 'Alienation and Anomie'. In P. Laslett and W. G. Runciman (eds) *Philosophy, Politics and Society.* Oxford: Oxford University Press.

Lukes, S. (1981) *Emile Durkheim: His Life and Work – A Historical and Critical Study.* Harmondsworth: Penguin.

Lukes, S. (1985) *Marxism and Morality.* Oxford: Oxford University Press.

Lupton, D. (ed.) (1999) *Risk and Sociocultural Theory: New Directions and Perspectives.* Cambridge: Cambridge University Press.

Lyman, S. (1991) *Militarism, Imperialism and Racial Accommodation: An Analysis and Interpretation of the Early Writings of Robert E. Park.* Fayetteville, AR: University of Arkansas Press.

Lyon, D. (2001) *Surveillance Society: Monitoring Everyday Life.* Buckingham, Open University Press.

Lyon, D. (ed.) (2006) *Theorizing Surveillance: The Panopticon and Beyond.* Cullompton, UK: Willan Press.

Lyotard, J. F. (1984) *The Postmodern Condition: A Report on Knowledge.* Translated by G. Bennington and B. Massumi. Foreword by F. Jameson. Manchester: Manchester University Press.

Lyotard, J. F. (1993) 'Answering the Question: What is Postmodernism?' In T. Docherty (ed.) *Postmodernism: A Reader.* London: Harvester Wheatsheaf.

McCarthy, T. (1984) *The Critical Theory of Jürgen Habermas.* Cambridge: Polity.

McCarthy, T. (1991) 'Complexity and Democracy: Or the Seducements of Systems Theory'. In A. Honneth and H. Joas (eds) *Communicative Action: Essays on Jürgen Habermas's 'The Theory of Communicative Action'.* Translated by J. Gains and D. L. Jones. Cambridge, MA: MIT Press.

McGrew, A. (2007) 'Globalization in Hard Times: Contention in the Academy and Beyond'. In G. Ritzer (ed.) *The Blackwell Companion to Globalization.* Oxford: Blackwell.

McHugh, P. (1974) 'On the Failure of Positivism'. In J. D. Douglas (ed.) *Understanding Everyday Life: Towards the Reconstruction of Sociological Knowledge*. London: Routledge & Kegan Paul.

McHugh, P., Raffel, S., Foss, D. C. and Blum, A. F. (1974) *On the Beginning of Social Inquiry*. London: Routledge & Kegan Paul.

MacIntyre, A. (1973) 'The Idea of a Social Science'. In A. Ryan (ed.) *The Philosophy of Social Explanation*. Oxford: Oxford University Press.

MacIntyre, A. (1985) *After Virtue: A Study in Moral Theory*, 2nd edn. London: Duckworth.

MacIntyre, A. (1988) *Whose Justice? Which Rationality?* London: Duckworth.

MacKinnon, C. (1988) 'Desire and Power: A Feminist Perspective'. In C. Nelson and L. Grossberg (eds) (1988) *Marxism and the Interpretation of Culture*. London: Macmillan.

McLellan, D. and Sayers, S. (eds) (1990) *Socialism and Morality*. London: Macmillan.

McLennan, G. (1995) *Pluralism*. Buckingham: Open University Press.

McLuhan, M. (1975) *Understanding Media: The Extensions of Man*, 3rd edn. Toronto: McGraw-Hill.

McNay, L. (1994) *Foucault: A Critical Introduction*. Cambridge: Polity.

McNay, L. (2000) *Gender and Agency: Reconfiguring the Subject in Feminist and Social Theory*. Cambridge: Polity.

McNay, L. (2001) 'Meditations on Pascalian Meditations'. *Economy and Society* 30(1): 139–154.

McNay, L. (2004) 'Agency, Anticipation, Indeterminacy in Feminist Theory'. *Feminist Theory* 4(2): 139–148.

McPhail, C. and Rexroat, C. (1979) 'Mead vs. Blumer: The Divergent Methodological Perspectives of Social Behaviourism and Symbolic Interactionism'. Reprinted in K. Plummer (ed.) *Symbolic Interactionism*, Volume 1, *Foundations and History*. Aldershot: Edward Elgar.

Mann, M. (2006) *The Dark Side of Democracy*. Cambridge: Cambridge University Press

Mannheim, K. (1952) *Essays on the Sociology of Knowledge*. Translated and edited by P. Kecskemeti. New York: Oxford University Press.

Manning, P. (1992) *Erving Goffman and Modern Sociology*. Cambridge: Polity.

Marcuse, H. (1964) *One-Dimensional Man: Studies in the Ideology of Advanced Industrial Society*. London: Routledge.

Marcuse, H. (1968a) *One Dimensional Man: The Ideology of Industrial Society*. London: Sphere.

Marcuse, H. (1968b) *Negations: Essays in Critical Theory*. Boston, MA: Beacon.

Marcuse, H. (1969) *Reason and Revolution: Hegel and the Rise of Social Theory*. London: Routledge & Kegan Paul.

Marshall, B. L. (1994) *Engendering Modernity: Feminism, Social Theory and Social Change*. Cambridge: Polity.

Marshall, B. and Witz, A. (2004) *Engendering the Social*. Maidenhead: Open University Press

Martin, J. R. (1994) 'Methodological Essentialism, False Difference, and Other Dangerous Traps'. *Signs* 19(3): 630–657.

Marx, K. (1961) *The Poverty of Philosophy*. Originally published in 1847. Edited by C. J. Arthur. London: Lawrence & Wishart.

Marx, K. (1964) *The German Ideology*. London: Lawrence & Wishart.

Marx, K. (1980) 'The Eighteenth Brumaire of Louis Bonaparte'. In K. Marx and F. Engels (1980) *Selected Works in One Volume*. London: Lawrence & Wishart.

Marx, K. (1981) *Economic and Philosophical Manuscripts of 1844*. London: Lawrence & Wishart.

Marx, K. (1983) *Capital: A Critique of Political Economy*, Volume 2, *The Process of Production of Capital*. Edited by F. Engels. Translated by S. Moore and E. Aveling. English edition first published in 1887. London: Lawrence & Wishart.

Marx, K. and Engels, F. (1953) *Selected Correspondence: 1843–1895*. London: Lawrence & Wishart.

Massey, D. (2005) *For Space*. London: Sage.

May, T. (1998) 'Reflexivity in the Age of Reconstructive Social Science'. *International Journal of Social Research Methodology: Theory and Practice* 1(1): 7–24.

May, T. (1999a) 'Reflexivity and Sociological Practice'. *Sociological Research Online*, special section on 'The Future of Sociology', 4(3). www.socresonline.org.uk/socresonline/4/3/may.html

May, T. (1999b) 'From Banana Time to Just-in-Time: Power and Resistance at Work'. *Sociology* 33(4): 767–783.

May, T. (2000) 'A Future for Critique? Positioning, Belonging and Reflexivity'. *European Journal of Social Theory* 3(2): 157–173.

May, T. (2001) 'Power, Knowledge and Organizational Transformation: Administration as Depoliticization', special issue on 'Social Epistemology and Knowledge Management'. *Social Epistemology* 15(3): 171–186.

May, T. (2002) 'The Discontented Epoch: Freedom and Security in Bauman's Postmodernity'. In P. Beilharz (ed.) *Zygmunt Bauman: 4 Volumes*. Volume 3, *The Postmodern*. London: Sage.

May, T. (2005) 'Transformations in Academic Production: Context, Content and Consequences'. *European Journal of Social Theory* 8(2): 193–209.

May, T. (2006) 'Transformative Power: A Study in Human Service Organization'. In H. Beynon and T. Nichols (eds) *Patterns of Work in the Post-Fordist Era*, Volume 2. Cheltenham: Edward Elgar.

May, T. and Marvin, S. (2008) 'Elected Regional Assemblies: Lessons for Better Policy Making'. In M. Sandford (ed.) *The Northern Veto*. Manchester: Manchester University Press.

May, T. and Perry, B. (2006) 'Cities, Knowledge and Universities: Transformations in the Image of the Intangible'. In special edition on 'Universities in the Knowledge Economy: Places of Expectation/Spaces for Reflection?', edited by T. May and B. Perry *Social Epistemology* 20(3–4): 259–282.

May, T. and Powell, J. L. (2007) 'Interpretive Analytics and the Constitution of the Social'. In T. Edwards (ed.) *Cultural Theory*. London: Sage.

May, T. and Williams, M. (2002) 'Rom Harré on Social Structure and Social Change'. *European Journal of Social Theory* 5(1): 107–111.

Mayer, T. (1994) *Analytical Marxism*. London: Sage.

Maynard, D. W. and Clayman, S. E. (1991) 'The Diversity of Ethnomethodology'. *Annual Review of Sociology* 17: 385–418.

Mead, G. H. (1910) 'What Social Objects Must Psychology Presuppose?' Reprinted in A. J. Reck (ed.) (1964) *Selected Writings: George Herbert Mead*. Chicago, IL: University of Chicago Press.

Mead, G. H. (1930) 'Cooley's Contribution to American Social Thought'. Reprinted in K. Plummer (ed.) *Symbolic Interactionism*, Volume 1, *Foundations and History*. Aldershot: Edward Elgar.

Meltzer, B. N. and Petras, J. W. (1973) 'The Chicago and Iowa Schools of Symbolic Interactionism'. In T. Shibutani (ed.) *Human Nature and Collective Behaviour: Papers in Honor of Herbert Blumer.* New Brunswick, NJ: Transaction.

Meltzer, B. N., Petras, J. W. and Reynolds, L. T. (1975) *Symbolic Interactionism: Genesis, Varieties and Criticism.* London: Routledge & Kegan Paul.

Mennell, S. (1975) 'Ethnomethodology and the New *Methodenstreit'. Acta Sociologica* 18(4): 287–302.

Mennell, S. (1992) *Norbert Elias: An Introduction.* Oxford: Blackwell.

Merlino, F. S. (1898) *Formes et essences de socialisme.* Paris: Giard & Brière.

Merton, R. (1968) *Social Theory and Social Structure.* New York: Free Press.

Meštrović, S. (1992) *The Coming Fin de Siècle: An Application of Durkheim's Sociology to Modernity and Postmodernity.* London: Routledge.

Meštrović, S. (1993) *The Barbarian Temperament: Towards a Critical Postmodern Theory.* London: Routledge.

Miles, S. and Miles, M. (2004) *Consuming Cities.* Basingstoke: Palgrave Macmillan.

Millett, K. (1969) *Sexual Politics.* New York: Avon.

Millett, K. (1992) 'Beyond Politics? Children and Sexuality'. In C. S. Vance (ed.) *Pleasure and Danger: Exploring Female Sexuality.* London: Pandora.

Mills, C. W. (1970) *The Sociological Imagination.* Originally published in 1959. Harmondsworth: Penguin.

Mitchell, J. (1966) 'Women: The Longest Revolution'. *New Left Review* 40: 11–37.

Mitchell, J. (1971) *Women's Estate.* London: Penguin.

Mitchell, J. (1974) *Woman's Estate.* Harmondsworth: Penguin.

Mitchell, J. (1986) 'Reflections on Twenty Years of Feminism'. In J. Mitchell and A. Oakley (eds) *What is Feminism?* Oxford: Blackwell.

Moi, T. (1991) 'Appropriating Bourdieu: Feminist Theory and Pierre Bourdieu's Sociology of Culture'. *New Literary History* 22: 1017–1049.

Mommsen, W. J. (1992) *The Political and Social Theory of Max Weber: Collected Essays.* Cambridge: Polity.

Monk, R. (1990) *Ludwig Wittgenstein: The Duty of Genius.* London: Vintage.

Morgan, K. (2001) 'The Exaggerated Death of Geography: Localized Learning, Innovation and Uneven Development'. Paper presented to the Future of Innovation Studies Conference, Eindhoven.

Mounce, H. O. (1997) *The Two Pragmatisms: From Peirce to Rorty*. London: Routledge.

Mouzelis, N. (1991) *Back to Sociological Theory: The Construction of Social Orders*. London: Macmillan.

Mouzelis, N. (2007) 'Cognitive Relativism'. In J. L. Powell and T. Owen (eds) *Reconstructing Postmodernism*. New York: Nova Science.

Mullan, B. (1987) *Sociologists on Sociology: Interviews with Contemporary Sociologists*. London: Croom Helm.

Munck, R. (2002) *Globalization and Labour*. London: Zed Books.

Murgatroyd, L. (1989) 'Only Half the Story: Some Blinkering Effects of "Malestream" Sociology'. In D. Held and J. Thompson (eds) *Social Theory of Modern Societies: Anthony Giddens and his Critics*. Cambridge: Cambridge University Press.

Mythen, G. (2007) 'The Postmodern Terrorist Risk: Plus ça change, plus c'est la même chose?' In J. Powell and T. Owen (eds) *Reconstructing Postmodernism: Critical Debates*. New York: Nova Science.

Nelson, C. and Grossberg, L. (eds) (1988) Marxism and the Interpretation of Culture. London: Macmillan.

Nisbet, R. (1970) The Sociological Tradition. London: Heinemann.

Norris, C. (1987) *Derrida*. London: Fontana.

Nuyen, A. T. (1990) 'Truth, Method, and Objectivity: Husserl and Gadamer on Scientific Method'. *Philosophy of the Social Sciences* 20(4): 437–452.

Oakley, A. (1974) *The Sociology of Housework*. Oxford: Martin Robertson.

Oberg, P. and Tornstam, L. (1999) 'Body Images among Men and Women of Different Ages'. *Ageing and Society* 19: 645–658.

Odih, P. (2007) *Gender and Work in Capitalist Economies*. Maidenhead: Open University Press.

Ohmae, K (2005) *The Next Global Stage: Challenges and Opportunities in Our Borderless World*. Upper Saddle River, NJ: Wharton.

Okin, S. M. (1980) *Women in Western Political Thought*. London: Virago.

Ollman, B. (1979) *Social and Sexual Revolution: Essays on Marx and Reich*. London: Pluto.

Ortner, S. B. (1982) 'Is Female to Male as Nature is to Culture?' In M. Evans (ed.) *The Woman Question: Readings on the Subordination of Women*. London: Fontana.

Osborn, R. (1937) *Freud and Marx: A Dialectical Study*. Introduction by J. Strachey. London: Gollancz.

Outhwaite, W. (1975) *Understanding Social Life: The Method Called 'Verstehen'*. London: Allen & Unwin.

Outhwaite, W. (1994) *Habermas*. Cambridge: Polity.

Owen, D. (1997) *Maturity and Modernity: Nietzsche, Weber, Foucault and the Ambivalence of Reason*. London: Routledge.

Owen, T. (2006) 'Genetic-social Science and the Study of Human Biotechnology'. *Current Sociology* 54(6): 897–917.

Owen, T. (2007) 'Towards a Post-Postmodern Social Science'. In J. L. Powell and T. Owen (eds.) *Reconstructing Postmodernism*. New York: Nova Science.

Paci, E. (1972) *The Function of the Sciences and the Meanings of Man*. Translated by P. Piccone and J. Hansen. Evanston, IL: Northwestern University Press.

Park, R. E. (1936) 'Human Ecology'. *American Journal of Sociology* 42: 1–15.

Park, R. E. (1972) *The Crowd and the Public and Other Essays*. Edited by H. Elsner.

Translated by C. Elsner. Chicago, IL: University of Chicago Press.

Parrott, W. G. (2003) 'Positioning and the Emotions'. In R. Harré and F. M. Moghaddam (eds) *The Self and Others: Positioning Individuals and Groups in Personal, Organizational, Political and Cultural Contexts*. Westport, CT: Praeger/ Greenwood.

Parsons, T. (1937) *The Structure of Social Action*. New York: McGraw-Hill.

Parsons, T. (1951) *The Social System*. New York: Free Press.

Parsons, T. (1965) 'An Outline of the Social System'. In T. Parsons, E. Shils, K. D. Naegele and J. R. Pitts (eds) *Theories of Society: Foundations of Modern Sociological Theory*. New York: Free Press.

Parsons, T., Shils, E., Naegele, K. D. and Pitts, J. R. (eds) (1965) *Theories of Society: Foundations of Modern Sociological Theory*. New York: Free Press.

Pearce, F. (1989) *The Radical Durkheim*. London: Unwin Hyman.

Perry, B. and May, T. (2006) 'Excellence, Relevance and the University: The "Missing Middle" in Socio-Economic Engagement'. *Journal of Higher Education in Africa* 4(3): 69–92.

Perry, B. and May, T. (2007). 'Governance, Science Policy and Regions: An Introduction'. In special edition on 'Governance, Science Policy and Regions', edited by B. Perry and T. May. *Regional Studies* 41(8): 1039–1050.

Petras, J. W. (1968) 'Psychological Antecedents of Sociological Theory in America: Williams James and James Mark Baldwin'. Reprinted in K. Plummer (ed.) *Symbolic Interactionism, Volume 1, Foundations and History*. Aldershot: Edward Elgar.

Phillipson, C. (2005) 'Globalization and the reconstruction of Old Age: New Challenges for Critical Gerontology'. In J. Hendricks, S. Biggs and A. Lowenstein (eds) *Theoretical Perspectives in Social Gerontology*. New York: Baywood Press.

Phillipson, C. and Powell, J. L. (2004) 'Risk, Social Welfare and Old Age'. In E. Tulle (ed.) *Old Age and Human Agency*. New York: Nova Science.

Plamenatz, J. (1963) *Man and Society*, Volume 1, *A Critical Examination of Some Important Social and Political Theories from Machiavelli to Marx*. London: Longman.

Pollner, M. (1991) 'Left of Ethnomethodology: The Rise and Decline of Radical Reflexivity'. *American Sociological Review* 56(3): 370–380.

Poulantzas, N. (1978) *State, Power, Socialism*. Translated by P. Camiller. London: New Left Books.

Porter M. (1990) *The Competitive Advantage of Nations*. New York: Free Press.

Powell, J. L. (2005) *Social Theory and Aging*. Lanham, MD: Rowman & Littlefield.

Powell, J. L. (2007) *Rethinking Social Theory and Later Life*. New York: Nova Science.

Powell, J. L. and Biggs, S. (2004) 'Aging, Technologies of Self, and Bio-Medicine: A Foucauldian Excursion'. *International Journal of Sociology and Social Policy* 23(13): 96–115.

Powell, J. L. and Moody, H. R. (2003) 'Habermas and Critical Theory'. *Theory and Science* 5(2): 1–10.

Powell, J. L. and Owen, T. (eds) (2007) *Reconstructing Postmodernism*. New York: Nova Science.

Powell, J. L and Wahidin, A (2006) *Foucault and Aging.* New York: Nova Science.

Powell, J. L., Wahidin, A. and Zinn, J. (2007) 'Understanding Risk and Old Age in Western Society'. *International Journal of Sociology and Social Policy* 27 (1–2): 65–76.

Ramazanoglu, C. (ed.) (1993) *Up against Foucault: Explorations of some Tensions between Foucault and Feminism.* London: Routledge.

Rasmussen, D. (1990) *Reading Habermas.* London: Blackwell.

Rawls, A. W. (1987) 'The Interaction Order *Sui Generis:* Goffman's Contribution to Social Theory'. *Sociological Theory* 5(2): 136–149.

Ray, L. and Reed, M. (eds) (1994) *Organizing Modernity: New Weberian Perspectives on Work, Organization and Society.* London: Routledge.

Reck, A. J. (ed.) (1964) *Selected Writings: George Herbert Mead.* Chicago, IL: University of Chicago Press.

Reich, W. (1975) *The Mass Psychology of Fascism.* Translated by V. R. Carfagno. Originally published in 1933. Harmondsworth: Penguin.

Rex, J. (1961) *Key Problems of Sociological Theory.* London: Routledge & Kegan Paul.

Rich, A. (1976) *Of Woman Born: Motherhood as Experience and Institution.* New York: Norton.

Rich, A. (1980) 'Compulsory Heterosexuality and Lesbian Existence'. *Signs: Journal of Women in Culture and Society* 5(4): 631–660.

Ricoeur, P. (1982) *Hermeneutics and the Human Sciences.* Edited and translated by J. B. Thompson. Cambridge: Cambridge University Press.

Ricoeur, P. (1994) *Oneself as Another.* Translated by K. Blamey. Chicago, IL: University of Chicago Press.

Risseeuw, C. (1991) 'Bourdieu, Power and Resistance: Gender Transformation in Sri Lanka'. In K. Davis, M. Leijenaar and J. Oldersma (eds) *The Gender of Power.* London: Sage.

Ritzer, G. (2000) 'Introduction'. In J. Baudrillard (ed.) *The Consumer Society: Myths and Structures.* London: Sage.

Ritzer, G. (2004) *The McDonaldization of Society.* Thousand Oaks, CA: Pine Forge Press.

Ritzer, G. and Goodman, D. (eds) (2001) *Sociological Theory.* London: Sage.

Ritzer, G. and Ryan, M. (2007) 'The Impossibility of Postmodernism'. In J. L. Powell and T. Owen (eds) *Reconstructing Postmodernism*. New York: Nova Science.

Robbins, D. (1991) *The Work of Pierre Bourdieu: Recognizing Society*. Buckingham: Open University Press.

Robertson, R. (1992) *Globalization: Social Theory and Global Culture*. London: Sage.

Rocher, G. (1974) *Talcott Parsons and American Sociology*. Translated by B. Mennell and S. Mennell. London: Thomas Nelson.

Rock, P. (1979) *The Making of Symbolic Interactionism*. London: Macmillan.

Roderick, R. (1986) *Habermas and the Foundations of Critical Theory*. London: Macmillan.

Rogers, K. M. (ed.) (1979) *Before their Time: Six Women Writers of the Eighteenth Century*. New York: Frederick Unger.

Rogers, M. F. (1983) *Sociology, Ethnomethodology, and Experience: A Phenomenological Critique*. Cambridge: Cambridge University Press.

Rogers, M. F. (1984) 'Everyday Life as Text'. In R. Collins (ed.) *Sociological Theory*. San Francisco, CA: Jossey-Bass.

Rojek, C. (2004) *Frank Sinatra*. Cambridge: Polity.

Rorty, R. (1982) *Consequences of Pragmatism: Essays 1972–1980*. Minneapolis, MN: University of Minneapolis Press.

Rorty, R. (1989) *Contingency, Irony and Solidarity*. Cambridge: Cambridge University Press.

Rorty, R. (1993) 'Cosmopolitanism without Emancipation: A Response to Lyotard'. In S. Lash and J. Friedman (eds) *Modernity and Identity*. Oxford: Blackwell.

Rose, J. (1990) 'Femininity and its Discontents'. In T. Lovell (ed.) *British Feminist Thought: A Reader*. Oxford: Blackwell.

Rose, N. (2006) *Biomedicine, Power, and Subjectivity in the Twenty-First Century*. Princeton, NJ: Princeton University Press.

Ross, D. (1991) *The Origins of American Social Science*. Cambridge: Cambridge University Press.

Rowbotham, S. (1973) *Woman's Consciousness, Man's World*. Harmondsworth: Penguin.

Rowland, R. and Klein, R. D. (1990) 'Radical Feminism: Critique and Construct'. In S. Gunew (ed.) *Feminist Knowledge: Critique and Construct.* London: Routledge.

Rubinstein, D. (1981) *Marx and Wittgenstein: Social Praxis and Social Explanation.* London: Routledge & Kegan Paul.

Runciman, W. G. (1973) 'What is Structuralism?' In A. Ryan (ed.) *The Philosophy of Social Explanation.* Oxford: Oxford University Press.

Russell, B. (1955) *History of Western Philosophy and its Connection with Political and Social Circumstances from the Earliest Times to the Present Day.* London: Allen & Unwin.

Ryan, A. (1986) *Property and Political Theory.* Oxford: Blackwell.

Sabini, J. and Silver, M. (1982). *Moralities of Everyday Life.* Oxford: Oxford University Press.

Sacks, H. (1963) 'Sociological Description'. *Berkeley Journal of Sociology* 8: 1–16.

Sacks, H. (1972) 'An Initial Investigation of the Usability of Conversational Data for Doing Sociology'. In D. Sudnow, D. (ed.) *Studies in Social Interaction.* New York: Free Press.

Sands, P. (2006) *Lawless World.* London: Penguin.

Sartre, J. P. (1960) *Critique of Dialectic Reason.* London: New Left Books.

Sarup, M. (1993) *An Introductory Guide to Post-Structuralism and Postmodernism,* 2nd edn. London: Harvester Wheatsheaf.

Sassen, S. (2001) *The Global City,* 2nd edn. Princeton, NJ: Princeton University Press.

Sassen, S. (2006) *Cities in a World Economy,* 3rd edn. Thousand Oaks, CA: Sage.

Saussure, F. de (1959) *Course in General Linguistics.* Translated by W. Baskin. Originally published in 1916. New York: Philosophical Library.

Savitch, H. (2002) 'What is New about Globalization and What does it Portend for Cities?' *International Social Science Journal* 54(172): 179–189.

Sayer, A. (1992) *Method in Social Science: A Realist Approach,* 2nd edn. London: Routledge.

Sayer, D. (1991) *Capitalism and Modernity: An Excursus on Marx and Weber.* London: Routledge.

Sayers, S. (1989) 'Knowledge as Social Phenomenon'. *Radical Philosophy* 52: 34–37.

Schneider, A. (2007) 'Masculinity as a Reproduction of Traditionalism, Feminist Reaction, and Egalitarianism'. In J. L. Powell and T. Owen (eds) *Reconstructing Postmodernism: Critical Debates*. New York: Nova Science.

Schutz, A. (1972) *The Phenomenology of the Social World*. Originally published in 1932. Translated by G. Walsh and F. Lehnert. Introduction by G. Walsh. London: Heinemann.

Schutz, A. (1979) 'Concept and Theory Formation in the Social Sciences'. In J. Bynner and K. Stribley (eds) *Social Research: Principles and Procedures*. Milton Keynes: Open University Press.

Schwartz, J. (1990) 'Antihumanism in the Humanities'. *Public Interest* 99: 29–44.

Sciulli, D. (1985) 'The Practical Groundwork of Critical Theory: Bringing Parsons to Habermas (and vice versa)'. In J. C. Alexander (ed.) *Neofunctionalism*. Beverly Hills, CA: Sage.

Segal, L. (1987) *Is the Future Female? Troubled Thoughts on Contemporary Feminism*. London: Virago.

Seidman, S. (1994a) 'The End of Sociological Theory'. In S. Seidman (ed.) *The Postmodern Turn: New Perspectives on Social Theory*. Cambridge: Cambridge University Press.

Seidman, S. (1994b) *Contested Knowledge: Social Theory in the Postmodern Era*. Oxford: Blackwell.

Seidman, S. (1998) *Contested Knowledge: Social Theory in the Postmodern Era*, 2nd edn. Oxford: Blackwell.

Seidman, S. (2001) *The New Social Theory Reader: Contemporary Debates*. London: Routledge.

Seidman, S. (2004) *Contested Knowledge: Social Theory Today*, 3rd edn. Oxford: Blackwell.

Sharrock, W. and Anderson, B. (1986) *The Ethnomethodologists*. London: Tavistock.

Shaw, M. (1994) *Global Society and International Relations*. Cambridge: Polity.

Shilling, C. (1993) *The Body and Social Theory*. London: Sage.

Shott, S. (1987) 'Emotion and Social Life: A Symbolic Interactionist Analysis'. Reprinted in K. Plummer (ed.) *Symbolic Interactionism*, Volume 2, *Contemporary Issues*. Aldershot: Edward Elgar.

Shotter, J. (1993) *Cultural Politics of Everyday Life: Social Constructionism, Rhetoric and Knowing of the Third Kind.* Buckingham: Open University Press.

Sibeon, R. (2004) *Rethinking Social Theory.* London: Sage

Sibeon, R. (2007) 'An Excursus in Post-post Postmodernism'. In J. L. Powell and T. Owen (eds) *Reconstructing Postmodernism.* New York: Nova Science.

Sibley, D. (2006) 'Negotiating the Spaces of Old Age'. In J. L. Powell and A. Wahidin (eds) *Foucault and Aging.* New York: Nova Science.

Simmie, J. (2002) 'Trading Places: Competitive Cities in the Global Economy'. *European Planning Studies* 10(2): 201–214.

Simons, J. (1995) *Foucault and the Political.* London: Routledge.

Simpson, D. (2002) *Situatedness, or, Why We Keep Saying Where We're Coming From.* Durham, NC: Duke University Press.

Singer, P. (1983) *Hegel.* Oxford: Oxford University Press.

Smart, B. (1990) 'Modernity, Postmodernity and the Present'. In B. S. Turner (ed.) *Theories of Modernity and Postmodernity.* London: Sage.

Smart, B. (1993) *Postmodernity.* London: Routledge.

Smart, B. (2007) '(Dis)interring Postmodernism or a Critique of the Political Economy of Consumer Choice'. In J. L. Powell and T. Owen (eds) *Reconstructing Postmodernism.* New York: Nova Science

Smith, C. W. (1983) 'A Case Study of Structuration: The Pure-Bred Beef Business'. *Journal for the Theory of Social Behaviour* 13: 4–18.

Smith, D. E. (1974) 'Theorizing as Ideology'. In R. Turner (ed.) *Ethnomethodology.* Harmondsworth: Penguin.

Smith, D. E. (1988) *The Everyday World as Problematic: A Feminist Sociology.* Milton Keynes: Open University Press.

Smith, D. E. (1993) *Texts, Facts and Femininity: Exploring the Relations of Ruling.* London: Routledge.

Smith, D.E. (1999) *Writing the Social: Critique, Theory and Investigations.* Toronto: University of Toronto Press.

Smith, D. E. (2005) *Institutional Ethnography: A Sociology for People.* New York: Rowman & Littlefield.

Smith, G. W. (2006) *Erving Goffman.* London: Routledge.

Smith, N. (1993) 'Putting Practice into Theory: A Review Essay'. *Radical Philosophy* 63: 42–44.

Sontag, S. (1991) *Illness as Metaphor and AIDS and its Metaphors*. London: Penguin.

Soper, K. (1993) 'Productive Contradictions'. In C. Ramazanoglu (ed.) *Up against Foucault: Explorations of some Tensions between Foucault and Feminism*. London: Routledge.

Spencer, H. (1969) *Herbert Spencer*. Edited with an introduction by A. Low-Beer. London: Macmillan.

Spender, D. (1980) *Man-Made Language*. London: Routledge & Kegan Paul.

Spender, D. (1983) *Women of Ideas (and What Men Have Done to Them)*. London: Ark.

Spybey, T. (1995) *Globalization and World Society*. Cambridge: Polity.

Stanley, L. and Pateman, C. (1991) *Feminist Interpretations and Political Theory*. Cambridge: Polity.

Star, S. L. (ed.) (1995) *Ecologies of Knowledge: Work and Politics in Science and Technology*. Albany, NY: State University of New York Press.

Stehr, N. (2005) *Knowledge Politics: Governing the Consequences of Science and Technology*. New York: Paradigm.

Steuerman, E. (1992) 'Habermas vs Lyotard: Modernity vs Postmodernity?' In A. Benjamin (ed.) *Judging Lyotard*. London: Routledge.

Stinchcombe, A. L. (1990) 'Milieu and Structure Updated: A Critique of the Theory of Structuration'. In J. Clark, C. Modgil and S. Modgil (eds) *Anthony Giddens: Consensus and Controversy*. Brighton: Falmer.

Stones, R. (2005) *Structuration Theory*. London: Palgrave Macmillan.

Storper, M. (1997) *The Regional World: Territorial Development in a Global Economy*. New York: Guilford Press.

Strange, S. (1986) *Casino Capitalism*. Oxford: Blackwell.

Strasser, S. (1985) *Understanding and Explanation: Basic Ideas Concerning the Humanity of the Human Sciences*. Pittsburgh, PA: Duquesne University Press.

Strauss, A. (1978) *Negotiations, Varieties, Contexts, Processes and Social Order*. San Francisco, CA: Jossey-Bass.

Strauss, A. (1982) 'Interorganizational Negotiation'. Reprinted in K. Plummer (ed.) *Symbolic Interactionism*, Volume 2, *Contemporary Issues*. Aldershot: Edward Elgar.

Stryker, S. (1980) *Symbolic Interactionism: A Social Structural Version.* Menlo Park, CA: Benjamin Cummings.

Swingewood, A. (1991) *A Short History of Sociological Thought,* 2nd edn. London: Macmillan.

Tannen, D. (ed.) (1993) *Gender and Conversational Interaction.* New York: Oxford University Press.

Taylor, C. (1981) 'Understanding in Human Science'. *Review of Metaphysics* 34: 25–38.

Taylor, C. (1992) *Sources of the Self: The Making of the Modern Identity.* Cambridge: Cambridge University Press.

Taylor, C. and Montefiore, A. (1980) 'From an Analytical Perspective'. Introductory essay G. Kortian, *Metacritique: The Philosophical Argument of Jürgen Habermas.* Translated by J. Raffan. Cambridge: Cambridge University Press.

Thomas, W. I. and Thomas, D. S. (1928) *The Child in America: Behavior Problems and Programs.* New York: Knopf.

Thomas, W. I. and Znaniecki, F. (1918–19) *The Polish Peasant in Europe and America,* 5 volumes. Boston, MA: Badger.

Thompson, J. B. (1981) *Critical Hermeneutics: A Study in the Thought of Paul Ricoeur and Jürgen Habermas.* Cambridge: Cambridge University Press.

Thompson, J. B. (1984) *Studies in the Theory of Ideology.* Cambridge: Polity.

Thompson, K. (1992) 'Social Pluralism and Postmodernity'. In S. Hall, D. Held and T. McGrew (eds) *Modernity and its Futures.* Cambridge: Polity.

Tiryakian, E. A. (1979) 'Emile Durkheim'. In T. Bottomore and R. Nisbet (eds) *A History of Sociological Analysis.* London: Heinemann.

Tomlinson, J. (1999) *Globalization and Culture.* Cambridge: Polity.

Tong, R. (1989) *Feminist Thought: A Comprehensive Introduction.* London: Unwin Hyman.

Toulmin, S. (1990) *Cosmopolis: The Hidden Agenda of Modernity.* Chicago: University of Chicago Press.

Toulmin, S. (2003) *Return to Reason.* Cambridge, MA: Harvard University Press.

Touraine, A. (2000) *Can We Live Together? Equality and Difference.* Cambridge: Polity.

Toynbee, A. (1954) *A Study of History: Volume 9*. London: Oxford University Press.

Turner, B. S. (1981) *For Weber: Essays on the Sociology of Fate*. London: Routledge & Kegan Paul.

Turner, B. S. (2006) *Vulnerability and Human Rights*. University Park, PA: Pennsylvania State University Press

Turner, B. S. and Robertson, R. (1991) 'How to Read Parsons'. In R. Robertson and B. S. Turner (eds) *Talcott Parsons: Theorist of Modernity*. London: Sage.

Turner, J. H. (1974) 'Parsons as a Symbolic Interactionist: A Comparison of Action and Interaction Theory'. Reprinted in K. Plummer (ed.) *Symbolic Interactionism*, Volume 1, *Foundations and History*. Aldershot: Edward Elgar.

Turner, R. (1974) 'Words, Utterances and Activities'. In R. Turner (ed.) *Ethnomethodology*. Harmondsworth: Penguin.

Twigg, J. (2000) 'Social Policy and the Body'. In G. Lewis, S. Gewirtz and J. Clarke (eds) *Rethinking Social Policy*. London: Sage.

Twigg, J. (2006) *The Body in Health and Social Care*. Basingstoke: Palgrave Macmillan.

Urry, J. (2000) *Sociology beyond Societies: Mobilities for the Twenty-First Century*. London: Routledge.

Urry, J. (ed.) (2005) *Automobilities*. London: Sage.

Vasishth, A. and Sloane, D. C. (2002) 'Returning to Ecology: An Ecosystem Approach to Understanding the City'. In M. J. Dear (ed.) *From Chicago to L.A.: Making Sense of Urban Theory*. Thousand Oaks, CA: Sage.

Visker, R. (1995) *Michel Foucault: Genealogy as Critique*. Translated by C. Turner. London: Verso.

Wacquant, L. (1992) 'The Structure and Logic of Bourdieu's Sociology'. In P. Bourdieu and L. J. Wacquant (1992) *An Invitation to Reflexive Sociology*. Cambridge: Polity.

Wacquant, L. (1993) 'Bourdieu in America: Notes on the Transatlantic Importation of Social Theory'. In C. Calhoun, E. LiPuma and M. Postone (eds) *Bourdieu: Critical Perspectives*. Cambridge: Polity.

Walby, S. (1990) *Theorizing Patriarchy*. Cambridge: Polity.

Walby, S. (2005) 'Gender Mainstreaming Theory'. *Social Politics: International Studies in Gender, State and Society* 12(3): 321–343.

Walker, A. and Naegelhe, G. (eds) (1999) *The Politics of Ageing in Europe*. Buckingham: Open University Press.

Walklate, S. and Mythen, G. (eds) (2007) *Beyond the Risk Society: Critical Reflections on Risk and Human Security*. Maidenhead: Open University Press.

Wallerstein, I. (1990) 'World-Systems Analysis'. In A. Giddens and J. Turner (eds) *Social Theory Today*. Cambridge: Polity.

Warren, M. (1992) 'Max Weber's Nietzschean Conception of Power'. *History of the Human Sciences* 5(3): 19–37.

Wasserman, J. and Faust, N. (1994) *Social Network Analysis*. Cambridge: Cambridge University Press.

Watson, S. (2001) 'The Public City'. In J. Eade and C. Mele (eds) *Urban Studies: Contemporary and Future Perspectives*. Oxford: Blackwell.

Weber, M. (1949) *The Methodology of the Social Sciences*. Edited by E. Shils and H. Finch Glencoe, IL: Free Press.

Weber, M. (1985) *The Protestant Ethic and the Spirit of Capitalism*. Originally published in 1930. London: Unwin.

Webster, F. (1995) *Theories of the Information Society*. London: Routledge.

Weinbaum, B. (1978) *The Curious Courtship of Women's Liberation and Socialism*. Boston, MA: South End Press.

Weinstein, D. and Weinstein, M. (1991) 'Georg Simmel: Sociological Fliineur Bricoleur'. In M. Featherstone (ed.) *Consumer Culture and Postmodernism*. London: Sage

West, C. and Zimmerman, D. H. (1983) 'Small Insults: A Study of Interruptions in Cross-Sex Conversations with Unacquainted Persons'. In B. Thorne, C. Kramerae and N. Henley (eds) *Language, Gender and Society*. Rowley, MA: Newbury House.

Wheen, F. (1999) *Karl Marx: A Life*. New York: Norton.

White, S. (1990) *The Recent Work of Jürgen Habermas: Reason, Justice and Modernity*. Cambridge: Cambridge University Press.

Whyte, D. (2007) 'The Crimes of Neo-liberal Rule in Occupied Iraq'. *British Journal of Criminology* 47(2): 177–195.

Wieder, D. L. (1974) 'On Meaning by Rule'. In J. D. Douglas (ed.) *Understanding Everyday Life: Towards the Reconstruction of Sociological Knowledge*. London: Routledge & Kegan Paul.

Wiggershaus, R. (1995) *The Frankfurt School: Its History, Theories and Political Significance.* Translated by M. Robertson. Cambridge: Polity.

Williams, F. (1993) 'Gender, Race and Class in British Welfare Policy'. In A. Cochrane and J. Clarke (eds) *Comparing Welfare States: Britain in International Context.* London: Sage.

Williams, M. and May, T. (1996) *Introduction to the Philosophy of Social Research.* London: UCL Press.

Williams, Raymond (1961) *Culture and Society: 1780–1950.* Harmondsworth: Penguin.

Williams, Robin (1980) 'Goffman's Sociology of Talk'. In J. Ditton (ed.) (1980) *The View from Goffman.* London: Macmillan.

Williams, Robin (1988) 'Understanding Goffman's Methods'. In P. Drew and A. Wootton (eds) *Erving Goffman: Exploring the Interaction Order.* Cambridge: Polity.

Williams, S. (2000) *Emotions and Social Theory.* London: Sage.

Wilson, B. (ed.) (1970) *Rationality.* Oxford: Blackwell.

Wilson, E. (1990) 'Psychoanalysis: Psychic Law and Order?' In T. Lovell (ed.) *British Feminist Thought: A Reader.* Oxford: Blackwell.

Winch, P. (1990) *The Idea of a Social Science and its Relation to Philosophy*, 2nd edn. Originally published in 1958. London: Routledge.

Wolff, K. H. (1979) 'Phenomenology and Sociology'. In T. Bottomore and R. Nisbet (eds) *A History of Sociological Analysis.* London: Heinemann.

Wolffensperger, J. (1991) 'Engendered Structure: Giddens and the Conceptualization of Gender'. In K. Davis, M. Leijenaar and J. Oldersma (eds) *The Gender of Power.* London: Sage.

Wollstonecraft, M. (1989) *A Vindication of the Rights of Women.* Originally published in 1792. Buffalo, NY: Prometheus.

Wooffitt, R. (2005) *Conversation Analysis and Discourse Analysis: A Comparative and Critical Introduction.* London: Sage.

Wright, E. O. (1989) 'Models of Historical Trajectory: An Assessment of Giddens' Critique of Marxism'. In D. Held and J. Thompson (eds) *Social Theory of Modern Societies: Anthony Giddens and his Critics.* Cambridge: Cambridge University Press.

Zimmerman, D. H. and Wieder, D. L. (1974) 'Ethnomethodology and the Problem of Order: Comments on Denzin'. In J. D. Douglas (ed.) *Understanding Everyday Life: Towards the Reconstruction of Sociological Knowledge*. London: Routledge & Kegan Paul.

awareness, social
as element in understanding of
reaction to change, 75–7
Baudrillard, J., 53, 223, 224–7, 231,
244, 255, 276
Bauman, Z., 9, 169, 217, 234, 236,
259, 277
Beauvoir, S. de, 59, 180
Beck, U., 238
Beechey, V., 178
Beloff, M., 15
Bendelow, G., 245
Bendix, R., 30
Bentham, J., 206
Berger, P., 40
Berman, M., 8, 218
Blumer, H., 77–80, 85–7
Bourdieu, P., 40, 48, 122–38, 244,
254–5, 274–5, 276
Brand, A., 169
Brenner, J., 193
Brentano, F., 38–9
Bronowski, J., 8
Brown, P., 60
Brubaker, R., 136
Brunkhorst, H., 31–2
biography (concept)
as method of interpreting
meaning of emotion, 243–4
'bio-power' (Foucault), 207
'black box' (metaphor)
relevance of as element in actor
network theory, 143–4
bodies, images of
impact on furtherance of feminist
theory, 187–9
borders, national
decline of as consequence of
globalization, 263–4, 266,
268–9
CA (conversational analysis), 94,
99–100, 102
Callinicos, A., 235
Callon, M., 143, 145, 147, 149
capital, social
as element in relationship
between agency and social
position, 127–8
see also habitas
capitalism

influence on feminist social
theory, 62–4, 177–9
understanding of as element in
development of social theory,
20–22
Castells, M., 140
centralization, as element in
development of postmodernism,
222
centuries, current
questionability of classification as
postmodern era, 233–8
change, social
interpretations of Park and
Thomas to individual reactions
concerning, 74–7
see also drivers eg globalization
chaos (phenomenon)
as element in development of
postmodernism, 222
Chicago School of Sociology, 77–80,
85–7
Chodorow, N., 183–4
Chomsky, N., 101
Cicourel, A., 100, 101
classical social theory, impact on
ideas of Bourdieu, 125–6
Cleaver, H., 223
Cohen, G., 19
communication (concept)
as element in concept of
'lifeworld', 163–4
as element in understanding of
reaction to social change, 75–7
communications, electronic
as driver for globalization spread,
265
communicative action theory
characteristics and historical
development of, 43, 160–65,
168–72
communicative reason
as philosophy underpinning
ideology of Habermas, 155–60
Comte, A., 16
consciousness
as element in understanding of
reaction to social change, 75–7
as element of hermoneutics and
phenomenology, 36–40

Index

accountability, socio-economic
changing nature of as feature of
globalization, 261
action, human
role in interpretation of concept
of 'emotion', 245
action, social
as element in pragmatist ideology,
42–3
as element in understanding of
reaction, 75–7
criticisms and limitations in
analysis of structuration theory,
116–21
interpretations as element in
understanding of symbolic
interaction, 78–9
views of structuration theory
concerning, 107–16
action theory
influence on ethnomethodology,
90–91
influence on understanding of
systems theory, 54–8
activity, economic
impact of globalization upon,
267–8
actor network theory (ANT)
evolution, definition and
characteristics, 139–41
strengths, weaknesses and
challenges, 149–51
value and importance of theory,
275

see also elements and concepts eg
actors, social; 'black box';
inscription; networks, social;
prescription; stablization
actors, social
relevance of as element in actor
network theory, 142–4
see also type eg intermediaries
Adorno, T., 34, 45, 46–7, 168, 248
agency, personal
influence on understanding of
feminism, 61–2
views of structuration theory
concerning, 107–16
weakness of when analysing
feminist social theory, 177–9
see also elements in understanding of
eg capital, social; 'field';
habitas; strategy
Akrich, M., 142
Albrow, M., 33
Alexander, J., 57
Althusser, L., 51–2, 273
Amin, A., 269
analysis, conversational (CA), 94,
99–100, 102
Anderson, R., 88
ANT see actor network theory
Anthony, S., 62
Appadurai, A., 261, 263
Archer, M., 118
Assister, A., 191
Astell, M., 14
Augustine, St., 9
Austin, J., 89, 163

as element of pragmatist ideology, 41
changing ideas of as element in development of social theory, 17–22
consumption, characteristics as element in postmodernism, 223–7
conversational analysis (CA), 94, 99–100, 102
conversations
    relevance as element in diversity of ethnomethodology, 98–100
    see also language
Cook, D., 9, 220
Coulanges, F de., 24
Coulter, J., 97–8
Craib, I., 119
critical realism, 52–3
critical theory
    evolution and characteristics, 43–9
    role of structuralist ideology within, 53
Crook, S., 222
culture and customs
    as element in understanding of reaction to social change, 75–7
    influence as element in interpretations of social theory, 29–30
    interpretation differences between postmodernism and earlier theory, 230–31
    role as element in history of social theory, 15
Darwin, C., 26
dasein (Heidegger), 39
Dean, M., 244
de-differentiation, as element in development of postmodernism, 221–2
Delphy, C., 178, 186
Denzin, N., 71–2, 245–6
Derrida, J., 53
Descartes, R., 10
'desire' (Lacan), 247–8
Dewey, J., 41
difference, individual
    influence on understanding of feminism, 61–2
Dilthey, W., 29, 37, 38

discourse
    relevance as element in diversity of ethnomethodology, 98–100
    see also language
dispersion (concept)
    as element in development of postmodernism, 222
distance (concept)
    impact of consequences of globalization upon, 263–9
Division of Labour in Society (Durkheim), 26
domination, male
    influence on understanding of feminism, 58–64
doubt, role within theory of rationalism, 10
Dreyfus, H., 210
Du Bois, W., 8
Durkheim, E., 22–7, 29, 30, 41, 126, 162–3, 244, 246, 247, 272
Dworkin, A., 181, 193
dynamicism, social
    as element in understanding of symbolic interaction, 78–9
economics
    impact of globalization upon, 267–8
egalitarianism
    role as element in history of social theory, 15
Eichenbaum, L., 251
Elias, N., 40, 244
embodiment (concept)
    role in interpretation of concept of 'emotion', 245, 251–5
emotion (concept)
    definitions, importance and interpretations of, 243–55, 276–7
emotionalism
    role in interpretation of concept of 'emotion', 247
empiricism
    role of experience and reason as elements in theory of, 11–13
Engels, F., 179–81
Enlightenment
    characteristics as catalyst for styles of social thinking, 7–13

evolution of sociological theory
during, 13–17
essentialism, as element informing
debate on feminist theories, 192–5
ethics, as element in understanding
of social theory, 22–7
ethnomethodology
evolution and characteristics of
philosophy of, 89–96
interpretations of, 96–103
value and importance of theory,
274
exchange and use value
characteristics as element in
postmodernism, 223–7
existence (being)
as element of hermoneutic and
phenomenology, 36–40
experience (concept)
role of within theory of
empiricism, 11–13
family, the
impact on feminist social theory,
177–9
Farganis, S., 64
feminism
evolution, characteristics and
importance of theory, 58–65,
176–87, 273
influence of Foucault's theories on
211–14
legacy for contemporary social
theory, 65–8
role as critique of social theory, 14
see also influences upon eg
essentialism; identities, social;
image, body; patriarchy;
relationships, gender
Ferguson, A., 15
Feuerbach, L., 19
'field' (concept)
as element in relationship
between agency and social
position, 131–3
finance
changing accountability of as
element of globalization, 261
Firestone, S., 179–81, 192
Fisher, B., 75
fluidity, social world

as element in understanding of
symbolic interaction, 78–9
Formes et essences du socialisme
(Merlino), 25
Foucault, M., 10, 40, 48–9, 194,
197–215, 244, 253, 276, 282
Fraser, N., 48, 171–2, 174, 179, 212
freedom (concept)
role of within theory of
empiricism, 11–13
role as element in evolution of
social theory, 15, 18–19
Freud, S., 27, 47–8, 182, 247, 252
Fromm, E., 48
Gadamer, H-G., 39–40
Gane, M., 226
Gellner, E., 216
'Gemeinslchaft' (Tönnies), 28
gender
impact on feminist social theory,
177–9
see also patriarchy
'Gessellschaft' (Tönnies), 28
Gibson-Graham J., 186
Giddens, A., 105–16, 170, 179, 234,
237, 244, 250, 261–2, 274
Giogione, 189
globalization
characteristics and importance,
257–8, 277–8
evolution and understanding of
within social world, 259–63
socio-economic and political
consequences, 263–9
Goffman, E., 80–87, 97, 244, 252, 274
governance, national
decline of as consequence of
globalization, 263–4, 266,
268–9
Gramski, A., 45–6
Griffiths, M., 60
Grosz, E., 187–8, 190
groups, role as element in history of
social theory, 15
Habermas, J., 40, 42, 43, 57, 154–74,
179, 219, 229, 236–7, 275–6
habitas, as element in relationship
between agency and social
position, 128–30
Hamilton, P., 7
Hare, P., 72

Harvey, D., 235, 237, 265–6
Hegel, G., 17–19
Heidegger, M., 39
Hekman, S., 176
Held, D., 258, 268–9
Heritage, J., 94
hermoneutics
    characteristics, importance and
        influence as social thought,
        36–40, 272–3
    Foucault's conceptualisation of,
        199–203, 214
    legacy for contemporary social
        theory, 65–8
heterogeneity
    as central to stable networks, 149
    as element of postmodernism, 220
Hindness, B., 209
history and historicism
    as element in evolution of social
        theory, 29
    as element of hermoneutics and
        phenomenology, 36–40
Hobbes, T., 25
Hochschild, A., 252
Hollinger, R., 235
Holton, R., 28
Honneth, A., 48, 170, 174
Horkheimer, M., 34, 44, 45, 46–7,
    248
Hughes, S., 8, 22
humanism, influence of Foucault's
    ideologies upon, 211–14
humans, role as element in history of
    social theory, 14
Hume, D., 11, 15
Husserl, E., 38
identities, social
    impact on furtherance of feminist
        theory, 187–9
ideologies, social see theories,
    sociological
image, body
    impact on furtherance of feminist
        theory, 187–9
images, stereotypical
    influence on understanding of
        feminism, 58–64
indexicality (concept)
    as element of
        ethnomethodological
        understanding, 95–6
indifference (concept)
    as element of
        ethnomethodological
        understanding, 95–6
individuals and individualism
    Foucault's conceptualisation of,
        198–203
    interpretations of Park and
        Thomas reactions to change
        concerning, 74–7
    role as element in history of social
        theory, 17
information technology (IT)
    as driver for globalization spread,
        265
inscription (concept)
    characteristics and relevance of as
        element in actor network
        theory, 145–6
institutions, socio-economic and
    political
    changing nature in relation to
        process of globalization, 261–3
integration, social
    as element in understanding of
        approach to social theory, 22–7
intentionality, as element in
    understanding of social
    interaction, 81–2
interaction, social
    Goffman's interpretation of micro
        and macro connectedness of,
        80–85
    influence on ethnomethodology,
        98–100, 102
    role in interpretation of concept
        of 'emotion', 251–5
interaction, symbolic
    comparison of Mead and Blumer
        interpretations, 77–80
    influences on history of, 71–7
    value and importance of theory,
        273
intermediaries, characteristics and
    relevance of as element in actor
    network theory, 146–9
internet, as driver for globalization
    spread, 265

interpretation (concept)
as element of
ethnomethodological
understanding, 95–6
as focus in understanding of
symbolic interaction, 79–80
IT (information technology)
as driver for globalization spread,
265
James, W., 41
Jameson, F., 235, 237
Joas, H., 41, 42
Johnson, L., 63
Jordanova, L., 60
Kant, I., 10–12, 18, 61, 199
Kellner, D., 66
Kinnaird, J., 14
Knorr-Cetina, K., 105
knowledge
as element in linguistic
philosophy, 92
interpretation differences of
postmodernism and earlier
theories, 228–9
Kroker, A., 9, 220
labourforce, changes within, as
consequence of globalization,
265–6
Lacan, J., 247–8
language
as element in concept of
'lifeworld', 163–4
Foucault's theoretical
understanding of, 202–3
influence on understanding of
structuralism, 50–51
interpretations of Bourdieu
concerning, 136–7
relevance as element in diversity
of ethnomethodology, 98–100
see also discourse
Lash, S., 134–5
Latour, B., 139–40, 141, 142–3, 147,
149, 151
Law, J., 143
Layder, D., 118
Leonard, D., 177–8, 186
Levi-Strauss, C., 51, 53, 124, 273
'lifeworld' (Habermas), 161–8
Lincourt, J., 72
Lindsay, A., 17

location
changing nature as element of
globalization, 259–61
impact of consequences of
globalization upon, 263–9
Lowenthal, L., 48
Lowith, K., 31
Luckmann, T., 40
Luhmann, N., 12, 140, 169, 170, 221
Lukács, G., 45
Lukes, S., 25
Lyotard, J., 217, 219–20, 228–9,
230–32, 234, 235–6
McCarthy, T., 168–9, 171
'McDonaldization'
as element in understanding of
concept of 'emotion', 250–51
McHugh, P., 102
MacIntyre, A., 21
McLuhan, M., 265
McNay, L., 60
Marcuse, H., 11, 45, 46
Marshall, B., 9–10, 244, 251
Marx, K., 7, 17–18, 20–23, 26, 30–31,
156–8, 177, 179–82, 185, 244, 247,
260, 272
Masculine Domination (Bourdieu),
134M
Mass Psychology of Facism, The
(Reich), 249
Mauss, M., 25
Mazlish, B., 8
Mead, G., 42, 72–4, 77–8, 85–7,
162–3, 252, 273
meanings, cultural
interpretation differences of
postmodernism and earlier
theories, 230–31
Merlino, F., 25
Meštrovi, S., 246
meta-narratives and narratives
interpretation differences of
postmodernism and earlier
theories, 230–32
Mill, J.S., 16–17, 62
Millar, J., 15
Mills, C., 43, 218–9, 243
Mitchell, J., 181–3, 191
modernity (concept)
characteristics as catalyst for styles
of social thinking, 7–13

understanding and interpretation
of, 27–32
Monod, G., 24
Montefiore, A., 154–5
Montesquieu, C., 15
morality, role as element in
understanding of social theory, 15
Murgatryd, L., 117
'myths' (Levi-Strauss), 51
narratives and meta-narratives
interpretation differences of
postmodernism and earlier
theories, 230–32
nationhood (concept)
decline of as consequence of
globalization, 263–4, 266,
268–9
see also spatiality
'natural attitude' (Schutz), 38, 91
network (concept)
relevance and role in actor
network theory, 144–5
see also elements of eg inscription;
prescription
networks, social
characteristics and relevance as
elements of actor network
theory, 146–9
Nietzsche, F., 27, 45, 202, 210
normative social theory (Durkheim),
23–4
Oakley, A., 59
Oberg, P., 188
objectivity
as driver in sociological ideas of
Bourdieu, 122–38
Odih, P., 59
Ohmae, K., 264
Ollman, B., 249
Orbach, S., 251
order, social
as element in understanding of
social interaction, 80–85
Park, R., 74–7, 81
Parsons, T., 54–8, 67, 89–91, 244, 273
'parts' (individuals)
influence on understanding of
structuralism, 51–2
patriarchy
as element informing debates on
feminist theories, 190–92

influence on understanding of
feminism, 62–4
Peirce, C., 41, 43
phenomenology
characteristics, importance and
influence as social thought,
36–40, 272–3
influence on ethnomethodology,
91–2
legacy for contemporary social
theory, 65–8
philosophy, linguistic
influence on ethnomethodology,
92–5
place
changing nature as element of
globalization, 259–61
impact of consequences of
globalization upon, 263–9
Plamenatz, J., 15
politics
decline of national as
consequence of globalization,
263–4, 266, 268–9
influence as element in
interpretations of social theory,
29–30
influence on understanding of
critical theory, 45
Portrait of an Old Woman (Giogione),
189
Postmodern Condition, The (Lyotard),
228
postmodernism
criticisms and weakness of, 233–8
definition and characteristics,
217–18
differences with earlier social
theory, 223–32
evolution and history, 218–23
value and importance of theory,
272–6
power
Foucault's interpretations of,
204–9
influence on understanding of
feminism, 58–64
strengths and weaknesses of,
134–7, 211–12, 213
pragmatism

characteristics, importance and
implications, 40–43, 272–3
legacy for contemporary social
theory, 65–8
'praxis' (Marx), 42, 44
prescription (concept)
characteristics and relevance of as
element in actor network
theory, 145–6
Presentation of Self in Everyday Life
(Goffman), 80
progress, social
role as element in history of social
theory, 16, 18–19
*Protestant Ethic and the Spirit of
Capitalism, The* (Weber), 248
psychologism, as element in history
of social theory, 29
Rabinow, P., 210
Ramas, M., 193
Rasmussen, D., 160
rationalism
role of doubt as element, 10
role of reason as element, 11–13
*see also outputs of approach eg
progress, social*
rationality and rationalization
as element in concept of
'lifeworld', 164–5
as element in development of
postmodernism, 219
as philosophy underpinning
ideology of Habermas, 155–60
influence as element in
ethnomethodology, 93–5
influence as element in
interpretation of social theory,
27–32
role in interpretation of concept
of 'emotion', 247–8
realism, critical, 52–3
reality (concept)
role as element in history of social
theory, 18–19
reason (concept)
role of within theory of
empiricism, 11–13
reason, communicative
as philosophy underpinning
ideology of Habermas, 155–60
reflexivity (concept)

as element of
ethnomethodological
understanding, 95–6
Reich, W., 249
relationships, gender
impact on feminist social theory,
177–9
see also patriarchy
relationships, social
influence on understanding of
feminism, 58–64
religion
as element in understanding of
social theory, 23–7
Renouvier, C., 24–5
Rich, A., 181, 189
Ricoeur, P., 37, 51
Rise of the Network Society, The
(Castells), 140
Ritzer, G., 250–51
Robertson, R., 263
Rock, P., 72
Roderick, R., 161
roles, social
as element in understanding of
social interaction, 82–3
Rorty, R., 43
Ross, E., 40
Russell, B., 41
Ryle, G., 89
Sacks. H., 94, 96
Saussure, F de, 49–50, 124, 273
Sayer, D., 21
Schaffle, A., 24
Schleiermacher, F., 37
Schopenhauer, A., 27, 45
Schutz, A., 40, 43, 91–2, 101
science
approach to adoption of scientific
thought as element of
understanding of, 27–8
role as element in history of social
theory, 16
Science in Action (Latour), 142
sciences, natural and social
characteristics and
commonalities, 36–40
Seidman, S., 26, 230, 233, 236
'self' (concept)
as element in understanding of
social interaction, 83–4

Foucault's conceptualisation of, 198–203
interpretations of Mead in formation of in social world, 72–4
Shotter, J., 14
Sibeon, R., 151, 262
Simmel, G., 28
Smith, A., 15
Smith, D., 61, 101, 184–5
social life *see* society
'social physics' (Comte), 16
Social System, The (Parsons), 55
society (concept)
    ethics and integration of as elements of social theory, 22–7
    influence on understanding of structuralism, 51–2
    interpretations of *see theory eg* symbolic interaction
    role in development of social theory, 13–17
    see also elements informing nature and development eg globalization; 'self'
'sociological epistemology' (Durkheim), 25
Sorel, G., 41
spatiality
    changing nature as element of globalization, 259–61
    impact of consequences of globalization upon, 263–9
specialization, as element in development of postmodernism, 219
speech *see* language
Spencer, H., 16–17
Spender, D., 190–91
spheres, public and private social
    influence on understanding of feminism, 61–2, 177–9
stablilization, need for in actor network theory, 148–9
Stanton, E., 62
stereotypes, influence on understanding of feminism, 58–64
Strange, S., 261
strategy (concept)

as element in relationship between agency and social position, 127–34
strengths and weaknesses of interpretation of, 134–7
stratification, impact on ideas of Bourdieu, 126–7
Strauss, A., 75
structuralism
    evolution and characteristics, 49–53
    Foucault's conceptualisation of, 199–203, 214
    impact on ideas of Bourdieu, 124–5
    legacy for contemporary social theory, 65–8
    value and importance of theory, 273
structuration theory
    characteristics and intellectual development, 106–16
    criticisms and limitations, 116–21
structures, social
    criticisms and limitations in analysis of structuration theory, 116–21
    role in interpretation of concept of 'emotion', 245, 246–7
    weaknesses of when analysing feminist social theory, 177–9
Stryker, S., 72
subjectivity
    as driver in sociological ideas of Bourdieu, 122–38
Sumner, W., 40
symbolic interaction
    comparison of Mead and Blumer interpretations, 77–80
    influences on history of, 71–7
    value and importance of theory, 273
symbolism
    impact on ideas of Bourdieu, 126
    role in interpretation of concept of 'emotion', 251–5
systems and institutions (concept)
    as element in history of social theory, 29
    changing nature in relation to process of globalization, 261–3

Habermas' view of relationship
with 'lifeworld', 165–8
influence of societal systems on
understanding of structuralism,
51–2
systems theory
evolution of characteristics, 53–8
legacy for contemporary social
theory, 65–8
utilization of in development of
ideology of communicative
action, 168–72
Taylor, C., 154–5
technology, information
as driver for globalization spread,
265
telecommunications, as driver for
globalization spread, 265
theories, sociological
changing ideas of consciousness as
element in development of,
17–22
Enlightenment as catalyst for,
7–13
future developmental pathways,
278–84
political and intellectual cultures
influencing, 13–17, 18–19, 29
see also influences eg capitalism;
culture; ethics; hermoneutics;
phemomenology; religion
see also name eg action theory;
actor network theory; classical
social theory; communicative
action theory; critical theory;
feminism; postmodernism;
pragmatism; structuration
theory; systems theory
Thomas, W., 74–7
Thompson, J., 101, 119–20, 136
Thompson, K., 227
thought and thinking, sociological
Enlightenment as catalyst for,
7–13
see also traditions of eg
hermoneutics; phenomenology
Thrift, N., 269
time and temporality, impact of
consequences of globalization
upon, 263–9

time period, current
questionability of classification as
postmodern era, 233–8
Tönnies, F., 28
Toulmin, S., 9, 13
Touraine, A., 281–2
Toynbee, A., 9
trust, as element in understanding of
concept of 'emotion', 249–50
truth (concept)
Foucault's conceptualisation of,
198–203
interpretation differences of
postmodernism and earlier
theories, 228–9
role of within theory of
empiricism, 11–13
Truth, S., 59
unpredictability, as element in
development of postmodernism,
222
Urry, J., 280–81
use and exchange value
characteristics as element in
postmodernism, 223–7
Veblen, T., 27
verstehen (Schutz), 38, 91
Vico, G., 14
Vindication of the Rights of Women
(Wollstonecraft), 62
wages, changing accountability of as
element of globalization, 261
Walby, S., 186–7
Weber, M., 27–32, 158–9, 209–10,
218, 244, 248, 272, 278
Webster, F., 226
Western Intellectual Tradition
(Bronowski), 8
Williams, S., 245
Winch, P., 40, 88–9, 93–4
Wittgenstein, L., 40, 88, 92–3
Witz, A., 244, 251
Wolff, K, 38
Woolf, V., 59
Wollstonecraft, M., 14, 62
workforce, changes within, as
consequence of globalization,
265–6

Cultural Change and Ordinary Life

Brian Longhurst

- How important are the media?
- How is culture changing?
- How is ordinary life being transformed?
- How do we belong?

This ground-breaking book offers a new approach to the understanding of everyday life, the media and cultural change. It explores the social pattern of ordinary life in the context of recent theories and accounts of social and cultural change.

Brian Longhurst argues that our social and cultural lives are becoming increasingly audienced and performed and that activities in everyday life are changing due to the ever-growing importance and salience of the media. These changes involve people forging new ways of belonging, where among other things they seek to distinguish themselves from others.

In *Cultural Change and Ordinary Life*, Longhurst evaluates changes in the media and ordinary life in the context of large-scale cultural change, especially with respect to globalization and hybridisation, fragmentation, spectacle and performance, and enthusing or fan-like activities. He makes the case that analysis of the media has to be brought into a more thorough dialogue with other forms of research that have looked at social processes.

Cultural Change and Ordinary Life is key reading for students and researchers of sociology, media studies, cultural studies and mass communication.

Contents: Introduction – Concepts and theories of everyday and ordinary life – Changing ordinary life – Understanding and theorizing cultural change – Globalizing, hybridizing and localizing: Processes of elective belonging – Imagining, performing and identifying: Class, identity and culture – Distinguishing and connecting 1: Capitals and the use of time – Distinguishing and connecting 2: The omnivore thesis- Enthusing – Conclusions

2007 192pp

978-0-335-22187-5 (Paperback) 978-0-335-22188-2 (Hardback)

Scoping the Social

Anthony Woodiwiss

Social theory is central to the disciplines of sociology, cultural studies, criminology and media studies. Many students, however, find it difficult to relate theory to their other courses, projects, dissertations and theses, let alone imagine themselves producing theory.

In contrast to conventional social theory textbooks that restrict themselves to the description and analysis of theories and what other professionals have said about them, this innovative book shows students how to use, criticise and contribute to the development of theory.

Treating theory as a variety of 'visual work' that is intimately connected with the process of empirical investigation, and with the help of clear diagrams and carefully chosen quotations, Part 1 provides an exceptionally clear introduction to the different ways of practicing social theory. Part 2 provides a practical example of how to theorise by producing and demonstrating the effectiveness of a new concept of reflexivity in the course of an outline of the history of the development of social theory since 1945.

This is important reading for students and researchers in sociology and related fields.

Contents: *Part One: The theory of social life – Visualizing the social – Looking for laws – Looking at models – Looking from the inside – Looking as work –*
Part Two: The social life of theory – Towards a realist reflexivity – Atlanticisim and the inward turn – The politicization of identity and the eclipse of class – Globalization and the reappearance of social structure – Conclusion: In praise of the ateliers of sociology

200pp

9798-0-335-21676-5 (Paperback)978-0-335-21677-2 (Hardback)